May It Please the Campus

Lawyers Leading Higher Education

Touro University Press Books

Series Editor
MICHAEL A. SHMIDMAN, PhD (Touro University, New York)
SIMCHA FISHBANE, PhD (Touro University, New York)

May It Please the Campus

Lawyers Leading Higher Education

Patricia E. Salkin

NEW YORK
2022

Library of Congress Control Number: 2022945223

Copyright © Touro University Press, 2022

Published by Touro University Press and Academic Studies Press.
Typeset, printed and distributed by Academic Studies Press.

ISBN 9798887190082 (hardback)
ISBN 9798887190495 (paperback)
ISBN 9798887190099 (adobe pdf)
ISBN 9798887190105 (epub)

Touro University Press
Michael A. Shmidman and Simcha Fishbane, Editors
320 West 31st Street, Fourth Floor,
New York, NY 10001, USA
tcpress@touro.edu

Book design by PHi Business Solutions
Cover design by Ivan Grave

Academic Studies Press
1577 Beacon Street
Brookline, MA 02446, USA

press@academicstudiespress.com
www.academicstudiespress.com

Contents

List of Tables and Charts	ix
Acknowledgements	xv
Methodology	xvii
Introduction: Higher Education in Crisis	1
1. Lawyers, Leadership, and Higher Education	9
Leadership Skills Needed in Times of Crisis	14
Lawyers Are Crisis Managers Adept at Navigating in the Unknown	16
Legal Challenges Have Always Existed in Higher Education	17
Litigation Floodgates Are Opening Demanding Both Preventive Law Strategies and Pragmatic Planning	20
What Are Campuses Searching for Today and Why These Skills Can Be Found in Lawyers	25
2. Historically, Lawyers Have Been at the Forefront of Higher Education	32
Early Higher Education Leaders	32
The Early 1900s Give Way to Academic Administrators	37
The 1950s, Civil Rights, Vietnam, and Campus Unrest Make Lawyers Once Again Attractive Education Leaders	39
The Rise of Legal Education	43
Why Law Professors Make Good Choices for Campus Presidencies	45
Law Deans as a Pathway to the Presidency	51
3. Lawyers Widely Accepted as Leaders across the Higher Education Landscape	60
Geographic Acceptance	62
Public vs Private Schools	75
Community Colleges	80
Religiously Affiliated Schools	82
Historically Black Colleges and Universities	84
Institutions with Law Schools	88

4. Characteristics of Lawyer Presidents ... 91
   Education and Training ... 91
   Does Where a Campus Leader Earned Their Law Degree Matter? ... 93
   Do Campus Presidents Need Degrees in Addition to
   the Juris Doctorate? ... 95
   On the Job Experience ... 98
   Prior Academic Experience ... 98
   Prior Experience as Law Dean ... 102
   Community Colleges ... 106
   Religiously Affiliated Schools ... 108
   Prior Experience as Provost ... 110
   Prior Experience as Government Lawyers ... 115
   Presidents with Prior Government Experience ... 116
   Not All Lawyer Presidents Come from Academia ... 126
   Fundraising Skills ... 127
   General Counsels Bring Seasoned Experience to the C-Suite ... 134
   Governing Board Lawyers Increasingly Tapped to Lead Campuses ... 142
   Lawyer Presidents and Race ... 150

5. Women Lawyers Emerging as Campus Presidents ... 154
   Geography and Women Lawyer Presidents ... 160
   Women Lawyer Presidents and Types of Schools ... 161
   Women Lawyer Presidents and Prior Academic Experience ... 162
   Women Lawyer Presidents and Prior Experience in Government,
   as General Counsel, Trustee and Fundraiser ... 175
   Women Leading Higher Education—Public Opinion ... 186
   Women Campus Presidents Matter ... 188

6. Lawyers Will Continue to Lead Campuses: What Does That Mean
   for the Future of Higher Education? ... 190
   Search Firms Are Buzzing About Lawyer Presidents ... 190
   Influencers and Appointing Authority ... 191
   Findings ... 192
      The Role of Legal Education ... 192
      Does Legal Education Teach Lawyers to be Leaders? ... 192
      Will Lawyer Presidents Dramatically Change the
      Course of Higher Education? ... 196

Appendices	199
Appendix 1. Lawyer Presidents, 1700s to 2019	199
Appendix 2. Lawyer Presidents, 2020 to 2021	225
Appendix 3. Women Lawyer Presidents by Name, School, School Type, and Location	228
Appendix 4. Lawyer Presidents of Community Colleges by Name, School, School Type, and Location	232
Appendix 5. Lawyer Presidents of Religiously Affiliated Schools by Name, School, and Location	235
Appendix 6. Lawyer Presidents of HBCUs by Name, School, and Location	242
Appendix 7. Appointments of Lawyer Presidents by Decade	244
Appendix 8. Lawyer Presidents by School Type and Decade, 1700 to 2019	273
Appendix 9. Lawyer Presidents and Where They Attended Law School, 1900–2019	295
Bibliography	311
Index	327

List of Tables, Charts and Maps

Table 1.1.	Presidents with JDs, All Survey Years	10
Table 1.2.	Appointments of Lawyer Presidents (by Decade)	11
Chart 1.1.	Distinct Lawyer Presidents Appointed by Decade	12
Table 1.3.	Lawyers Serving as Presidents in Each Decade	12
Chart 1.2.	All Appointments of Lawyer Presidents by Decade	14
Chart 2.1.	Appointments of Lawyer Presidents (1800s)	37
Chart 2.2.	Appointments of Lawyer Presidents (by Half-Century)	38
Chart 2.3.	Lawyer Presidents with Prior Law Professor Experience (1900–2019)	47
Chart 2.4.	Lawyer Presidents at Public Institutions with Prior Law Professor Experience (1900–2019)	49
Chart 2.5.	Lawyer Presidents at Private Institutions with Prior Law Professor Experience (1900–2019)	50
Chart 2.6.	Lawyer Presidents at Community Colleges with Prior Law Professor Experience (1900–2019)	51
Chart 2.7.	Lawyer Presidents at Religiously Affiliated Institutions with Prior Law Professor Experience (1900–2019)	52
Chart 2.8.	Lawyer Presidents with Prior Law Dean Experience (1900–2019)	53
Chart 2.9.	Lawyer Presidents at Public Institutions with Prior Law Dean Experience (1900–2019)	54
Chart 2.10.	Lawyer Presidents at Private Institutions with Prior Law Dean Experience (1900–2019)	55
Chart 2.11.	Lawyer Presidents at Community Colleges with Prior Law Dean Experience (1900–2019)	56
Chart 2.12.	Lawyer Presidents at Religiously Affiliated Institutions with Prior Law Dean Experience (1900–2019)	57
Table 3.1.	Number of U. S. Postsecondary Institutions, by Level of Institution, and Region: Academic Year 2016–17	61
Table 3.2.	Number of Lawyer Appointments by State (1900–2019)	62
Chart 3.1.	Top States for Lawyer Presidents (1900–2019)	64
Map 3.1.	Number of Lawyer Appointments by State (1900–2019)	64
Chart 3.2.	Top States for Lawyer Presidents (2010–2019)	66

Map 3.2.	Number of Lawyer Appointments by State (2010–2019)	67
Table 3.3.	Number and Percentage of Schools by State (2018)	68
Map 3.3.	Number of Lawyer Appointments at Public Institutions by State (2010–2019)	70
Map 3.4.	Number of Lawyer Appointments at Public Institutions by State (1900–2019)	70
Map 3.5.	Number of Lawyer Appointments at Private Institutions by State (2010–2019)	71
Map 3.6.	Number of Lawyer Appointments at Private Institutions by State (1900–2019)	72
Map 3.7.	Number of Lawyer Appointments at Community Colleges by State (2010–2019)	72
Map 3.8.	Number of Lawyer Appointments at Community Colleges by State (1900–2019)	73
Map 3.9.	Number of Lawyer Appointments at Religiously Affiliated Institutions by State (2010–2019)	74
Map 3.10.	Number of Lawyer Appointments at Religiously Affiliated Institutions by State (1900–2019)	74
Chart 3.3.	Public and Private Institutions with Lawyer Presidents (2010–2019)	76
Chart 3.4.	Public and Private Institutions with Lawyer Presidents (1900–2019)	76
Table 3.4.	Share of Institutional Control Led by JD Holding Presidents	77
Table 3.5.	JD Holding Presidents, by Carnegie Classification and Year	78
Table 3.6.	Distribution of JD Holding Presidents, by Carnegie Classification and Year	78
Table 3.7.	Percentage of Presidents holding JDs, by Carnegie and Control	78
Table 3.8.	Distribution of JD Holding Presidents Each Year, by Carnegie and Control	79
Table 3.9.	Percentage Distribution of Grand Total of U. S. Postsecondary Institutions, by Level of Institution, and Region: Academic Year 2016–17	80
Chart 3.5.	Community Colleges with Lawyer Presidents (1940–2019)	82
Chart 3.6.	Religiously Affiliated Institutions with Lawyer Presidents (1900–2019)	84
Chart 3.7.	Historically Black Colleges and Universities with Lawyer Presidents (1900–2019)	87

Chart 3.8.	Historically Black Colleges and Universities with Lawyer Presidents (2010–2019)	88
Chart 3.9.	Institutions with Law Schools Who Have Had Lawyer Presidents (2010–2019)	89
Chart 3.10.	Institutions with Law Schools Who Have Had Lawyer Presidents (1900–2019)	89
Chart 4.1.	Top Schools Attended by Lawyer Presidents (1900–2019)	93
Table 4.1.	Presidents Who Hold Additional Post-BA Degrees, among All Presidents	95
Table 4.2.	Presidents Who Hold Additional Post-BA Degrees, among JD Holding Presidents	95
Table 4.3.	JD Plus Other Degrees (1900–2019)	96
Table 4.4.	Prior Presidencies Held among All Presidents	98
Table 4.5.	JD Holding Presidents by Prior Presidency	98
Table 4.6.	Distribution of JD Holding Presidents by Prior Positions for Each Survey Year	99
Table 4.7.	Distribution of All Presidents by Prior Positions for Each Survey Year	99
Chart 4.2.	Lawyer Presidents with Prior Academic Experience (1900–2019)	100
Chart 4.3.	Lawyer Presidents at Public Institutions with Prior Academic Experience (1900–2019)	101
Chart 4.4.	Lawyer Presidents at Private Institutions with Prior Academic Experience (1900–2019)	102
Chart 4.5.	Lawyer Presidents at Community Colleges with Prior Academic Experience (1900–2019)	103
Chart 4.6.	Lawyer Presidents at Religiously Affiliated Institutions with Prior Academic Experience (1900–2019)	104
Chart 4.7.	Lawyer Presidents with Prior Dean Experience (1900–2019)	105
Chart 4.8.	Lawyer Presidents at Public Institutions with Prior Dean Experience (1900–2019)	106
Chart 4.9.	Lawyer Presidents at Private Institutions with Prior Dean Experience (1900–2019)	107
Chart 4.10.	Lawyer Presidents at Community Colleges with Prior Dean Experience (1900–2019)	108
Chart 4.11.	Lawyer Presidents at Religiously Affiliated Institutions with Prior Dean Experience (1900–2019)	109
Chart 4.12.	Lawyer Presidents with Prior Provost Experience (1900–2019)	111

Chart 4.13.	Lawyer Presidents at Public Institutions with Prior Provost Experience (1900–2019)	112
Chart 4.14.	Lawyer Presidents at Private Institutions with Prior Provost Experience (1900–2019)	113
Chart 4.15.	Lawyer Presidents at Community Colleges with Prior Provost Experience (1900–2019)	114
Chart 4.16.	Lawyer Presidents at Religiously Affiliated Institutions with Prior Provost Experience (1900–2019)	115
Chart 4.17.	Lawyer Presidents with Prior Government Experience (1900–2019)	121
Chart 4.18.	Lawyer Presidents at Public Institutions with Prior Government Experience (1900–2019)	122
Chart 4.19.	Lawyer Presidents at Private Institutions with Prior Government Experience (1900–2019)	123
Chart 4.20.	Lawyer Presidents at Community Colleges with Prior Government Experience (1900–2019)	124
Chart 4.21.	Lawyer Presidents at Religiously Affiliated Institutions with Prior Government Experience (1900–2019)	125
Chart 4.22.	Lawyer Presidents with Prior Fundraiser Experience (1900–2019)	129
Chart 4.23.	Lawyer Presidents at Public Institutions with Prior Fundraiser Experience (1900–2019)	130
Chart 4.24.	Lawyer Presidents at Private Institutions with Prior Fundraiser Experience (1900–2019)	131
Chart 4.25.	Lawyer Presidents at Community Colleges with Prior Fundraiser Experience (1900–2019)	132
Chart 4.26.	Lawyer Presidents at Religiously Affiliated Institutions with Prior Fundraiser Experience (1900–2019)	133
Chart 4.27.	Lawyer Presidents with Prior General Counsel Experience (1900–2019)	137
Chart 4.28.	Lawyer Presidents at Public Institutions with Prior General Counsel Experience (1900–2019)	138
Chart 4.29.	Lawyer Presidents at Private Institutions with Prior General Counsel Experience (1900–2019)	139
Chart 4.30.	Lawyer Presidents at Community Colleges with Prior General Counsel Experience (1900–2019)	140
Chart 4.31.	Lawyer Presidents at Religiously Affiliated Institutions with Prior General Counsel Experience (1900–2019)	141

Chart 4.32.	Lawyer Presidents Who Were Prior Board of Trustees Members (1900–2019)	146
Chart 4.33.	Lawyer Presidents at Public Institutions Who Were Prior Board of Trustees Members (1900–2019)	147
Chart 4.34.	Lawyer Presidents at Private Institutions Who Were Prior Board of Trustees Members (1900–2019)	148
Chart 4.35.	Lawyer Presidents at Community Colleges Who Were Prior Board of Trustees Members (1900–2019)	149
Chart 4.36.	Lawyer Presidents at Religiously Affiliated Institutions Who Were Prior Board of Trustees Members (1900–2019)	150
Table 4.8.	Distribution of Race among JD Holding Presidents, by Survey Year	151
Table 4.9.	Distribution of Race among All Presidents, by Survey Year	151
Table 4.10.	American Bar Association, National Lawyer Population Survey, Resident Active Attorney Demographics, Race/Ethnicity, 2011–2021	152
Table 5.1.	Distribution of JD Holding Presidents Each Year, by Sex	154
Table 5.2.	Distribution of Presidents Each Year, by Sex	155
Chart 5.1.	Lawyer Presidents—Gender (2010–2019)	155
Chart 5.2.	Lawyer Presidents—Gender (1900–2019)	156
Chart 5.3.	Appointments of Female Lawyer Presidents (by Decade)	157
Chart 5.4.	Female Lawyer Presidents (Last Decade)	158
Chart 5.5.	Female Lawyer Presidents (by Decade)	159
Map 5.1.	Schools with Female Lawyer Presidents by State (1970–2019)	160
Chart 5.6.	Institutions with Female Lawyer Presidents (1970–2019)	161
Chart 5.7.	Institutions with Lawyer Presidents (1970–2019)	162
Chart 5.8.	Female Lawyer Presidents with Prior Academic Experience (by Decade)	163
Chart 5.9.	Lawyer Presidents with Prior Academic Experience (by Decade and Gender)	164
Chart 5.10.	Female Lawyer Presidents with Prior Academic Experience (1970–2019)	165
Chart 5.11.	Female Lawyer Presidents with Prior Law Professor Experience (by Decade)	166
Chart 5.12.	Lawyer Presidents with Prior Law Professor Experience (by Decade)	167
Chart 5.13.	Female Lawyer Presidents with Prior Law Professor Experience (1970–2019)	168

Chart 5.14. Female Lawyer Presidents with Prior Law Dean Experience (by Decade) 169
Chart 5.15. Lawyer Presidents with Prior Law Dean Experience (by Decade) 170
Chart 5.16. Female Lawyer Presidents with Prior Law Dean Experience (1970–2019) 171
Chart 5.17. Female Lawyer Presidents with Prior Provost Experience (by Decade) 172
Chart 5.18. Lawyer Presidents with Prior Provost Experience (by Decade) 173
Chart 5.19. Female Lawyer Presidents with Prior Provost Experience (1970–2019) 174
Chart 5.20. Female Lawyer Presidents with Prior Government Experience (by Decade) 175
Chart 5.21. Lawyer Presidents with Prior Government Experience (by Decade) 176
Chart 5.22. Female Lawyer Presidents with Prior Government Experience (1970–2019) 177
Chart 5.23. Female Lawyer Presidents with Prior General Counsel Experience (by Decade) 178
Chart 5.24. Lawyer Presidents with Prior General Counsel Experience (by Decade) 179
Chart 5.25. Female Lawyer Presidents with Prior General Counsel Experience (1970–2019) 180
Chart 5.26. Female Lawyer Presidents with Prior Fundraiser Experience (by Decade) 181
Chart 5.27. Lawyer Presidents with Prior Fundraiser Experience (by Decade) 182
Chart 5.28. Female Lawyer Presidents with Prior Fundraiser Experience (1970–2019) 183
Chart 5.29. Female Lawyer Presidents Who Were Prior Board of Trustees Members (by Decade) 184
Chart 5.30. Lawyer Presidents Who Were Prior Board of Trustees Members (by Decade) 185
Chart 5.31. Female Lawyer Presidents Who Were Prior Board of Trustees Members (by Decade) 186

Acknowledgements

This book is based on my 2022 doctoral dissertation at the University of the Arts. There are many people to thank and acknowledge who made this project possible. First, my colleagues at Touro University who supported my pursuit of a PhD in Creativity that resulted in the research and manuscript that formed the basis of this work. Next, the Touro University team, starting with President Dr. Alan Kadish, whose unwavering support was critical in my ability to undertake this journey, and Evan Hoberman, whose data organization skills made possible the visualization of the illustrative charts and graphs. Thank you also to Irene McDermott, director of the Gould Law Library at Touro University Jacob D. Fuchsberg Law Center, whose help in tracking down resources was invaluable. Special thanks to Adam Lubatkin, Aisha Scholes, Judiana Olvera, Beth Chamberlain, Ryan Kothe, Wendy Rokhsar, Laura Ross, and Michael Tatonetti for helping me to pour through the websites of more than 4,000 colleges and universities in the quest to identify past and present lawyer presidents.

I am indebted for the guidance and support of each member of my dissertation committee, all of whom are legends in their fields, and each one a distinguished scholar: Dr. Paul Finkelman (chair), Dr. John Sexton, and Stephen Trachtenberg, JD.

Thank you to the academic leadership of the University of the Arts, without whose vision and perseverance to develop the country's first PhD program in Creativity, this manuscript would not have been achieved, including Dr. Jonathan Fineberg and professors Buzz Spector and Zach Savich.

Last and most important, thank you to my husband Howard Gross and our children Sydney and Jordan for their support, love, and constant encouragement.

Methodology

There is little literature with only a small number of recent studies focused on non-traditional or unconventional leadership in higher education,[1] with a scant few that discuss lawyers as college and university presidents.[2] None of these bodies of work has attempted to collect and analyze comprehensive empirical data to track and explore the rise of the lawyer presidents within the academy. They also do not attempt to categorize the unique backgrounds and experiences that these lawyer presidents bring to the campus, factors that clearly contribute to their overall ability to meet the complex needs of the modern university.

---

1   See, for example, Laura B. Klein, "Understanding the Experiences of Non-Traditional University Leadership in Higher Education: A Qualitative Study Using a Triangular Theoretical Approach" (PhD diss., Oakland University, Rochester, MI, 2016), accessed October 30, 2019, https://www.proquest.com/dissertations-theses/understanding-experiences-non-traditional/docview/1826914039/se-2?accountid=30558; Joanne L. Ivory, "A Review of Nontraditional Presidents in Higher Education: Benefits and Challenges of Change Agents in Colleges and Universities" (PhD diss., Benedictine University, Lisle, IL, 2017), https://www.proquest.com/dissertations-theses/review-nontraditional-presidents-higher-education/docview/1914898658/se-2?accountid=30558; Jonathan Peri, "The Wisdom of Employed General Counsel In Higher Education," *Widener Law Journal* 18 (2008), https://heinonline.org/HOL/Page?handle=hein/journals/wjpl18&id=193&collection=journals (Peri's research included a leadership theory analysis of one lawyer president who had a distinguished career in the public, private, and non-profit sectors as well as service on the college board of trustees prior to appointment as president); Scott Cochran Beardsley, "The Rise of the Nontraditional Liberal Arts College President: Context, Pathways, Institutional Characteristics, Views of Search Firm Executives, and Lessons Learned by Presidents Making the Transitions" (PhD diss., University of Pennsylvania, Philadelphia, PA, 2015), https://www.proquest.com/dissertations-theses/rise-nontraditional-liberal-arts-college/docview/1727125953/se-2?accountid=30558 (Beardsley's research included an interview with attorney Lawrence Schall who became president of Oglethorpe University).

2   Thomas T. Nguyen, "Perceptions of Lawyers on Career Transition, Transferable Skills, and Preparation for Community College Leadership" (PhD diss., Florida Atlantic University, Boca Raton, FL, 2014), https://www.proquest.com/dissertations-theses/perceptions-lawyers-on-career-transition/docview/1547946174/se-2?accountid=30558; Jermaine Johnson, "Led by Lawyers: Perceptions of Legal Training and Experience and Their Effect upon Leadership" (PhD diss., Iowa State University, Ames, IA, 2017), https://lib.dr.iastate.edu/etd/16725/; and Seth P. Wall, "Characteristics of Nontraditional College and University Presidents in New England" (PhD diss., New England College, Henniker, NH, 2015), https://www.proquest.com/dissertations-theses/characteristics-nontraditional-college-university/docview/1682466631/se-2?accountid=30558.

Instead, most of the studies reflect original research gained from interviewing five to twelve people and drawing conclusions based on this very limited sample.

The research approach that forms the basis of this work is largely data-driven, but also employs direct observations from lawyer presidents and comments concerning lawyer leaders from observers in secondary sources. The author's own informed observations, as an attorney for thirty-four years, including time as a government lawyer and as a law professor, law school dean, and university provost, also serve to enrich the research and bring a pragmatic view and analysis. For purposes of this study, a person was identified as a lawyer if they practiced law or if they received an academic law degree that qualified them to practice law.

The data included in Appendix 1 contains detailed information on lawyer presidents of colleges and universities from the 1700s through the end of 2021. The illustrative charts, graphs, and maps throughout the first five chapters emanate from this data and were created by importing the data from Excel spreadsheets into a Tableau database. Appendix 2 contains only data about lawyer presidents appointed at the start of the new decade (2020 and 2021), which is discussed in chapter six. Appendix 3 focuses on women lawyer presidents, which is the subject of chapter four. Focusing on specific types of schools in chapter three, Appendix 4 provides the data for lawyer presidents of community colleges, Appendix 5 contains the data for lawyer presidents at religiously affiliated schools, and Appendix 6 provides the data for lawyer presidents at Historically Black Colleges and Universities. Appendices 7 and 8 show the appointment of lawyer presidents by the decade and by school type, respectively, discussed in chapters one and three. Appendix 9 shows where lawyer presidents went to law school, discussed in chapter four. Charts and tables throughout the manuscript reflect data mined through June 2022.

The research undertaken herein focuses on the 4,324 Carnegie Classified Institutions (degree-granting)[3] and not the 7,310 Title IV institutions recognized by the U. S. Department of Education.[4] As explained in their 2018 Update, "The Carnegie Classifications includes all U.S. degree-granting, Title IV eligible

---

[3] Indiana University Center for Postsecondary Research, "2018 Update Facts & Figures," *Carnegie Classification of Institutions of Higher Education*, last modified March 19, 2021, accessed August 31, 2021, https://carnegieclassifications.iu.edu/downloads/CCIHE2018-FactsFigures.pdf.

[4] U.S. Department of Education, "DataLab," *IES-NCES National Center for Education Statistics*, accessed November 14, 2021, https://nces.ed.gov/Datalab/TablesLibrary/TableDetails/12129?releaseYear=0&dataSource=IPEDS&subjectId=2&topicId=3&rst=true.

postsecondary institutions that granted at least one degree in the target year."⁵ The precise number of degree-granting institutions is a moving target. This is in part because it depends upon how branch and satellite campuses are accounted for, and in today's challenging COVID-19 pandemic climate, schools are merging and ceasing operations with disarming frequency.⁶

The empirical data collection was accomplished by reviewing the websites of every Carnegie Classified Institution to determine whether the sitting president is a lawyer. Additionally, where campus websites contained historical information about past presidents, these identifiable individuals were researched to determine whether any of them were lawyers. Most schools did not provide historical records of prior administrations. Additional names were identified through internet searches focusing on media reports and press releases, various databases, as well as through conversations with leaders in higher education and in legal education about this research. The data was locked for purposes of this study in early June 2022, and any additional names and new appointments are maintained by the author for future updates.

It is important to note that no previous studies exist that identify the names, schools, and other data points about campus presidents who are or were lawyers.⁷ While the American Council on Education (ACE) has been publishing a study on American College Presidents roughly every five years since 1988 (last published in 2017) the aggregate data is based on the return of voluntary surveys sent to campus presidents.⁸ The data in the 2017 report results from 1,546 survey responses to 3,615 presidents for a 43% return rate.⁹

For reasons of confidentiality, ACE research staff could not share data that included names of lawyer presidents and the names of institutions that employed

---

5   Indiana University Center for Postsecondary Research, "2018 Update Facts & Figures."
6   Josh Moody, "A Guide to the Changing Number of U.S. Universities: The U.S. Department of Education Lists Nearly 4000 Degree-Granting Academic Institutions," *U.S. News and World Report, Best Colleges*, last modified April 27, 2021, accessed August 29, 2021, https://www.usnews.com/education/best-colleges/articles/how-many-universities-are-in-the-us-and-why-that-number-is-changing.
7   Note: there are law professors who are legal historians/scholars but never attended law school and later became college and university presidents, such as Dr. Paul Finkelman (President of Gratz College, 2017–2021) and Dr. Kermit Hall (President of the University at Albany, 2005–2006).
8   Jonathan S. Gagliardi et al., *American College President Study 2017*, American College President Study Series 8 (Washington, DC: American Council on Education, TIAA Institute, 2017), accessed November 14, 2021, https://www.aceacps.org/.
9   Jonathan S. Gagliardi et al., *American College President Study 2017*, American College President Study Series 8 (Washington, DC: American Council on Education, TIAA Institute, 2017), 1, accessed November 14, 2021, https://www.aceacps.org/.

lawyer presidents. Therefore, while it was impossible to compare data or verify whether all of the names used for this study were included in the ACE study, this study identifies a greater number of lawyer presidents than the ACE study reveals.

One key difference between the ACE study and this research is that ACE was able to perform a survey that asked their members to identify their race and ethnicity. Since the research here did not involve a survey in which presidents could self-identify, it was not possible to include a robust discussion in the present study. However, in chapter four the ACE diversity data is compared with data from the American Bar Association about diversity in the profession to draw limited comparisons.

Another challenge for the analysis was the labeling of religiously affiliated schools. The organizations that are responsible for the classification process do not share common definitions or processes. So, although the Carnegie Classification is employed throughout this study, in determining religiously affiliated schools it did not prove as useful. This is largely due to that fact that the Carnegie Classification lists "special focus" schools as "religious." Yet other schools, such as Notre Dame, Liberty University, Pepperdine, Touro University, American Jewish University, and Yeshiva University, just to name a few, are not on the Carnegie list. In the end, the author of this study chose to visit the websites of the colleges and universities with lawyer presidents to see whether they self-identified on their website as being affiliated with, or in the tradition of, a religious group.

Finally, while for most lawyer presidents, biographical information was obtainable through a variety of sources, for some individuals, certain data points discussed in the aggregate were not readily discoverable and therefore unable to be factored in certain analyses.

Introduction: Higher Education in Crisis

In the opening of their 2017 American College President Study report, the American Council on Education asserted that "college and university presidents occupy a leadership role unlike any other. They play a critical role in ensuring their institution's success, especially as internal and external pressures have grown at a time of resource instability and demographic change."[1] No statement could be truer. Today's higher education leaders, and particularly presidents, are facing challenges their predecessors never imagined. From the COVID-19 pandemic, to increasing issues of racial injustice, to shrinking enrollment, to the ever-growing financial pressures that are both long term and brought on by inflation, the landscape facing presidents is not what it was even a decade ago. As L. Jay Lemons, President and Senior Consultant of Academic Search, wrote, "the realities of today make college and university leadership more challenging, more vexing and more uncertain than perhaps ever before. In this COVID-19 era, when institutions may be only one leader away from shutting their doors forever," schools must be careful in whom they select and the processes they use to do so.[2] Even the celebrated Ivy League has not escaped these evolving challenges. In 2022, Harvard faced questions about its connections to slavery and the slave trade. The situation ended up with the university establishing a $100 million fund, "to implement the recommendations includes resources both for current use and to establish an endowment to sustain the work in perpetuity."[3]

Importantly, these ever increasing and mutating challenges, which college and university presidents face, call into question the qualifications they must now

---

1 Julie Johnson, "The Law; Universities Looking to Lawyers for Leadership," *New York Times*, December 25, 1987, sec. B, https://www.nytimes.com/1987/12/25/us/the-law-universities-looking-to-lawyers-for-leadership.html.
2 Jay L. Lemons, "Another Wave of Presidential Departures," March 10, 2021, accessed June 14, 2022, https://www.insidehighered.com/views/2021/03/10/more-presidents-may-be-leaving-will-their-colleges-be-ready-it-opinion.
3 Alvin Powell, "Dual Message of Slavery Probe: Harvard's Ties Inseparable from Rise, and Now University Must Act," *The Harvard Gazette*, April 26, 2022, accessed July 6, 2022, https://news.harvard.edu/gazette/story/2022/04/slavery-probe-harvards-ties-inseparable-from-rise/.

bring to the job in order to be successful. One recent study that focused on the pathway to the modern campus presidency revealed that the traditional pathways are no longer the norm and that the demands of unique skill sets warrant searches for candidates that include people who are: strategists, communicators and storytellers, fundraisers, collaborators, and who possess financial and operational acumen. Ranking last as important among current presidents surveyed was being a leader who is an academic and intellectual.[4]

Today's campus presidents are "multidisciplinarians" who face challenges of inequality among students and institutions, shifting government relationships and the impact of technology on higher education[5] and lawyers are often associated as individuals who have honed skills suited to meet these challenges. Instead of being the more classic academics who transition into administration and then climb the ladder to a presidency, lawyers are trained to sort through conflict and emotion. Their problem-solving skills and strategies, including the skills gleaned from negotiation, mediation, and client counseling, are important parts of the toolbox that they bring to the campus to aid in addressing these campus challenges.

Yet, as late as 2012, *The Chronicle of Higher Education* underreported that the trend of lawyers serving as college presidents was still relatively rare.[6] While the author estimated that the jump in lawyer presidents doubled since the last decade,[7] had he waited until the end of this decade, the number would actually have tripled. According to Scott Beardsley, who studied this trend, "you have traditional and you have nontraditional presidents at all types of universities, whether they're high-ranked or low-ranked. It's just that the proportion tended to indicate that smaller or lower-ranked institutions had a greater probability today of having nontraditional leaders."[8] In addition to the challenges that

---

4 Deloitte's Center for Higher Education Excellence and Georgia Tech's Center for 21st Centur Universities, *Pathways to the University Presidency: The Future of Higher Education Leadership* (n.p.: Deloitte University Press, 2017), accessed August 31, 2021, https://www2.deloitte.com/us/en/insights/industry/public-sector/college-presidency-higher-education-leadership.html. *See also* Kelly Field, "The Successful President of Tomorrow: The Five Skills Future Leaders Will Need," *Chronicle of Higher Education*, 2019, 34.
5 Deloitte's Center for Higher Education Excellence and Georgia Tech's Center for 21st Century Universities, *Pathways to the University Presidency*.
6 Peter Schmidt, "A Lawyer Takes an Uncommon Path to a University Presidency," *Chronicle of Higher Education*, January 1, 2012, accessed August 31, 2021, https://www.chronicle.com/article/a-lawyer-takes-an-uncommon-path-to-a-university-presidency/.
7 Ibid.
8 Rick Seltzer, "Defending Nontraditional Presidents," *Inside Higher Ed*, last modified August 30, 2017, accessed September 29, 2021, https://www.insidehighered.com/news/2017/08/30/new-book-examines-developments-hiring-nontraditional-college-presidents.

confront campuses, presidential search committees that are headed by lawyers may be more likely to yield a campus lawyer leader.⁹

Scholars and statisticians have been predicting for some time that, based upon declining birthrates and trends in enrollment, the business of higher education is headed for troubled times.¹⁰ In 2017, Harvard Business School professor Clayton Christensen predicted that 50% of U. S. colleges and universities will be bankrupt in ten to fifteen years.¹¹ Although this dire prediction may not materialize, it also does not take into account the number of new schools that may open and the number of schools that may merge. In 2018–2019, a staggering 236 colleges and universities closed their doors.¹² The 2018–2019 figures were double the number that closed in 2016–2017 and more than ten times the number of schools that closed in 2010–2011.¹³ This was even *before* the COVID-19 pandemic led to enormous financial pressure on higher education.

By the summer of 2020, NYU professor Scott Galloway examined about 10% of U. S. colleges and universities. He predicted that 89 of them could close as a direct result of the pandemic and identified another 129 that will struggle.¹⁴ This is consistent with the opinion of University of Pennsylvania professor Robert Zemsky, who estimates that about 200 private liberal arts institutions are likely

---

9   Julie Johnson, "The Law; Universities Looking to Lawyers for Leadership," *New York Times*, December 25, 1987, sec. B, https://www.nytimes.com/1987/12/25/us/the-law-universities-looking-to-lawyers-for-leadership.html.
10 Lauren Camera, "The Higher Education Apocalypse: A Steady Drip of Crises in Massachusetts and across New England May Just Signal Its Arrival," *U.S. News & World Report*, last modified March 22, 2019, accessed August 29, 2021, https://www.usnews.com/news/education-news/articles/2019-03-22/college-closings-signal-start-of-a-crisis-in-higher-education.
11 Abigail Johnson Hess, "Harvard Business School Professor: Half of American Colleges Will Be Bankrupt in 10–15 Years," *CNBC Make It: Careers*, last modified August 30, 2018, accessed August 29, 2021, https://www.cnbc.com/2018/08/30/hbs-prof-says-half-of-us-colleges-will-be-bankrupt-in-10-to-15-years.html.
12 "Table 317.50. Degree-Granting Postsecondary Institutions that have Closed Their Doors, by Control and Level of Institution: 1969–1970 through 2018–2019," *National Center for Education Statistics: Digest of Education Statistics*, accessed August 29, 2021, https://nces.ed.gov/programs/digest/d19/tables/dt19_317.50.asp?current=yes.
13 Ibid.
14 Scott Galloway, "U.SS University," *No Mercy/No Malice*, last modified July 17, 2020, accessed August 29, 2021, https://www.profgalloway.com/uss-university/. Some, such as Baylor University Dean Jeff Doyle, were quick to question the methodology of Galloway's research, in terms of which variables he chose to include and which he left out. See Jeff Doyle, "Should We Believe Scott Galloway's Predictions of Soon-To-Perish Colleges," *University Business*, last modified July 27, 2020, accessed August 29, 2021, https://universitybusiness.com/should-we-believe-scott-galloways-predictions-of-soon-to-perish-colleges/.

to close.[15] If these futurists are correct, it could signal closures for 10–20% of all institutions of higher education. However, this too is misleading as to real impact. For example, if twenty small colleges with average enrollments of 750 students per school close, that might barely cover the increase of enrollment at some very large state universities.

As enormous pressures weigh on all of higher education and many schools fight for survival, the COVID-19 pandemic continues to deal economic blows to the sector. According to the National Student Clearinghouse, as of March 25, 2021, spring 2021 enrollments were in the steepest decline since the start of the pandemic.[16] Most schools are heavily dependent on tuition and room and board revenues to cover budgeted operations.[17] With enrollment continuing to decline and mounting pressures to avoid increases and even cut tuition, thousands of schools face the prospect of severe deficits. The State University of New York told its sixty-four-campus network to expect a 25% reduction in state aid that year, on top of mounting revenue shortfalls from empty dorm rooms and lackluster out-of-state and foreign student enrollment.[18]

Changes in federal and state leadership add to the positive and negative infusion of cash to support higher education. One year into the pandemic, with rising costs and decreasing revenues, numerous colleges such as Becker College

---

15 Kai Ryssdal, "COVID-19: Some Small Colleges are Closing their Doors for Good amid Pandemic," August 20, 2020, in *Marketplace*, narrated by Sasha Asianian, podcast, audio, accessed August 29, 2021, https://www.marketplace.org/2020/08/20/some-small-colleges-closing-for-good-covid19/.

16 "As of March 25—three months into the spring semester, undergraduate enrollment is in its steepest decline so far since the pandemic began (–5.9%). Community college enrollment fell by double digits (–11.3%) for the first time in this pandemic. Graduate enrollment, on the other hand, continues to grow this spring (+4.4%). Overall postsecondary enrollment is down 4.2 percent from a year ago. Students aged 18–20, comprising over 40 percent of all undergraduates, saw the largest enrollment decline of any age group this spring (–7.2%), with the steepest drop occurring at community colleges (–14.6%). There is still no sign of any recession-related increase in adult enrollment at community colleges." COVID-19, Stay Informed with the Latest Enrollment Information: Spring 2021 Enrollment (As of March 25)," *National Student Clearinghouse Research Center*, last modified April 29, 2021, accessed August 29, 2021, https://nscresearchcenter.org/stay-informed/.

17 However, schools without dormitories, dining halls, and competitive league sports teams have not faced the same economic pressures.

18 Carl Campanile and Bernadette Hogan, "SUNY Campuses Prepare for 25 percent Cut in State Aid Amid Pandemic," *New York Post*, September 27, 2020, accessed October 14, 2020, https://nypost.com/2020/09/27/suny-campuses-face-25-percent-cut-in-state-aid-amid-pandemic/.

(MA),[19] Concordia College (NY),[20] MacMurray College (IL),[21] Urbana University (OH),[22] Holy Family College (WI),[23] and Judson College (AL)[24] had already announced permanent closures. Other schools, such as Wells College (NY),[25] publicly announced that they might not survive the pandemic, and Wesley College (DE) after struggling with enrollment and finances was acquired by Delaware State University in 2021.[26]

The Pennsylvania State University system announced plans to combine six of their fourteen schools into two (leaving ten schools in the system),[27] and in July 2021 Saint Leo University and Marymount California University announced an

---

19 Chris Burt, "Becker College Will Permanently Close after 237 Years, but Esports Will Survive," *University Business*, March 29, 2021, accessed August 29, 2021, https://universitybusiness.com/becker-college-will-permanently-close-after-237-years/?eml=20210330&oly_enc_id=9918E4543589E5D.

20 Ryan Santistevan, "Concordia College to Close: Iona College to Acquire Bronxville Campus," *Iohud*, January 28, 2021, accessed August 29, 2021, https://www.lohud.com/story/news/education/2021/01/28/concordia-college-closes-iona-college-acquires-bronxville-campus/4292059001/.

21 Ryssdal, "COVID-19."

22 Jennifer Smola, "Urbana University in Ohio Closing due to Coronavirus Challenges, Low Enrollment," *Cincinnati.com: The Enquirer*, April 22, 2020, accessed September 1, 2021, https://www.cincinnati.com/story/news/2020/04/22/urbana-university-ohio-closing-permanently-coronavirus/3002171001/.

23 Patti Zarling, "'Sad Situation': Manitowoc Mayor, College Leaders React to Holy Family College Closing," *Herald Times Reporter*, last modified May 6, 2020, accessed August 29, 2021, https://www.htrnews.com/story/news/2020/05/06/manitowoc-holy-family-college-closing-mayor-justin-nickels-leaders-react/5171455002/.

24 Jennifer David Rash, "Judson College Board of Trustees Votes to Close School," *The Alabama Baptist*, May 6, 2021, accessed August 29, 2021, https://thealabamabaptist.org/judson-college-board-votes-to-close-school/.

25 Emma Whitford, "Frank Assessment from a Private College," *Inside Higher Ed*, last modified May 15, 2020, accessed August 29, 2021, https://www.insidehighered.com/news/2020/05/15/wells-college-exemplifies-which-institutions-stand-lose-most-pandemic.

26 Elizabeth Redden, "A Cross-Town Acquisition," *Inside Higher Ed*, last modified July 2, 2021, accessed August 29, 2021, https://www.insidehighered.com/news/2021/07/02/delaware-state-university-finalizes-acquisition-neighboring-wesley-college?utm_source=Inside+Higher+Ed&utm_campaign=01799623bd-DNU_2021_COPY_02&utm_medium=email&utm_term=0_1fcbc04421-01799623bd-197546157&mc_cid=01799623bd&mc_eid=8696d9ba4f.

27 Bill Schnackner, "In Historic Vote, State System of Higher Education Sets Plan in Motion to Combine 6 Schools into 2," *Pittsburg Post-Gazette*, April 28, 2021, accessed August 30, 2021, https://www.post-gazette.com/news/education/2021/04/28/California-Clarion-Edinboro-university-colleges-merger-Pennsylvania-State-System-of-Higher-Education-Bloomsburg-Lock-Haven-Mansfield/stories/202104280084?utm_source=Iterable&utm_medium=email&utm_campaign=campaign_2277141_nl_Daily-Briefing_date_20210429&cid=db&source=ams&sourceId=4587547.

agreement to merge.²⁸ While noting the temporary help of the COVID relief aid from the federal government, in October 2021, three four-year colleges within the Vermont State College system merged under one name effective July 1, 2023—Vermont State University—to combat what was described as chronic underfunding and declining enrollment.²⁹

Compounding the tuition shortfall are staggering revenue losses from the cancellation of athletic events along with lost lucrative television and other media contracts, tickets sales, and without fans in seats, closed concession stations and a smaller demand for licensed team-wear for the roughly two dozen colleges and universities who generate substantial revenue from sports. Additionally, lost or reduced room fees for on-campus housing, cancellation of student charges for meal plans, the burden of cancelled or postponed theater and other events that yield revenue from ticket sales, parking, and other related sources (such as philanthropic support and advertising) is forcing schools to grapple with ever more challenging financial and legal issues, compounded by losses in the stock market that have decreased endowments in 2022.

The story is the same on both public and private university and college campuses throughout the United States. The ripple effects of the growing economic typhoon will be felt for years to come as each institution struggles to recover from the lasting impacts of COVID-19, even with the help of federal CARES Act (Coronavirus Aid Relief and Economic Recovery Act, 2020) and HEERF Act (Higher Education and Emergency Relief Fund Act, 2021) support. Compounding the problems in higher education that have already been highlighted, a 2021 survey of turnover rates in higher education found that, over the last thirty-six months, college and university presidents have turned over at a rate of 36%.³⁰

* * *

---

28   Emma Whitford, "Saint Leo University to Merge with Marymount California," *Inside Higher Ed*, last modified July 30, 2021, accessed August 30, 2021, https://www.insidehighered.com/news/2021/07/30/saint-leo-university-will-acquire-marymount-california?utm_source=Inside+Higher+Ed&utm_campaign=46c2c0cfa1-DNU_2021_COPY_02&utm_medium=email&utm_term=0_1fcbc04421-46c2c0cfa1-199790317&mc_cid=46c2c0cfa1&mc_eid=ef35c4ecbc.

29   Susan Greenberg, "3 Campuses Unite to Become Vermont State University," *Inside Higher Ed*, last modified October 1, 2021, accessed November 8, 2021, https://www.insidehighered.com/quicktakes/2021/10/01/3-campuses-unite-become-vermont-state-university?utm_source=Inside+Higher+Ed&utm_campaign=903c7d9065-DNU_2021_COPY_02&utm_medium=email&utm_term=0_1fcbc04421-903c7d9065-199790317&mc_cid=903c7d9065&mc_eid=ef35c4ecbc.

30   "College Administrator Data/Turnover Rates 2018-Present," *HigherEd Direct*, last modified March 31, 2021, accessed August 30, 2021, https://hepinc.com/newsroom/college-administrator-data-turnover-rates-2018-present/?utm_source=Iterable&utm_

The campus president is the face of the college or university. Their responsibility for vision, decision making, and communication makes them ultimately responsible for the short-term and possibly long-term fate of the institution. Presidents with legal training can put the lawyer's tool kit to good use making tough decisions, navigating legal complexities of compliance, and addressing issues arising from programmatic, human resources, and contractual obligations to help chart a sustainable course for the campus and the community it serves. This is likely why an increasing number of schools are discovering that lawyers often have the qualifications needed to succeed as presidents in the twenty-first century.

Yet, despite this trend and the large number of studies that have examined the leadership qualities of campus presidents, there is scant literature on the subject of lawyers leading higher education, leaving many important questions unexamined. This multi-year study on lawyer presidents, performed between 2019 and the first half of 2022, reveals that institutions increasingly are turning to lawyers to help lead during challenging times. This should not be surprising as a law degree has now been referred to as the modern "renaissance degree."[31] It not only examines the increasing abundance of lawyer presidents, with sixty new lawyer president appointments between January 2020 and June 2022, but it also reveals how this trend influences the diversity of presidents in terms of their educational backgrounds, professional experience, and demographics.

The goal of this undertaking is to demonstrate the value that lawyers may bring to the campus presidency. It is not to assert that only lawyers make great leaders in higher education. Rather, it demonstrates that lawyers should no longer be viewed as unconventional candidates, as they possess the requisite skill set to effectively lead a campus. Even the data suggests that by the end of the 2020s lawyers will occupy the presidency at 10% of Carnegie classified colleges and universities in the Unites States. While this trend has not yet been fully recognized in the literature or the higher education news, this book provides the historical and factual data to support the importance of considering lawyers as leaders in the campus C-suite.

---

medium=email&utm_campaign=campaign_2175853_nl_Daily-Briefing_date_20210402&cid=db&source=ams&sourceId=4587547.

31 Mark Curriden, "CEO, Esq.," *ABA Journal*, May 1, 2010, accessed August 30, 2021, https://www.abajournal.com/magazine/article/ceo_esq/ (quoting James Bradford, dean of the Owen School of Management at Vanderbilt University, who stated, "The law degree is today's renaissance degree").

CHAPTER 1

Lawyers, Leadership, and Higher Education

Lawyers have historically been viewed as change agents for better laws, public policy, and business decisions. When attorney Gloria Cordes Larson became president of Bentley University, she reflected that the experience she gained from a diverse career in law, government, business, and then higher education taught her that real change happens when people shake up the status quo.[1] Similarly, Benedict College lawyer President Roslyn Carter Artis said that "... as the higher education landscape continues to evolve—and in many instances becomes even more unstable—the calm, critical and analytical approach that most lawyers tend to apply will be even more useful in the future."[2]

In 2015, attorney Lawrence Schall, who served as President of Oglethorpe College, reflected: "Ten years ago I was a nontraditional president. Today I'm not. . . . There are so many presidents who haven't done [the traditional provost route] that I think the use of traditional and nontraditional is probably not the right terminology."[3] In September 2021, when St. John's College in Annapolis, Maryland appointed veteran law dean Nora Demleitner as their next president, the announcement by the board chair prioritized the importance of her legal experience, stating that "The Board of Visitors and Governors is proud to appoint a great legal mind, prolific writer, strategic leader, and

---

1 Gloria Larson, "From 'Recovering Lawyer' to University President: Q and A with Gloria Larson," *HuffPost*, August 16, 2017, accessed August 30, 2021, https://www.huffpost.com/entry/from-recovering-lawyer-to-university-president-q_b_599451d4e4b0a88ac1bc38a4?guccounter=1.
2 Lyle Moran, "Lawyers Find Their Skill Sets Make Them Ideal Candidates for College Presidencies," *ABA Journal*, April/May 2021, 61.
3 Beardsley, "The Rise of the Nontraditional Liberal Arts College President."

dedicated teacher as the first woman to be president of the third oldest college in America."[4]

Data shown in Table 1.1 below from the American Council on Education, culled from their recent American College President Study, reveals an increasing percentage of presidents who hold law degrees.[5]

Table 1.1. Presidents with JDs, All Survey Years

	President Holds JD		President Does Not Have JD		Total Sample
	N	%	N	%	N
2002	119	5.04%	2,240	94.96%	2,359
2007	118	5.69%	1,957	94.31%	2,075
2012	116	7.01%	1,539	92.99%	1,655
2017	122	7.89%	1,424	92.11%	1,546
Total	475		7,160		7,635

Note: Table shows the percentage of presidents who hold JD degrees in each survey.

Set in greater context, more comprehensive research shows that the last several decades have seen an exponential explosion of lawyers being appointed to college and university presidencies. Since the 1980s, the number of lawyers appointed as presidents has almost doubled every decade, starting with 50 in the 1980s and reaching a new high of 290 in the 2010s. With 60 appointments already in the first eighteen months of this decade, the extrapolated data suggests that by the end of the 2020s there will be 400 new lawyer presidents appointed, added to the number serving and accounting for retirements and resignations, suggesting that at least 10% of presidents of Carnegie classified colleges and universities will be lawyers. This is illustrated in the tables and charts on the next two pages.

---

4   "Nora Demleitner Appointed President of St. John's College, Annapolis," *St. John's College*, last modified September 24, 2021, accessed November 8, 2021, https://www.sjc.edu/news/nora-demleitner-appointed-president-st-johns-college-annapolis.

5   Jonathan Turk, "ACPS Data Request," email message to author, February 21, 2020; Jonathan Turk, "ACPS Data Request," email message to author, February 28, 2020.

Table 1.2. Appointments of Lawyer Presidents (by Decade)

Time Periods	# Distinct Presidents	# Total Appointments
1700s	1	1
1720s	1	1
1770s	1	1
1780s	2	2
1790s	1	1
1800s	2	2
1820s	3	3
1830s	8	8
1840s	10	11
1850s	7	8
1860s	7	7
1870s	9	9
1880s	19	22
1890s	11	11
1900s	13	14
1910s	5	5
1920s	9	9
1930s	12	12
1940s	15	18
1950s	15	15
1960s	32	33
1970s	40	50
1980s	44	50
1990s	70	76
2000s	131	148
2010s	251	290
2020s	60	60

Note: There is an acknowledged gap in the table from 1720 through 1770 and in the 1810s. While there is no way to be certain that there were no lawyer presidents appointed during this time, the research methodology used for this study did not reveal any appointments. The real focus of the research was in the last century leading through the 2010s. It should also be noted that the 2020s only accounts for appointments through August 2021.

The number of active presidents in 2020 and 2021 (292) was already more than three-quarters the number of active presidents for all of the 2010s (351 or 83.1%). This is further evidence foreshadowing an even greater number of lawyer presidents by the end of the 2020s than in each of the prior decades.

Chart 1.1. Distinct Lawyer Presidents Appointed by Decade

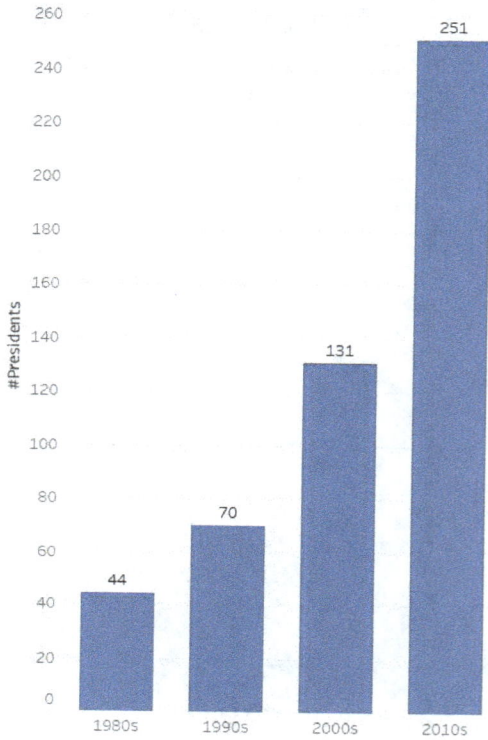

Notes
- Each appointment within a decade is counted by the start of a president's term.
- If a president was appointed twice in the same decade, they are only counted once.
- If a president was appointed in two different decades, they are counted in each decade.
- Appointments do not include presidents of private independent law schools.
- Appointments include presidents, chancellors, and CEOs.
- Interim positions are also included, and, if known, are generally considered as separate appointments from permanent positions.
- Presidents who started their appointment in 2020 and after are not included within this graph.
- Two current presidents have unidentified start dates for their terms. They are not included in this graph.

Table 1.3. Lawyers Serving as Presidents in Each Decade

Time Periods	# Distinct Presidents	# Total Appointments	# Active Presidents
1700s	1	1	1
1710s	0	0	1
1720s	1	1	2
1730s	0	0	1
1770s	1	1	1

Time Periods	# Distinct Presidents	# Total Appointments	# Active Presidents
1780s	2	2	3
1790s	1	1	4
1800s	2	2	5
1810s	0	0	3
1820s	3	3	4
1830s	8	8	11
1840s	10	11	16
1850s	7	8	13
1860s	7	7	13
1870s	9	9	18
1880s	19	22	27
1890s	11	11	24
1900s	13	14	25
1910s	5	5	20
1920s	9	9	21
1930s	12	12	22
1940s	15	18	26
1950s	15	15	29
1960s	32	33	43
1970s	40	50	66
1980s	44	50	71
1990s	70	76	110
2000s	131	148	196
2010s	251	290	351
2020s	60	60	292

Chart 1.2 is even more illustrative as each column represents the number of lawyer presidents who are actively serving during a specific decade. For example, if someone was appointed in 1980 and left in 2019, that president is counted in the last column in the 1980s, 1990s, 2000s, and 2010s. This provides a more accurate picture of how many lawyer presidents were actually active during a decade, irrespective of the decade of their appointment (which also tells a separate but equally important story).

Chart 1.2. All Appointments of Lawyer Presidents by Decade

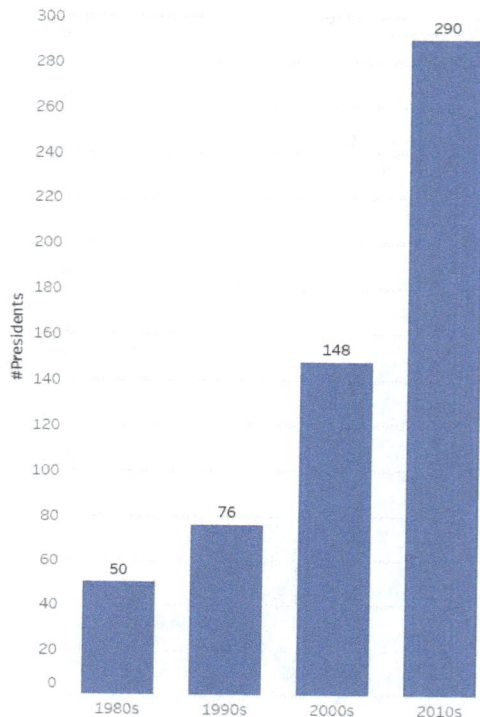

Notes
- Each appointment within a decade is counted by the start of a president's term.
- If a president was appointed twice in the same decade, they are counted for each appointment.
- If a president was appointed in two different decades, they are counted in each decade.
- Appointments do not include presidents of private independent law schools.
- Appointments include presidents, chancellors, and CEOs.
- Interim positions are also included, and, if known, are generally considered as separate appointments from permanent positions.
- Presidents who started their appointment in 2020 and after are not included within this graph.
- Two current presidents have unidentified start dates for their terms. They are not included in this graph.

Leadership Skills Needed in Times of Crisis

In "The Successful President of Tomorrow: The Five Skills Future Leaders Will Need,"[6] author Kelly Field argued that presidents of the future must be people, "... who will make difficult, data-driven decisions ... an innovator and risk-taker

---

6   Field, "The Successful President of Tomorrow," 2019.

who will reinvent the business model while staying true to institutional mission."[7] Field concluded that schools will "... require an expert communicator—someone who can make the case for change, calm the campus culture wars, and convince the public that college is indeed worth it."[8] The five essential skills distilled from interviews with more than three dozen presidents and leadership experts are: "analyzing the business; innovating; building relationships; careful communicating; and managing a crisis."[9] These are all core skills that most lawyers possess, or at least should have learned in law school or in practice.

As crises on college campuses escalated in the 2010s, differences were noticed in the ways in which lawyers and non-lawyers handled difficult situations. For example, one author described how business executive turned president, Timothy Wolfe, at the University of Missouri, did little to deescalate student tensions on campus, failed to consult with faculty and students on major decisions, and basically functioned in an autocratic manner.[10] This ultimately led to his resignation after less than three years.[11]

In her writing on the topic, Field contrasted Wolfe's style to that of Princeton president and lawyer Christopher Eisgruber (the first Princeton president to not have earned a PhD), who when faced with a campus crisis over racial justice issues "quickly met with student protesters, agreeing to consider or otherwise implement their demands, including that Woodrow Wilson's name be removed from school buildings and that the school create a mandatory class on 'the history of marginalized peoples.' He asked the Board of Regents to form a sub-committee that would collect information about Wilson's legacy, issued a long memo to the entire college that recognized their concerns and laid out detailed plans for the future."[12]

In assessing how these leaders chose to approach problem solving on their campuses, it is important to consider their prior professional backgrounds. President Eisgruber was a law professor at New York University for eleven years prior to joining the faculty at Princeton University where he served as director of the Program in Law and Public Affairs and later as provost. President Wolfe had no prior academic experience, and although he was president of Novell

---

7   Ibid., 5.
8   Ibid.
9   Ibid.
10 Laura McKenna, "Why Are Fewer College Presidents Academics?," *The Atlantic*, December 3, 2015, accessed August 30, 2021, https://www.theatlantic.com/education/archive/2015/12/college-president-mizzou-tim-wolfe/418599/.
11 Ibid.
12 Ibid.

Americas, the C-suite experience in the private sector was not enough to ensure his success in academia.

Lawyers Are Crisis Managers Adept at Navigating in the Unknown

Lawyers, due to the very nature of the job, must learn to work in the "grey area," where the law may not be precisely defined. After all, if the answers were clear-cut, there would be little need for clients to retain lawyers to explain to courts or other decision makers how the particular facts of a scenario ought to be applied under the existing body of law. This is why lawyers are often comfortable navigating in the unpredictability of the higher education arena, particularly in times of crisis, when their campus communities look for leadership signs of strength, vision, and security. Indeed, it has been noted by scholars in the field that one of the most significant advantages non-traditional presidents bring to the job are problem-solving approaches that employ fresh perspectives, thinking outside of the box, and freedom from focusing solely on the way things were done before.[13]

As discussed more fully in chapter four, an overwhelming number of lawyer presidents have had prior government experience. In the current fiscal crisis, these individuals have a distinct advantage in effectively advocating for funding for higher education as a whole and for the individual programs on their campuses that may qualify for support from diverse funding streams/programs within governments (for example, not a single higher education budget allocation but rather funding from housing, transportation, health, economic development, and other agencies or legislative interests at various levels of government, not to mention research grants). Notably, many of these former government lawyers turned campus leaders also have a great deal of experience fundraising for political candidates, demonstrating an ability to ask for contributions and opening a vast untapped network of wealthy givers who could easily become college donors. Their varied legal experience is often buttressed with business acumen and fiscal management experience from running law firms, leading corporations, and even from serving as general counsel inside higher education.

---

13 Daryl Delabbio and Louann Palmer, "A 360° View of Non-Traditional University Presidents," *Academic Leadership: The Online Journal* 7, no. 1 (Winter 2009): n.p., accessed August 30, 2021, https://scholars.fhsu.edu/cgi/viewcontent.cgi?article=1245&context=alj.

Legal Challenges Have Always Existed in Higher Education

Legal issues in higher education have been present dating to colonial times. One scholar posits that no other industry may be as heavily regulated as higher education, and that the scope of regulation is continually expanding as various stakeholders seek to hold colleges and universities accountable for their actions.[14] Even in an era of deregulation, the higher education experience has been the opposite, with government regulation impacting nearly all aspects of campus operations.[15]

By 1914, as a result of early tension challenging academic freedom, 18 professors from Johns Hopkins issued a call to colleagues at nine other universities to organize a national association in support of academic freedom.[16] In 1915, 867 professors from sixty colleges and universities became charter members of the resulting American Association of University Professors and issued the Declaration of Principles on Academic Freedom and Academic Tenure.[17]

It was not until the mid-1940s, after three centuries of higher education, that the landscape began to change as government began funding research conducted on university campuses leading to compliance requirements and then other areas of oversight and regulation.[18] Perhaps it is a small price to pay for the post-World War II funding to promote access to higher education, which has contributed more than $400 billion for more than twenty-five million students,[19] the National Defense Education Act (NDEA) enacted in 1958 that provided funding to promote postsecondary education,[20] and the Pell Grant

---

14   Barbara A. Lee, "Fifty Years of Higher Education Law: Turning the Kaleidoscope," *Journal of College and University Law* 36, no. 3 (2010): 649–690, https://heinonline.org/HOL/Print?collection=journals&handle=hein.journals/jcolunly36&id=699.

15   Stephen S. Dunham, "Government Regulation of Higher Education: The Elephant in the Middle of the Room," *Journal of College and University Law* 36, no. 1 (2009): 749–790, https://heinonline.org/HOL/Print?collection=journals&handle=hein.journals/jcolunly36&id=799.

16   Judith Areen and Peter F. Lake, *Higher Education and the Law*, 2nd ed., University Casebook Series (n.p.: Foundation Press, 2014), 87. While this is their position, it is acknowledged that other industries, such as nuclear power, airlines, food, drugs, and health care are also highly regulated.

17   Ibid., 88, citing American Association of University Professors, Declaration of Principles on Academic Freedom and Academic Tenure, 1 AAUP Bulletin, 17–39 (December 1915).

18   Dunham, "Government Regulation of Higher Education."

19   "75th Anniversary of the GI Bill," *U.S. Department of Veterans Affairs*, accessed August 30, 2021, https://benefits.va.gov/gibill/75th-anniversary.asp.

20   Thomas C. Hunt, "National Defense Education Act, United States [1958]," *Britannica*, last modified August 26, 2021, accessed September 30, 2021, https://www.britannica.com/topic/National-Defense-Education-Act.

program started in the early 1970s that, taken together with other financial aid programs, has exceeded $95 million in student support.[21]

Beginning in 1965 with the Higher Education Act,[22] followed by increased protections extended to higher education employees through the Equal Employment Opportunity Act[23] in the early 1970s, which extended Title VII of the Civil Rights Act of 1964 to institutions of higher education,[24] the amount of regulation continues to build. While today Title IX is a major enforcement/compliance area for higher education, it has roots with the passage of the Title IX Amendments of 1972[25] and the 1973 Rehabilitation Act.[26] It is true that since World War II, higher education, like dozens of other industries, has experienced increasing complexities, but other issues such as minors on campus, federal aid, food service, student housing, and the presence of campus police, may make for a far more complicated legal environment than many other businesses.

Even the leading luminaries in higher education have found it difficult to navigate legal storms on their college campuses, which can be influenced as well by local and state partisan politics. For example, former University of California president Clark Kerr, who, among other things, served as chairman and director of the Carnegie Commission on Higher Education and was credited with the philosophy underpinning of the 1972 Basic Educational Opportunity Grant (known as Pell grants) that all should be entitled to higher education regardless of ability to pay, was fired as UC president by then Governor Ronald Reagan for his handling of the Free Speech movement that swept the Berkeley campus during his tenure as chancellor.[27] Each time that a presidency is derailed, it likely

---

21 Dunham, "Government Regulation of Higher Education," 754.
22 Higher Education Act of 1965, Pub. L. No. 89–329, 86 Stat. 1219 (November 8, 1965), codified as amended 20 U.S.C. §1001 et seq.
23 Equal Employment Opportunity Act of 1972, Pub. L. No. 92–261, 86 Stat. 103 (March 24, 1972).
24 Title VII, Civil Rights Act of 1964, Pub. L. No. 88–352, 78 Stat. 253 (July 2, 1964), codified as amended 42 U.S.C. §2000e et seq.
25 Title IX of Educational Amendments of 1972, Pub. L. No. 92–318, 86 Stat. 235 (June 22, 1972).
26 Rehabilitation Act of 1973, Pub. L. No. 93–112, 87 Stat. 355 (September 26, 1973), codified as amended 29 U.S.C. §701 et seq.
27 "Although Mr. Kerr transformed the shape and the scope of public higher education, his contribution was partly eclipsed by the turbulent ending of his reign as chancellor of the Berkeley campus from 1952 to 1958 and as head of the full university from 1958 to 1967. His towering reputation as a leader of 20th-century American education was tarnished by his handling of the Free Speech Movement that swept the Berkeley campus in 1964. Caught in a crossfire from students on the left and politicians on the right, he was ousted in 1967 by the new governor, Ronald Reagan." Grace Hechinger, "Clark Kerr, Leading Public Educator and Former Head of California's Universities, Dies at 92," *New York Times*, December 23, 2003,

costs the campus community millions of dollars due to the resulting tarnished image, impacts on campus morale, and costs associated with the particulars of the incident leading to the demise of the leader.[28]

The increase in legal and regulatory challenges on college and university campuses has not let up in intensity.[29] The legalistic and litigious environment can be traced to many factors including, but not limited to: increasing consumer-driven expectations of students and their parents; increasing transparency enabled by data that allows consumers to compare and contrast institutions; increased political savvy of students and faculty; increasing sophistication of various advocacy groups; greater diversity of students and faculty as well as increasing demands for diversity, equity, and inclusion; greater acceptance and enforcement of civil rights; technology advances that impact intellectual property, privacy, and free speech issues.[30]

In addition, the rise of the regulatory state has generated federal, state, and local laws as well as agency rulemaking that contribute to complex compliance challenges in dozens of everyday campus business issues including: student records, student and campus safety, equal opportunity and communications.[31] Title IX, inter-collegiate sports, employment issues, disability accommodation, cybersecurity, and financial aid can be added to the growing list of hot-button legal issues on campus.[32] Not properly managed, each of these issues pose real threats of scandal and crisis that can severely damage the reputation and sustainability of campuses within hours of occurrence due to the internet and social media users, leaving little time for appropriate responses.[33] Leaders in higher education are also facing challenges with lower enrollments,[34] stagnant and decreasing government funding, and consumer-savvy students and parents who push back on tuition.[35] In this context, it is no surprise that campuses are increasingly turning

---

https://www.nytimes.com/2003/12/02/us/clark-kerr-leading-public-educator-former-head-california-s-universities-dies-92.html.

28 Stephen Joel Trachtenberg, Gerald B. Kauvar, and E. Grady Bogue, *Presidencies Derailed: Why University Leaders Fail and How to Prevent It* (n.p.: The Johns Hopkins University Press, 2013).
29 William A. Kaplin and Barbara A. Lee, *The Law of Higher Education*, 5th ed. (n.p.: Jossey-Bass, 2013), 3.
30 Ibid., 3–4.
31 Ibid., 4.
32 See, for example, Americans with Disabilities Act of 1990, 42 U.S.C. §12101 et seq.; Title VII of the Civil Rights Act of 1964, 42 U.S.C. §2000e et seq.; Age Discrimination in Employment Act 29 U.S.C. §621 et seq.; Rehabilitation Act of 1973 (Section 504 codified as amended), 29 U.S.C. §794; Equal Pay Act (Fair Labor Standards Act), 29 U.S.C. §206(d); Title IX of the Educational Amendments Act of 1972, 20 U.S.C. §1681 et seq.
33 Field, "The Successful President of Tomorrow," 4.
34 Ibid., 5 (noting that the number of high school graduates is expected to plummet in 2025).
35 Ibid., 4.

to lawyer-leaders. Placed in a larger context, more comprehensive research demonstrates that the last several decades have seen an exponential explosion of lawyers being appointed to college and university presidencies. Since the 1980s, the number of lawyers appointed as presidents has almost doubled every decade, starting with 47 in the 1980s and reaching a new high of 289 in the 2010s.

Litigation Floodgates Are Opening Demanding Both Preventive Law Strategies and Pragmatic Planning

Legal complaints against higher education institutions have become routine. As previously noted, issues surrounding laws such as Title IX, ADA compliance, other Civil Rights claims and Free Speech claims often cause students, faculty, staff and surroundings communities to bring legal actions against universities.

In this litigious environment, schools now spend significant resources constructing strategies to avoid or mitigate costly legal action. These strategies include the development of campus policies, language for handbooks and catalogs targeted at stakeholders, and a wide range of trainings, in the hopes of preventing legal issues from arising in the first place. These tasks not only rest on the shoulders of the campus counsel/compliance officers. Protecting the institution is also part of the fiduciary responsibility of board members, and it is the job of the president.

In fact, with growing complexities and increasing numbers of decision makers, college and university counsel find it increasingly difficult to identify who their client is—is it the board of trustees, the chancellor, the president, the college or university as a corporate entity, a dean or someone else who has made a decision subject of a lawsuit?[36] Roslyn Clark Artis, a lawyer-president at Benedict College, used her legal training and experience during the COVID crisis in spring 2020 to make critical campus decisions, noting, "The lawyer voice in me says, 'avoid liability at all costs and to the extent that you can, protect and preserve life at all costs.' . . . [S]o most of my decision-making is made against that backdrop."[37]

More than one hundred lawsuits have already been filed against colleges and universities stemming from decisions made in response to keeping campus communities safe during COVID-19. Litigation, thus far, ranges from class action suits seeking recovery of tuition for programs that pivoted from in-person to remote instruction to the refund of on-campus housing costs as well

---

36 Lee, "Fifty Years of Higher Education Law," 649–690.
37 Moran, "Lawyers Find Their Skill Sets," 55.

as a range of fees including lab fees, athletic fees, and student activity fees.[38] The pandemic also brought lawsuits over issues such as COVID-19 vaccine requirements and penalties for violating the code of conduct related to student behavior. Education Dive asked six campus leaders what their greatest challenges are in 2020, and their responses included: unpredictability,[39] maintaining affordability and advancing digitally,[40] making sure students feel welcome and respected in a national climate of conflict and disagreement,[41] and adapting the higher education model to different kinds of students—adult learners.[42]

In 2021, the National Association of College and University Attorneys list, among other things, the following categories of cases and developments on their website for campus general counsel: Accreditation, Authorizations and Higher Education Act; Athletics and Sports; Campus Police, Safety and Crisis Management; Compliance and Risk Management; Constitutional Issues; Contracts; Discrimination, Accommodation and Diversity; Ethics; Faculty and Staff; General Counsel; Governance; Immigration and International Activities; Intellectual Property; Investigations; Real Property, Facilities and Construction; Sexual Misconduct and Other Campus Violence; Students; Tax; and Technology.[43]

These issues, taken together, and if not properly managed, could have serious consequences for the educational mission of institutions of higher education changing dynamics of relationships between and among students, faculty, staff, and alumni, and shifting financial resources from educational purposes to legal

---

38 Patricia E. Salkin and Pamela Ko, "Should I Stay or Should I Go? Student Housing, Remote Instruction, Campus Policies," *The Urban Lawyer* 50, no. 3 (February 2021): 371–399, https://papers.ssrn.com/sol3/papers.cfm?abstract_id=3748864.
39 "7 College Presidents Share Their Biggest Challenges for 2020," *Higher Ed Dive*, last modified February 6, 2020, accessed August 31, 2021, https://www.highereddive.com/news/7-college-presidents-share-their-biggest-challenges-for-2020/571856/ (Carolyn Stefanco, College of St. Rose, discusses dealing with the free tuition programs, and mentions that Mary Marcy of Dominican College has stated, "One of the biggest challenges I expect to face at Dominican, and indeed expect most of higher education will be facing, is the challenge of unpredictability—in the national political climate, in the changes to enrollment practices, in the pressures on free speech and contested speech, and in the challenges to our business model. In the midst of this unpredictability, it will be essential for us to continue to implement those practices that we know are most effective for student and institutional success. It will also be important for us to continue to innovate in response to the volatile environment").
40 Ibid. (by Astrid Tuminez of Utah Valley University).
41 Ibid. (Freeman Hrabowski III of the University of Maryland, Baltimore County).
42 Ibid.
43 See the website of National Association of College and University Attorneys, accessed August 31, 2021, https://www.nacua.org/about-nacua.

and compliance matters.[44] This has led at least one scholar to recommend law-related training and education for faculty and academic administrators.[45]

While the earliest college counsel's office can be traced to the University of Alabama in 1925,[46] campus leaders began to recognize the significance of the legal environment within which they worked by the 1960s when 50 campuses had an in-house legal or general counsel.[47] Forty years later, in 2004, the number of campus lawyers who were National Association of College and University Attorneys (NACUA) members increased to 2,058,[48] and today, membership includes more than 1,850 campuses and more than 5,000 lawyers.[49]

Economist Clark Kerr, former president of the University of California, and a non-lawyer who dealt with controversial First Amendment issues on his own campus, commented in the late 1980s that with the increase in litigation surrounding college campuses, a president needs to have a lawyer by their side. He also noted that lawyers are accustomed to living with controversy, which has become routine for college presidents.[50] Dr. Ruth Weintraub, who was vice president for executive search for the Academy of Educational Development, believed that the trend that began in the 1980s of selecting lawyers to head universities was "something that could not have happened 10 years ago," as this phenomenon was "a response to the litigiousness of the 1970s that brought lawyers to the front."[51] The fact remains that campuses are no longer insulated from the litigious nature of society.[52]

The American Council on Higher Education confirmed this in their 2017 study on the American College President, noting in the foreword, "Now more than ever, leading an institution of higher education is a difficult and complicated endeavor."[53] As lawyer Thomas Ehrlich assumed the presidency of the University

---

44 See Le Von E. Wilson, "The Value of Law-Related Education for Faculty and Academic Administrators in Higher Education: The Challenge of Educating Educators," *Academy of Educational Leadership Journal* 11, no. 1 (2007): 34, https://www.proquest.com/docview/214227083/fulltextPDF/58F2C2FFC6AC453DPQ/1?accountid=30558, citing H. T. Edwards and V. D. Norton, *Higher Education and the Law* (Cambridge, MA: Institute for Educational Management, Harvard University, 1979). https://www.proquest.com/docview/214227083/fulltextPDF/58F2C2FFC6AC453DPQ/1?accountid=30558.
45 Wilson, "The Value of Law-Related Education," 25–41.
46 Robet D. Bickel and Peter H. Ruger, "The Ubiquitous College Lawyer," *Chronicle of Higher Education*, last modified June 25, 2004, accessed August 31, 2021, https://www.chronicle.com/article/the-ubiquitous-college-lawyer/.
47 Ibid.
48 Ibid.
49 See the website of National Association of College and University Attorneys.
50 Johnson, "The Law."
51 Ibid.
52 Wilson, "The Value of Law-Related Education."
53 Gagliardi et al., *American College President Study 2017*; Johnson, "The Law."

of Indiana in 1987, he told the *New York Times* that "Lawyers are trained to take a problem, break it into its component parts, work through the issues and put it all back together again."[54]

New pathways to the college presidency have opened in response to challenges and a changing job description that no longer supports the traditional notions of career academics moving up the ladder to the top leadership position on campus. A typical path began with a faculty member who became a dean and then a dean who became a provost, and provosts were thought of as the steppingstone to the presidency. According to a 1986 study sponsored by the Carnegie Corp and published by the Association of Governing Boards, "Almost 95 percent of presidents have administrative experience as department chairpersons, deans or provosts, as vice presidents inside academic life or administrators in nonacademic life."[55] This is no longer sacrosanct.

Further, the data demonstrates that it is no longer the case that schools are looking more favorably upon people who have served in the role as campus president in the past.[56] Nearly three-quarters of all college presidents appointed are new to the office of the president having never served in the role at another institution.[57]

With continuous, rapid, and accelerating changes in higher education, it is not a surprise that an increasing number of search committees and appointing boards are choosing lawyers to lead institutions of higher education. In recent decades, lawyers have been tapped to run some of the country's most elite institutions including Barnard, Berkeley, Chicago, Columbia, Dartmouth, George Washington University, Harvard, Johns Hopkins, New York University, Princeton, Stanford, Tufts, and Yale, as well as the State Universities of California, Chicago, Florida, Indiana, Iowa, Minnesota, Texas, and Virginia.

With over 4,000 institutions of higher education in the United States, there is a robust body of literature on leadership in higher education. Presidents have been studied and critiqued by biographers and by scholars, yet as noted, little attention has been paid to the trend of lawyers assuming the campus leadership position.[58] With, the number of lawyer president appointments more than doubling in each

---

54 Johnson, "The Law."
55 Clark Kerr and Marian L. Gade, *The Many Lives of Academic Presidents* (Washington, DC: Association of Governing Boards of Universities and Colleges, 1986), accessed August 30, 2021, https://files.eric.ed.gov/fulltext/ED267704.pdf.
56 Field, "The Successful President of Tomorrow," 34.
57 Trachtenberg, Kauvar, and Bougue, *Presidencies Derailed*, 13.
58 Valerie Strauss, "Lawyers Are Leading U.S. Colleges and Universities More than Ever Before. Is That Good or Bad for Higher Education?," *Washington Post*, January 15, 2020, accessed August 30, 2021, https://www.washingtonpost.com/education/2020/01/15/lawyers-are-leading-us-colleges-universities-more-than-ever-before-is-that-good-or-bad-higher-education/.

decade of the last three, and a staggering 159 lawyers appointed in the 2010s at this rate, by 2029, lawyers will account for roughly 400 presidents or more than 10% of all sitting presidents. Considering that, from 1900 to 1989, fewer than 1% of college presidents were lawyers, these numbers are astonishing.

Lawyers have always been leaders in society. They have played pivotal leadership roles in government. The majority of United States presidents have been lawyers and close to half of the members of Congress are lawyers.[59] While less than 0.5% of the American population are lawyers, as a profession, lawyers have been leaders at all levels of government and have been the heads of public, private, and non-profit corporations.[60] It should therefore be no surprise that lawyers have increasingly been tapped to lead institutions of higher education.

Roughly thirty-five years ago, on December 25, 1987, the *New York Times* reported that the complexities of running colleges and universities have resulted in schools looking beyond academia to recruit the best person for the campus presidency.[61] Noting that, by the end of 1987, lawyers were running prestigious schools such as Yale, Harvard, and Columbia, as well as dozens of smaller schools, experts were not yet ready to declare it a trend.[62] Yet, Dr. Ronald Stead, who served as director of presidential search for the Association of Governing Boards of Colleges and Universities, observed that by 1987 the campus presidency has become much more complicated that it had been two decades earlier.[63]

The job of the college president today encompasses ensuring campus compliance with federal, state and local regulations; advocating in the public policy arena for desired and needed higher education reforms; and resource generation from the public, private, and non-profit sectors all tied to ensuring the economic sustainability of the institution. Presidents have to be flexible to adapt to changing landscapes and they must be able to quickly assess opportunities and challenges. Lawyers tend to be comfortable navigating in these waters. They also bring creativity and problem-solving skills, political prowess, collaborative management approaches, preventive law strategies, and communication and negotiation skills, the ability to react quickly and strategically to the unexpected, and the ability to manage difficult personalities, honed from experience. Some lawyer presidents have been tapped by up to three or more different institutions to serve as their leader, and one of them, E. Gordon Gee, has served the most

---

59 Deborah L. Rhode, *Lawyers as Leaders* (New York: Oxford University Press, 2013), 1.
60 Johnson, "The Law."
61 Ibid.
62 Rhode, *Lawyers as Leaders*, 1.
63 Johnson, "The Law."

institutions of any college president, having been appointed president seven times at five different schools.

Another reason that lawyers have become desirable candidates to lead the campus are the political, financial, and managerial skills they bring to the table.[64] The politicization of the campus presidency continues to play out across the country on campuses of all sizes and shapes. For example, Carol Folt, chancellor of the University of North Carolina at Chapel Hill, announced her intention to resign in the wake of the "Silent Sam" Confederate monument controversy, a case that surely highlights the difficult waters college presidents navigate between a trend of ideologically driven governance board and increasingly activist campus constituencies.[65]

While the political influences at public institutions of higher education have always been in the background, sometimes even becoming somewhat public, such as Governor Ronald Regan's "war" on the University of California, today there are a barrage of headlines accusing university and college governing boards of being controlled by the governors who appointed them. Issues surrounding governing boards have existed since the start of higher education, pre-dating the American Revolution. The colonists adopted a new form of governance, not found at Oxford and Cambridge, when they established governing boards that consisted of political and religious leaders rather than academic faculty and vested the boards with authority over campus matters.[66]

What Are Campuses Searching for Today and Why These Skills Can Be Found in Lawyers

As the job of the campus president has changed as described herein, boards of trustees and campus stakeholders have sought a different skill set in their leaders. According to Paul Hsun-Ling Chou, co-managing director and senior client partner of the Korn Ferry Global Education Practice, "Before many presidents got promoted because of their records of scholarly achievement. Now presidents

---

64 Ibid.
65 Adam Harris, "Who Wants to Be a College President? Probably Not Many Qualified Candidates," *The Atlantic*, January 24, 2019, accessed November 12, 2021, https://www.theatlantic.com/education/archive/2019/01/how-politics-are-reshaping-college-presidency/581077/.
66 As compared to the governance structure at Oxford, which consists of a twenty-six-member Council that makes policy on some matters but the final responsibility rests with the Congregation, which is made up of about 4,000 members of the faculty and academic staff. See Areen and Lake, *Higher Education and the Law*, 32.

have to have a diverse background in managing complexity.... They need to be capable at managing governance and persuading the board, faculty and the general public of their strategy, and have access to networks of powerful people who can make it happen."[67]

Chou notes that among the skills university leaders need to be successful today are: complex problem solving, critical thinking, emotional intelligence, cognitive flexibility, people management, and collaborating with others.[68] Not coincidentally, these are found among the myriad skills that effective lawyers bring to the table. Lawyers are trained to be creative problem solvers who must be persuasive with opposing counsel, jurors, and judges. Critical thinking is a key component of legal education, as is emotional intelligence, which is necessary not just for client counseling, but also as part of the power of persuasion.

Collaboration and team-based approaches are critical as lawyers in government, in-house counsel, and those practicing in medium to large-size and multinational law firms must effectively collaborate to bring expertise from different perspectives to the fore, to analyze and assess problem solving from all angles. Lawyers manage people every day—from clients to associates, support staff, expert witnesses, and others who are needed to effectively run a law office and represent client interests. Chou also points to the importance of managing governance and access to networks of powerful people who can make things happen, and this is reflected in the backgrounds of many lawyer presidents who have experience working in government. This dimension of the lawyer presidency will be discussed further in chapter four.

Higher education search consultants Ginny Schaefer Horvath, former president of the State University of New York at Fredonia, and Maya Ranchod Kishore, both with Academic Search, report that, as we enter the new decade, senior leaders for colleges and universities must have or develop the following ten essential skills for current and anticipated changes in higher education: financial acuity, cultural competency, technological deftness, crisis management, entrepreneurial mindset, political savviness, empathy and respect, multi-genre communication skills, high emotional intelligence, and agility.[69] In examining

---

67 Paul Hsun-Ling Chou, "The Dark Spots on the Ivory Tower: Leaders in Higher Education Are Facing More Scrutiny, Higher Stress and Lower Job Security," *Korn Ferry*, accessed August 31, 2021, https://www.kornferry.com/insights/this-week-in-leadership/the-dark-spots-on-the-ivory-tower.
68 Ibid.
69 Ginny Schaefer Horvath and Maya Ranchod, "Sharpening the Lens for Hiring Leaders," *2020 Vision Academic Search*, last modified 2020, accessed August 31, 2021, https://academicsearch.org/wp-content/uploads/formidable/8/ASI-2020-Vision-Article.pdf.

each of these ten requirements, they are either part of overt legal education or skills honed through legal practice. For example, financial acuity is acquired by lawyers in formal education in courses including business/corporate law, tax law, trusts and estates, family law, antitrust law, and accounting for lawyers, where law students must work with balance sheets, audited financial statements, economic forecasting, stocks and investing, pensions, marital assets/equitable distribution, and tax returns. In practice, lawyers apply these skills to serve their individual, corporate, or nonprofit clients. In addition, running a law firm or a law office requires business financial acumen for budgeting, forecasting, real estate investments, personnel matters, and other related transactions.

The authors' second required skill set is cultural competency. Law students have historically acquired this as part of an ingrained commitment to access to justice and social justice. They have also learned about civil rights and equality through constitutional law courses, labor and employment law, immigration law, and more specialized courses focusing on diversity, equity, and inclusion. The American Bar Association's Council on Legal Education recently issued proposed changes to the Standards for Legal Education that would require, among other things, that law schools provide training and education to law students on bias, cross-cultural competency, and racism both at the start of their formal program of legal education and at least once before graduation.[70]

In addition, following a resolution adopted by the American Bar Association House of Delegates in 2017,[71] many states have amended their continuing education requirements to mandate training in diversity, inclusion and the elimination of bias.[72] This is an example of the changing legal landscape that lawyer

---

70 ABA Standards Committee to The Council (Council on Legal Education), memorandum, "Proposed Changes to Standards 205, 206, 303, 507 and 508," May 7, 2021, accessed August 31, 2021, https://www.americanbar.org/content/dam/aba/administrative/legal_education_and_admissions_to_the_bar/council_reports_and_resolutions/may21/21-may-standards-committee-memo-proposed-changes-with-appendix.pdf. See also Karen Sloan, "ABA Pushes Forward with Racism Training Requirement for Law Schools," Law.com, May 17, 2021, accessed August 31, 2021, https://www.law.com/2021/05/17/aba-pushes-forward-with-racism-training-requirement-for-law-schools/.

71 "American Bar Association, Resolution (Adopting the Model Rule for Minimum Legal Education and Accompanying Report)," *American Bar Association*, last modified February 6, 2017, accessed August 31, 2021, https://www.americanbar.org/content/dam/aba/directories/policy/2017_hod_midyear_106.pdf.

72 For example, in 2020 the Supreme Court of New Jersey amended its CLE requirements to mandate coursework for licensed attorneys in diversity, inclusion, and the elimination of bias. Stuart Rabner, Chief Justice, and Glen A. Grant, J.A.D., "Notice to the BAR and Order" (Continuing Legal Education Requirement of Two Hours [per Two-year Reporting Cycle] of Courses in Diversity, Inclusion, and Elimination of Bias; Judiciary to Offer Real-time Virtual Courses on Implicit Bias and Elimination of Bias), *Supreme Court of New Jersey*, last modified

leaders must navigate and while successful lawyer presidents possess cultural competencies that enable them to lead with authenticity, whether this sensitivity is innate or learned, it is clear that for future generations of lawyer leaders it will be reinforced as part of formal legal education.

The third skill identified is technological deftness. The legal profession was early in ensuring that licensed lawyers are tech savvy as attorney professionalism requires this knowledge and law practice cannot survive without it. In 2012, the American Bar Association amended its Model Rules of Professional Conduct adding a comment to Rule 1.1 addressing competency that provides: "To maintain the requisite knowledge and skill, a lawyer should keep abreast of changes in the law and its practice, including the risks associated with relevant technology. . . ."[73] This competency requires, among other things, that lawyers demonstrate: a level of proficiency regarding cybersecurity and safeguarding information; electronic discovery including its use and the responsibility to retain and provide electronic information; the need for back-ups; using technology to deliver client services including use of electronic court scheduling and the ability to electronically communicate with courts and other counsel including the appropriate sharing of files; understanding metadata and how it is used and how to protect client and office information through encryption; using technology in the courtroom; the use of electronic case and document management systems; and using technology as a source to gather relevant facts and information.[74] For campus presidents, it may mean being able to make the right hire for a competent chief information officer as lawyers may be more sensitized to technology issues from practice and professionalism requirements than

---

October 20, 2020, accessed August 31, 2021, https://www.njcourts.gov/notices/2020/n201021e.pdf?c=c2f. New Jersey joins California, Illinois, Maine, Minnesota, Missouri, New York, Oregon and others. See Christine Hernández and Annie Martínez, "Leading the Way to a Diversity-Focused CLE Requirement," *Colorado Lawyer*, last modified December 2020, accessed August 31, 2021, https://k794ovkhls2hdtl419uu4dcd-wpengine.netdna-ssl.com/wp-content/uploads/2020/11/Dec2020_Welcome-PM.pdf.

73 "ABA Model Rules of Professional Conduct, Rule 1.1, Competence Comment," *American Bar Association*, accessed August 31, 2021, https://www.americanbar.org/groups/professional_responsibility/publications/model_rules_of_professional_conduct/rule_1_1_competence/comment_on_rule_1_1/.

74 Don Macauley, "What Is A Lawyer's Duty Of Technology Competence?," *National Jurist*, February 2, 2019, accessed August 31, 2021, http://www.nationaljurist.com/smartlawyer/what-lawyers-duty-technology-competence. See also Melinda J. Bentley, "Ethics: The Ethical Implications of Technology in Your Law Practice: Understanding the Rules of Professional Conduct Can Prevent Potential Problems," *The Missouri Bar*, February 17, 2020, accessed August 31, 2021, https://news.mobar.org/ethics-the-ethical-implications-of-technology-in-your-law-practice-understanding-the-rules-of-professional-conduct-can-prevent-potential-problems/.

perhaps a non-lawyer campus president whose academic discipline may not have required such attention.

Crisis management, the fourth required skill noted, is a space where most lawyers are comfortable navigating. Lawyers learn through formal Socratic education, problem solving, and law and public policy experiences to function well in unknown space by applying information and skills. Lawyers are trained to take charge in crisis situations by analyzing the facts and helping to develop and chart a decisive (but well-thought-out) course forward. The leadership exhibited by lawyers can, and often does, have a calming effect for otherwise anxious or excited clients or stakeholders.

Possessing an entrepreneurial mindset, the fifth desired skill, is also a requirement for successful lawyers in general. While, in the past, many lawyers did not necessarily possess the entrepreneurial mindset as they largely focused on rules and deadlines, today a new breed of lawyers are running law firms and legal start-ups as entrepreneurs would—demonstrating tenacity, resourcefulness, flexibility, measured risk taking, and the ability to move quickly.[75]

The sixth desired skill, political savviness, is another skill many lawyers possess. Horvath and Kirkhope posit that campus leaders today must be able to navigate on both sides of the political aisle, and work through relationships and messaging not just with government officials but also with donors, employees, and families who may express strong and/or controversial political views.[76] As the data in chapter four reveals, many lawyer presidents have worked as staff in the legislative and executive branches of government, and a good number have been elected officials, often at very high level. Thus, they have insight and experience gained from these positions and have relationships that are highly desirable to help advance the campus economically, programmatically, and reputationally.

Empathy and respect, the seventh trait identified by Horvath and Kirkhope, combined with high emotional intelligence, the ninth trait, are also qualities found in lawyers. Lawyers are taught to be sincere and honest and to have empathy and respect for others, including opposing counsel while in law school through client counseling experiences in clinics and externships. Through pro

---

75 Adriana Gardella, "The Secret of Lawyers-Turned-Entrepreneurs?," *Forbes*, last modified April 10, 2015, accessed September 1, 2021, https://www.forbes.com/sites/adriana-gardella/2015/04/10/the-secret-of-lawyers-turned-entrepreneurs/?sh=24e83d067cec. See also Jonathan Tobin, "Q&A: Lawyer As Entrepreneur," *Law Technology Today*, last modified April 17, 2015, accessed September 1, 2021, https://www.lawtechnologytoday.org/2015/04/qa-lawyer-as-entrepreneur/.
76 Schaefer Horvath and Ranchod, "Sharpening the Lens for Hiring Leaders."

bono and community engagement work, many lawyers volunteer to help people struggling to maintain decent shelter, obtain food, and defend themselves when confronted by the power of the state through the police and prosecutors. The pro bono ethic that is instilled in many law students[77] is a contributing factor to a lawyer's ability to demonstrate authentic concern and humanity in interactions with all people. While many in the legal profession have not always scored as well in the area of emotional intelligence, the American Bar Association has focused attention to better educate lawyers of the importance of this skill.[78]

The eighth desirable skill, multi-genre communication skills, is an area where ideally lawyers are particularly adept since without these skills lawyers cannot be successful. Lawyers have to communicate effectively with many different people on a routine basis—clients, professional and support staff, other lawyers, witnesses (who may sometimes be reluctant and adverse), regulators, judges, the public, the media, and vendors. Lawyers communicate through multiple modalities—in person, via phone, through email, and by formal letters. In face-to-face communications, lawyers have to speak, listen, and observe body language. Further, the communication skills honed through trial practice are easily transferred to administering a college. Lawyers consider their audience to shape and frame the facts and to explain the narrative in a manner to connect with the intended receiver of the information. Through communication, lawyers are taught to exude honesty, confidence, and emotional intelligence, among other messages that leadership requires. As members of the bar, they are obligated to be honest and at least never to lie to courts or clients.[79] Most of all, the business of lawyering is often one of

---

[77] See, for example, Court of Appeals, State of New York, "Rule 520.16, Pro Bono Requirement for Bar Admission" (22 N.Y. Comp. Codes R. & Regs. §520.16), last amended 2012, current through October 15, 2020, *Westlaw, New York Codes, Rules and Regulations*, accessed September 1, 2021, https://govt.westlaw.com/nycrr/Document/I14be86f14dbb11e2b9e30000845b8d3e?viewType=FullText&originationContext=documenttoc&transitionType=CategoryPageItem&contextData=(sc.Default), mandating that essentially every applicant admitted to the bar in New York on or after January 1, 2015 must first complete fifty hours of qualifying pro bono service prior to filing an application for admission.

[78] Ronda Muir, "Emotional Intelligence for Lawyers," *ABA Career Center* (blog), accessed September 1, 2021, https://www.americanbar.org/careercenter/blog/emotional-intelligence-for-lawyers/; Gray Robinson, "Family Lawyers and Emotional Intelligence," *Family Lawyer Magazine.com*, August 26, 2021, accessed September 1, 2021, https://familylawyer-magazine.com/family-lawyers-and-emotional-intelligence/.

[79] When lawyers fail to meet this standard, they may lose their license to practice law, as Rudy Giuliani did. See Nicole Hong, William K. Rosenblaum, and Ben Protess, "Court Suspends Giuliani's Law License, Citing Trump Election Lies," *The New York Times*, June 24, 2021, accessed September 30, 2021, https://www.nytimes.com/2021/06/24/nyregion/giuliani-law-license-suspended-trump.html.

persuasion, requiring lawyers to convince others that they are advancing the correct or best solution to a particular challenge. All aspects of lawyering communication are helpful and necessary for campus presidents.

Agility, the final key skill, is found in lawyers who are trained to think quickly on their feet, pivot as necessary, perfect the art of compromise, and routinely become quick learners of new subjects.

Richard Vedder, who directs the Center for College Affordability and Productivity, points out the desirability of legal training for campus presidents. An adjunct scholar at the American Enterprise Institute, he compiled the Forbes Best 75 Colleges List, noting that, "good university presidents also need to have good interpersonal communication skills, honesty, integrity, innate intelligence, discipline, a strong work ethic, et cetera. Additionally, it may well be that presidents from some other disciplines are disproportionately represented among presidents—law, for example, may well be a useful field for university presidents to have had acquired knowledge."[80]

As this chapter and the rest of this book will demonstrate, not only were these non-traditional presidents not nearly as rare as they are portrayed, but, then and now, lawyers offer higher educational institutions many skills that can help them succeed in a constantly changing environment. This includes expert crisis management, the ability to navigate government regulation, and the ability to deal with the increasing litigation college and universities face. Given this, it is critical to have a fuller understanding the rise of the lawyer presidents, both quantitatively and qualitatively—as this book offers its readers.

---

80 Richard Vedder, "Training to Be a College President," *Forbes*, last modified August 30, 2016, accessed September 1, 2021, https://www.forbes.com/sites/ccap/2016/08/30/training-to-be-a-college-president/?sh=cd7c7a171a1f.

CHAPTER 2

Historically, Lawyers Have Been at the Forefront of Higher Education

---

Having lawyers serve as leaders is not new in higher education. Rather, there is a long history connecting the legal profession to academia. The key is to recognize the changes in society that required leaders to have different backgrounds and skills than those a traditional academic background would offer a president. This is particularly seen in periods such as the Industrial Revolution in the late nineteenth century and the Civil Rights Movement of the 1950s and 1960s. These moments in time saw higher educational institutions needing leaders who could effectively navigate changes in social structures and in the relationship between the government and educational institutions, not unlike some of the challenges presently confronting campuses in the second decade of the current century.

Early Higher Education Leaders

While higher education and the modern university dates back to twelfth-century Europe,[1] higher education has been part of the fabric of this country since the founding of Harvard College in 1636, followed by College of William and Mary in 1693[2] and the Collegiate School (which was renamed Yale College)

---

1   U.S. Department of Education, *Reform in American Public Higher Education*, by Harriett J. Robles, research report no. ED 426746 (1998), 3, accessed November 8, 2021, https://files.eric.ed.gov/fulltext/ED426746.pdf, noting that "Forms of specialized learning, principally in law and medicine, were created in response to social needs and demands. . . ."
2   Ibid.

in 1701.³ By the beginning of the American Revolution, nine colleges had been formed: Harvard, William and Mary, Yale, Princeton, King's or Columbia, The University of Pennsylvania, Brown, Dartmouth, and Queen's, which became Rutgers.⁴ North Carolina established the first public university in 1795,⁵ followed by Ohio with the University in Athens in 1802.⁶ By 1851, the United States had 120 institutions of higher education. The first research universities opened in 1852, signaling an increased professionalization of the academic faculty who possessed PhD degrees.⁷

In the eighteenth century, most colleges were led by members of the clergy. This is not surprising given that the early financial support for higher education was tied to upholding religious beliefs such as Puritanism.⁸ These early presidents set the tone for an "... American model of a strong president under the authority of an external governing board with a relatively weak faculty."⁹

Both John Leverett of Harvard and Elisha Williams at Yale were lawyers who set a pattern of the strong college presidency.¹⁰ Leverett was also noted for moving Harvard toward a more secular rather than divinity focused school.¹¹ A few colleges at the time had a lawyer president such as:

- John Leverett, Harvard University (1708–1724);
- Elisha Williams, Yale University (1726–1739);
- Jonathan Dickinson, College of New Jersey (Princeton) (1747);
- William Samuel Johnson, Columbia University (1787–1800);

---

3   Roger L. Geiger, "The First Century of the American College, 1636–1740," in his *The History of American Higher Education: Learning and Culture from the Founding to World War II* (Princeton: Princeton University Press, 2014), accessed September 1, 2021, http://assets.press.princeton.edu/chapters/s10320.pdf.
4   "Colleges in the Colonial Times. A Lecture by Prof. Tyler—Harvard's Tariff for College Sins," *The Harvard Crimson* (Boston, MA), April 20, 1883, accessed September 30, 2021, https://www.thecrimson.com/article/1883/4/20/colleges-in-the-colonial-times-prof/. See also U.S. Department of Education, *Reform in American Public Higher Education*, 4, noting about these early institutions, "All colleges were public because they were integral to the colonies and chartered by civic government."
5   Areen and Lake, *Higher Education and the Law*, 58–59.
6   Ibid., 56.
7   Ibid., 72.
8   Geiger,"The First Century of the American College."
9   Ibid.
10 Ibid.
11 "John Leverett, Educator, Lawyer, Politician," *Prabook*, accessed September 1, 2021, https://prabook.com/web/john.leverett/2231353.

- Abraham Baldwin, University of Georgia (1785–1801); and
- David Kerr, University of North Carolina (1794–1796).
- Bishop James Madison, College of William and Mary (1777–1812) (whose namesake cousin was the more famous U. S. President), was admitted to the bar but never practiced.

As law and medicine began to attract more educated New Englanders than the pulpit between 1700 and 1760,[12] over time, fewer academically talented New Englanders were choosing ministry upon college graduation.[13] The training of lawyers during this era was influenced by the English attorney and solicitor model, involving an apprenticeship with a lawyer for a period of time coupled with a written exam before being admitted to practice.[14] In the Northern states, such as Massachusetts, the apprenticeship could be as much as five years (with a one-year reduction if the apprentice was a college graduate), historian Robert Stevens suggests that ". . . at the time of independence the American bar may have had an even firmer structure, at least in requirements for preparation, than either branch of the legal profession in England."[15] The motivation, preparation, and focus to successfully complete this training is indicative of the work ethic required to successfully pursue a legal career.

By the nineteenth century, colleges and universities were appointing a handful of lawyers to the presidency, but the professionalization of the academy made faculty members from within more desirable candidates for the assignment. Noted nineteenth-century lawyer presidents include:

- Josiah Meigs, University of Georgia (1801–1810);
- Asa Messer, Brown University (1802–1826);
- William DeLancy, University of Pennsylvania (1828–1834);
- Josiah Quincy, Harvard University (1829–1845);
- Peter Clark, Washington College (1829–1832);
- William Alexander Deur, Columbia University (1829–1842);
- David Elliott, Washington College (1830–1831);

---

12 James W. Schmotter, "Ministerial Careers in Eighteenth-Century New England: The Social Context, 1700–1760," *Journal of Social History* 9, no. 2 (Winter 1975): 249–267, http://www.jstor.org/stable/3786254.
13 Ibid., 251.
14 Robert Bocking Stevens, *Law School: Legal Education in America from the 1850s to the 1980s* (Chapel Hill, NC: University of North Carolina Press, 1983), 3.
15 Ibid.

- David Lowry Swain, University of North Carolina (1835–1868);
- Ignatius Alphonso Few, Emory University (1836–1839);
- William Maxwell, Hampden-Sydney (1838–1845);
- Abraham Bruyn Hasbrouck, Rutgers University (1840–1850);
- Augustus Baldwin Longstreet, Emory University (1840–1848);
- Nathaniel Fish Moore, Columbia University (1842–1849);
- Robert Emory, Dickinson College (1842–1843 interim; 1845–1847);
- Robert Jefferson Breckinridge, Jefferson College (1845–1847);
- Theodore Dwight Wolsey, Yale University (1846–1871);
- George Foster Pierce, Emory University (1848–1854);
- Theodore Frelinghuysen, Rutgers University (1850–1862);
- Andrew J. Sutton, Washington College (1860–1867);
- William Henry Purnell, University of Delaware (1870–1875);
- Charles Henry Fowler, Northwestern University (1873–1876);
- Kent Plummer Battle, University of North Carolina (1876–1891);
- Oliver Marcy, Northwestern University (1876–1881, 1890);
- Joseph Cummings, Northwestern University (1881–1890);
- Lyon Gardiner Tyler, College of William and Mary (1888–1919);
- Henry Wade Rogers, Northwestern University (1890–1900); and
- Walter Barnard Hill, University of Georgia (1899–1905).

The 1880s represented a "building boom" for colleges and universities with more than 200 new institutions charted.[16] Spurred in part by the Morrill Land-Grant Act of 1862, which authorized the sale of federal lands to finance colleges with offerings, including, among other things, agriculture and mechanic arts.[17] As the charts that follow demonstrate, from the 1830s through the 1870s, the number of lawyer campus presidents was relatively stable at roughly eight or nine per decade. However, the number more than doubled in the 1880s.

This change in president qualifications coincided with the industrial revolution in the United States, which challenged higher education to address shifting social and economic conditions.[18] Education in just the classics declined

---

16 John R. Thelin et al., "Higher Education in the United States: Historical Development, System," *Education Encyclopedia—StateUniversity.com*, https://education.stateuniversity.com/pages/2044/Higher-Education-in-United-States.html.
17 U.S. Department of Education, *Reform in American Public Higher Education*, 6.
18 Cengage, "1878–1899: Education: Overview," *Encyclopedia.com*, accessed September 1, 2021, https://www.encyclopedia.com/history/news-wires-white-papers-and-books/1878-1899-education-overview.

as scientific approaches, including Darwin's theory of evolution slowly made its way into the curriculum.[19] Moreover, during this time, thousands of young men and a few women went to Europe, and Germany in particular, to access postgraduate opportunities. They returned home to help reshape American colleges into research universities.[20] By the end of the 1880s, the federal government increased financial support for the land grant colleges, helping to further increase the stature of higher education.[21] A second Morrill Land-Grant Act was enacted in 1890 providing federal financial support to land-grant colleges.[22]

With law recognized as a learned profession, though at that time one not requiring higher education (as evidenced by the small number of law schools) and with the challenge of change upon the education sector, given the leadership traits associated with the legal profession, the increase in lawyer presidents during the 1880s is explainable. However, as shown on the chart below, the number of lawyer presidents decreased by 50% in the 1890s. During this decade, the evolution of higher education witnessed a decrease in emphasis on the liberal arts and an increase in technical and professional schools.[23] The 1870s through the 1910s have been referred to by some historians as the "gilded age" of higher education.[24]

---

19 Ibid.
20 Ibid.
21 Thelin et al., "Higher Education in the United States."
22 U.S. Department of Education, *Reform in American Public Higher Education*, 6.
23 Cengage, "1878–1899: Education: Overview."
24 Ibid. However, it was not the "gilded age" for everyone as Jewish immigrants in the early 1900s experienced antisemitism in the form of raised admissions standards at some institutions of higher education. Ibid., 7. See also Helen Lefkowitz Horowitz, "The 1960s and the Transformation of Campus Cultures," *History of Education Quarterly* 26, no. 1 (Spring 1986): 1–38, https://www.jstor.org/stable/368875, noting that when student Walter Lippman arrived at Harvard in 1910, "He quickly learned that no major athletic team took Jews, nor did the *Crimson*, nor did any of the final clubs that confirmed college social prestige."

Chart 2.1. Appointments of Lawyer Presidents (1800s)

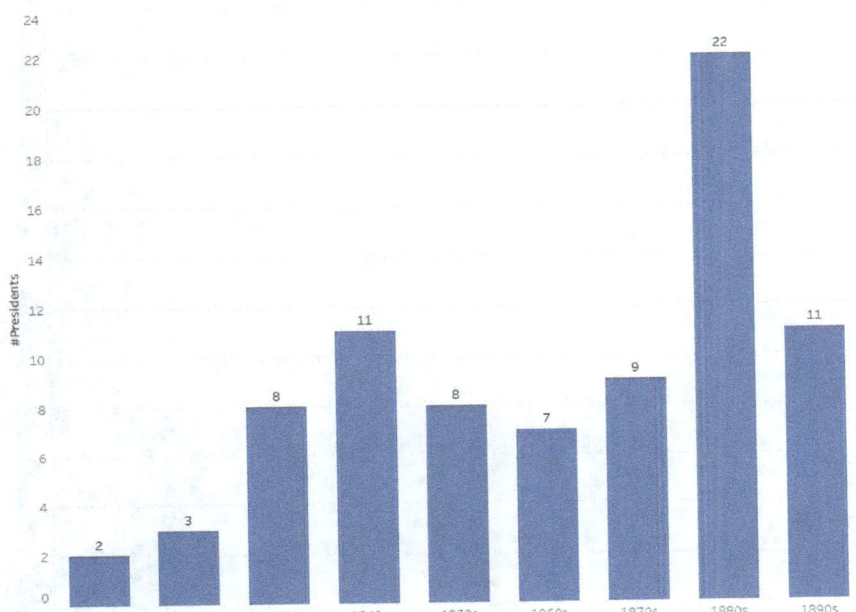

Notes
- Each appointment within a decade is counted by the start of a president's term.
- If a president was appointed twice in the same decade, they are counted for each appointment.
- If a president was appointed in two different decades, they are counted in each decade.
- Appointments do not include presidents of private independent law schools.
- Appointments include presidents, chancellors, and CEOs.
- Interim positions are also included, and, if known, are considered as separate appointments from permanent positions.
- Presidents who started their appointment in 2020 and after are not included within this graph.
- Two current presidents have unidentified start dates for their terms. They are not included within this graph.

The Early 1900s Give Way to Academic Administrators

By the late 1800s and early 1900s, colleges and universities began the development of administrative organizational structures that resemble the modern institution of higher education.[25] In 1900, presidents of fourteen institutions established the Association of American Universities. Their goal was to create

---

25 Philo A. Hutcheson, *A People's History of American Higher Education* (New York: Routledge, 2020), 68.

Chart 2.2. Appointments of Lawyer Presidents (by Half-Century)

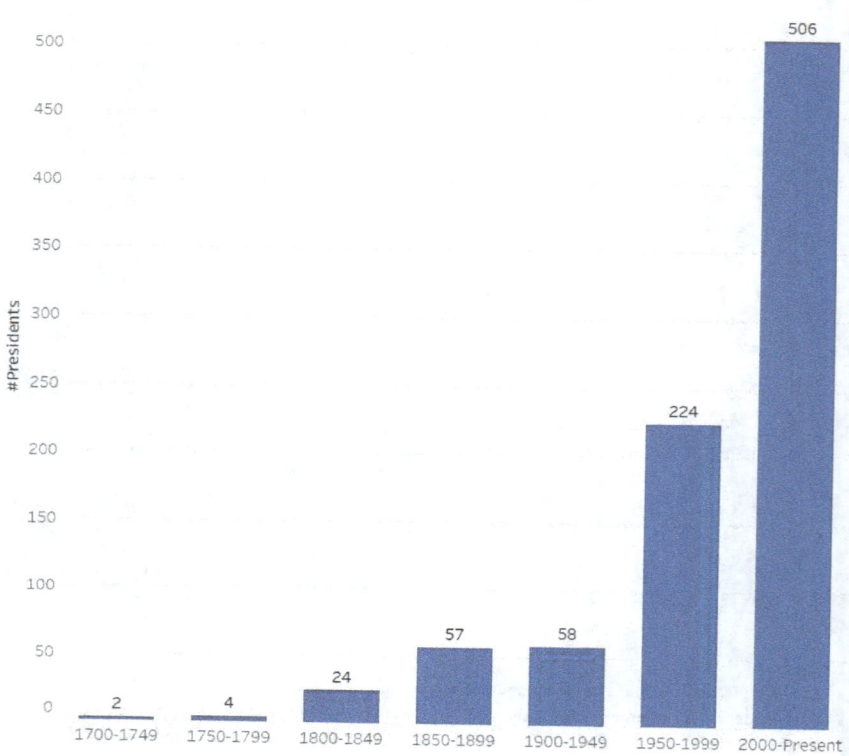

Notes
- Each appointment within each time period is counted by the start of a president's term.
- If a president was appointed twice in the same time period, they are counted for each appointment.
- If a president was appointed in two different time periods, they are counted in each time period.
- Appointments do not include presidents of private independent law schools.
- Appointments include presidents, chancellors, and CEOs.
- Interim positions are also included, and, if known, are generally considered as separate appointments from permanent positions.
- Presidents who started their appointment in 2020 are included within this graph as 2000–Present.
- Two current presidents have unidentified start dates for their terms. They are included within this graph as 2000–Present.

greater uniformity in U. S. higher education and to provide a better option for the students leaving the country for higher education in Europe.[26] The presidents

---

26   Letter by Harvard University et al., "The Letter of Invitation to the Founding Conference of AAU," January 1900, accessed September 1, 2021, https://www.aau.edu/sites/default/files/AAU%20Files/Key%20Issues/Budget%20%26%20Appropriations/FY17/Invit.pdf.

desired to strengthen the doctoral degree and improve the public opinion about American higher education.[27]

During the first half of the 1900s, the number of lawyer presidents remained relatively stable as compared to the last half of the 1800s. Higher education experienced many changes and challenges throughout the twentieth century, impacted by among other things, two world wars, the Korean and Vietnam wars, and national economic turmoil.[28] If the late 1800s was viewed as the "gilded age" in higher education, the "golden age" occurred in the mid-nineteen hundreds. This included unprecedented financial support from the Servicemen's Readjustment Act of 1944 (GI Bill), which by the 1950s and 1960s was the impetus for more than two million veterans to enroll in colleges and universities.[29] This combined with federal student loan programs in 1965 and the 1972 need-based grant program (first called Basic Educational Opportunity Grants and later Pell Grants) made higher education more accessible.[30]

The 1970s, however, witnessed significant changes and challenges for higher education as government financial support began to wane and financial aid shifted from large grants to fewer outright grants and to guaranteed student loans.[31]

The 1950s, Civil Rights, Vietnam, and Campus Unrest Make Lawyers Once Again Attractive Education Leaders

Student protests on college campuses date back to 1638 when students at Harvard expressed unhappiness over the discipline meted out by their president, Nathaniel Eaton, which led to his dismissal.[32] In the early 1800s there were

---

27 Ibid.
28 U.S. Department of Education, *Reform in American Public Higher Education*, 10.
29 Keith W. Olsen, "The G.I. Bill and Higher Education: Success and Surprise," *American Quarterly* 25, no. 5 (1973): 596–610, https://www.jstor.org/stable/2711698, noting that although the public acknowledges the GI Bill as support for individual service members, the real impetus behind the program was to create an economic adjustment to avoid another depression. See also John Bound and Sarah Turner, "Going to War and Going to College: Did World War II and the G.I. Bill Increase Educational Attainment for Returning Veterans?," *Journal of Labor Economics* 20, no. 4 (October 2002): 784, https://www.jstor.org/stable/pdf/10.1086/342012.pdf.
30 U.S. Department of Education, *Reform in American Public Higher Education*, 16.
31 Ibid., 16–17.
32 "The beginnings of the college were not happy. Nathaniel Eaton, the first head, had every qualification on paper for a successful president; but he used the rod more freely than college students were willing to put with even in those rough days. . . ." Frank L. Ellsworth and Martha A. Burns, *Student Activism in American Higher Education*, Student Personnel Series 10 (Washington, D.C:

student rebellions at Harvard, Princeton, Yale, and the University of Virginia, leading some to liken the atmosphere to a revolutionary brawl.[33]

In the early 1800s student unrest led to the death of a professor at the University of Virginia, the removal of a faculty member at Williams College, and difficulties with Greek-letter fraternities at Amherst College.[34] By the 1900s, students had been able to establish systems of student government, helping to create a more organized voice to advocate for greater student perspective in higher education.[35] Yet, the student college rebellion, grown out of students viewing themselves as nonconformists, started at Harvard in 1910, was active at Columbia by 1920, and lead to the formation of a national college rebels organization that continued into the 1930s.[36]

In the first half of the twentieth century higher education emerged as a greater player in the economy, and "The college president became a fund-raiser, politician, negotiator, and organization man, rather than just a teacher, father and friend."[37] During the Great Depression student unrest increased with students protesting about poor quality food, lack of rights and discontent with myriad campus life issues.[38] Students protested in the 1920s against ROTC, college curriculum that was viewed as pro-establishment, and against foreign policy that was viewed as imperialistic.[39] While there were student strikes in the 1930s against the war, there were few serious clashes between students and campus leaders and law enforcement.[40]

There was notably less unrest and more calm across campuses from the 1940s until the early 1960s, with some opining that this "silent generation" was partially a reflection of the Cold War.[41] Students in the 1950s, 1960s, and 1970s

---

American College Personnel Association, 1970), 9, accessed September 1, 2021, http://story.myacpa.org/img/carousel/STUDENT%20ACTIVISM%20IN%20AMERICAN%20HIGHER%20EDUCATION.pdf.

33 Ibid.
34 Ibid., 10.
35 Ibid.
36 Lefkowitz Horowitz, "The 1960s and the Transformation of Campus Cultures."
37 Ellsworth and Burns, *Student Activism*, 10.
38 U.S. Department of Health Education and Welfare, *The Report of the President's Commission on Campus Unrest*, report no. ED083899 (Washington, DC: U.S. Government Printing Office, 1970), accessed November 8, 2021, https://files.eric.ed.gov/fulltext/ED083899.pdf. See also Ellsworth and Burns, *Student Activism*, 11.
39 U.S. Department of Health Education and Welfare, *The Report of the President's Commission on Campus Unrest*.
40 Ibid.
41 Ibid. See also Philip G. Altbach, "From Revolution to Apathy: American Student Activism in the 1970s," *Higher Education* 8, no. 6 (November 1979): 612, https://www.jstor.org/stable/3446222, noting, "The Cold War, which probably began in earnest with the Truman

organized in different ways to draw attention to their concerns about politics and society, including protesting the Vietnam War and selective service and advocating for civil rights, nuclear disarmament, environmental issues, and free speech. Their protests went from peaceful to violent, earning the students the label of "activists."[42]

For example, in 1960 four college students entered the Greensboro Woolworth and sat at the lunch counter where they were denied their request for coffee, sparking similar actions in thirty-one cities in seven southern states.[43] This event ignited what historians recount as student sit-ins during the struggle for civil rights.[44] The 1964 University of California–Berkeley student revolt ended when the governor called in the police to end a campus sit-in resulting in mass student arrests that led to even stronger support of the Free Speech Movement.[45]

Student protests on campuses across the nation over the Cambodian incursion led in some cases to skirmishes with law enforcement and resulted in the 1970 deaths of students at Kent State and Jackson State University, drawing national attention to the significance of student unrest.[46] This was followed by a bombing at the University of Wisconsin-Madison, with one researcher killed and four others injured, and the perpetrators warning of more action if their demands were not met.[47]

The Report of the President's Commission on Campus Unrest examined, among other things, the student protests in the 1960s, the Black student movement, and how institutions of higher education were responding to campus disorder after the events at Kent State and Jackson State.[48] The 1970 Commission

---

Doctrine in 1947, dealt a serious blow to student activism, which did not resume to any significant degree until the end of the 1950s."

42 Ellsworth and Burns, *Student Activism in American Higher Education*, 12; see also Lynn M. Lombardo, "A Comprehensive Examination of Student Unrest at Buffalo State College 1966–1970" (Master's thesis, Buffalo State College, Buffalo, NY, 2011), https://digitalcommons.buffalostate.edu/cgi/viewcontent.cgi?article=1005&context=buffstate-history.

43 "The Greensboro Sit-Ins: Nearly Four Decades Ago, Well-Mannered, Well-Dressed, and Courteous Black College Kids Launched a Lunch Counter Revolution in the United States," *Journal of Blacks in Higher Education* 15 (Spring 1997): 135. See also Deidre B. Flowers, "The Launching of the Student Sit-in Movement: The Role of Black Women at Bennett College," *The Journal of African American History* 90, no. 1/2 (Winter 2005): 52.

44 Flowers, "The Launching of the Student Sit-in Movement," 54.

45 U.S. Department of Health Education and Welfare, *The Report of the President's Commission on Campus Unrest*.

46 Lombardo, "A Comprehensive Examination"; see also U.S. Department of Health Education and Welfare, *The Report of the President's Commission on Campus Unrest*.

47 U.S. Department of Health Education and Welfare, *The Report of the President's Commission on Campus Unrest*.

48 Ibid.

Report described the crisis on college campuses as having two components—a crisis of violence and a crisis of understanding—and, among other things, suggested that defects of universities had fueled student unrest, and that the nation had been slow to resolve issues related to war and race.[49] The Report supported the notion of campuses serving as open fora for all points of view, stating, "The area of permitted speech and conduct should be at least as broad as that protected by the First Amendment."[50] At the same time the Commission urged campuses to enact codes of conduct with consequences for violations, and while respecting the rights of the members of the campus communities to express their views, it advised, ". . . universities as institutions must remain politically neutral. . . ."[51] Universities were also advised to increase student and faculty participation in governance areas, and students were reminded to avoid language that offends.[52]

Statements in this 1970 report could have been written fifty years later, specifically recommendations that the president ". . . point out the importance of diversity and coexistence to the nation's health," and that president ". . . renew the national commitment to full social justice, and to be aware of the increasing charges of repression."[53]

Over the years, students have demanded a greater voice in administrative decisions and have become an important stakeholder constituency that college and university presidents must negotiate with.[54] With the start of the second decade of the new century, issues drawing student activism include racism and anti-racism, campus safety, steering of campus investments away from certain companies and countries with poor records on worker rights, the environment, human rights, the cost of higher education and student debt, and cancel culture.

In the last decade, student free speech on college campuses has also drawn substantial attention from campus leaders and from Congress.[55] Given the challenges with political unrest, the desires to advance law and public policy both at home on the national stage, and the limits of constitutionally protected free

---

49 Ibid.
50 Ibid.
51 Ibid.
52 Ibid.
53 Ibid. The report also recommended, among other things, increased financial support for Black colleges and universities and continuing efforts to recruit minority students.
54 Genevieve Carlton, "Student Activism in College: A History of Campus Protests," *Best Colleges* (blog), entry posted May 18, 2020, accessed September 1, 2021, https://www.bestcolleges.com/blog/history-student-activism-in-college/.
55 See, for example, Orrin Hatch, "Protecting Freedom of Speech Where It Matters Most, on the College Campus," *National Review*, February 7, 2018, accessed September 1, 2021, https://www.nationalreview.com/2018/02/free-speech-college-campuses-legislation-ensure-it/.

speech, it makes sense that during the last half of the 1900s the number of lawyer presidents nearly quadrupled, and the strong record of recruitment and appointment of lawyer presidents continues to this day. Lawyer presidents are also able to explain and navigate thorny First Amendment and other constitutional issues that surface as part of advocacy. This skill and legal acumen may provide comfort to certain campus constituencies.

The Rise of Legal Education

Another significant contributing factor to the increasing number of lawyer presidents, starting in the late nineteenth century and moving forward in the early twentieth, was the expansion of legal education. From the late 1700s through the 1800s, formal legal education was not a robust part of the development of higher education. While the reopening of Harvard Law School in 1829 is often cited as the founding of modern legal education,[56] the first full-time chair in law was held by George Wythe at the College of William and Mary beginning in 1779. His student, St. George Tucker, succeeded him in 1789. At that time, lectures in law were delivered to students based on Blackstone.[57] Teaching appointments followed at the College of Philadelphia, Harvard, Transylvania University, the University of Maryland, and Columbia College,[58] and in 1784 the first independent school for the study of law, the Litchfield Law School, was founded by Judge Tapping Reeve.[59] By the time the school closed in 1833 it had trained just over one thousand men in the practice of law.[60]

In addition to the independent law schools, by 1840 there were nine colleges that had law schools, although these connections were routinely made and abandoned, and in the 1860s a handful of part-time schools began to open for students who were working full-time in other fields.[61] Other law schools existed at the time that catered to the less affluent, such as YMCA schools (first established

---

56   Andrew Siegel, "'To Learn and Make Respectable Hereafter:' The Litchfield Law School in Cultural Context," *New York University Law Review* 73 (December 1998): 1978–2028, accessed September 1, 2021, https://digitalcommons.law.seattleu.edu/faculty/644/.
57   Albert J. Harno, *Legal Education in the United States* (San Francisco: Bancroft-Whitney Company, 1953), 23; see also Stevens, *Law School*, 3.
58   Harno, *Legal Education*, 23–25.
59   Harno, *Legal Education*, 28–30.
60   Harno, *Legal Education*.
61   Stevens, *Law School*, 8, 74.

in Boston) where immigrants also found a welcoming opportunity, and a small number of schools that admitted Black people and women.[62]

Yet, although there was a greater appearance of legal education and higher education in general was growing in the United States, there were still only a mere fifteen law schools by 1850. This number rose to twenty-one in 1860, and ten more were added by 1870.[63] During this same time period, the legal profession was in a growth mode: with approximately 23,939 lawyers in 1850, the number grew to 40,376 in 1870, and by 1880 there were roughly 64,137 lawyers.[64] As the number of lawyers grew, the requirements for practice did as well, and the states still held to a required period of apprenticeship for all regardless of obtaining a formal classroom legal education.[65]

In 1878, the American Bar Association was established, and the first formal Section created in 1893 was Legal Education and Admission to the Bar.[66] In 1922, delegates to a special conference on legal education endorsed two principles: obligatory graduation from an approved law school and successful completion of an independent examination to practice law.[67]

By 1920, the number of law schools had grown, and "by 1931, 77 U.S. law schools had received ABA approval. There were many other law schools that operated without ABA approval since they allowed immigrants, blacks, women and Jews to study law at the time when this was not accepted by the elitists in the profession."[68] "By 1951, 124 were approved, and of those, 107 were also members of the Association of American Law Schools (AALS)."[69] In the years that followed World War II, veterans created a spike in legal education. By 1947,

---

62 Ibid., 73–84.
63 Ibid., 21.
64 Ibid., 22.
65 Ibid., 25.
66 "About the American Bar Association, ABA Timeline," *American Bar Association*, accessed September 1, 2021, https://www.americanbar.org/about_the_aba/timeline/. See also Simeone E. Baldwin, "The Founding of the American Bar Association," *American Bar Association Journal* 3 (1917): 658, accessed September 1, 2021, https://digitalcommons.law.yale.edu/cgi/viewcontent.cgi? referer=https://www.google.com/&httpsredir=1&article=5 323&context=fss_papers.
67 Alfred Z. Reed, *Review of Legal Education in the United States and Canada for the Years 1926 and 1927* (New York City: The Carnegie Foundation for the Advancement of Teaching, 1928), 3, accessed September 1, 2021, https://www.americanbar.org/content/dam/aba/publications/misc/legal_education/Standards/standardsarchive/1926_1927_review.pdf.
68 Stevens, *Law School*, 92–130.
69 Thomas D. Morgan, "The Changing Face of Legal Education: Its Impact on What It Means to Be a Lawyer," *Akron Law Review* 45, no. 4 (2011–2012): 811–842.

there were approximately 47,000 students enrolled in law school, and by 2018, the number was almost triple at 112,882 students.[70]

The legal profession has increased more than sixfold: from 200,000 in 1945 to about 1,338,678 lawyers today.[71] As of 2021, there were 203 American Bar Association approved law schools,[72] along with 32 non-ABA approved schools.[73] With the increase in the number of law students and law schools, came an increase in the number of law faculty. In 1947, there were 991 full-time professors at 111 ABA accredited law schools, and by 2007–2008 the number swelled to 8,142 full-time law professors at 197 ABA accredited law schools.[74]

Why Law Professors Make Good Choices for Campus Presidencies

Historically, the typical path to the college presidency began with a faculty member who served as a department chair or dean, and then became a provost or held some other senior leadership post in the central administration. Given this, is it important to consider the pipeline of law professors that has swelled over the last three decades to meet the demand for legal education. By 2010, the number of law professors was 40% greater than the decade before.[75]

---

70 Section on Legal Education and Admission to the Bar, "Various Statistics on ABA Approved Law Schools," *American Bar Association*, accessed September 2, 2021, https://www.americanbar.org/groups/legal_education/resources/aba_approved_law_schools/.
71 "ABA National Lawyer Population Survey: Lawyer Population by State," *American Bar Association*, last modified 2021, accessed September 22, 2021, https://www.americanbar.org/content/dam/aba/administrative/market_research/2021-national-lawyer-population-survey.pdf.
72 Section on Legal Education and Admission to the Bar, "List of ABA Approved Law Schools," *American Bar Association*, accessed September 2, 2021, https://www.americanbar.org/groups/legal_education/resources/aba_approved_law_schools/. As of February 2020; one of the 203 is provisionally approved, one is the U. S. Army Judge Advocate General School, which only offers an LLM degree; and five schools are currently approved but are in a teach-out to close.
73 "Non-ABA-Approved Law Schools," *Law School Admission Council*, accessed September 30, 2021, https://www.lsac.org/choosing-law-school/find-law-school/non-aba-approved-law-schools.
74 Elizabeth Mertz, Katherine Barnes, and Wamucii Njogu, *After Tenure: Post-Tenure Law Professors in the United States* (n.p.: American Bar Foundation, 2011), accessed October 30, 2019, http://www.americanbarfoundation.org/uploads/cms/documents/after_tenure_report-_final-_abf_4.1.pdf.
75 Jack Crittenden, "Law School Faculties 40% Larger than 10 Years Ago," *The National Jurist*, last modified March 9, 2010, accessed September 2, 2021, http://www.nationaljurist.com/content/law-school-faculties-40-larger-10-years-ago.

With more law professors and more academic administrative positions within the law schools such as associate deans for academic affairs, student affairs, research and scholarship, experiential education, and diversity and inclusion, more law professors have gained experience in the administrative realm making them even more desirable candidates for deanships and for provost or vice president of academic affairs positions, all potential steppingstones to the college presidency. In addition, a growing number of these law professors are skipping over the traditional step of becoming a law dean prior to ascending to either a provost or president position.

It is not surprising that many law professors make attractive and competitive candidates for the role of campus leader. After all, many of the doctrinal fields taught and studied by law faculty are essential to the skill set of effective presidents. Administrative law, state and local government law, tax law and policy, and other federalism courses are good background for the public policy and compliance skills that college presidents need to gain public sector economic support for the campus and higher education in general. Alternative dispute resolution, mediation, and team-based problem-solving skills are also key for resolving conflicts between and among various campus stakeholders and for bringing the various campus constituencies together. Likewise, trial advocacy skills can come in handy to help frame the campus narrative in compelling ways for donors, prospective students, alumni, and other influencers, as could trusts and estates when making the case for various forms of planned giving. Faculty who teach in the contracts, corporate, and business law fields also bring a sense of financial acumen and business entrepreneurship essential for a successful president, and labor law faculty can offer unique perspectives in the area of human resource management and appropriate accommodations. Those in the real estate arena can be valuable for campuses in need of further development and/or redevelopment. Formal legal education includes foundational courses that focus on procedure, and as a result, lawyers understand process. This is an important skill that allows them to work with faculty, boards and other stakeholders. One of the cornerstones of the legal profession is the sense of ethics and professionalism that is taught to every law student. This is one reason why law faculty have a unique tendency to exhibit high levels of ethics, professionalism, and transparency when leading institutions of higher education.

Lastly, there are a growing number of law schools with courses focused on leadership for law students. This was recently recognized with the introduction of a new section of the American Association of Law Schools on Leadership in 2017.[76]

---

76 "Section on Leadership," *Association of American Law Schools*, accessed September 2, 2021. https://www.aals.org/sections/list/leadership/.

Historically, Lawyers Have Been at the Forefront of Higher Education | 47

This trend has caused law students and lawyers to discuss their role as leaders in various sectors, both within and outside the profession.

Chart 2.3 illustrates the number of lawyer presidents who previously held appointments as law professors. In the 1980s, as the number of law schools was swelling, the percentage of presidents who had been law professors was at a peak of 44%. In the 1990s and 2000s, the percentage was closer to the 1960s and 1970s, hovering at around 30%. By the 2010s, as the number of lawyer presidents was at an all-time high, the percentage of these presidents who were law professors dropped to just under 25%. It may be that law professors as a group are less interested in leading a campus, and it may also be true that other non-traditional pathways for lawyers to the campus presidency exist.

Chart 2.3. Lawyer Presidents with Prior Law Professor Experience (1900–2019)

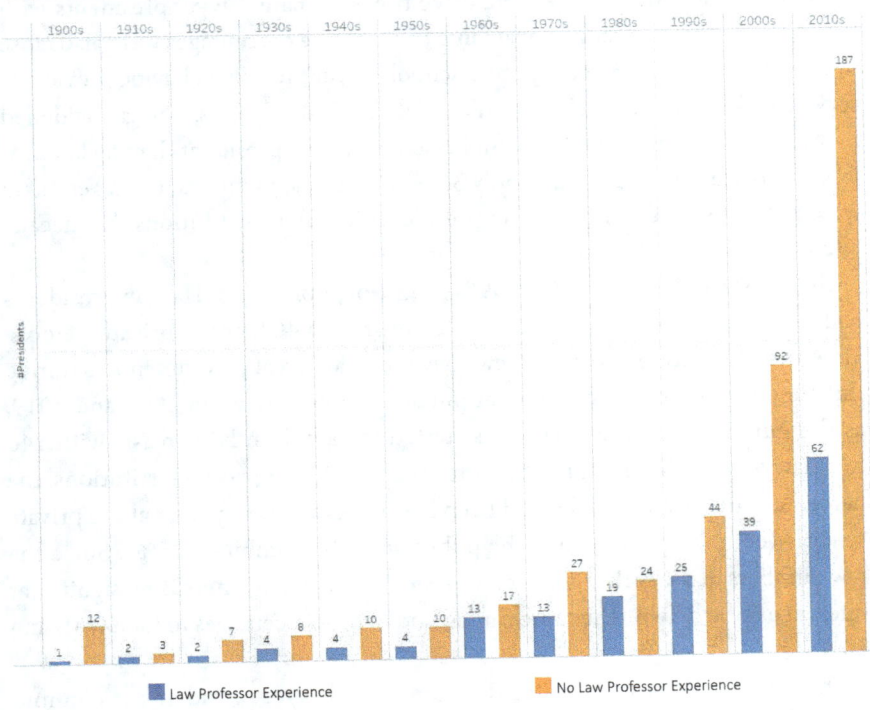

Notes
- Each appointment within a decade is counted by the start of a president's term.
- If a president was appointed twice in the same decade, they are only counted once.
- If a president was appointed in two different decades, they are counted in each decade.
- Appointments do not include presidents of private independent law schools.
- Appointments include presidents, chancellors, and CEOs.
- Interim positions are also included, and, if known, are generally considered as separate appointments from permanent positions.
- Presidents who started their appointment in 2020 and after are not included within this graph.
- Two current presidents have unidentified start dates for their terms. They are not included in this graph.

The next two charts compare the number of lawyer presidents with prior law professor experience at public and private institutions (excluding community colleges). Since the 1950s, in raw numbers, there have been more lawyer presidents with no prior law professor experience private institutions (246) than at public institutions (160). In comparing percentages for the same decades of the number of lawyer presidents who did have prior law professor experience, for most decades the numbers are fairly close. For example, in the 1950s, 25% of the lawyer presidents at public schools had prior law professor experience, compared to 28% at private schools (but in both cases the raw number was only 2).

In the 1960s, the percentage of lawyer presidents with law professor experience at public institutions was 50% and at private institutions it was 47%, yet the raw numbers show there were three times as many lawyer presidents with law professor experience at private institutions. The percentages were also close in the 1970s, with 35% of the public-school lawyer presidents having previously served as law professors, compared to 30% at private schools. The gap widened in the 1980s with almost 58% of public-school lawyer presidents having law professor experience, compared to only 36% in the private school setting. Yet, there were only a total of 19 new lawyer presidents in public institutions that decade as compared to 25 at private institutions.

The gap started to close in the 1990s as 35% of public-school lawyer presidents had prior law professor experience as compared to 40% at the private schools. However, there were still more new lawyer presidents at private schools during this time (40 as compared to 31 at public schools). Between 2000 and 2019, as the number of lawyer presidents started to significantly increase, with 146 total lawyer presidents at public institutions and 237 at private institutions, the percentage of presidents who had been law professors was greater at the private schools (combined 28%) than the public schools (combined 25%). Since the raw numbers in the earlier decades were small, statistically there is no significant inference to be drawn. The same can be said of the percentages in the 2000s and 2010s.

The following chart illustrates the number of lawyer presidents at community colleges. A more detailed discussion of community colleges is discussed in chapter three. Interestingly, none of these presidents had prior law professor experience. The most plausible explanation for this is that community colleges, as two-year institutions, do not have law schools attached to them, so there would be no traditional law professors (defined as those who work full-time at an ABA-accredited law school) associated with community college

Chart 2.4. Lawyer Presidents at Public Institutions with Prior Law Professor Experience (1900–2019)

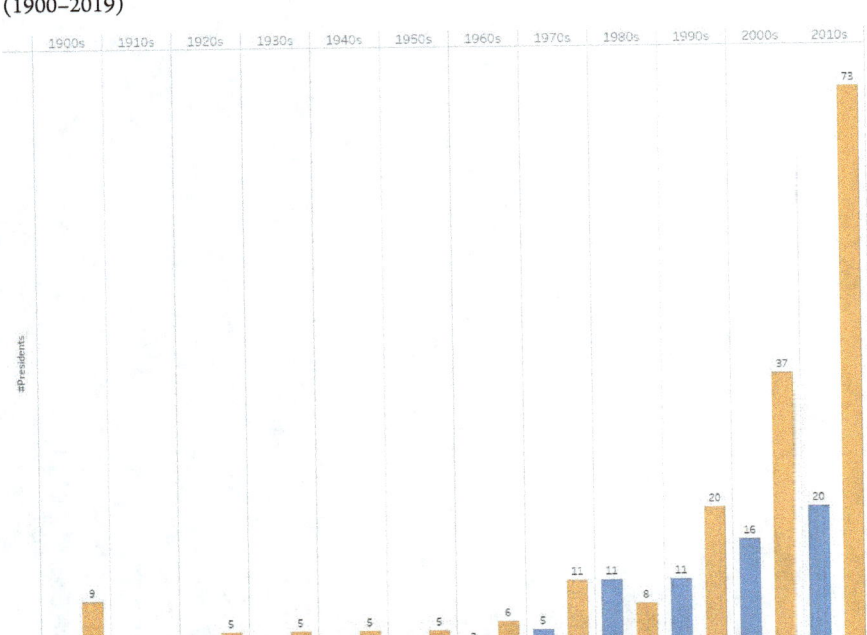

Notes
- Each appointment within a decade is counted by the start of a president's term.
- If a president was appointed twice in the same decade, they are only counted once.
- If a president was appointed in two different decades, they are counted in each decade.
- Appointments do not include presidents of private independent law schools.
- Appointments include presidents, chancellors, and CEOs.
- Interim positions are also included, and, if known, are generally considered as separate appointments from permanent positions.
- Presidents who started their appointment in 2020 and after are not included within this graph.
- Two current presidents have unidentified start dates for their terms. They are not included in this graph.

education, as their experience would be at four-year and higher degree-granting institutions.

Further, community college search committees may not dismiss lawyer candidates due to lack of law professor experience. Community colleges tend to value leaders who are able to navigate the local community, build local relationships and partnerships and understand the business of community college education. These lawyer presidents often come from the private sector, government, or have experience teaching in non-law academic departments.

Chart 2.5. Lawyer Presidents at Private Institutions with Prior Law Professor Experience (1900–2019)

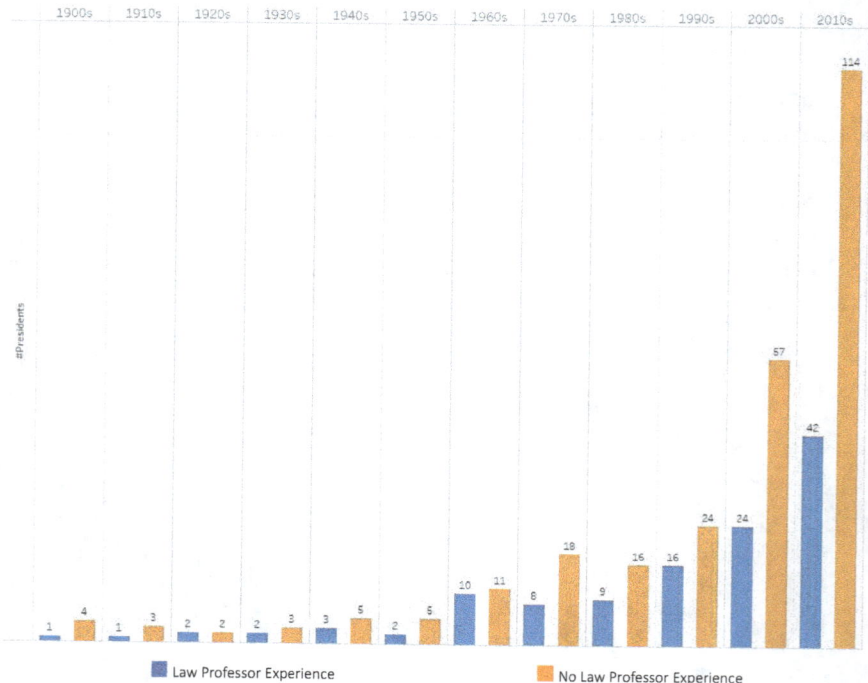

Notes
- Each appointment within a decade is counted by the start of a president's term.
- If a president was appointed twice in the same decade, they are only counted once.
- If a president was appointed in two different decades, they are counted in each decade.
- Appointments do not include presidents of private independent law schools.
- Appointments include presidents, chancellors, and CEOs.
- Interim positions are also included, and, if known, are generally considered as separate appointments from permanent positions.
- Presidents who started their appointment in 2020 and after are not included within this graph.
- Two current presidents have unidentified start dates for their terms. They are not included in this graph.

Chart 2.7 shows the number of lawyer presidents at religiously affiliated institutions who have prior law professor experience (religiously affiliated schools are discussed in more detail in chapter three). While the number are steady and relatively small for forty years (1950s through the 1990s), they more than doubled from the 1990s to the 2000s and it doubled from the 2000s through the 2010s. Also, during the last two decades, the number of lawyer presidents dramatically increased from numbers that hovered under ten each decade throughout the last century to shooting up to thirty-two in the 2000s to a total of seventy-four in the 2010s. The next chapter discusses some of the complex legal issues with

Chart 2.6. Lawyer Presidents at Community Colleges with Prior Law Professor Experience (1900–2019)

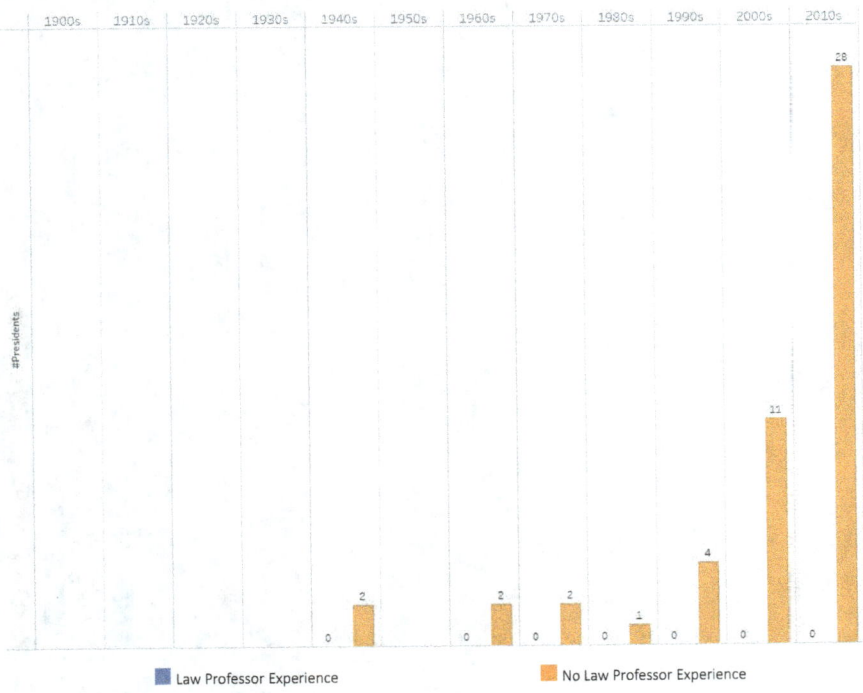

Notes
- Each appointment within a decade is counted by the start of a president's term.
- If a president was appointed twice in the same decade, they are only counted once.
- If a president was appointed in two different decades, they are counted in each decade.
- Appointments do not include presidents of private independent law schools.
- Appointments include presidents, chancellors, and CEOs.
- Interim positions are also included, and, if known, are generally considered as separate appointments from permanent positions.
- Presidents who started their appointment in 2020 and after are not included within this graph.
- Two current presidents have unidentified start dates for their terms. They are not included in this graph.

religiously affiliated schools including federal financial aid, Title IX, and free speech, that make presidents with legal acumen desirable candidates to help navigate the nuanced challenges.

Law Deans as a Pathway to the Presidency

The series of charts that follow show the number of law deans who were appointed as a college or university president. Law deans are often selected from the law

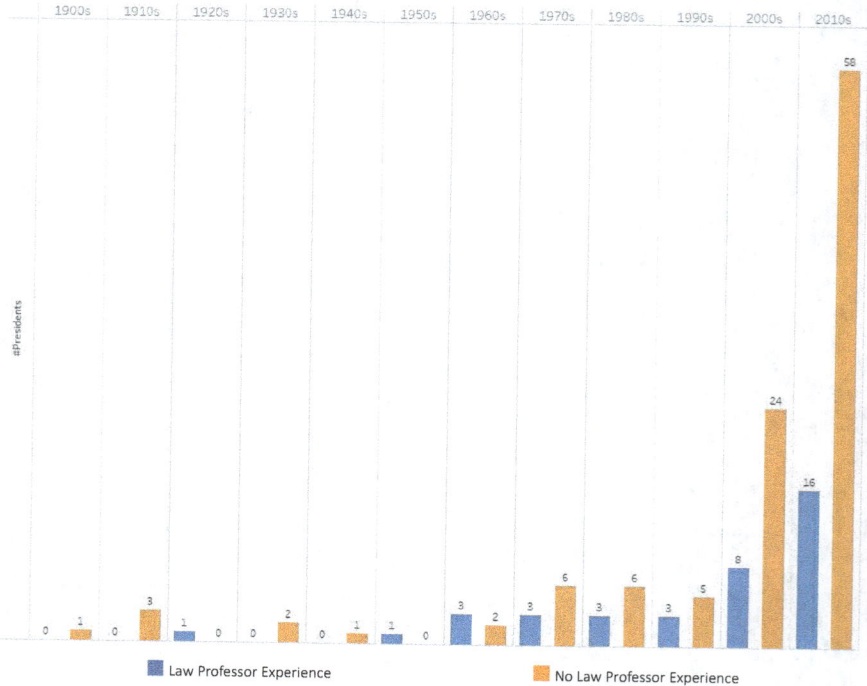

Chart 2.7. Lawyer Presidents at Religiously Affiliated Institutions with Prior Law Professor Experience (1900–2019)

Notes
- Each appointment within a decade is counted by the start of a president's term.
- If a president was appointed twice in the same decade, they are only counted once.
- If a president was appointed in two different decades, they are counted in each decade.
- Appointments do not include presidents of private independent law schools.
- Appointments include presidents, chancellors, and CEOs.
- Interim positions are also included, and, if known, are generally considered as separate appointments from permanent positions.
- Presidents who started their appointment in 2020 and after are not included within this graph.
- Two current presidents have unidentified start dates for their terms. They are not included in this graph.

faculty, including faculty who have assumed great administrative responsibility. Chart 2.8 shows that, in raw numbers, in each decade from the 1980s through the 2010s, the number of law deans who have become campus presidents has increased; however, the percentage of lawyer presidents with law dean experience has decreased in each of these decades from a high of 30% in the 1980s to just 14% in the 2010s when ironically the number of lawyer presidents was at an all-time high. This may be surprising in the context that a number of law schools beginning in the 2000s started looking outside the academy to recruit and hire

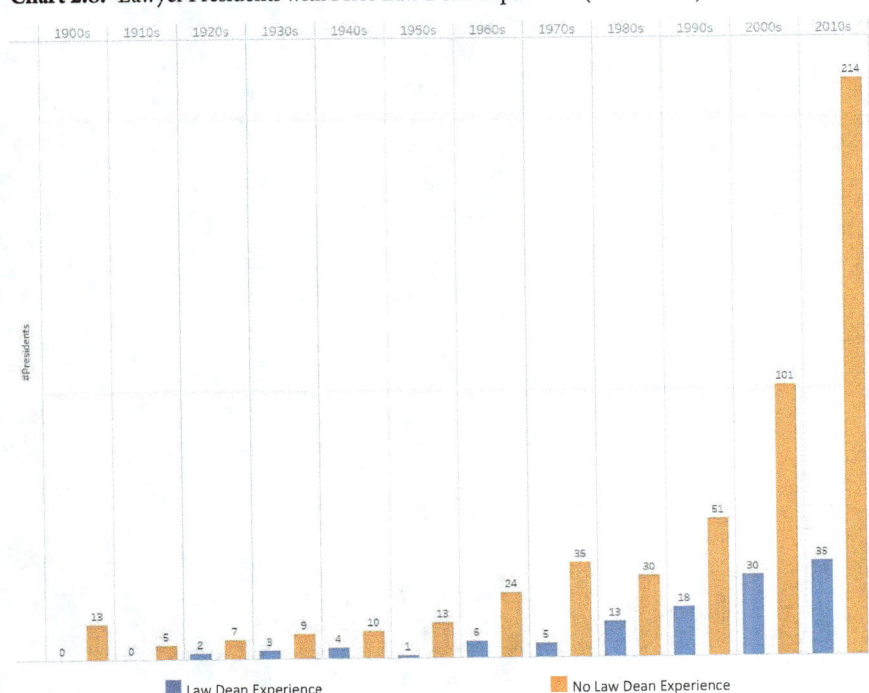

Chart 2.8. Lawyer Presidents with Prior Law Dean Experience (1900–2019)

Notes
- Each appointment within a decade is counted by the start of a president's term.
- If a president was appointed twice in the same decade, they are only counted once.
- If a president was appointed in two different decades, they are counted in each decade.
- Appointments do not include presidents of private independent law schools.
- Appointments include presidents, chancellors, and CEOs.
- Interim positions are also included, and, if known, are generally considered as separate appointments from permanent positions.
- Presidents who started their appointment in 2020 and after are not included within this graph.
- Two current presidents have unidentified start dates for their terms. They are not included in this graph.

"non-traditional" deans who came from business, retired government officials, retired judges, practitioners and university counsel.[77]

---

77   See, for example, Jacqueline Lipton, "Non-Traditional Law Deans and Tenure," *The Faculty Lounge* (blog), entry posted October 3, 2009, accessed September 2, 2021, https://www.thefacultylounge.org/2009/10/nontraditional-law-deans-and-tenure.html; Jack M. Weiss, "A Causerie on Selecting Law Deans in an Age of Entrepreneurial Deaning," *Louisiana Law Review* 70, no. 3 (Spring 2010): 923–944, accessed September 2, 2021, https://digitalcommons.law.lsu.edu/cgi/viewcontent.cgi?article=6345&context=lalrev.

Chart 2.9. Lawyer Presidents at Public Institutions with Prior Law Dean Experience (1900–2019)

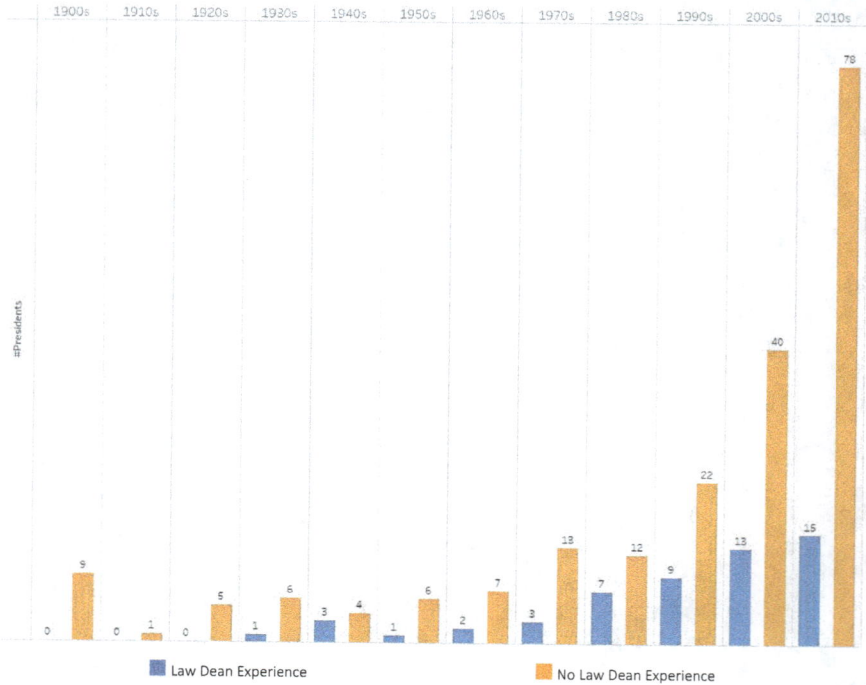

Notes
- Each appointment within a decade is counted by the start of a president's term.
- If a president was appointed twice in the same decade, they are only counted once.
- If a president was appointed in two different decades, they are counted in each decade.
- Appointments do not include presidents of private independent law schools
- Appointments include presidents, chancellors, and CEOs.
- Interim positions are also included, and, if known, are generally considered as separate appointments from permanent positions.
- Presidents who started their appointment in 2020 and after are not included within this graph.
- Two current presidents have unidentified start dates for their terms. They are not included in this graph.

Charts 2.9 and 2.10 show that, in raw numbers, there are more presidents who were law deans at private schools than at public schools, but in reality, there are more lawyer presidents at private schools. Just like there were no law professors who became presidents at community colleges, there were no former law deans either as depicted in chart 2.11. Yet, as the number of lawyer presidents at religiously affiliated institutions has increased substantially in the last decade, chart 2.12 shows that nearly 11% of these presidents are former law deans. More lawyer presidents were law professors who have not had experience as law deans

Chart 2.10. Lawyer Presidents at Private Institutions with Prior Law Dean Experience (1900–2019)

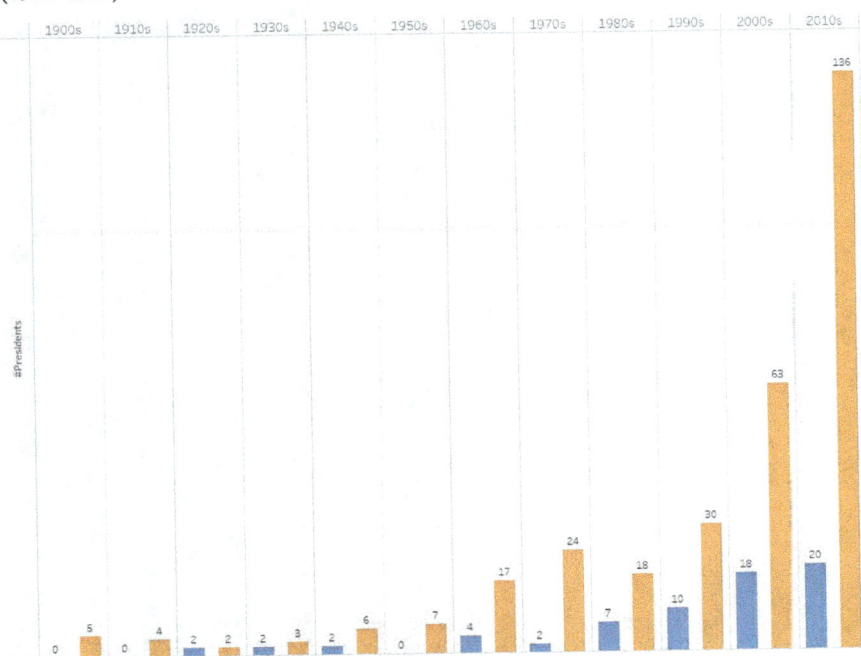

Notes
- Each appointment within a decade is counted by the start of a president's term.
- If a president was appointed twice in the same decade, they are only counted once.
- If a president was appointed in two different decades, they are counted in each decade.
- Appointments do not include presidents of private independent law schools
- Appointments include presidents, chancellors, and CEOs.
- Interim positions are also included, and, if known, are generally considered as separate appointments from permanent positions.
- Presidents who started their appointment in 2020 and after are not included within this graph.
- Two current presidents have unidentified start dates for their terms. They are not included in this graph.

prior to leading the campus (see chart 4.7 in chapter four) than those who were first law school deans.

It is important to point out that law deans offer additional skills needed for a successful presidency than those who simply served as faculty. For example, most law deans have experience in the areas of fundraising and philanthropy. Further, law deans have operated in an environment of shared governance with the faculty, an excellent training ground for shared governance practices throughout the campus. Deans are also part of the chief academic officer's

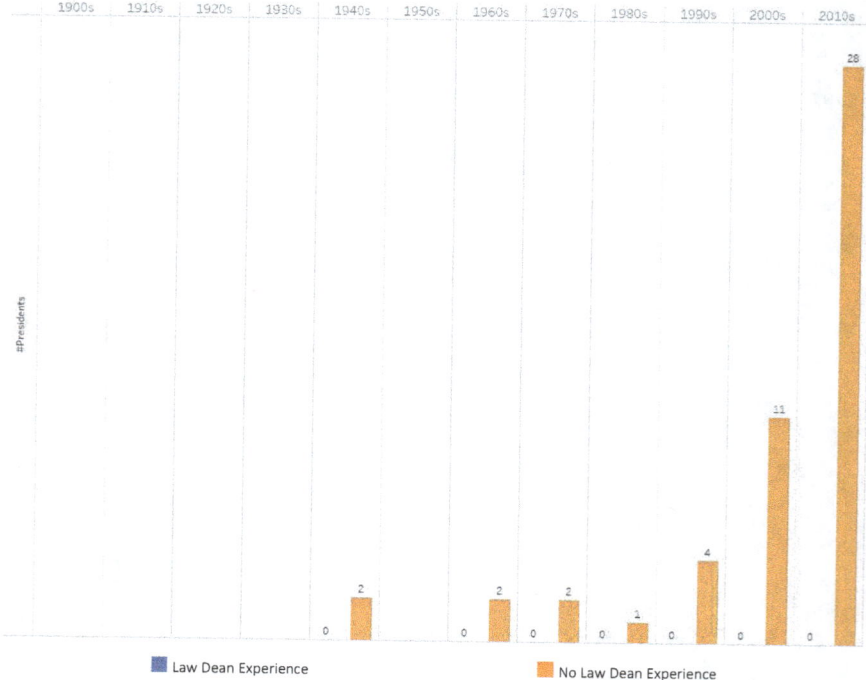

Chart 2.11. Lawyer Presidents at Community Colleges with Prior Law Dean Experience (1900–2019)

Notes
- Each appointment within a decade is counted by the start of a president's term.
- If a president was appointed twice in the same decade, they are only counted once.
- If a president was appointed in two different decades, they are counted in each decade.
- Appointments do not include presidents of private independent law schools.
- Appointments include presidents, chancellors, and CEOs.
- Interim positions are also included, and, if known, are generally considered as separate appointments from permanent positions.
- Presidents who started their appointment in 2020 and after are not included within this graph.
- Two current presidents have unidentified start dates for their terms. They are not included in this graph.

leadership cabinet, responsible for development and overseeing a sizable budget, and they are often part of the formulation and implementation of significant campus policies and strategic direction.

Bill Howard, vice president and search consultant with Academic Search, shared his view that law deans may be "more so of a mini-CEO than some of the university-wide positions."[78] Likewise, WittKieffer senior partner Werner

---

78 Moran, "Lawyers Find Their Skill Sets," 59.

Chart 2.12. Lawyer Presidents at Religiously Affiliated Institution with Prior Law Dean Experience (1900–2019)

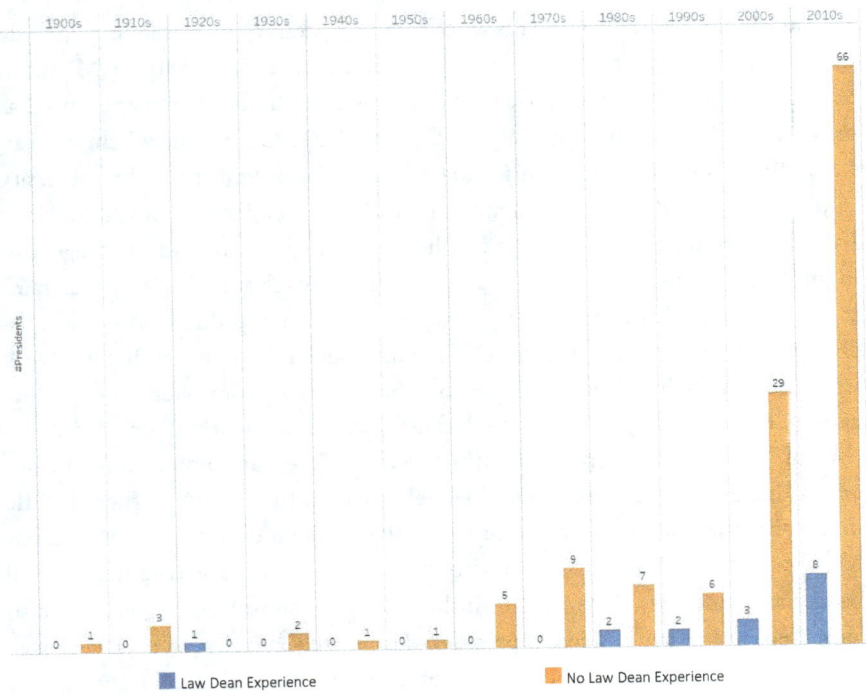

Notes
- Each appointment within a decade is counted by the start of a president's term.
- If a president was appointed twice in the same decade, they are only counted once.
- If a president was appointed in two different decades, they are counted in each decade.
- Appointments do not include presidents of private independent law schools.
- Appointments include presidents, chancellors, and CEOs.
- Interim positions are also included, and, if known, are generally considered as separate appointments from permanent positions.
- Presidents who started their appointment in 2020 and after are not included within this graph.
- Two current presidents have unidentified start dates for their terms. They are not included in this graph.

Boel, who routinely conducts law dean searches, commented, "If you can manage a cantankerous law faculty, you can pretty much do anything in the world."[79] Judith Areen, executive director and CEO of the American Association of Law Schools, predicts that more law deans are likely to be tapped as campus presidents in the near future because, as colleges and universities are looking for

---

79   Ibid.

increased diversity at the top, the current cohort of law deans is the most diverse the profession has seen.[80]

A number of notable law deans who have ascended to the presidency include Lee Bollinger who previously served as dean of the University of Michigan School of Law and then president of the University before being appointed as president of Columbia University. In October 2021 Cornell Law School dean Eduardo Peñalver announced his plans to become president at Seattle University in July 2021,[81] and L. Song Richardson, dean at the University of California at Irvine, announced plans to leave for the presidency of Colorado College also in July 2021.[82] Peñalver believes that service as a law school dean is a great training ground for advancing in higher education leadership due to the multidisciplinary nature of legal education.[83] Similarly, Richardson noted that her work with the Law School's leadership team that includes admissions, budgeting, career development, and others, will transfer well to her work as president.[84]

While historically a smattering of lawyers has been appointed to lead campuses, this number had remained relatively small until the 1980s. There is little doubt that the rise of the regulatory state that really took off in the 1980s, has had a major impact on the business of higher education. It is true that, as will be demonstrated in chapter four, in-house legal counsel positions have also increased and that non-lawyer presidents often rely heavily on their counsel, whether in-house and/or on retainer. Still, presidents with legal training may be able to more easily navigate the morass of statutes, regulations, and case law to effectively work with campus counsel to ensure appropriate preventive law strategies and responses to daily challenges.

Lawyer presidents may also be appointed during particularly challenging legal times on certain campuses as a way to offer needed comfort and confidence to a campus community in search of greater stability and community. This is no

---

80   Ibid. For example, as of May 2021 there are twenty-seven Black women law deans, see Paul Caron, "There Are Now 27 Black Women Law School Deans," *TaxProf Blog*, entry posted May 5, 2021, accessed September 2, 2021, https://taxprof.typepad.com/taxprof_blog/2021/05/there-are-now-27-black-women-law-school-deans.html; and 2019 saw a record-setting number of women deans, see Sloan, "ABA Pushes Forward."
81   James Dean, "Peñalver, Law School Dean, Named Seattle University President," *Cornell Law School*, last modified October 22, 2020, accessed September 2, 2021, https://www.lawschool.cornell.edu/news/penalver-law-school-dean-named-seattle-university-president/.
82   Hal S. Stern, "Law Dean L. Song Richardson Named President of Colorado College," UCI Office of the Provost and Executive Vice Chancellor, accessed September 2, 2021, https://provost.uci.edu/2020/12/09/law-dean-l-song-richardson-named-president-of-colorado-college/.
83   Moran, "Lawyers Find Their Skill Sets," 58.
84   Ibid., 59.

different from a noticeable observed increase in the number of presidents who have been appointed during the COVID-19 pandemic who have medical and public health training in their backgrounds. As colleges increasingly face financial constraints and look to solutions like the mergers already mentioned, it will be interesting to observe how this may also influence the qualifications university leaders will be expected to bring to their positions. Indeed, some lawyer presidents also hold MBA degrees, and some bring significant business world experience to the position.

CHAPTER 3

Lawyers Widely Accepted as Leaders across the Higher Education Landscape

It is important to note that it is not just the top echelon of higher education institutions that has sought to have lawyer presidents. The data collected for this study reveals that lawyers have been tapped to lead all categories of colleges—community colleges, four-year colleges, comprehensive universities, public colleges, private colleges, religiously affiliated colleges, and Historically Black colleges and universities. While, as discussed in the prior chapter, many of the lawyer presidents "moved up" in the academic ranks from law professor to law dean and then either to provost or president, by 2012, about 20% of all college presidents, including those who possessed a law degree, came from outside of the academy.[1]

According to the 2018 Carnegie Classification database, there were a total of 4,324 U. S. postsecondary institutions that conferred at least one degree during the 2016–2017 academic year (as reported through the National Center for Education Statistics IPEDS).[2] Table 3.1 from the Carnegie Classification database shows that of these 4,324 schools, 1,666 were public schools, 1,742 were private non-profit schools, and 916 schools were private for-profit.[3]

---

1 McKenna, "Why Are Fewer College Presidents Academics?"
2 Indiana University Center for Postsecondary Research, "2018 Update Facts & Figures," *Carnegie Classification of Institutions of Higher Education*, last modified March 19, 2021, accessed August 31, 2021, https://carnegieclassifications.iu.edu/downloads/CCIHE2018-FactsFigures.pdf.
3 Ibid.

Table 3.1. Number of U. S. Postsecondary Institutions, by Level of Institution, and Region: Academic Year 2016–17

	Control of Institution			
Level of Institution	Public	Private Not-For-Profit	Private For-Profit	Total
4- or More-Year	**784**	**1,641**	**447**	**2,872**
U. S. Service Schools	17	0	0	17
New England CT ME MA NH RI VT	42	143	7	192
Mideast DE DC MD NJ NY PA	120	342	45	507
Great Lakes IL IN MI OH WI	100	267	47	414
Plains IA KS MN MO NE ND SD	67	171	40	278
Southeast AL AR FL GA KY LA MS NC SC TN VA WV	195	342	114	651
Southwest AZ NM OK TX	82	90	60	232
Rocky Mountains CO ID MT UT WY	36	33	31	100
Far West AK CA HI NV OR WA	107	206	92	405
Outlying Areas AS FM GU MH MP PR PW VI	18	47	11	76
At Least 2-Year but Less than 4-Year	**881**	**101**	**467**	**1,449**
U. S. Service Schools	2	0	0	2
New England CT ME MA NH RI VT	44	5	4	53
Mideast DE DC MD NJ NY PA	88	29	72	189
Great Lakes IL IN MI OH WI	116	8	58	182
Plains IA KS MN MO NE ND SD	105	5	25	135
Southeast AL AR FL GA KY LA MS NC SC TN VA WV	239	24	150	413
Southwest AZ NM OK TX	113	7	67	187
Rocky Mountains CO ID MT UT WY	33	6	18	57
Far West AK CA HI NV OR WA	134	13	65	212
Outlying Areas AS FM GU MH MP PR PW VI	7	4	8	19
Less than 2-Year		**1**	**2**	**3**
Southeast AL AR FL GA KY LA MS NC SC TN VA WV		1		1
Southwest AZ NM OK TX			2	2
Grand Total	**1,665**	**1,743**	**916**	**4,324**

Geographic Acceptance

From the 1900s to present, colleges and universities on the East Coast, and the Northeast in particular, have welcomed more lawyers to the president's office (just over 140). New York leads the trend with 65, followed by Pennsylvania with 42 and Massachusetts with 38. Some include Ohio in the Northeast region, and if that is the case, the combined total jumps to about 170 lawyer presidents concentrated in four states. California is second only to New York with 47 lawyer president appointments during this time.

Table 3.2 illustrates the number of lawyer presidents in each decade by state. Map 3.1 shows this data on a map of the United States with the size of the circle corresponding to the number of lawyer presidents in each state. Interestingly, every state has had at least one school since the 1900s that has had a lawyer president. The four states with just one lawyer president are Delaware, North Dakota, New Mexico, and Wyoming. In addition, the U. S. Virgin Islands has a school with a lawyer president. Two United States-based schools that operate campuses in other countries have also appointed a lawyer president (in Kosovo and Kuwait), and there have been five lawyer presidents in the territory of Puerto Rico. Chart 3.1 illustrates the states that have colleges and universities who appointed the greatest number of lawyer presidents between 1900 and 2019.

Table 3.2. Number of Lawyer Appointments by State (1900–2019)

State	1900s	1910s	1920s	1930s	1940s	1950s	1960s	1970s	1980s	1990s	2000s	2010s	Grand Total
AK											1	2	3
AL	2			2			1		2		2	4	13
AR	3			1				1	2		3	7	17
AZ					1					1		4	6
CA		1			2	1		1	4	6	8	24	47
CO				1	2	1			1	2	5	4	16
CT						1	2	3	2			1	9
DC						1	1	1	2	1		3	9
DE												1	1
FL							2	4	3	3	2	10	24
GA							1				3	10	14
HI									1			2	3
IA						1			2	3	3	5	14
ID												4	4
IL			1		1		4	2		1	4	10	23

State	1900s	1910s	1920s	1930s	1940s	1950s	1960s	1970s	1980s	1990s	2000s	2010s	Grand Total
IN			1						3		5	9	18
Kosovo												1	1
KS						1				1		1	3
Kuwait												1	1
KY		1	1					2		1	1	6	12
LA				1			1	1				10	13
MA	2			1	1		1	3	3	6	6	15	38
MD		1							2		3	3	6	15
ME					1		1				1	6	9
MI						1		4	1	3	4	4	17
MN					1				2	1		9	13
MO			1		1	1	1			2	2	6	14
MS	2			1						1	1	1	6
MT						1	1						2
NC						1	2	3	1	1	2	10	20
ND												1	1
NE												4	4
NH										1	1	2	4
NJ	1			1	1		1	2		2	2	6	16
NM												1	1
NV					1					1		1	3
NY	2					2	3	4	4	12	16	22	65
OH								2	1	1	13	12	29
OK				1				1		3	3	3	11
OR			1			1	1	1		3	4	3	14
PA	2	1	2	1	1	1	1	3	3	4	6	17	42
PR								1		1	3		5
RI									1		3	1	5
SC						1	1			1		5	8
SD											1	1	2
TN			1	1	1			2			2	6	5	18
TX		1		1				3	1		2	11	10	29
UT						1	1	1			2	2	7
VA					3		4	1	4		3	13	10	38
VI											1		1
VT						1	1	2		1		1	6
WA										1		1	4	6
WI										2		2	3	7
WV		1							1	2	4	4	12
WY								1					1
Grand Total	14	5	9	12	18	15	31	48	47	75	147	289	720

Chart 3.1. Top States for Lawyer Presidents (1900–2019)

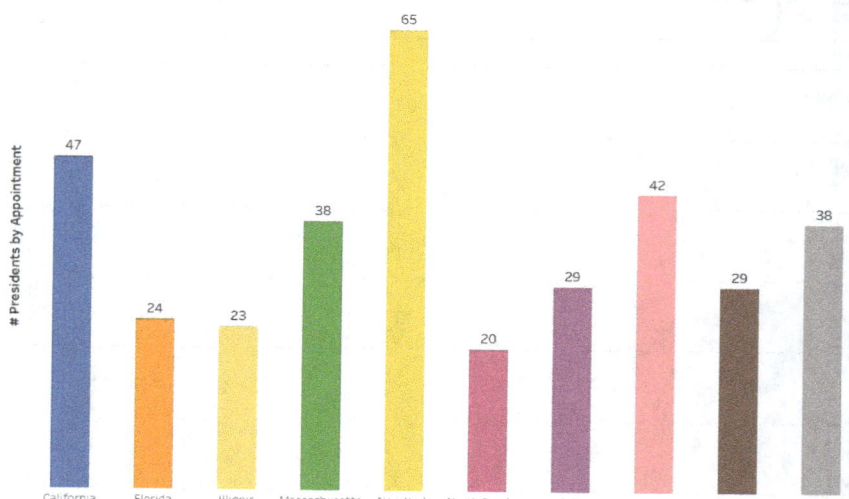

Notes
- Each appointment is counted by the start of a president's term.
- If a president was appointed twice in the same state, they are counted for each appointment.
- If a president was appointed in two different states, they are counted in each state.
- Appointments do not include presidents of private independent law schools.
- Appointments include presidents, chancellors, and CEOs.
- Interim positions are also included, and, if known, are considered as separate appointments from permanent positions.
- Presidents who started their appointment in 2020 and after are not included within this graph.
- Two current presidents have unidentified start dates for their terms. They are not included within this graph.

Map 3.1. Number of Lawyer Appointments by State (1900–2019)

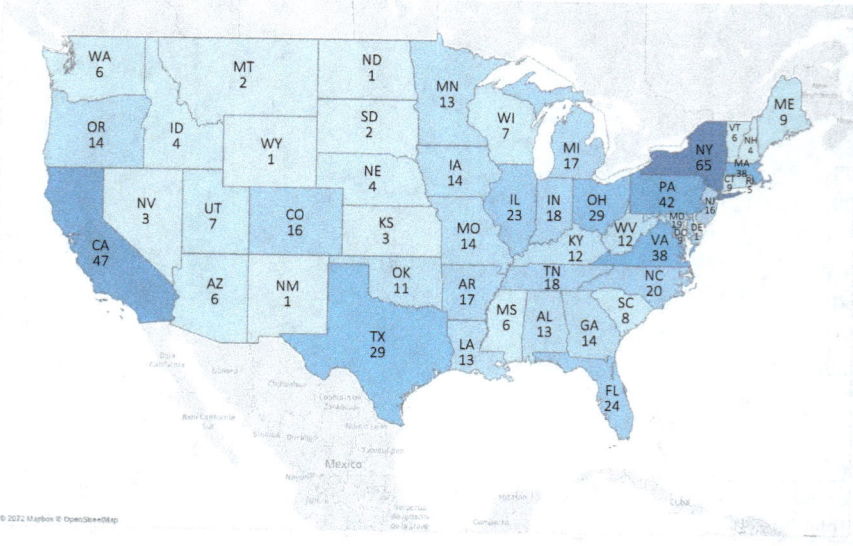

Notes
- Each appointment is counted by the start of a president's term.
- Presidents are counted for each of their appointments.
- A president can be appointed more than once in a state, at either the same school or a different one.
- If a president was appointed in two different states, they are counted in each state.
- Appointments do not include presidents of private independent law schools.
- Appointments include presidents, chancellors, and CEOs.
- Interim positions are also included, and, if known, are generally considered as separate appointments from permanent positions.
- Presidents who started their appointment in 2020 and after are not included within this graph.
- Two current presidents have unidentified start dates for their terms. They are not included in this graph.
- Appointments in fifty U. S. states are included.
- Darker shades of colors represent a higher number of appointments.

Chart 3.2 below focuses on the states that are home to institutions with the greatest number of lawyer presidents during the last decade (Map 3.2 illustrates the same data without the raw numbers apparent). Although longitudinally over time New York schools have had more lawyer presidents, in the last decade California schools slightly outpaced New York. Pennsylvania and Massachusetts continued to hold their third- and fourth-place spots, but appointments in Ohio slightly exceeded Virginia (see Table 3.2). The remaining eight states (Florida, George, Illinois, Louisiana, North Carolina, Texas, and Virginia) all saw ten lawyer president appointments during the decade. In comparing charts 3.1 and 3.2, schools in Florida and Illinois appointed almost half of the lawyer presidents in those states just in the last decade.

These findings are particularly interesting when compared to the states with the greatest number of institutions of higher education according to the Carnegie Classification (see Table 3.3). For example, the states with the highest number of colleges and universities are California (432); New York (299); Texas (250); Pennsylvania (243); Florida (191); Ohio (181); Illinois (171); North Carolina (143); Virginia (124); and Georgia (118). Using the total number of Carnegie schools (4,324), about 10% of the institutions of higher education in the United States are located in California, with about 6.9% located in New York, and roughly 5.8% and 5.6% in Texas and Pennsylvania, respectively. Florida and Ohio are home to just over 4% of all colleges and universities each. Of the total number of lawyer presidents appointed between 1900 and 2019, California (47) and New York (65) combined account for nearly one-third in the top ten states for lawyer presidents. While Massachusetts is ranked eleventh for the number of colleges and universities it houses, in raw numbers it ranked fourth for the highest number of lawyer president appointments between 1900 and 2019. In just the last decade, while California slightly outpaced New York, Pennsylvania and Massachusetts retained their third and fourth place spots in the number of lawyer president appointments.

It is possible that California and New York occupy first places simply because they have the greatest number of schools, and the odds are that such appointments would be similarly proportional. In looking at the number of law schools in each of these states, California leads the country with 20 ABA-approved law schools, followed by New York with 15.[4] In continuing to examine the list of top states with lawyer presidents, Florida has the next highest number of law schools (11) followed by Ohio (9) and Texas (9), Massachusetts (8) and Virginia (8), and North Carolina and Pennsylvania (7).[5] All of these states are in the top jurisdictions for the appointment of lawyer presidents.

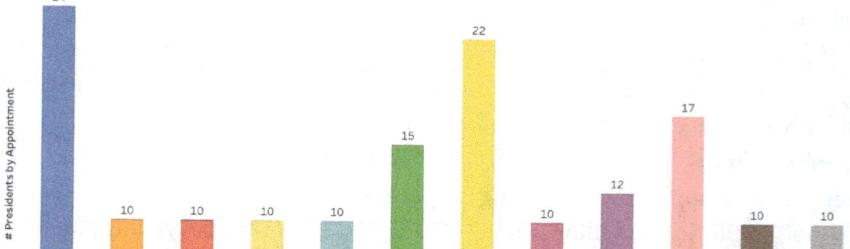

Chart 3.2. Top States for Lawyer Presidents (2010–2019)

Notes

- Each appointment is counted by the start of a president's term.
- If a president was appointed twice in the same state, they are counted for each appointment.
- If a president was appointed in two different states, they are counted in each state.
- Appointments do not include presidents of private independent law schools.
- Appointments include presidents, chancellors, and CEOs.
- Interim positions are also included, and, if known, are considered as separate appointments from permanent positions.
- Presidents who started their appointment in 2020 and after are not included within this graph.
- Two current presidents have unidentified start dates for their terms. They are not included within this graph.

---

4 "Browse Law Schools by State," *Law School Numbers*, accessed September 2, 2021, http://schools.lawschoolnumbers.com/states.
5 Ibid.

While on the surface it could be that many of the lawyer presidents went to law school in the state or worked at a law school in the state, lawyer presidents are also appointed with academic experience and credentials from other states, and, as will be discussed in chapter four, there are more lawyer presidents in total appointed at universities that do not have law schools than universities that do have law schools attached to them.

Map 3.2. Number of Lawyer Appointments by State (2010–2019)

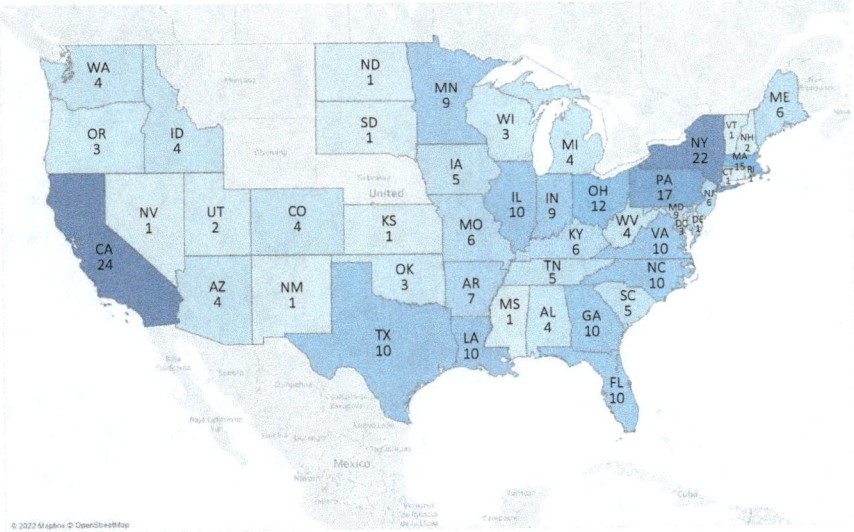

Notes
- Each appointment is counted by the start of a president's term.
- Presidents are counted for each of their appointments.
- A president can be appointed more than once in a state, at either the same school or a different one.
- If a president was appointed in two different states, they are counted in each state.
- Appointments do not include presidents of private independent law schools.
- Appointments include presidents, chancellors, and CEOs.
- Interim positions are also included, and, if known, are generally considered as separate appointments from permanent positions.
- Presidents who started their appointment in 2020 and after are not included within this graph.
- Two current presidents have unidentified start dates for their terms. They are not included in this graph.
- Appointments in fifty U. S. states are included.
- Darker shades of colors represent a higher number of appointments.

Table 3.3. Number and Percentage of Schools by State (2018)[6]

State	# of Public Schools	# of Private Not-For-Profit Schools	# of Private For-Profit Schools	Total	
				N	%
AK	4	3	1	8	0.19%
AL	39	21	10	70	1.62%
AR	33	15	3	51	1.18%
AS	1			1	0.02%
AZ	29	11	36	76	1.76%
CA	154	154	124	432	9.99%
CO	29	15	33	77	1.78%
CT	19	17	3	39	0.90%
DC	5	12	5	22	0.51%
DE	3	4	1	8	0.19%
FL	43	69	79	191	4.42%
FM	1			1	0.02%
GA	50	39	29	118	2.73%
GU	2	1		3	0.07%
HI	10	6	4	20	0.46%
IA	24	34	4	62	1.43%
ID	8	7	2	17	0.39%
IL	60	84	27	171	3.95%
IN	16	41	18	75	1.73%
KS	34	24	8	66	1.53%
KY	24	26	10	60	1.39%
LA	32	13	13	58	1.34%
MA	30	80	6	116	2.68%
MD	32	19	7	58	1.34%
ME	17	13	1	31	0.72%
MH	1			1	0.02%
MI	46	41	7	94	2.17%
MN	43	35	14	92	2.13%

---

6   Indiana University Center for Post-Secondary Research, "CCIHE 2018 Public Data File," *Carnegie Classifications of Institutions of Higher Education*, last modified 2018, http://carnegieclassifications.iu.edu/downloads/CCIHE2018-PublicDataFile.xlsx.

State	# of Public Schools	# of Private Not-For-Profit Schools	# of Private For-Profit Schools	Total N	%
MO	28	52	32	112	2.59%
MP	1			1	0.02%
MS	23	9	6	38	0.88%
MT	17	5	1	23	0.53%
NC	75	50	18	143	3.31%
ND	14	5	1	20	0.46%
NE	18	19	3	40	0.93%
NH	13	12		25	0.58%
NJ	32	32	10	74	1.71%
NM	28	3	9	40	0.93%
NV	7	5	10	22	0.51%
NY	81	183	35	299	6.91%
OH	61	75	45	181	4.19%
OK	30	13	12	55	1.27%
OR	25	26	6	57	1.32%
PA	63	121	59	243	5.62%
PR	17	50	19	86	1.99%
PW	1			1	0.02%
RI	4	10		14	0.32%
SC	33	22	17	72	1.67%
SD	12	7	3	22	0.51%
TN	23	47	30	100	2.31%
TX	108	70	72	250	5.78%
UT	8	11	13	32	0.74%
VA	42	45	37	124	2.87%
VI	1			1	0.02%
VT	5	16	1	22	0.51%
WA	43	25	12	80	1.85%
WI	34	34	8	76	1.76%
WV	22	10	12	44	1.02%
WY	8	1		9	0.21%
Total	1666	1742	916	4324	100.00%

Map 3.3. Number of Lawyer Appointments at Public Institutions by State (2010–2019)

Notes
- Each appointment is counted by the start of a president's term.
- Presidents are counted for each of their appointments.
- A president can be appointed more than once in a state, at either the same school or a different one.
- If a president was appointed in two different states, they are counted in each state.
- Appointments do not include presidents of private independent law schools.
- Appointments include presidents, chancellors, and CEOs.
- Interim positions are also included, and, if known, are generally considered as separate appointments from permanent positions.
- Presidents who started their appointment in 2020 and after are not included within this graph.
- Two current presidents have unidentified start dates for their terms. They are not included in this graph.
- Appointments in fifty U. S. states are included.
- Darker shades of colors represent a higher number of appointments.

Map 3.4. Number of Lawyer Appointments at Public Institutions by State (1900–2019)

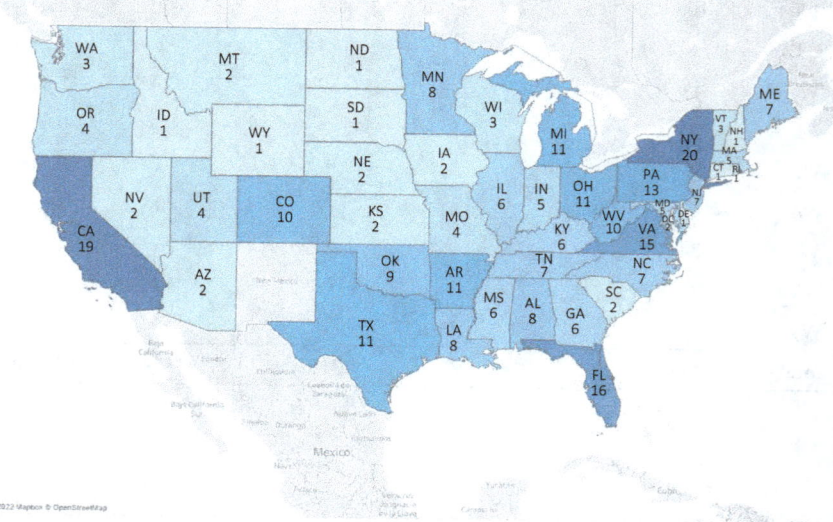

Notes

- Each appointment is counted by the start of a president's term.
- Presidents are counted for each of their appointments.
- A president can be appointed more than once in a state, at either the same school or a different one.
- If a president was appointed in two different states, they are counted in each state.
- Appointments do not include presidents of private independent law schools.
- Appointments include presidents, chancellors, and CEOs.
- Interim positions are also included, and, if known, are generally considered as separate appointments from permanent positions.
- Presidents who started their appointment in 2020 and after are not included within this graph.
- Two current presidents have unidentified start dates for their terms. They are not included in this graph.
- Appointments in fifty U. S. states are included.
- Darker shades of colors represent a higher number of appointments.

Map 3.5. Number of Lawyer Appointments at Private Institutions by State (2010–2019)

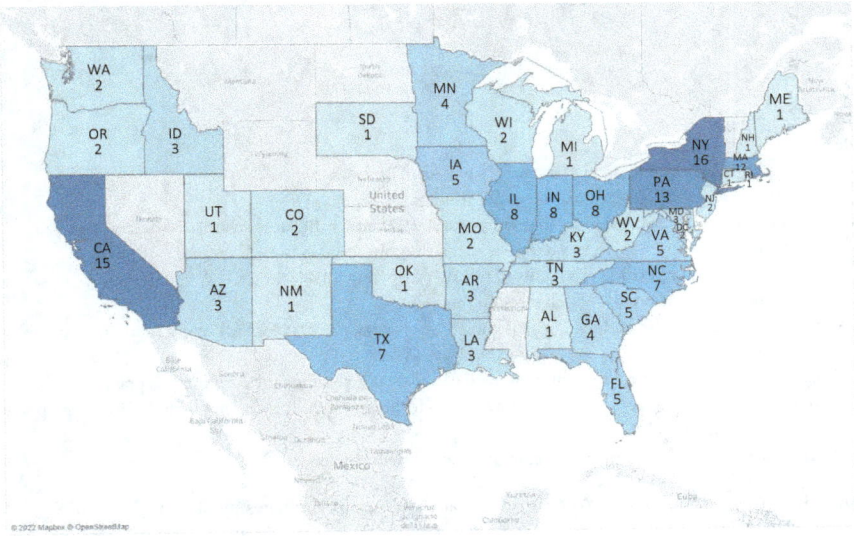

Notes

- Each appointment is counted by the start of a president's term.
- Presidents are counted for each of their appointments.
- A president can be appointed more than once in a state, at either the same school or a different one.
- If a president was appointed in two different states, they are counted in each state.
- Appointments do not include presidents of private independent law schools.
- Appointments include presidents, chancellors, and CEOs.
- Interim positions are also included, and, if known, are generally considered as separate appointments from permanent positions.
- Presidents who started their appointment in 2020 and after are not included within this graph.
- Two current presidents have unidentified start dates for their terms. They are not included in this graph.
- Appointments in fifty U. S. states are included.
- Darker shades of colors represent a higher number of appointments.

Map 3.6. Number of Lawyer Appointments at Private Institutions by State (1900–2019)

Notes
- Each appointment is counted by the start of a president's term.
- Presidents are counted for each of their appointments.
- A president can be appointed more than once in a state, at either the same school or a different one.
- If a president was appointed in two different states, they are counted in each state.
- Appointments do not include presidents of private independent law schools.
- Appointments include presidents, chancellors, and CEOs.
- Interim positions are also included, and, if known, are generally considered as separate appointments from permanent positions.
- Presidents who started their appointment in 2020 and after are not included within this graph.
- Two current presidents have unidentified start dates for their terms. They are not included in this graph.
- Appointments in fifty U. S. states are included.
- Darker shades of colors represent a higher number of appointments.

Map 3.7. Number of Lawyer Appointments at Community Colleges by State (2010–2019)

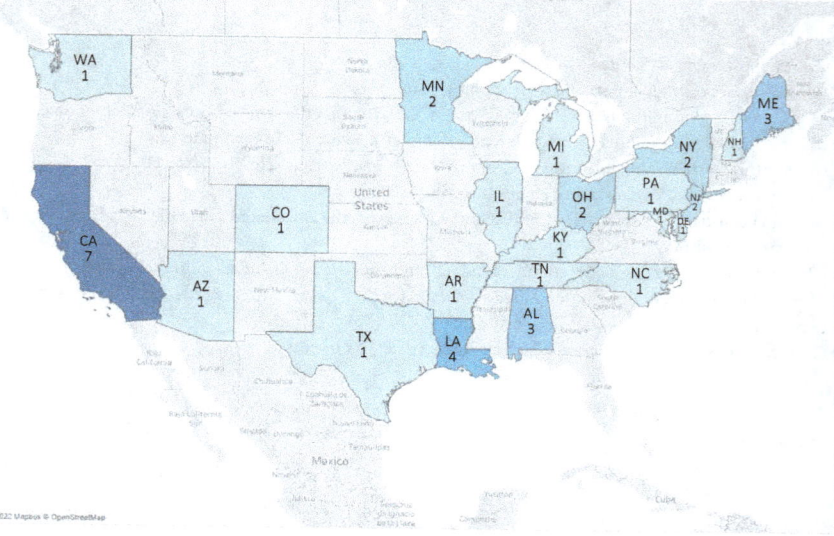

Notes
- Each appointment is counted by the start of a president's term.
- Presidents are counted for each of their appointments.
- A president can be appointed more than once in a state, at either the same school or a different one.
- If a president was appointed in two different states, they are counted in each state.
- Appointments do not include presidents of private independent law schools.
- Appointments include presidents, chancellors, and CEOs.
- Interim positions are also included, and, if known, are generally considered as separate appointments from permanent positions.
- Presidents who started their appointment in 2020 and after are not included within this graph.
- Two current presidents have unidentified start dates for their terms. They are not included in this graph.
- Appointments in fifty U. S. states are included.
- Darker shades of colors represent a higher number of appointments.

Map 3.8. Number of Lawyer Appointments at Community Colleges by State (1900–2019)

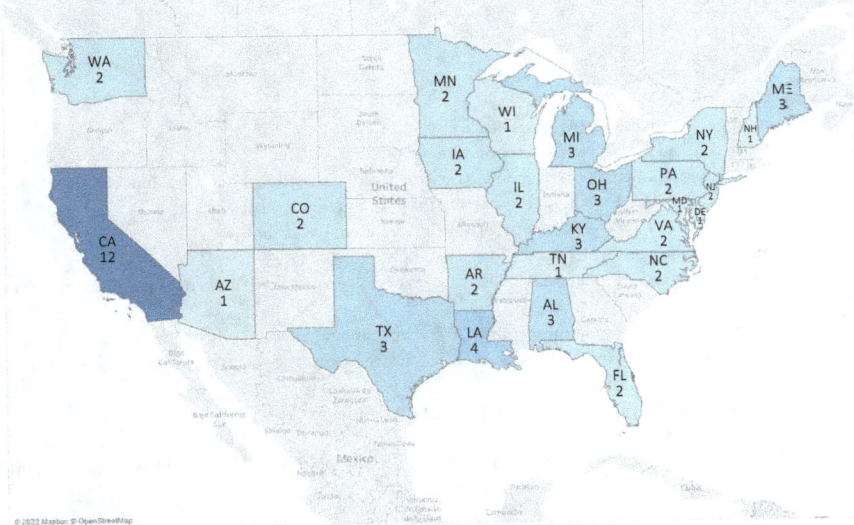

Notes
- Each appointment is counted by the start of a president's term.
- Presidents are counted for each of their appointments.
- A president can be appointed more than once in a state, at either the same school or a different one.
- If a president was appointed in two different states, they are counted in each state.
- Appointments do not include presidents of private independent law schools.
- Appointments include presidents, chancellors, and CEOs.
- Interim positions are also included, and, if known, are generally considered as separate appointments from permanent positions.
- Presidents who started their appointment in 2020 and after are not included within this graph.
- Two current presidents have unidentified start dates for their terms. They are not included in this graph.
- Appointments in fifty U. S. states are included.
- Darker shades of colors represent a higher number of appointments.

Map 3.9. Number of Lawyer Appointments at Religiously Affiliated Institutions by State (2010–2019)

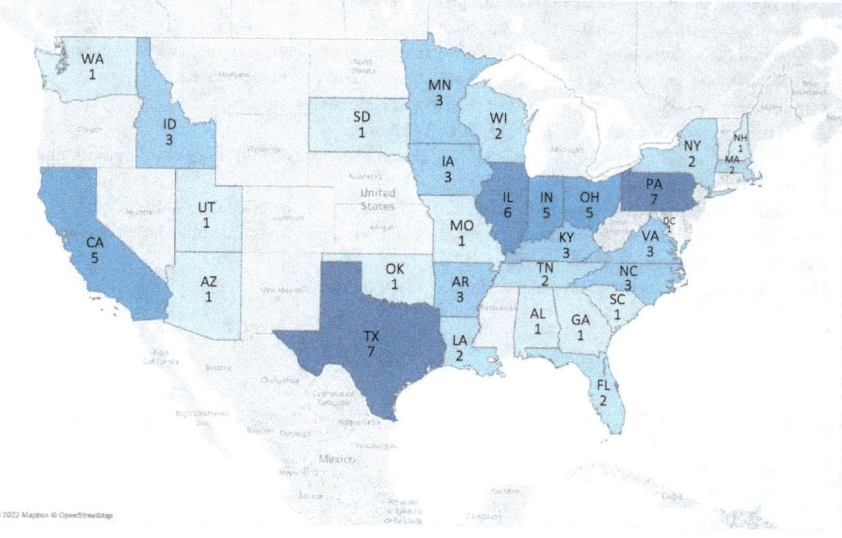

Notes
- Each appointment is counted by the start of a president's term.
- Presidents are counted for each of their appointments.
- A president can be appointed more than once in a state, at either the same school or a different one.
- If a president was appointed in two different states, they are counted in each state.
- Appointments do not include presidents of private independent law schools.
- Appointments include presidents, chancellors, and CEOs.
- Interim positions are also included, and, if known, are generally considered as separate appointments from permanent positions.
- Presidents who started their appointment in 2020 and after are not included within this graph.
- Two current presidents have unidentified start dates for their terms. They are not included in this graph.
- Appointments in fifty U. S. states are included.
- Darker shades of colors represent a higher number of appointments.

Map 3.10. Number of Lawyer Appointments at Religiously Affiliated Institutions by State (1900–2019)

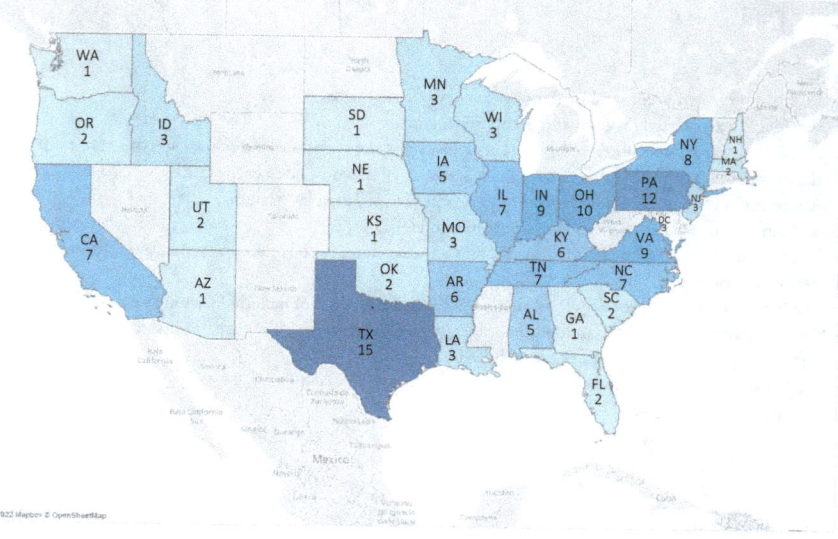

Notes
- Each appointment is counted by the start of a president's term.
- Presidents are counted for each of their appointments.
- A president can be appointed more than once in a state, at either the same school or a different one.
- If a president was appointed in two different states, they are counted in each state.
- Appointments do not include presidents of private independent law schools.
- Appointments include presidents, chancellors, and CEOs.
- Interim positions are also included, and, if known, are generally considered as separate appointments from permanent positions.
- Presidents who started their appointment in 2020 and after are not included within this graph.
- Two current presidents have unidentified start dates for their terms. They are not included in this graph.
- Appointments in fifty U. S. states are included.
- Darker shades of colors represent a higher number of appointments.

Public vs. Private Schools

According to the latest data (2018) from the Carnegie Classification, of the 4,324 colleges and universities 1,666 are public schools, 1,742 are private not-for-profit, and 916 are private for-profit.[7] Chart 3.3 shows that between 2010 and 2019, lawyer presidents were appointed at 109 unique public institutions, and at 161 unique private institutions. Among the private institutions, 75 were religiously affiliated and 86 had no religious affiliation. Chart 3.4 shows that, since the 1900, 228 public institutions appointed a lawyer president, and 324 private institutions appointed lawyer presidents, with 128 of those private institutions being religiously affiliated. The percentage of lawyer presidents at unique public institutions between 2010 and 2019 was 40%, roughly the same percentage over the last 120 years (1900–2019)—41%. The overall percentage of lawyer presidents at private institutions also remained constant during these timeframes, with an almost 5% increase in the number of lawyer presidents appointed at religiously affiliated institutions in 2010–2019. One likely reason for the uptick in lawyer presidents at religiously affiliated schools may be traced to potential legal and regulatory challenges some religious institutions face in their efforts to enforce policies that may otherwise be discriminatory but for closely held religious values and beliefs.

---

7   Ibid.

Chart 3.3. Public and Private Institutions with Lawyer Presidents (2010–2019)

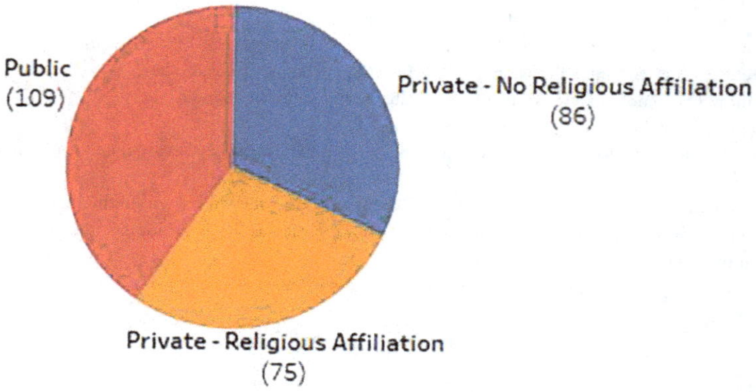

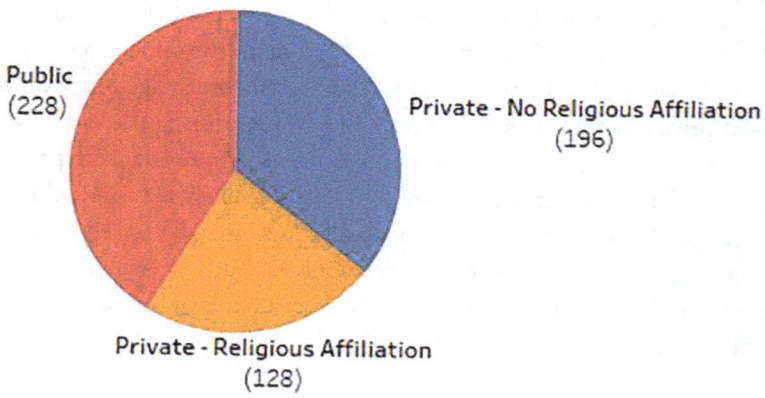

Notes
- This graph counts each school only once, even if there are multiple appointments.
- Appointments do not include presidents of private independent law schools.
- Appointments include presidents, chancellors, and CEOs.
- Interim positions are also included, and, if known, are generally considered as separate appointments from permanent positions.
- Presidents who started their appointment in 2020 and after are not included within this graph.
- Two current presidents have unidentified start dates for their terms. They are not included in this graph.

Chart 3.4. Public and Private Institutions with Lawyer Presidents (1900–2019)

Notes
- This graph counts each school only once, even if there are multiple appointments.
- Appointments do not include presidents of private independent law schools.
- Appointments include presidents, chancellors, and CEOs.
- Interim positions are also included, and, if known, are generally considered as separate appointments from permanent positions.
- Presidents who started their appointment in 2020 and after are not included within this graph.
- Two current presidents have unidentified start dates for their terms. They are not included in this graph.

The next five tables below present data from the American Council on Education's last four studies on the American College President with respect to institutions led by presidents holding juris doctorate (JD) degrees. While the data collected for this more recent research effort discovered more lawyer presidents than the ACE data, these charts are instructive in context for showing overall percentages of institutions controlled by lawyer presidents in public and private sectors. The ACE data in Table 3.4 shows that although the percentage of public institutions headed by lawyer presidents has remained relatively constant between 2002 and 2017, the percentage of private institutions (not-for-profit and for-profit ones) headed by lawyers during the same timeframe has steadily increased from about 14% in 2002 to almost 21% in 2017. Table 3.5 shows the percentage of institutions who were led by lawyer presidents according to their Carnegie Classification in the same time period. Appointments of lawyer presidents increased over time at Associates, Bachelors, Masters, and "Other" institutions, but decreased at "Doctorate" and "Special-Focus" schools. Among the largest jump were appointments of lawyers to Associate degree-granting institutions. This is discussed in greater detail in the next section, which will deal with community colleges. The increase at "Other" institutions may be explained in part because of the increasing regulatory and economic pressures on for-profit/proprietary schools and the benefits that might come from skilled attorneys. Table 3.6 presents the data based on percentage of lawyers leading the same institutions as compared to the percentage of institutions in the previous table.

Table 3.4. Share of Institutional Control Led by JD Holding Presidents

Control of institution	2002	2007	2012	2017
Public	3.74%	4.32%	5.38%	5.25%
Private, Not-For-Profit	6.26%	6.77%	8.64%	10.92%
For-Profit	7.79%	10.39%	9.62%	9.68%

Note: The table shows the share of institutional control of institutions led by JD holding presidents for each survey year. For example, in 2002 JD holding presidents made up 3.74% of presidents leading Public institutions, compared to the remaining 96.26% (not shown) who led these institutions but did not hold JD degrees.

Table 3.5. JD Holding Presidents, by Carnegie Classification and Year

Carnegie Classification	2002	2007	2012	2017
Associates	1.79%	2.89%	4.01%	4.03%
Bachelors	6.42%	7.02%	9.42%	9.28%
Masters	3.73%	5.88%	7.77%	10.60%
Doctorate	12.50%	11.17%	9.40%	10.06%
Special-Focus	8.01%	6.41%	7.98%	6.21%
Other	5.35%	9.09%	8.11%	12.50%

Note: The table shows for each survey year the percentage of presidents who hold JDs within each Carnegie classification. For example, 1.79% of presidents of Associate degree-granting institutions in 2002 held JDs, compared to 98.21% who did not. The data in this table include presidents leading for-profit institutions.

Table 3.6. Distribution of JD Holding Presidents, by Carnegie Classification and Year

Carnegie Classification	2002	2007	2012	2017
Associates	11.76%	17.80%	19.13%	15.57%
Bachelors	25.21%	24.58%	26.96%	26.23%
Masters	12.61%	21.19%	26.09%	31.97%
Doctorate	19.33%	18.64%	12.17%	13.93%
Special-Focus	22.69%	15.25%	13.04%	7.38%
Other	8.40%	2.54%	2.61%	4.92%
Total	100%	100%	100%	100%

Note: The table shows the share of institutional Carnegie classifications led by JD holding presidents for each survey year. For example, in 2002 11.76% of all JD holding presidents led Associate degree-granting institutions, while 25.21% led Bachelor degree-granting institutions, and so forth. The data in this table include presidents leading for-profit institutions.

Table 3.7. Percentage of Presidents Holding JDs, by Carnegie and Control

Carnegie by Control	2002	2007	2012	2017
Doctoral Public	11.38%	9.77%	8.99%	9.01%
Doctoral Private	14.75%	14.29%	10.34%	12.28%
Masters Public	4.52%	6.97%	8.19%	5.66%
Masters Private	2.76%	4.98%	7.55%	14.08%
BA Public	9.84%	6.78%	5.88%	4.84%
BA Private	5.91%	7.16%	10.49%	10.11%
AA Public	1.50%	2.22%	3.59%	3.88%
AA Private	2.70%	2.17%	7.41%	8.70%
Special Focus Public	4.26%	2.70%	7.14%	0.00%

Carnegie by Control	2002	2007	2012	2017
Special Focus Private	8.36%	6.58%	6.83%	7.32%
Other Public	3.57%	0.00%	10.20%	12.12%
Other Private	4.88%	11.11%	8.99%	10.00%
For-Profit	7.79%	10.39%	10.34%	9.63%

Note: The table shows for each survey year the percentage of presidents who hold JDs within each Carnegie and Control Classification. For example, 11.38% of presidents of Doctoral Public institutions in 2002 held JDs, compared to 88.62% who did not.

Table 3.8. Distribution of JD Holding Presidents Each Year, by Carnegie and Control

Carnegie by Control	2002	2007	2012	2017
Doctoral Public	12.17%	11.21%	7.14%	8.20%
Doctoral Private	7.83%	7.76%	5.36%	5.74%
Masters Public	8.70%	12.07%	12.50%	7.38%
Masters Private	4.35%	9.48%	14.29%	23.77%
BA Public	5.22%	3.45%	2.68%	2.46%
BA Private	20.87%	21.55%	25.00%	22.95%
AA Public	8.70%	12.07%	16.07%	13.93%
AA Private	1.74%	0.86%	1.79%	1.64%
Special Focus Public	1.74%	0.86%	0.89%	0.00%
Special Focus Private	20.00%	12.93%	9.82%	7.38%
Other Public	1.74%	0.00%	0.00%	3.28%
Other Private	1.74%	0.86%	0.00%	0.82%
For-Profit	5.22%	6.90%	4.46%	2.46%
Total	**100%**	**100%**	**100%**	**100%**

Note: The table shows for each survey year the proportion of presidents who hold JDs within each Carnegie and Control Classification, among JD holding presidents only. For example, 12.17% of all JD holding presidents in 2002 led Doctoral Public institutions.

Community Colleges

Roughly 34% of post-secondary institutions are two-year degree-granting institutions (See Table 3.9 below).[8] In 2018, there were 1,449 two-year schools (See Table 3.1).[9] Of the 1,449 "at least two-year but less than four-year" institutions, 881 were public, 101 were private not-for-profit, and 467 were private for-profit.[10]

Table 3.9. Percentage Distribution of Grand Total of U. S. Postsecondary Institutions, by Level of Institution and Region: Academic Year 2016–17

Level of Institution	Control of Institution			Total
	Public	Private Not-For-Profit	Private For-Profit	
4- or More-Year	**18.13%**	**37.95%**	**10.34%**	**66.42%**
U. S. Service Schools	0.39%	0.00%	0.00%	0.39%
New England CT ME MA NH RI VT	0.97%	3.31%	0.16%	4.44%
Mideast DE DC MD NJ NY PA	2.78%	7.91%	1.04%	11.73%
Great Lakes IL IN MI OH WI	2.31%	6.17%	1.09%	9.57%
Plains IA KS MN MO NE ND SD	1.55%	3.95%	0.93%	6.43%
Southeast AL AR FL GA KY LA MS NC SC TN VA WV	4.51%	7.91%	2.64%	15.06%
Southwest AZ NM OK TX	1.90%	2.08%	1.39%	5.37%
Rocky Mountains CO ID MT UT WY	0.83%	0.76%	0.72%	2.31%
Far West AK CA HI NV OR WA	2.47%	4.76%	2.13%	9.37%
Outlying Areas AS FM GU MH MP PR PW VI	0.42%	1.09%	0.25%	1.76%
At Least 2-Year but Less than 4-Year	**20.37%**	**2.34%**	**10.80%**	**33.51%**
U. S. Service Schools	0.05%	0.00%	0.00%	0.05%
New England CT ME MA NH RI VT	1.02%	0.12%	0.09%	1.23%
Mideast DE DC MD NJ NY PA	2.04%	0.67%	1.67%	4.37%
Great Lakes IL IN MI OH WI	2.68%	0.19%	1.34%	4.21%
Plains IA KS MN MO NE ND SD	2.43%	0.12%	0.58%	3.12%
Southeast AL AR FL GA KY LA MS NC SC TN VA WV	5.53%	0.56%	3.47%	9.55%
Southwest AZ NM OK TX	2.61%	0.16%	1.55%	4.32%
Rocky Mountains CO ID MT UT WY	0.76%	0.14%	0.42%	1.32%
Far West AK CA HI NV OR WA	3.10%	0.30%	1.50%	4.90%
Outlying Areas AS FM GU MH MP PR PW VI	0.16%	0.09%	0.19%	0.44%

8 Ibid.
9 Ibid.
10 Ibid.

	Control of Institution			Total
Level of Institution	Public	Private Not-For-Profit	Private For-Profit	
Less than 2-Year	0.00%	0.02%	0.05%	0.07%
Southeast AL AR FL GA KY LA MS NC SC TN VA WV	0.00%	0.02%	0.00%	0.02%
Southwest AZ NM OK TX	0.00%	0.00%	0.05%	0.05%
Grand Total	38.51%	40.31%	21.18%	100.00%

Community colleges are two-year schools that grant associates degrees. The interest in community colleges was ignited in the early twentieth century as an avenue for students who desired to earn a bachelor's degree but needed a lower cost option closer to home before transferring to a four-year college.[11] After World War II, more vocational training was added to the offerings as well as shorter training programs often in collaboration with local businesses.[12] Although the growth in the number of students enrolled in community colleges has far outpaced four-year colleges, completion rates are much lower.[13] Faculty at community colleges are different than the typical four-year college faculty in that they are less likely to hold PhDs and are more likely to not be full-time professors but rather teach in addition to other employment.[14]

Although lawyers have also been tapped to lead community colleges, it is surprising given the more unconventional credentials of the faculty that there have not been more lawyers at the helm. As chart 3.5 shows, while the number of lawyer presidents at community colleges has increased at a slightly higher rate than lawyer presidents at four-year colleges (more than tripling from the 1990s to the 2000s and close to tripling between 2000 and the 2010s), the percentage of community college lawyer presidents serving in the 2010s is just 13% of all lawyer presidents in office, despite the fact that community colleges represent about one-third (34%) of all institutions of higher education.

---

11 Derek Bok, "The American System of Higher Education," in his *Higher Education in America*, revised ed., The William G. Bowen Memorial Series in Higher Education (n.p.: Princeton University Press, 2013), 11, https://doi.org/10.2307/j.ctv7h0rts.34.
12 Ibid.
13 Ibid.
14 Ibid.

Chart 3.5. Community Colleges with Lawyer Presidents (1940–2019)

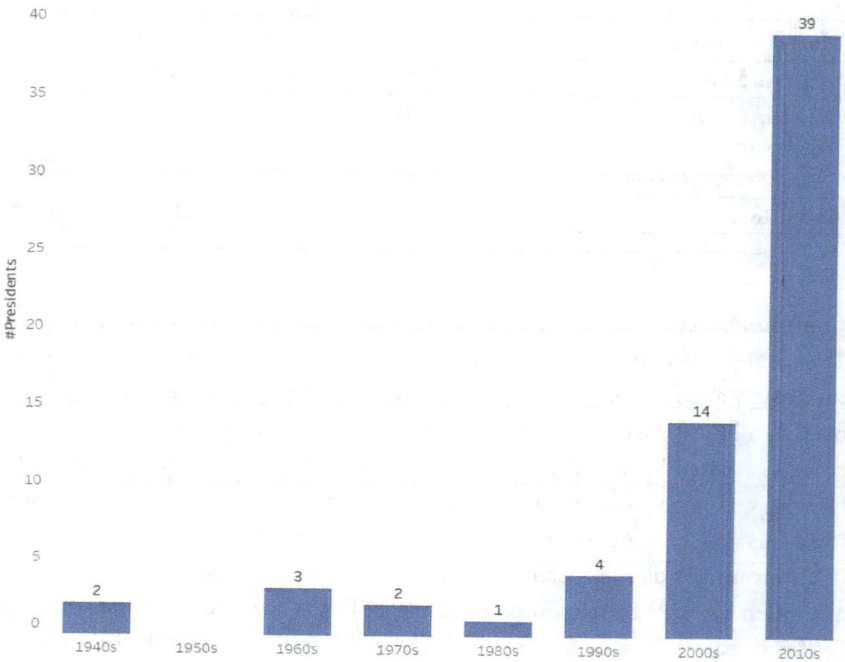

Notes
- Each appointment within a decade is counted by the start of a president's term.
- If a president was appointed twice in the same decade, they are counted for each appointment.
- If a president was appointed in two different decades, they are counted in each decade.
- Appointments do not include presidents of private independent law schools.
- Appointments include presidents, chancellors, and CEOs.
- Interim positions are also included, and, if known, are considered as separate appointments from permanent positions.
- Presidents who started their appointment in 2020 and after are not included within this graph.
- Two current presidents have unidentified start dates for their terms. They are not included within this graph.

Religiously Affiliated Schools

As discussed in chapter one, beginning with the development of higher education during colonial times, early institutions of higher education were established and run by the Church.[15] Of the 4,324 Carnegie classified Title

---

15 Thelin et al., "Higher Education in the United States."

IV degree-granting institutions in 2018, 300 or about 6.9% are identified as faith-related institutions.[16] As chart 3.6 demonstrates, just over one quarter (27%) of presidents serving in the 2010s at religiously affiliated colleges and universities were lawyers. Similar to community college lawyer presidents, the number of lawyer presidents serving at religiously affiliated schools tripled from the 1990s to the 2000s, and more than doubled from the 2000s to the 2010s.

This trend makes sense given the delicate legal relationship between church and state—the desire of the institutions generally to enable their students to receive federal financial and other governmental institutional economic support, while not being mandated to comply with government requirements that would be antithetical to basic tenets of religious belief. In twenty-one states, religiously affiliated colleges are exempt from higher education licensing process, leaving these schools, in almost half of the states, to deal with sometimes difficult compliance issues that may conflict with closely held religious beliefs.[17]

---

16 Indiana University Center for Postsecondary Research, "Distribution of Institutions and Enrollments by Classification Category," *CCIHE2018 Summary Tables*, last modified 2018, accessed September 22, 2021, https://view.officeapps.live.com/op/view.aspx?src=https%3A%2F%2Fcarnegieclassifications.iu.edu%2Fdownloads%2FCCIHE2018-SummaryTables.xlsx&wdOrigin=BROWSELINK.

17 "Talking Points: State Authorization of Religious Colleges," *WCET*, last modified January 2016, accessed September 2, 2021, https://wcet.wiche.edu/documents/talking-points/state-auth-religious-colleges; Connecticut General Assembly Office of Legislative Research, *Exemptions from the Higher Education Licensing Process for Religious Colleges*, by Rute A. Pinhel, report no. 2007-R-0023, January 9, 2007, accessed September 2, 2021, https://www.cga.ct.gov/2007/rpt/2007-R-0023.htm.

Chart 3.6. Religiously Affiliated Institutions with Lawyer Presidents (1900–2019)

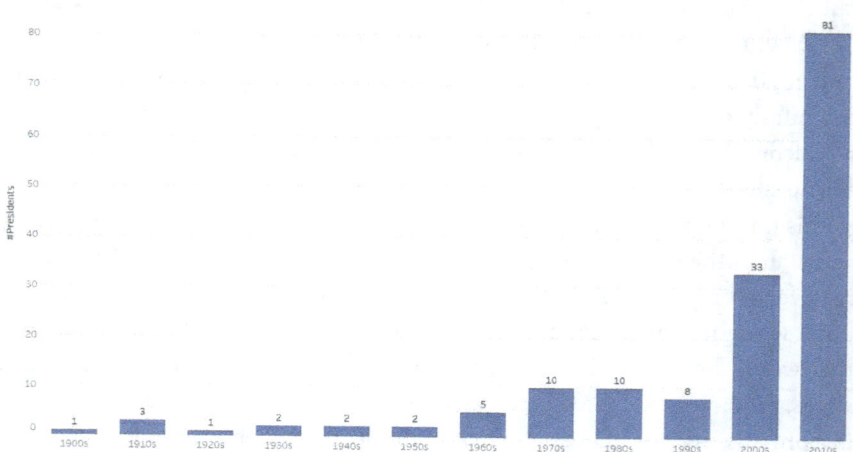

Notes
- Each appointment within a decade is counted by the start of a president's term.
- If a president was appointed twice in the same decade, they are counted for each appointment.
- If a president was appointed in two different decades, they are counted in each decade.
- Appointments do not include presidents of private independent law schools.
- Appointments include presidents, chancellors, and CEOs.
- Interim positions are also included, and, if known, are considered as separate appointments from permanent positions.
- Presidents who started their appointment in 2020 and after are not included within this graph.
- Two current presidents have unidentified start dates for their terms. They are not included within this graph.

Historically Black Colleges and Universities

Historically Black Colleges and Universities (HBCUs) are defined as schools established prior to 1964 with the principal mission of educating Black Americans.[18] "HBCUs have a special and important place in the fabric of higher education in the United States and bear a legacy like no other set of universities. They continue to serve as centers of diversity and access for low-income, first-generation college students. They are also symbolic of the African-American

---

18 "Status and Trends in the Education of Racial and Ethnic Minorities" (Snapshot: Enrollment in Historically Black Colleges and Universities, Hispanic Serving Institutions, and Tribal Colleges), *National Center for Education Statistics*, last modified 2017, accessed September 9, 2021, https://nces.ed.gov/pubs2010/2010015/indicator6_24.asp#snapshot.

quest for educational excellence and social equity."[19] Currently there are 101 HBCUs located in 21 states plus the District of Columbia and the U. S. Virgin Islands, with a split of 50 of these schools public and 51 private not-for-profit.[20]

Between the 2000s and the 2010s, the number of lawyer presidents appointed at HBCUs quadrupled, as shown on chart 3.7. Like other institutions of higher education, HBCUs are experiencing numerous challenges. A 2014 report of the Association of Governing Boards of Universities and Colleges (AGB) identified seven pressing priorities for HBCUs: enrollment and the value proposition; educational quality and degree offerings; student success and completion; finances and affordability; infrastructure; federal and state policy; and governance and leadership.[21]

On leadership, the report notes that, "Over the past few years, a number of HBCUs have faced governance difficulties that have garnered substantial national press for issues ranging from highly scrutinized presidential searches and compensation issues the to loss of accreditation and financial difficulties."[22] In interviews with HBCU presidents, it was reported that "Many presidents point to the lack of a presidential pipeline. One public president stated during the national conference that high presidential turnover and the general instability of the HBCU presidency is quite concerning."[23]

The relatively small number of lawyers leading HBCUs must be viewed in the context of Black lawyers in America. J. Clayton Smith, Jr. in his book *Emancipation: The Making of the Black Lawyer, 1844–1944* (1993) notes that, "Black lawyers were one of the last group of professionals to emerge as a class in the black community," and that preachers consistently outnumbered the number of Black lawyers in the South.[24] In 1844, Macon Bolling Allen became the first Black lawyer in the United States, having secured an apprenticeship in the Maine office of a white lawyer.[25] It was not until 1868 that George Lewis Ruffin, a Black student, enrolled at Harvard University School of Law,[26] and ten years after that when Yale Law School admitted its first Black student,

---

19 Kristin Hodge Clark and Brandon D. Daniels, *Top Strategic Issues Facing HBCUs, Now and into the Future* (Washington, DC: Association of Governing Boards of Universities and Colleges, 2014), 15, https://eric.ed.gov/?id=ED549731.
20 Indiana University Center for Post-Secondary Research, "CCIHE 2018 Public Data File."
21 Clark and Daniels, *Top Strategic Issues*.
22 Ibid.
23 Ibid.
24 J. Clay Smith, Jr, *Emancipation: The Making of the Black Lawyer, 1844–1944* (Philadelphia: University of Pennsylvania Press, 1993), 4.
25 Ibid., 33.
26 Ibid.

Edwin Archer Randolph.[27] Howard University called upon John Mercer Langston, the first Black lawyer to be admitted to the Ohio bar (and indeed one of the first Black lawyers to practice law in the nation), to organize its law department in 1868.[28]

Although five Black law schools were established between 1881 and 1896, all but one closed by 1914.[29] By 1939, nineteen Black law schools had been formed.[30] However, membership in the organized bar was unwelcoming to early Black lawyers. When word spread in 1912 that three Black lawyers had been admitted to the American Bar Association, Southern white lawyers who viewed the Association as a social organization, forced the issue of membership for Black lawyers to be addressed at the annual convention.[31] The political pressure mounted as U. S. Attorney General George Wickersham wrote to the ABA urging them not to disqualify at least one of the lawyers, William Henry Lewis, for membership (who happened to also be an assistant U. S. Attorney) based on, among other reasons, the fact that the ABA constitution did not discriminate.[32] Wickersham did not exactly prevail as the Association "compromised," by requiring applicants to indicate race on their application, leading to the general understanding that these three Black lawyers would be the last Black ABA members.

Thanks to movement from white Northern lawyers that began in 1938, the color ban was finally broken by a resolution of the Association in 1943.[33] According to the 1920 census, there were 955 Black male lawyers (plus 4 female Black lawyers) as compared to 120,341 white male lawyers.[34] By 1930, the number of Black male lawyers increased to 1,223 (plus 24 female Black lawyers) while the number of white male lawyers increased to 155,431.[35] The numbers of Black male lawyers dipped in 1940 to 1,013 (plus 39 female Black lawyers) while the number of white male lawyers increased to 172,329 (plus 4,146 female white lawyers).[36] By 2008, the U. S. Bureau of Labor Statistics reported that of

---

27 Ibid., 37.
28 Ibid., 42.
29 Ibid., 58.
30 Ibid., 65.
31 Ibid., 542.
32 Ibid., 542–543.
33 Ibid., 544–545.
34 Ibid., 630.
35 Ibid., 631–633.
36 Ibid., 634–637.

1,014,000 lawyers, only 7% were Black or African American.[37] According to the 2017 ACE Study on the Presidency, only 17% of all college presidents are racial minorities, with 8% being Black or African American.[38]

Chart 3.7. Historically Black Colleges and Universities with Lawyer Presidents (1900–2019)

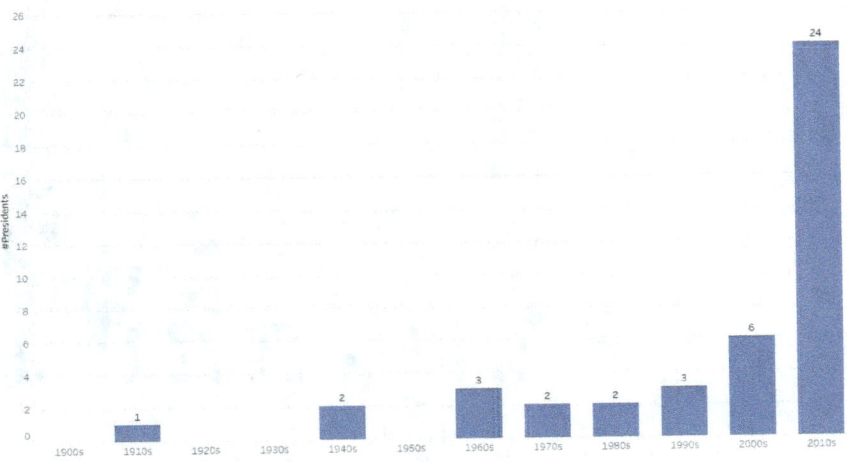

Notes
- Each appointment within a decade is counted by the start of a president's term.
- If a president was appointed twice in the same decade, they are counted for each appointment.
- If a president was appointed in two different decades, they are counted in each decade.
- Appointments do not include presidents of private independent law schools.
- Appointments include presidents, chancellors, and CEOs.
- Interim positions are also included, and, if known, are considered as separate appointments from permanent positions.
- Presidents who started their appointment in 2020 and after are not included within this graph.
- Two current presidents have unidentified start dates for their terms. They are not included within this graph.

---

37 "Table 6. Employed Persons by Detailed Occupation, Race, and Hispanic or Latino Ethnicity, 2008 Annual Averages," table, *U.S. Bureau of Labor Statistics*, November 2009, accessed September 9, 2021, https://www.americanbar.org/content/dam/aba/administrative/market_research/cpsaat11.pdf.

38 "2017 Overview, Minority Presidents, Demographics," *American Council on Education*, accessed August 29, 2021, https://www.aceacps.org/minority-presidents/#demographics.

Chart 3.8. Historically Black Colleges and Universities with Lawyer Presidents (2010–2019)

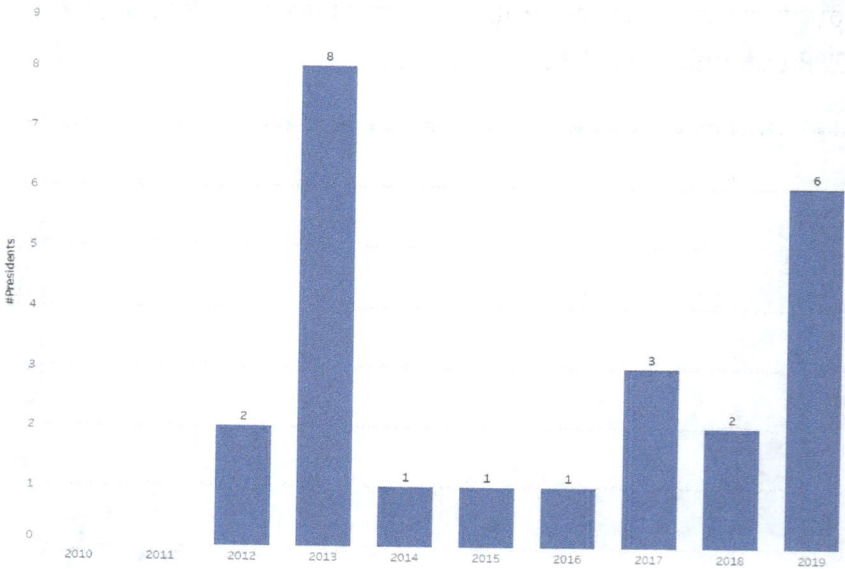

Notes
- Each appointment within a decade is counted by the start of a president's term.
- If a president was appointed twice in the same decade, they are counted for each appointment.
- If a president was appointed in two different decades, they are counted in each decade.
- Appointments do not include presidents of private independent law schools.
- Appointments include presidents, chancellors, and CEOs.
- Interim positions are also included, and, if known, are considered as separate appointments from permanent positions.
- Presidents who started their appointment in 2020 and after are not included within this graph.
- Two current presidents have unidentified start dates for their terms. They are not included within this graph.

Institutions with Law Schools

Although intuitively one might surmise that colleges and universities that have law schools might be more likely to have lawyer presidents, the data suggests otherwise. Chart 3.9 shows that in 2010–2019 the percentage of unique institutions that had both a law school and a lawyer president was 20%. This number is slightly less than the longitudinal number of 25% between 1900 and 2019. One reason for the small shift may be that lawyers are now more widely accepted as viable presidential candidates in general, and they may not require the validation that could come from colleagues and stakeholders more familiar with law school faculty and administrators from interactions on their campus.

Chart 3.9. Institutions with Law Schools Who Have Had Lawyer Presidents (2010–2019)

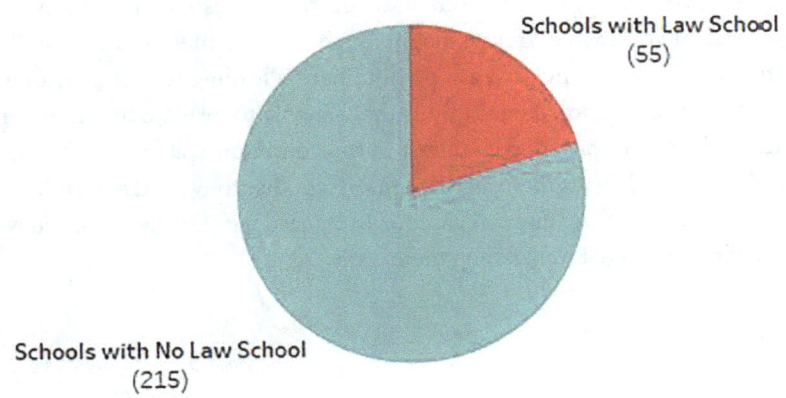

Notes
- This graph counts each school only once, even if there are multiple appointments.
- Appointments do not include presidents of private independent law schools.
- Appointments include presidents, chancellors, and CEOs.
- Interim positions are also included, and, if known, are generally considered as separate appointments from permanent positions.
- Presidents who started their appointment in 2020 and after are not included within this graph.
- Two current presidents have unidentified start dates for their terms. They are not included in this graph.

Chart 3.10. Institutions with Law Schools Who Have Had Lawyer Presidents (1900–2019)

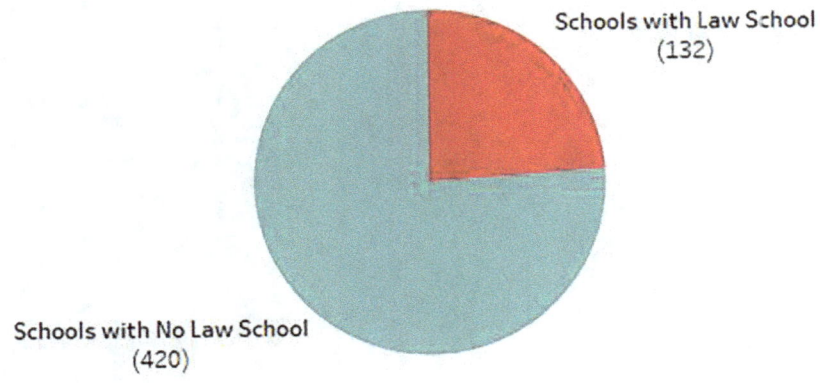

Notes
- This graph counts each school only once, even if there are multiple appointments.
- Appointments do not include presidents of private independent law schools.
- Appointments include presidents, chancellors, and CEOs.
- Interim positions are also included, and, if known, are generally considered as separate appointments from permanent positions.
- Presidents who started their appointment in 2020 and after are not included within this graph.
- Two current presidents have unidentified start dates for their terms. They are not included in this graph.

Although it is impossible to be certain, the consistent rise in lawyer presidents across all types of higher educational institutions does lead to a fairly strong hypothesis that it is the external factors, such as those mentioned in the introduction and chapter one, that are predominantly leading to this development. There are few educational institutions that are able to insulate themselves from issues such as free speech, civil unrest in the community at large, or economic turbulence, which leads them all to question whether they need a president who can not only lead their internal campus but guard against the rising tides that could, if not managed well, sweep them away.

CHAPTER 4

Characteristics of Lawyer Presidents

Roger Martin, a former (non-lawyer) president of Moravian College and Randolph-Macon College who serves as a senior consultant with R. H. Perry & Associates, opines that "Generally, successful candidates for a college presidency are, among other things, experienced and proven leaders who have strong communication skills and are people of high moral integrity. Must they have a doctorate? Most college presidents do, but others just have a terminal degree. The most crucial ingredient for a successful presidency is not a particular credential but experience raising money, balancing budgets and managing a complex organization."[1]

Noting the increase in the number of lawyers who are being appointed campus presidents, Martin comments, "... successful candidates increasingly come from outside the academy and are business leaders, attorneys and even retired military officers (what we call 'nontraditional' candidates). Key for nontraditional candidates is that they have a deep understanding of what makes a college or university different from other organizations. For example, many nontraditional candidates have served as college trustees and understand the distinct concept of shared governance."[2]

Education and Training

Consideration of academic credentials for unconventional leaders may be important to some search committees and appointing bodies, but it is not the

---

1. Rodger Martin, "So You Want to Become a College President," *Inside Higher Ed*, last modified March 19, 2018, accessed September 13, 2021, https://www.insidehighered.com/advice/2018/03/19/myths-and-misconceptions-about-presidential-searches-opinion.
2. Ibid.

case uniformly. While the majority of lawyer presidents do not possess post-Baccalaureate degrees beyond the juris doctorate, the number of lawyer presidents with multiple post-Baccalaureate degrees is steadily increasing.

As is the case with most who hold the position, the majority of lawyer presidents have had some type of prior academic experience, although some colleges and universities are increasingly hiring nontraditional presidents (defined as presidents who did not rise up through the faculty ranks). According to Scott Beardsley, who studied this trend, "You have traditional and you have nontraditional presidents at all types of universities, whether they're high-ranked or low-ranked," Beardsley said. "It's just that the proportion tended to indicate that smaller or lower-ranked institutions had a greater probability today of having nontraditional leaders."[3]

In addition to exploring traditional prior academic experience for lawyer presidents, this study adds to the literature by expanding Beardsley's consideration of presidents with traditional academic experience as simply those who rise up through the professorial ranks to including those who hold other positions inside academia such as in-house general counsel for colleges and universities, lawyers with experience as senior administrators responsible for institutional advancement (which includes fundraising, government, and community relations), and lawyers who have served college and university board of trustees. While not specifically analyzed in this chapter, another emerging trend gleaned from the short biographies of lawyer presidents is experience serving in the role of chief of staff to other college presidents as another steppingstone to the presidency.

Although the scope of this research does not analyze the experiences lawyer presidents who came completely form outside academia (for example, a small group who came from corporate America and from law firms without any prior connection to academia), this study does explore the strongest commonality in the non-academic background of lawyer presidents—experience in government. As will be discussed, some lawyer presidents had distinguished careers as well-known elected public officials, others as senior appointed public servants, many had prior military experience and a number served in the judiciary as law clerks.

---

3   Seltzer, "Defending Nontraditional Presidents."

Does Where a Campus Leader Earned Their Law Degree Matter?

Studies have shown that where someone goes to college is not a strong predictor of future success.[4] In relation to the research here, this does lead to the question of whether the same is true for lawyer presidents. Can one be successful regardless of where a law degree was earned or does pedigree matter? Chart 4.1 illustrates the law schools where the greatest number of lawyer presidents earned either their JD degree (including LLB and LLD) or some other law degree (including LLM and JSD).

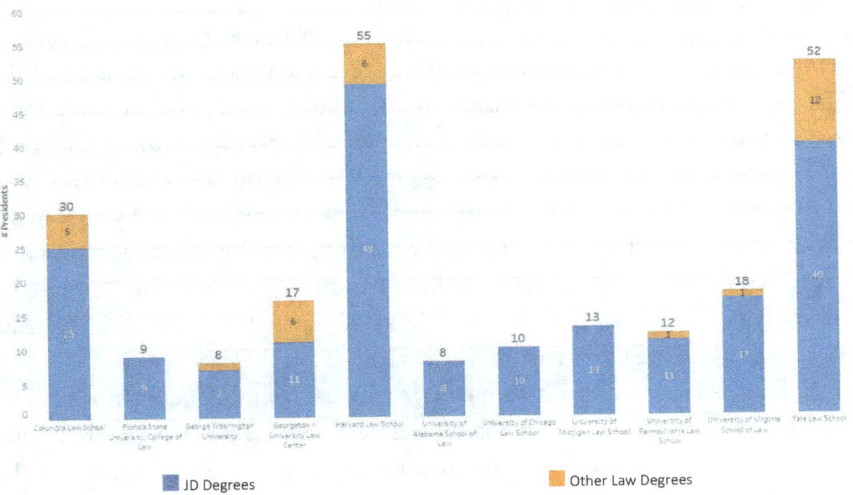

Chart 4.1. Top Schools Attended by Lawyer Presidents (1900–2019)

Notes
- "JD Degrees" includes: JD, LLB, or LLD.
- "Other Law Degrees" includes: JSD or LLM.
- Each president is counted once within in each school. If a lawyer earned both a JD and another law degree at the same school, they will be classified as JD.
- Appointments do not include presidents of private independent law schools.
- Appointments include presidents, chancellors, and CEOs.
- Interim positions are also included, and, if known, are generally considered as separate appointments from permanent positions.
- Presidents who started their appointment in 2020 and after are not included within this graph.
- Two current presidents have unidentified start dates for their terms. They are not included in this graph.

---

4 Gregg Easterbrook, "Who Needs Harvard?," *Brookings*, last modified October 1, 2004, accessed September 9, 2021, https://www.brookings.edu/articles/who-needs-harvard/.

While over a broad span of decades, no one law school can claim to be the "college president maker," three of the five Ivy League law schools hold the top spots for counting among its alumni the largest number of college and university presidents: Harvard Law School has fifty-five alumni presidents, Yale Law School has fifty-two, and Columbia University School of Law follows with thirty. The University of Pennsylvania School of Law trailed with twelve college and university presidents, and Cornell Law School did not make the list of the top eleven law schools for alumni who have held campus presidencies.

Using the lens of national law school rankings by U. S. News and World Report,[5] out of the 197 law schools ranked in 2021, the top eleven law schools that produced the greatest number of campus presidents were ranked in the top fifty, and all but two (George Washington University and Florida State University) were ranked in the top twenty-five.

In rank order, according to U. S. News and World Report, the top eleven schools that produced the greatest number of campus presidents were: Yale (#1), Harvard (#3), University of Chicago and Columbia (tied at #4), University of Pennsylvania (#7), University of Virginia (#8), University of Michigan (#10), Georgetown (#15), Alabama (#25), George Washington University (#27), and Florida State University (#48). Law Schools ranked in the top ten by U. S. News and World Report that did not make the list of the top eleven schools for graduating lawyer presidents included Stanford (ranked #2), New York University (ranked #6), University of California–Berkeley (ranked #9), and Duke (ranked #10 in a tie with the University of Michigan).

While it is always difficult to quantify whether members of campus leader search committees, appointing boards, and even search firms who might recruit candidates, put significant weight into where people earned their degrees, the fact that many in higher education pay attention to school rankings (love them or hate them) means that there is at least an implicit reaction to the schools that candidates attended. However, as the data in Appendix 9 reveal, lawyer presidents have earned their JDs at a wide array of schools, including at institutions unranked in the U. S. News and World Report survey.

---

5 "2022 Best Law Schools (Ranked in 2021)," *U.S. News and World Report*, accessed September 13, 2021, https://www.usnews.com/best-graduate-schools/top-law-schools/law-rankings.

Do Campus Presidents Need Degrees in Addition to the Juris Doctorate?

The 2017 American College President Study reports that in 2016, 79.5% of presidents had a PhD or EdD.[6] Table 4.1 below from the ACE study reveals that, out of the pool of all presidents, very few had earned both a juris doctorate and an additional doctoral degree, with the peak being just 2% in 2012, but this amount dipped back to under 1.5% by 2017. In contrast, by examining just the cohort of lawyer presidents, Table 4.2 from the same ACE study reveals that, among the group of presidents with a juris doctorate, the number of presidents who hold a second doctoral degree is consistently rising, starting with the baseline of just over 17% in 2002 and exceeding 30% in 2017. Table 4.3 presents data collected as part of the empirical research for this study and it reveals, in raw numbers, that from 1990 to the 2010s the number of lawyers with post-JD doctoral degrees has tripled from 10 to 31.

Table 4.1. Presidents Who Hold Additional Post-BA Degrees, among All Presidents

	2002	2007	2012	2017
No JD	94.96%	94.31%	92.99%	92.11%
JD but no additional-post-BA degree	3.18%	3.13%	3.69%	5.17%
JD and Masters Degree	0.97%	1.16%	1.27%	1.23%
JD and Doctoral Degree	0.89%	1.40%	2.05%	1.49%
Total	100%	100%	100%	100%

Note: The table shows the share of JD degree holders among all presidents, and JD holders with additional post-BA degrees. Doctoral degrees include PhDs, EdDs, and MDs (which include other health degrees such as DDS, DVM, and so forth).

Table 4.2. Presidents Who Hold Additional Post-BA Degrees, among JD Holding Presidents

	2002	2007	2012	2017
JD but no additional post-BA degree	63.03%	55.08%	52.59%	56.34%
JD and Masters Degree	19.33%	20.34%	18.10%	13.38%
JD and Doctoral Degree	17.65%	24.58%	29.31%	30.28%
Total	100%	100%	100%	100%

Note: The table shows the share of degrees held, among JD holders specifically. Doctoral degrees include PhDs, EdDs, and MDs (which include other health degrees such as DDS, DVM, and so forth).

---

6 Gagliardi et al., *American College President Study 2017*, 4.

Table 4.3. JD Plus Other Degrees (1900–2019)

Degree Type	Degree Category	1900s	1910s	1920s	1930s	1940s	1950s	1960s	1970s	1980s	1990s	2000s	2010s	Grand Total
Divinity	Divinity						1				1		1	3
Doctoral	Doctoral-Divinity												1	1
	Doctoral-EdD								2	2	1	8	14	20
	Doctoral-Medical									2		1	4	5
	Doctoral-Other												2	2
	Doctoral-PhD	1	1	1	1	2	1	2	3	4	10	22	31	58
Masters	Masters-Business						1	2	1		2	8	14	23
	Masters-Divinity						1			1		4	4	9
	Masters-Economics								1		1			2
	Masters-Education								1				3	4
	Masters-other	1	1	2		6	4	1	4	7	12	23	35	79
Post JD	Post JD-JSD							3	1	1	2	2		11
	Post JD-LLM					1	3	3	5	7	10	12	18	48
Grand Total		**2**	**2**	**2**	**2**	**7**	**7**	**8**	**15**	**15**	**27**	**53**	**91**	**186**

Notes

- Each appointment within a decade is counted by the start of a president's term.
- If a president was appointed twice in the same decade, they are only counted once per degree.
- If a president was appointed in two different decades, they are counted in each decade.
- If a president received more than one degree, it will be represented in this chart.
- Appointments do not include presidents of private independent law schools.
- Appointments include presidents, chancellors, and CEOs.
- Interim positions are also included, and, if known, are generally considered as separate appointments from permanent positions.
- Presidents who started their appointment in 2020 and after are not included within this graph.
- Two current presidents have unidentified start dates for their terms. They are not included in this graph.

There are a number of reasons for this rise in dual-post-degree presidents. A study by Vanderbilt law professors Joni Hersch and W. Kip Viscusi suggests that law schools are beginning to hire faculty who possess not just the JD degree, but also a PhD.[7] Examining the faculties at the twenty-six top-tier law schools, they reported that ". . . 361 of 1,338 current law professors (27%) have Ph.D. degrees. Thirteen percent (13%) of faculty members have Ph.D. degrees in the social sciences other than economics; 7% have degrees in economics; and 7% have them in other fields ranging from English to chemistry. Slightly more than 18% of law professors with Ph.D. degrees (65) possess a Ph.D. degree but no law degree. However, most law professors with Ph.D. degrees (296) hold both a law degree and a Ph.D."[8] Their work further reveals that, "Northwestern University appears to have gone further than any other school in this regard, and 50% of its law faculty now hold Ph.D. degrees. Other law schools with high percentages of Ph.D. professors include Pennsylvania (43%); UC-Berkeley (42%); Yale (40%); Cornell (40%); and Stanford (39%)."[9] As the number of law faculty with PhDs rises, and where law professors may choose the conventional route to the presidency (rising up through the academic ranks), there may be more people who simply possess the credentials. Another explanation is offered by former Oglethorpe President Lawrence Schall who commented that he enrolled in an executive doctorate in higher education program because he ". . . thought his chances of and a tool kit for becoming a president would be enhanced with a doctorate."[10]

---

7   Joni Hersch and W. Kip Viscusi, "Law and Economics as a Pillar of Legal Education," *Review of Law and Economics* 8, no. 2 (October 2012): 487–510, accessed September 9, 2021, https://law.vanderbilt.edu/files/archive/2012_Hersch&Viscusi_Law-and-Economics-as-a-Pillar-of-Legal-Education_RLE-Oct-2012.pdf. Hersch and Viscusi wrote the article as they launched the first law-school housed doctoral program in law and economics in the United States at Vanderbilt Law School and their data further explored the value of the PhD in Economics at top tier law schools.
8   J. Gordon Hylton, "What Should Be the Prerequisites for Becoming a Law Professor," *Marquette University Law School Faculty Blog*, entry posted September 8, 2011, accessed September 9, 2021, https://law.marquette.edu/facultyblog/2011/09/what-should-be-the-prerequisites-for-becoming-a-law-professor/.
9   Ibid.
10 Beardsley, "The Rise of the Nontraditional Liberal Arts College President," 268.

On-the-Job Experience

While search committees may be attracted to presidential candidates with prior experience in the position, this is not as significant factor in today's higher education environment as many might think. In 2017, of those presidents who responded to the American College President Study conducted by the American Council on Education, only 25% reported having held the same position at another institution, previous to their current appointment (see Table 4.4). When it comes to lawyer presidents, as Table 4.5 shows, the number of lawyer presidents who held a prior presidency before their current appointment was only slightly higher (27%), not a significant variance from the general data.

Table 4.4. Prior Presidencies Held among All Presidents

Prior Presidency	2002	2007	2012	2017
Had Not Been a President Before	71.05%	70.37%	74.55%	74.53%
Held a Prior Presidency	28.95%	29.63%	25.45%	25.47%
Total	100%	100%	100%	100%

Note: The table shows how many presidents in each survey year had been a president before.

Table 4.5. JD Holding Presidents by Prior Presidency

Prior Presidency	2002	2007	2012	2017
Had Not Been a President Before	86.09%	81.03%	81.73%	72.95%
Held a Prior Presidency	13.91%	18.97%	18.27%	27.05%
Total	100%	100%	100%	100%

Note: The table shows how many JD holding presidents in each survey year had been a president before.

Prior Academic Experience

Historically, the typical path to the college presidency began with faculty who may later have been promoted to department chair or dean, followed by appointment as provost or some other senior leadership position in the central administration, as demonstrated in chapter two. The following tables prepared by Dr. Jonathan M. Turk of the American Council on Education begin to reveal the type and frequency of prior experience of college presidents who both possess and do not possess a juris doctorate degree.

Table 4.6. Distribution of JD Holding Presidents by Prior Positions for Each Survey Year

Five Categories of Prior Position	2002	2007	2012	2017
President/Interim President	12.61%	13.16%	12.39%	22.03%
Chair/Faculty	3.36%	4.39%	6.19%	2.54%
Chief Academic Officer or Provost/Dean/Other Senior Executive in Academic Affairs	34.45%	28.95%	27.43%	27.97%
Other Senior Executive in Higher Education	21.01%	21.93%	14.16%	15.25%
Outside of Higher Education	28.57%	31.58%	39.82%	32.20%
Total	100%	100%	100%	100%

Note: The table shows the share of prior positions held by JD holding presidents for each survey year. For example, in 2002 12.61% of all JD holding presidents had previously served as a president/interim president in their prior position, while 3.36% had been a chair/faculty member in their previous position, and so forth.

Table 4.7. Distribution of All Presidents by Prior Positions for Each Survey Year

Five Categories of Prior Position	2002	2007	2012	2017
President/Interim President	20.37%	21.34%	19.53%	23.88%
Chair/Faculty	4.40%	4.11%	3.50%	2.11%
Chief Academic Officer or Provost/Dean/Other Senior Executive in Academic Affairs	40.81%	43.77%	44.78%	42.72%
Other Senior Executive in Higher Education	19.70%	17.28%	11.86%	16.26%
Outside of Higher Education	14.72%	13.51%	20.33%	15.03%
Total	100%	100%	100%	100%

Note: The table shows the share of prior positions held by all presidents for each survey year. For example, in 2002 20.37% of all presidents had previously served as a president/interim president in their prior position, while 4.40% had been a chair/faculty member in their previous position, and so forth.

Chart 4.2 that follows shows the number of lawyer presidents with prior academic experience based on a review of their biographies. While the number has doubled in each of the last three decades, there is a growing trend, albeit with small numbers, of lawyer presidents who are emerging entirely from outside the academy. There are a number of lawyer presidents whose prior academic experience does not come from experience inside law schools, but rather from other disciplines such as business and public administration, or from administrative experiences including vice presidents for student affairs, institutional advancement, diversity and inclusion, and as general counsel to colleges and universities.

Chart 4.2. Lawyer Presidents with Prior Academic Experience (1900–2019)

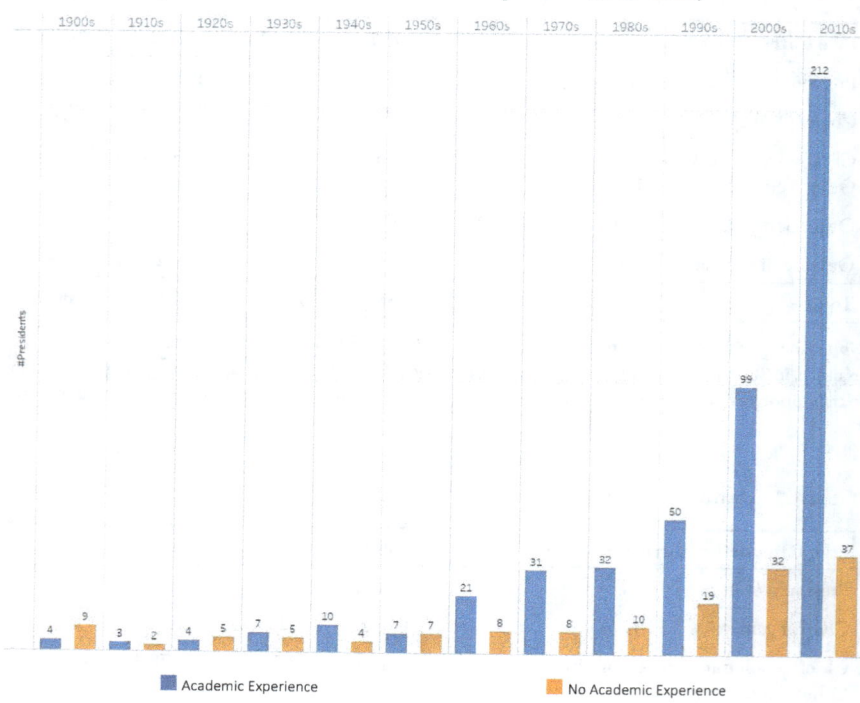

Notes
- Each appointment within a decade is counted by the start of a president's term.
- If a president was appointed twice in the same decade, they are only counted once.
- If a president was appointed in two different decades, they are counted in each decade.
- Appointments do not include presidents of private independent law schools.
- Appointments include presidents, chancellors, and CEOs.
- Interim positions are also included, and, if known, are generally considered as separate appointments from permanent positions.
- Presidents who started their appointment in 2020 and after are not included within this graph.
- Two current presidents have unidentified start dates for their terms. They are not included in this graph.

Charts 4.3 through 4.6 illustrate the number of lawyer presidents at public, private, community colleges, and religiously affiliated colleges who did and did not have academic experience prior to their presidential appointment. In all four settings, it is clear that the overwhelming majority of campus presidents possess some type of prior academic experience.

In the last decade, there is no discernable difference in the percentage of lawyer presidents appointed to public and private institutions who had no prior academic experience, with both at about 15% (see charts 4.3 and 4.4). While chart 4.6 shows this number was about the same for lawyer presidents at religiously affiliated schools (13.5%), at community colleges, only about 1% of lawyer presidents in the last decade had no prior academic experience (see chart 4.5); yet, in the 2000s, roughly 36% of community college lawyer presidents had no prior academic experience. However, the sample from the 2000s (total of 11 lawyer presidents) is much smaller than the sample from the 2010s (total of 28 lawyer presidents).

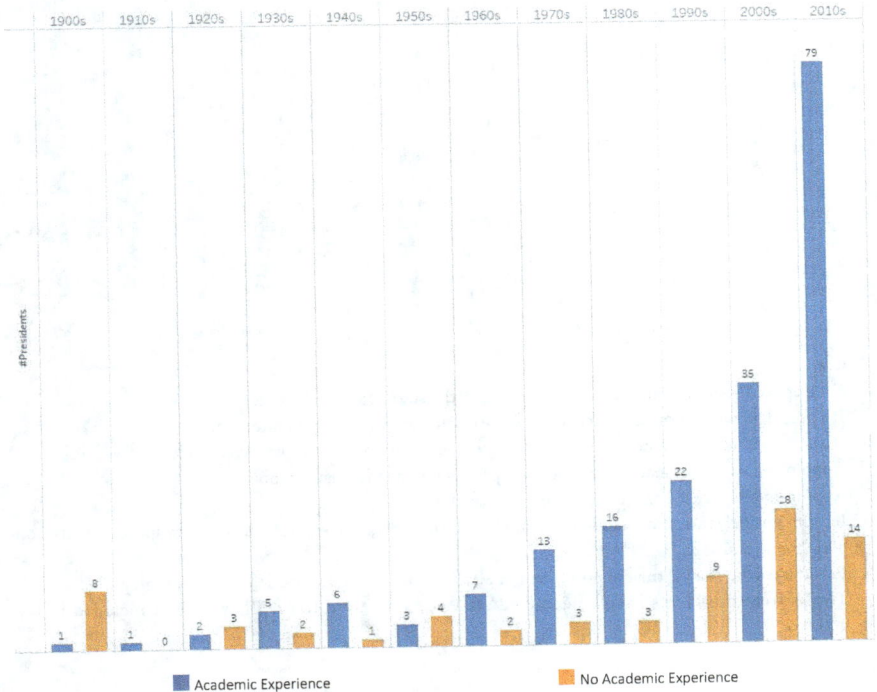

Chart 4.3. Lawyer Presidents at Public Institutions with Prior Academic Experience (1900–2019)

Notes
- Each appointment within a decade is counted by the start of a president's term.
- If a president was appointed twice in the same decade, they are only counted once.
- If a president was appointed in two different decades, they are counted in each decade.
- Appointments do not include presidents of private independent law schools.
- Appointments include presidents, chancellors, and CEOs.
- Interim positions are also included, and, if known, are generally considered as separate appointments from permanent positions.
- Presidents who started their appointment in 2020 and after are not included within this graph.
- Two current presidents have unidentified start dates for their terms. They are not included in this graph.

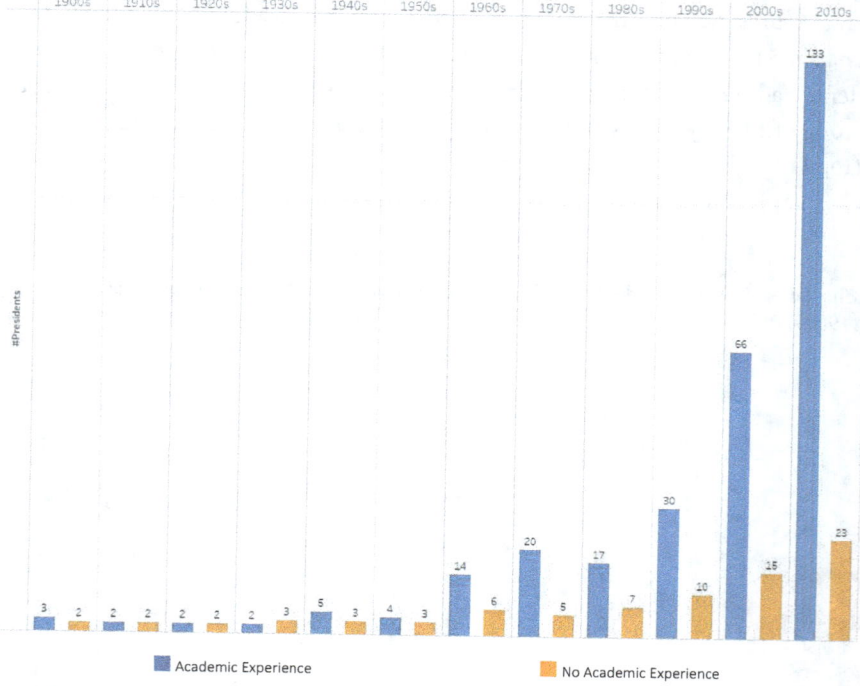

Chart 4.4. Lawyer Presidents at Private Institutions with Prior Academic Experience (1900–2019)

Notes
- Each appointment within a decade is counted by the start of a president's term.
- If a president was appointed twice in the same decade, they are only counted once.
- If a president was appointed in two different decades, they are counted in each decade.
- Appointments do not include presidents of private independent law schools.
- Appointments include presidents, chancellors, and CEOs.
- Interim positions are also included, and, if known, are generally considered as separate appointments from permanent positions.
- Presidents who started their appointment in 2020 and after are not included within this graph.
- Two current presidents have unidentified start dates for their terms. They are not included in this graph.

Prior Experience as Law Dean

Considering the conventional pathway of "climbing the academic ladder," presidents might have served as dean leading the faculty in their chosen field. Chart 4.7 shows the number of law deans who have been appointed as a college

Chart 4.5. Lawyer Presidents at Community Colleges with Prior Academic Experience (1900–2019)

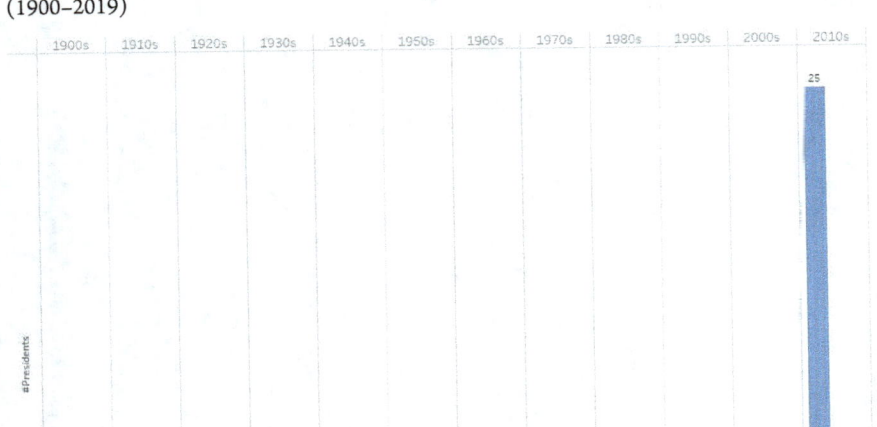

Notes
- Each appointment within a decade is counted by the start of a president's term.
- If a president was appointed twice in the same decade, they are only counted once.
- If a president was appointed in two different decades, they are counted in each decade.
- Appointments do not include presidents of private independent law schools.
- Appointments include presidents, chancellors, and CEOs.
- Interim positions are also included, and, if known, are generally considered as separate appointments from permanent positions.
- Presidents who started their appointment in 2020 and after are not included within this graph.
- Two current presidents have unidentified start dates for their terms. They are not included in this graph.

or university president.[11] In the 1980s the number of lawyer presidents with decanal experience was close to 50%. By the 2010s, as the number of lawyer presidents was at an all-time high, the percentage with decanal experience had

---

11 Note that some lawyer presidents may have been deans of other departments, such as business or political science/public administration. For purposes of this study, the focus in on legal education.

Chart 4.6. Lawyer Presidents at Religiously Affiliated Institutions with Prior Academic Experience (1900–2019)

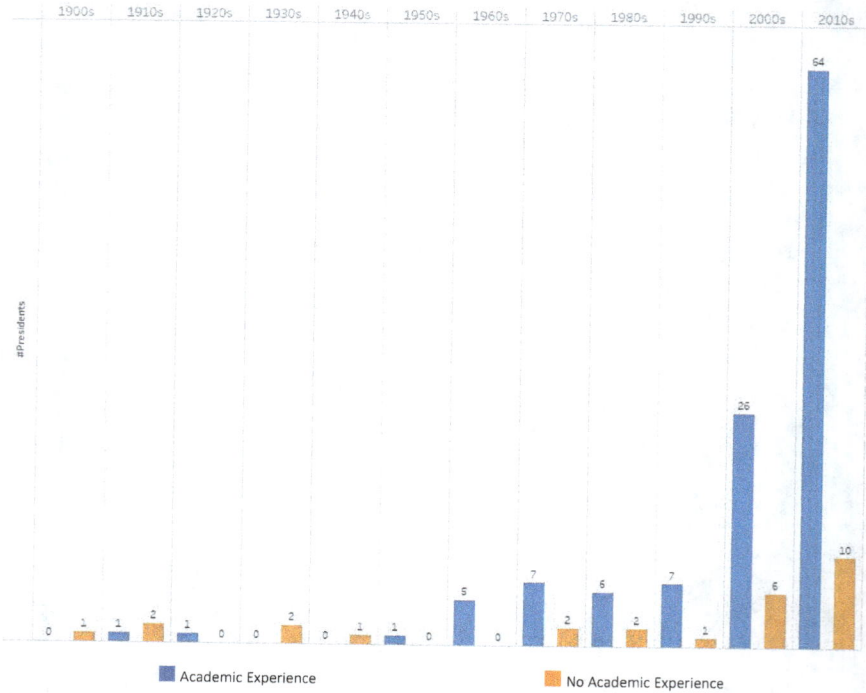

Notes
- Each appointment within a decade is counted by the start of a president's term.
- If a president was appointed twice in the same decade, they are only counted once.
- If a president was appointed in two different decades, they are counted in each decade.
- Appointments do not include presidents of private independent law schools.
- Appointments include presidents, chancellors, and CEOs.
- Interim positions are also included, and, if known, are generally considered as separate appointments from permanent positions.
- Presidents who started their appointment in 2020 and after are not included within this graph.
- Two current presidents have unidentified start dates for their terms. They are not included in this graph.

dropped to only 14%. It is noteworthy to compare this data to the chart 2.3, which illustrates the number of law professors who became college and university presidents. In the 1980s the number of presidents who were law professors was also close to 50%, but by the 2010s, the number of lawyer presidents who were former law professors was 24.5%, or 10% more than those with experience as a dean. This finding is surprising given the wider breadth of administrative experience and exposure to campus-wide issues that law deans enjoy. The earlier

Chart 4.7. Lawyer Presidents with Prior Dean Experience (1900–2019)

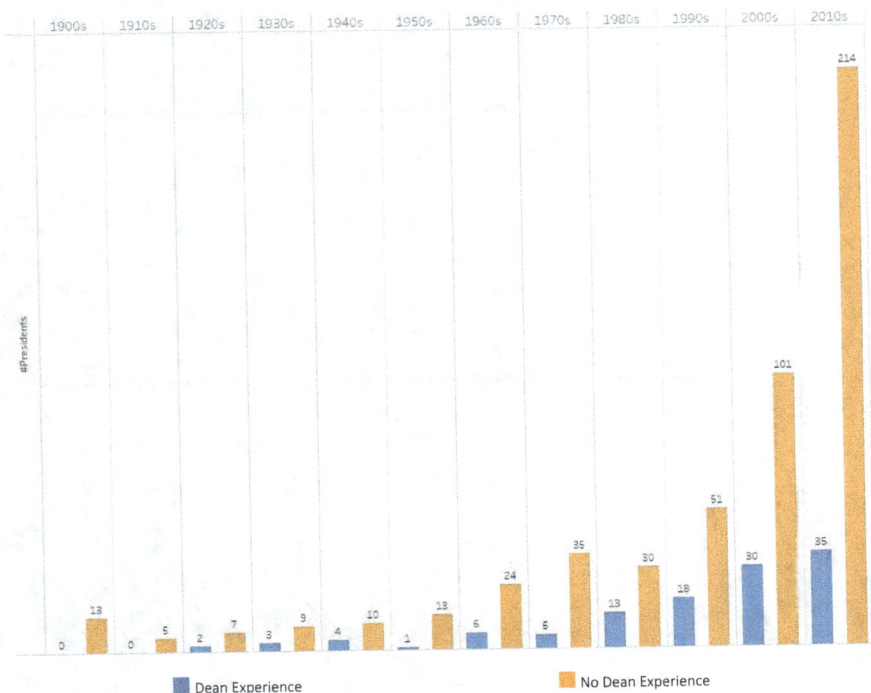

Notes
- Each appointment within a decade is counted by the start of a president's term.
- If a president was appointed twice in the same decade, they are only counted once.
- If a president was appointed in two different decades, they are counted in each decade.
- Appointments do not include presidents of private independent law schools.
- Appointments include presidents, chancellors, and CEOs.
- Interim positions are also included, and, if known, are generally considered as separate appointments from permanent positions.
- Presidents who started their appointment in 2020 and after are not included within this graph.
- Two current presidents have unidentified start dates for their terms. They are not included in this graph.

discussion in chapter two sets forth the rationale as to why prior experience as a law dean may be desirable.

In looking to determine whether public or private institutions had any discernible difference in attitude about whether prior dean experience was desirable for a lawyer president, the data in charts 4.8 and 4.9 demonstrate only a slightly higher percentage of presidents at public institutions from the 1980s through 2019 (22%), compared to those at private institutions (18%), bringing this specific experience to their presidencies.

Chart 4.8. Lawyer Presidents at Public Institutions with Prior Dean Experience (1900–2019)

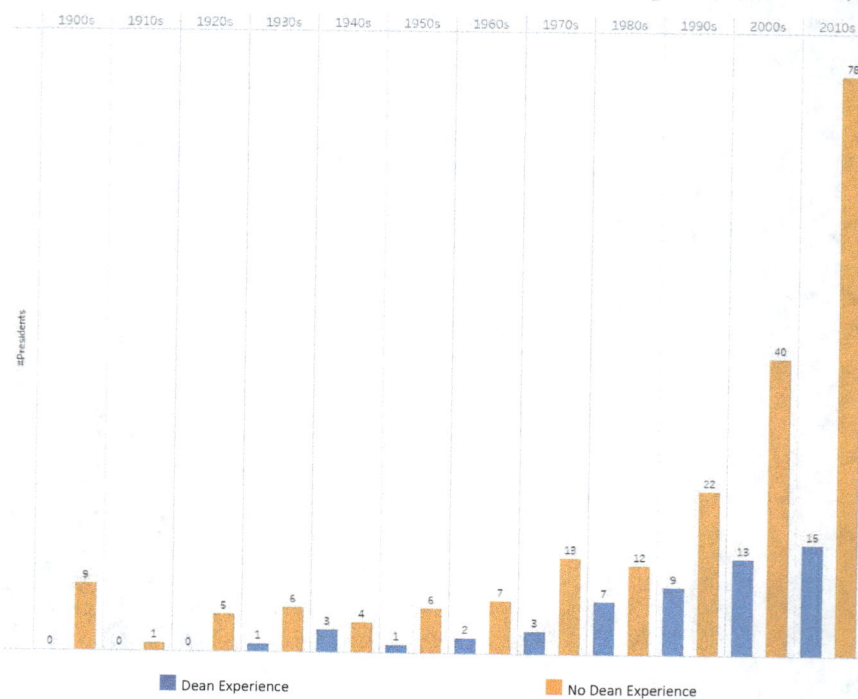

Notes
- Each appointment within a decade is counted by the start of a president's term.
- If a president was appointed twice in the same decade, they are only counted once.
- If a president was appointed in two different decades, they are counted in each decade.
- Appointments do not include presidents of private independent law schools.
- Appointments include presidents, chancellors, and CEOs.
- Interim positions are also included, and, if known, are generally considered as separate appointments from permanent positions.
- Presidents who started their appointment in 2020 and after are not included within this graph.
- Two current presidents have unidentified start dates for their terms. They are not included in this graph.

Community Colleges

As illustrated in chart 4.10, no community college lawyer president has had prior experience as a law dean. This finding shows that at the community level, the pathway to the presidency for lawyers is even more unconventional. This may be because community colleges are not comprehensive universities and they therefore do not have law schools. Law school deans may be less likely to set

Chart 4.9. Lawyer Presidents at Private Institutions with Prior Dean Experience (1900–2019)

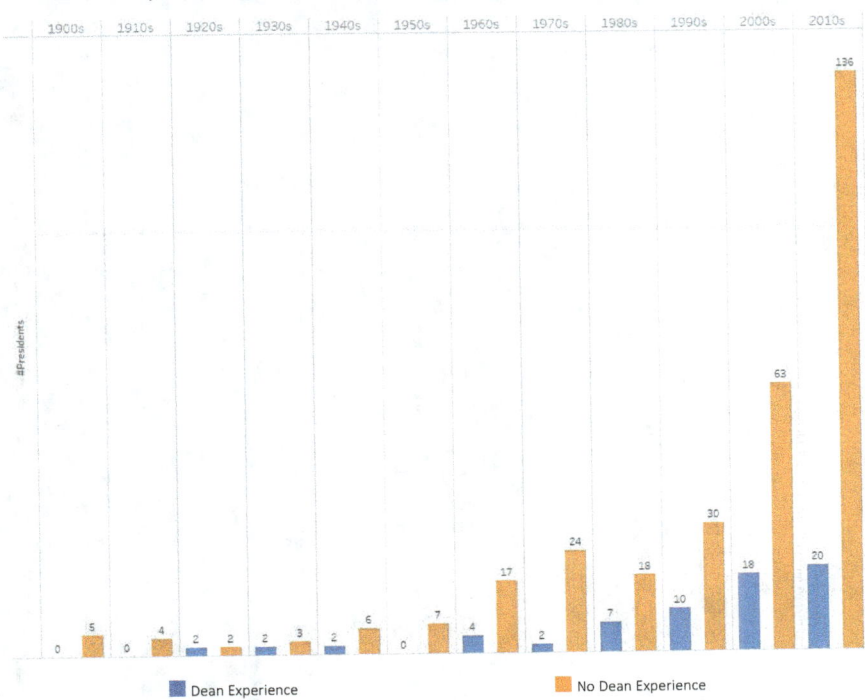

Notes
- Each appointment within a decade is counted by the start of a president's term.
- If a president was appointed twice in the same decade, they are only counted once.
- If a president was appointed in two different decades, they are counted in each decade.
- Appointments do not include presidents of private independent law schools.
- Appointments include presidents, chancellors, and CEOs.
- Interim positions are also included, and, if known, are generally considered as separate appointments from permanent positions.
- Presidents who started their appointment in 2020 and after are not included within this graph.
- Two current presidents have unidentified start dates for their terms. They are not included in this graph.

their sights on community colleges because their "sense of place" in higher education has been shaped by institutions that offer four-year and graduate degree programs. While a number of community colleges do offer programs in legal studies leading to a paralegal degree, community colleges have few lawyers on the full-time faculty, and no conventional "law professors." Nor are there many lawyers who lead academic departments (that is, function as deans) at community colleges except for legal studies programs.

Chart 4.10. Lawyer Presidents at Community Colleges with Prior Dean Experience (1900–2019)

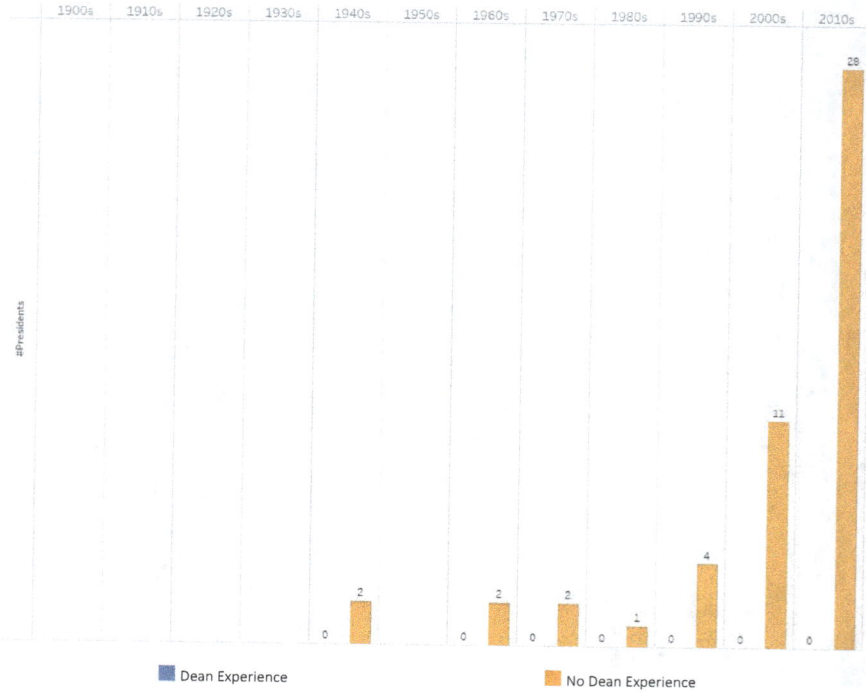

Notes
- Each appointment within a decade is counted by the start of a president's term.
- If a president was appointed twice in the same decade, they are only counted once.
- If a president was appointed in two different decades, they are counted in each decade.
- Appointments do not include presidents of private independent law schools.
- Appointments include presidents, chancellors, and CEOs.
- Interim positions are also included, and, if known, are generally considered as separate appointments from permanent positions.
- Presidents who started their appointment in 2020 and after are not included within this graph.
- Two current presidents have unidentified start dates for their terms. They are not included in this graph.

Religiously Affiliated Schools

An examination of the number of lawyer presidents at religiously affiliated institutions reveals a small number with prior law dean experience. As illustrated by chart 4.11, in the 2010s the number is just 1%. Although the percentage was higher in the three prior decades, the raw numbers were substantially smaller and therefore not a statistically valid comparator. This number is not surprising given the small number of religiously affiliated universities that have law schools.[12] Further, as previously noted, given the rise in the regulatory state and the legal challenges faced by religiously affiliated institutions who may be required to take positions inconsistent with government mandates based on religious beliefs, it is also not surprising that lawyers may be desirable candidates for campus leadership positions.

Chart 4.11. Lawyer Presidents at Religiously Affiliated Institutions with Prior Dean Experience (1900–2019)

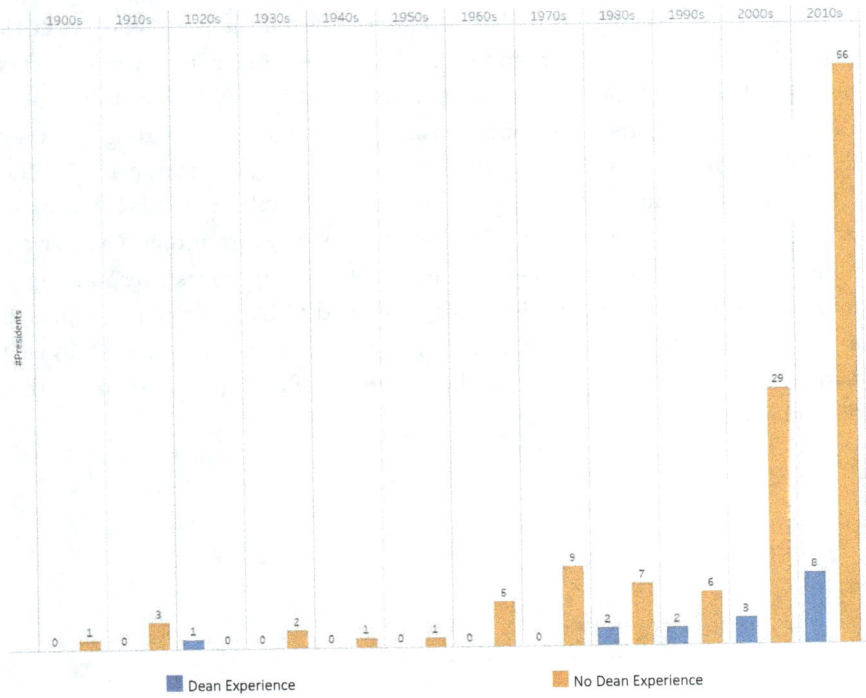

Notes
- Each appointment within a decade is counted by the start of a president's term.
- If a president was appointed twice in the same decade, they are only counted once.
- If a president was appointed in two different decades, they are counted in each decade.
- Appointments do not include presidents of private independent law schools.
- Appointments include presidents, chancellors, and CEOs.
- Interim positions are also included, and, if known, are generally considered as separate appointments from permanent positions.
- Presidents who started their appointment in 2020 and after are not included within this graph.
- Two current presidents have unidentified start dates for their terms. They are not included in this graph.

---

12 Steven M. Barkan, "The First Conference of Religiously Affiliated Law Schools: An Overview," *Marquette Law Review* 78, no. 2 (Winter 1995): 247–254, https://scholarship.law.marquette.edu/cgi/viewcontent.cgi?article=1568&context=mulr.

Prior Experience as Provost

A provost is the chief academic officer for a college or university, and has been historically viewed as a springboard position for a campus presidency. However, recent studies have suggested that, while many provosts may still be sought after as candidates for presidential searches, today, candidates who have dean experience may be just as desirable, if not more, for the campus leader post.[13] The reasons cited for this shift include the fact that today's provosts typically possess skills that complement, rather than replicate, those of the president.[14] A 2019 survey by the Council of Independent Colleges (CIC) of chief academic officers revealed that only 16% of respondents indicated that they believed their next career step was to pursue a campus presidency, with 37% responding that they would not pursue that path, and 31% indicating that they were undecided.[15] The CIC study is the most current source for information related to this topic; however, it is limited in scope to just 214 usable responses from their 652 private independent institutions.[16] The study reports 91% of all provosts responding at four-year colleges and universities had an earned PhD, while others reported earning an EdD, theological degrees, health profession degrees, and JDs as well as more than one terminal degree.[17] Less than 1% of respondents reported that their major field of study was law.[18]

---

13 Carl J. Strikwerda, "Do Deans Make Better Presidents?" *Inside Higher Ed*, last modified February 17, 2017, accessed September 13, 2021, https://www.insidehighered.com/advice/2017/02/02/encouraging-both-deans-and-provosts-become-college-presidents-essay#:~:text=Working%20or%20consulting%20with%20provosts,Provosts%20handle%20internal%20matters.&text=Deans%2C%20by%20contrast%2C%20especially%20at,like%20presidents%20of%20small%20colleges.

14 Deloitte's Center for Higher Education Excellence and Georgia Tech's Center for 21st Century Universities, *Pathways to the University Presidency*, 3.

15 Lesley McBain et al., *A Study of Chief Academic Officers at Independent Colleges and Universities, 2009–2019* (n.p.: Council of Independent Colleges, 2019), 10, accessed September 13, 2021, https://www.cic.edu/r/cd/Pages/cao-report-2019.aspx.

16 Ibid., 8.

17 Ibid., 16.

18 Ibid.

Chart 4.12 that follows shows that only a small percentage of lawyer presidents have had prior provost experience, with the number doubling from the 2000s to the 2010s (ten to twenty-two lawyer presidents) with past provost experience. This means that the overwhelming number of lawyer presidents took a different path to the presidency.

Chart 4.12. Lawyer Presidents with Prior Provost Experience (1900–2019)

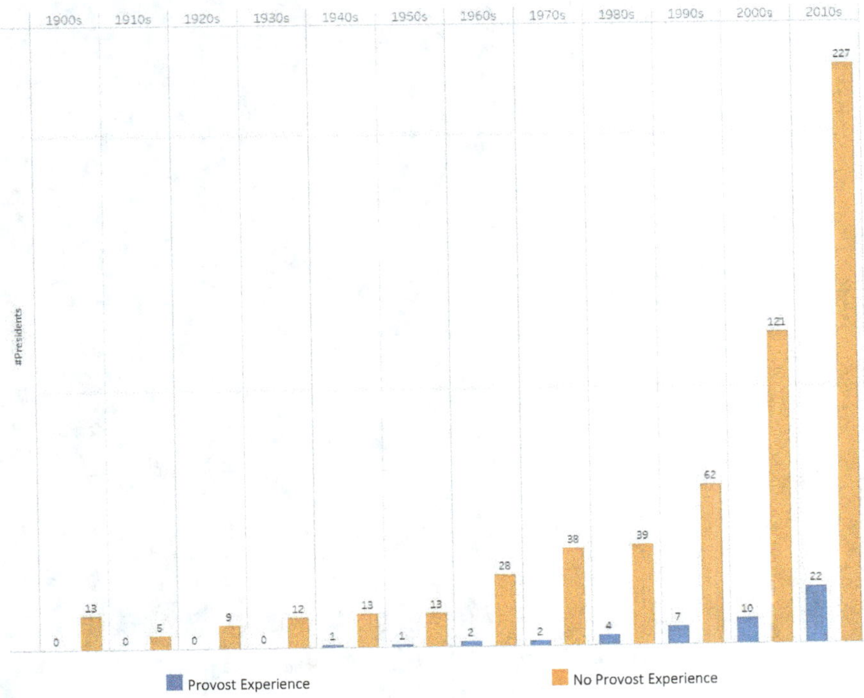

Decade	Provost Experience	No Provost Experience
1900s	0	13
1910s	0	5
1920s	0	9
1930s	0	12
1940s	1	13
1950s	1	13
1960s	2	28
1970s	2	38
1980s	4	39
1990s	7	62
2000s	10	121
2010s	22	227

Notes
- Each appointment within a decade is counted by the start of a president's term.
- If a president was appointed twice in the same decade, they are only counted once.
- If a president was appointed in two different decades, they are counted in each decade.
- Appointments do not include presidents of private independent law schools.
- Appointments include presidents, chancellors, and CEOs.
- Interim positions are also included, and, if known, are generally considered as separate appointments from permanent positions.
- Presidents who started their appointment in 2020 and after are not included within this graph.
- Two current presidents have unidentified start dates for their terms. They are not included in this graph.

Charts 4.13 and 4.14 show a slightly higher number of lawyer presidents with provost experience at private institutions over the last twenty years than at public institutions (nineteen at private schools versus thirteen at public schools). With numbers so small, there is little to discern by way of trends or explanation.

Chart 4.13. Lawyer Presidents at Public Institutions with Prior Provost Experience (1900–2019)

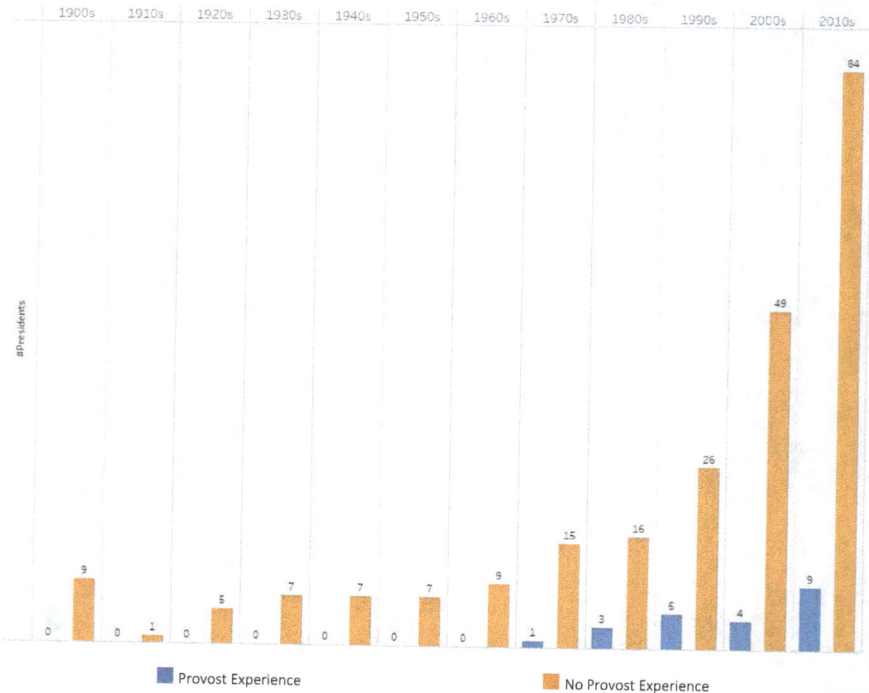

Notes
- Each appointment within a decade is counted by the start of a president's term.
- If a president was appointed twice in the same decade, they are only counted once.
- If a president was appointed in two different decades, they are counted in each decade.
- Appointments do not include presidents of private independent law schools.
- Appointments include presidents, chancellors, and CEOs.
- Interim positions are also included, and, if known, are generally considered as separate appointments from permanent positions.
- Presidents who started their appointment in 2020 and after are not included within this graph.
- Two current presidents have unidentified start dates for their terms. They are not included in this graph.

Characteristics of Lawyer Presidents 113

Chart 4.14. Lawyer Presidents at Private Institutions with Prior Provost Experience (1900–2019)

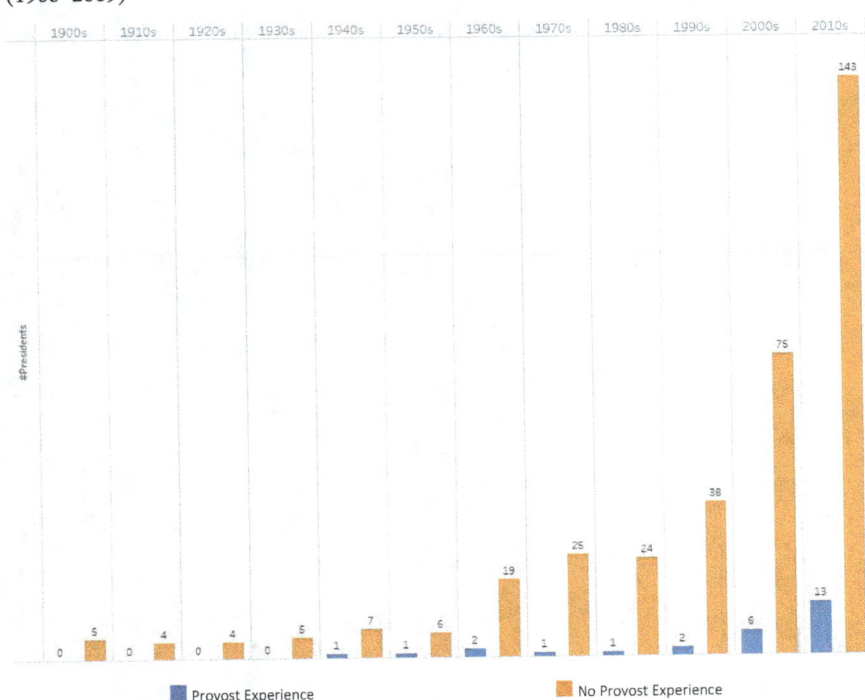

Notes
- Each appointment within a decade is counted by the start of a president's term.
- If a president was appointed twice in the same decade, they are only counted once.
- If a president was appointed in two different decades, they are counted in each decade.
- Appointments do not include presidents of private independent law schools.
- Appointments include presidents, chancellors, and CEOs.
- Interim positions are also included, and, if known, are generally considered as separate appointments from permanent positions.
- Presidents who started their appointment in 2020 and after are not included within this graph.
- Two current presidents have unidentified start dates for their terms. They are not included in this graph.

Chart 4.15 reveals that of all of the lawyer presidents leading community colleges, only one served as a provost. This is not a surprise since most community college lawyer presidents have come from non-traditional backgrounds.

Chart 4.15. Lawyer Presidents at Community Colleges with Prior Provost Experience (1900–2019)

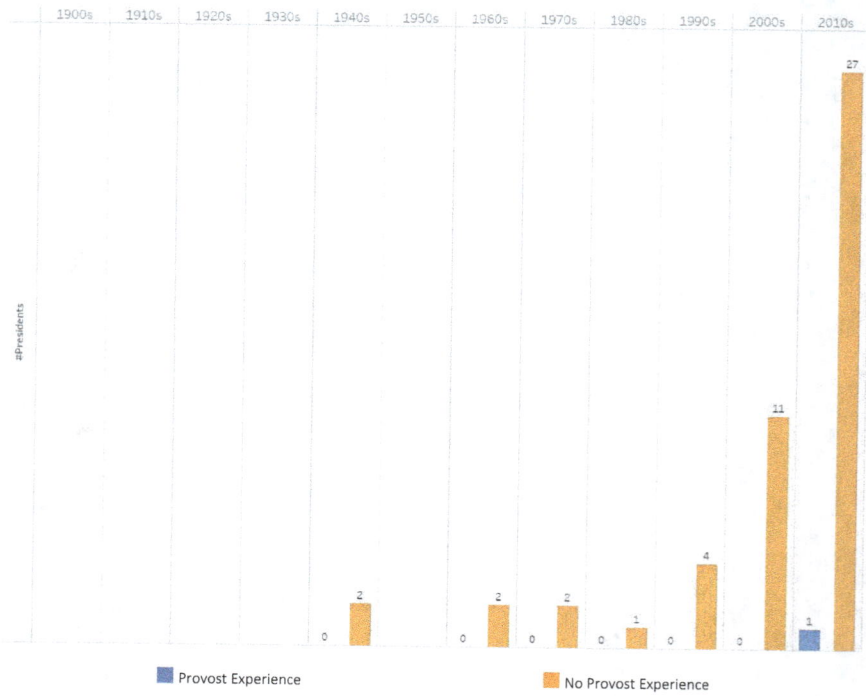

Notes
- Each appointment within a decade is counted by the start of a president's term.
- If a president was appointed twice in the same decade, they are only counted once.
- If a president was appointed in two different decades, they are counted in each decade.
- Appointments do not include presidents of private independent law schools.
- Appointments include presidents, chancellors, and CEOs.
- Interim positions are also included, and, if known, are generally considered as separate appointments from permanent positions.
- Presidents who started their appointment in 2020 and after are not included within this graph.
- Two current presidents have unidentified start dates for their terms. They are not included in this graph.

Chart 4.16 shows that about 8.1% (six out of seventy-four) of lawyer presidents at religiously affiliated institutions in the 2010s had prior provost experience. This is an interesting break from the decades prior when none of the lawyer presidents at these institutions had that experience. While the raw number is not large enough to draw conclusions about a trend, the academic regulatory and compliance issues that provosts deal with may be a factor.

Chart 4.16. Lawyer Presidents at Religiously Affiliated Institutions with Prior Provost Experience (1900–2019)

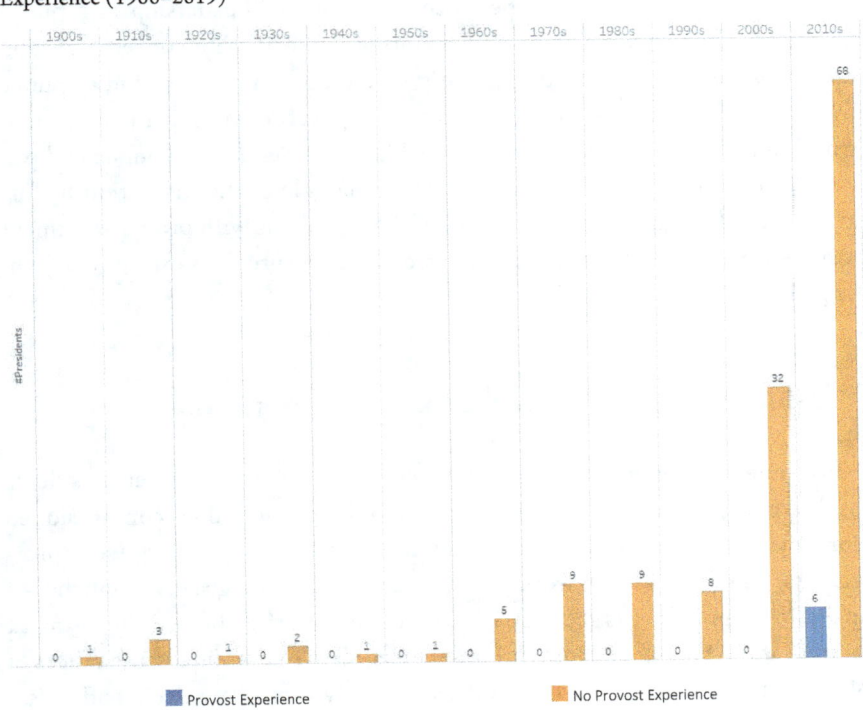

Notes
- Each appointment within a decade is counted by the start of a president's term.
- If a president was appointed twice in the same decade, they are only counted once.
- If a president was appointed in two different decades, they are counted in each decade.
- Appointments do not include presidents of private independent law schools.
- Appointments include presidents, chancellors, and CEOs.
- Interim positions are also included, and, if known, are generally considered as separate appointments from permanent positions.
- Presidents who started their appointment in 2020 and after are not included within this graph.
- Two current presidents have unidentified start dates for their terms. They are not included in this graph.

Prior Experience as Government Lawyers

There are many pathways to the presidency for lawyers, but one strong commonality in the background of the modern lawyer president is experience in government. This is not surprising, given the shared skillset required for successful government lawyers and successful campus leaders. In a recent 360 study of qualitative skills possessed by non-traditional campus presidents, one president with government experience commented, "Leadership in a public university involves recognizing and honoring the legitimate concerns of multiple constituencies. . . . And that's very much the same as any kind of public leadership."[19] Another lawyer president with government experience in that study concluded that his law degree plus his background in the public and private sectors were helpful in his current campus role as the institution had its share of legal and financial issues.[20] All of the presidents with prior government experience ". . . agreed their success hinged on having previous exposure to public policy and service work."[21]

Presidents with Prior Government Experience

Government experience comes in a variety of forms. Some lawyer presidents have completed military service as JAG officers and other commissioned appointments, some clerked for a federal or state judge, others were prosecutors, and the majority worked in the executive and legislative branches—including appointments at the U. S. Department of Justice, the U. S. Department of Education, the White House, counsel to legislative committees, the offices of state attorneys general, and as chiefs of staff or advisors to key elected officials.

In some instances, elected officials who are lawyers have been tapped for campus presidencies. For example, Dannel P. Malloy, former governor of Connecticut and mayor of Stamford, began his tenure in 2019 as the chancellor of the University of Maine System.[22] William Bulger, president of the Massachusetts Senate for eighteen years, became president of the University of Massachusetts in 1995.[23] Mitchell E. Daniels, Jr., the former lawyer governor of Indiana, was tapped to lead Purdue University in 2012.[24] Cathy Cox

---

19 Delabbio and Palmer, "A 360° View of Non-Traditional University Presidents," 5.
20 Ibid.
21 Ibid.
22 University of Southern Maine, Office of Public Affairs, "Former Connecticut Governor Dannel Malloy to Lead University of Maine System," news release, May 30, 2019, accessed September 22, 2021, https://usm.maine.edu/publicaffairs/former-connecticut-governor-dannel-malloy-lead-university-maine-system.
23 William H. Honan, "An Icon of State Politics is Picked to Lead U. Mass.," *New York Times*, November 29, 1995, 79, https://timesmachine.nytimes.com/timesmachine/1995/11/29/issue.html.
24 "Mitchell E. Daniels, Jr.: Biography," *Purdue University: Office of the President*, accessed September 22, 2021, https://www.purdue.edu/president/about/biography.php.

was the president of Young Harris College, and the recently appointed president of Georgia College and State University,[25] after she served as Georgia secretary of state and ran unsuccessfully for governor. Janet Napolitano, governor of Arizona and head of homeland security, became president of the University of California System in 2013.[26] Paul McNulty, who was appointed by President Bush as deputy attorney general, is the president of Grove City College,[27] and Glenn McConnell served as president of the College of Charleston after serving as lieutenant governor of South Carolina.[28]

While lawyers may enter public service at different times in their careers, as well as at different points of entry and levels of government, successful government lawyers possess basic leadership qualities, traits, and experiences that transfer well into the higher education space. For example, government lawyers must often confront media headlines and crises, which require strategic, thoughtful, and appropriate responses. So too, the college president must be prepared for the unexpected. Recent higher education headlines about admissions scandals, historical ties to slavery, allegations of racism, clashes over free speech and hate speech, allegations of harassment and campus safety, and other improprieties must all be swiftly addressed by the campus leader.

Additionally, just as government officials must provide answers and information to the public, college presidents must be excellent timely communicators for their constituents—a body that includes students, faculty, staff, alumni, parents, and donors, as well as the general public. Attorneys are trained in oral advocacy and communication skills from the very start of law school, and they hone these skills throughout their careers. In both government and higher education, the most important communications statements are typically vetted by attorneys who review them for accuracy, truthfulness, and potential unintended consequences. This training and innate awareness on the part of the lawyer president can make all the difference when managing crisis communications, especially

---

25 University of Georgia, Communications, "Cathy Cox Named President of Georgia College & State University," news release, August 19, 2021, accessed September 22, 2021, https://www.usg.edu/news/release/cathy_cox_named_president_of_georgia_college_state_university.

26 UC Berkeley, Public Affairs, "Janet Napolitano Selected as New UC president," news release, July 12, 2013, accessed September 24, 2021, https://news.berkeley.edu/2013/07/12/janet-napolitano-selected-as-new-uc-president/.

27 "McNulty Chosen as GCC President," *Allied News* (Grove City, PA), May 28, 2014, accessed September 22, 2021, https://www.alliednews.com/news/local_news/mcnulty-chosen-as-gcc-president/article_afada688-78c3-5f36-8551-43229559448f.html.

28 College of Charleston, "President Elect Glenn McConnell: Lt. Gov. Glenn McConnell Is 22nd President of College of Charleston," news release, accessed September 22, 2021, https://cofc.edu/president-elect/.

in situations that can have positive or negative long-term ramifications for the institution.

With a reputation for being creative problem solvers, government lawyers often operate in the space of the unknown. They learn to draw on precedent, consider multi-level potential, positive and negative ramifications, and abide by the rule of law when making recommendations and decisions. Their analytical skills play a key role in their successes. Likewise, campus presidents must be able to view unexpected challenges critically through multiple lenses, and to quickly make informed and reasoned decisions based on full analysis of facts and data.

Effective government lawyers also possess excellent management skills, as they often supervise direct reports and teams. To accomplish tasks within short timeframes, they must possess excellent interpersonal skills and be able to motivate their colleagues. Similarly, campus presidents manage direct reports and must handle delicate relationships with faculty and boards, as well as with students, staff, donors and community leaders.

Lawyers who work in government must perfect the art of compromise. Rarely is the original draft of a piece of legislation or proposed rulemaking the same as the version that gets adopted, thanks to input—both solicited and not—from a wide variety of stakeholders who often disagree. College presidents experience something similar. They must work with various campus and community stakeholders to develop and refine policies and procedures that will appeal to all parts of the campus community. While peaceful protests are expected in halls of statehouses, peaceful protests on campus are more apt to make the national news. Knowing when and how to compromise is an essential leadership skill.

Simply understanding how government works is of great value to campus leaders. After all, they must navigate the world of public funding at all levels of government to successfully deliver needed resources to their schools for capital and programmatic priorities. Yet, equal if not even more important is their ability to advocate for the individual campus's role in the higher education space. Public policy and public budget decisions can have a tremendous impact on the sustainable health of individual institutions and on higher education in general. Presidents with government backgrounds may have an advantage when developing strategies targeted at the policy and public sectors.

Given the similarities in general leadership skills required for both government lawyers and for campus presidents, the fact that many of the lawyers appointed to the presidency have government experience is not a surprise. For example, former Hawaii attorney general David M. Louie, in writing about leadership in the public service, reflected on his experience as a newly appointed attorney general.[29] He commented on how he quickly had to be proficient in many areas of law as he also became "the chief executive for the largest law firm in the state, with 185 deputies, 750 employees and a $70 million annual budget."[30] He posited, "While there are many similarities and common themes about leadership in all sectors, government institutions in the United States are markedly different from private business institutions in terms of motivations, politics, processes, constituencies, special interests and being affected by the media."[31]

Public sector leaders are quite often evaluated on what appears to be ambiguous scales, when it comes to whether they are "doing the right thing" or representing their constituents correctly on a host of issues for which they may have responsibility. This varies greatly from the private sector—where most large businesses today are driven by the dictates of the market and their stock prices, which place a premium on short-term metrics like quarterly earnings and profits. Business leaders must justify their decision making through the lens of profitability.

Governments, however, must pay attention not simply to money and balanced budgets. The functions undertaken by government are varied and complex, so that making money is not the main factor. Policy issues, political initiatives, regulations, and social problems that affect the public and different constituencies are important factors that leaders must understand and navigate."[32] In speaking about this topic, Louie further notes, "Government institutions are ultimately subject to politics and democracy, a process that requires the consent of the governed in regular elections. Most business institutions are governed by owners, either directly or through corporate elections and boards of directors, but they are not subject to the same type of political processes that affect government."[33]

In the press announcements about the appointment of former government lawyers to lead the campus, many of the traits discussed in this chapter were specifically mentioned. For example, The University of Maine System Board of Trustees chair commented about Dannell Malloy, "As governor he delivered reforms and structural changes to state government that were not always

---

29 David M. Louie, "Leadership in Public Service," in *Leadership for Lawyers*, ed. Francisco Ramos, Jr (Elmhurst, IL: Federation of Defense & Corporate Counsel, 2017), accessed September 9, 2021, https://cdn.ymaws.com/thefederation.site-ym.com/resource/resmgr/docs/Leadeship_for_Lawyers_Dec2017/V1.02_Leadership_for_Lawyers.pdf.
30 Ibid.
31 Ibid.
32 Ibid.
33 Ibid.

popular, and certainly not expedient, but that advanced the long-term interest of his state and its citizens."[34] This was followed by a statement from the chancellor that acknowledged they system needed a president who could address needed reforms, as he said, "The Strategic Priorities the Board adopted ... and the selection of Dan Malloy as our nest chancellor are clear indications of the Board's resolve to expedite our One University reforms."[35] When William Bulger was selected as president of the University of Massachusetts, the *New York Times* opined that "In doing so, they put the five-campus system in the hands of a man who many believe can provide the political clout it has long lacked with the State Legislature."[36] Chair of the Board of Trustees, Daniel Taylor, a Boston lawyer, commented that "... the choice of Senator Bulger ... was motivated by a recognition that if the university was to 'rise to the first rank,' improved relationships with the State Legislature were vital."[37] Also, a recognition that public officials have to be successful fundraisers for their campaigns, the chair of the trustees' search committee, Peter Lewenberg, noted about Bulger that his "... access to private and corporate philanthropy is just as important as his connections with the State Legislature."[38]

As illustrated in chart 4.17, the number of lawyer presidents with prior government experience has nearly doubled in each of the last three decades. In the 1980s and 1990s, the percentage of lawyer presidents with government experience was about 50%, but by the 2010s, there were slightly more lawyer presidents who had prior government experience than those who did not. This is not surprising given the enormous economic and regulatory pressures on higher education, and the experience gained from work in the public sector as previously discussed.

---

34 University of Southern Maine, Office of Public Affairs, "Former Connecticut Governor Dannel Malloy to Lead University of Maine System."
35 Ibid.
36 Honan, "An Icon of State Politics," 79.
37 Ibid.
38 Ibid.

Chart 4.17. Lawyer Presidents with Prior Government Experience (1900–2019)

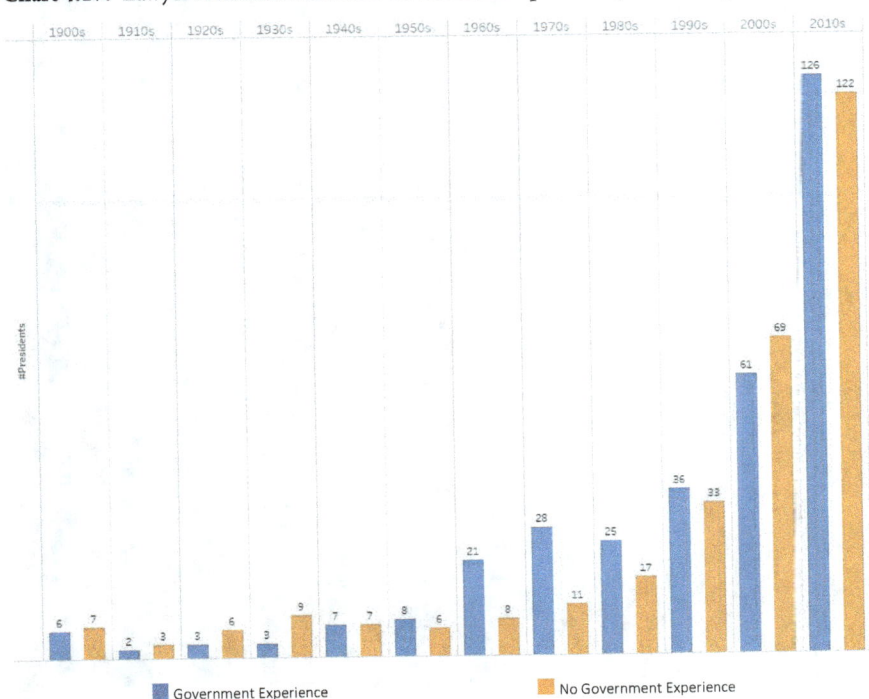

Notes
- Each appointment within a decade is counted by the start of a president's term.
- If a president was appointed twice in the same decade, they are only counted once.
- If a president was appointed in two different decades, they are counted in each decade.
- Appointments do not include presidents of private independent law schools.
- Appointments include presidents, chancellors, and CEOs.
- Interim positions are also included, and, if known, are generally considered as separate appointments from permanent positions.
- Presidents who started their appointment in 2020 and after are not included within this graph.
- Two current presidents have unidentified start dates for their terms. They are not included in this graph.

Charts 4.18 and 4.19 offer comparisons of the number of lawyer presidents with prior government experience at both public and private institutions. In the 2010s approximately 57% of the lawyer presidents at public institutions had prior government experience, while 10% less shared this background at private institutions (about 47%). Other than in the 1990s, when the spread was only about a 5% difference, in the 1980s and the 2000s the difference was about 10%. The most significant takeaway is the fact that so many lawyer presidents do have prior government experience and that is a desirable factor in the background of candidates for campus leadership.

Chart 4.18. Lawyer Presidents at Public Institutions with Prior Government Experience (1900–2019)

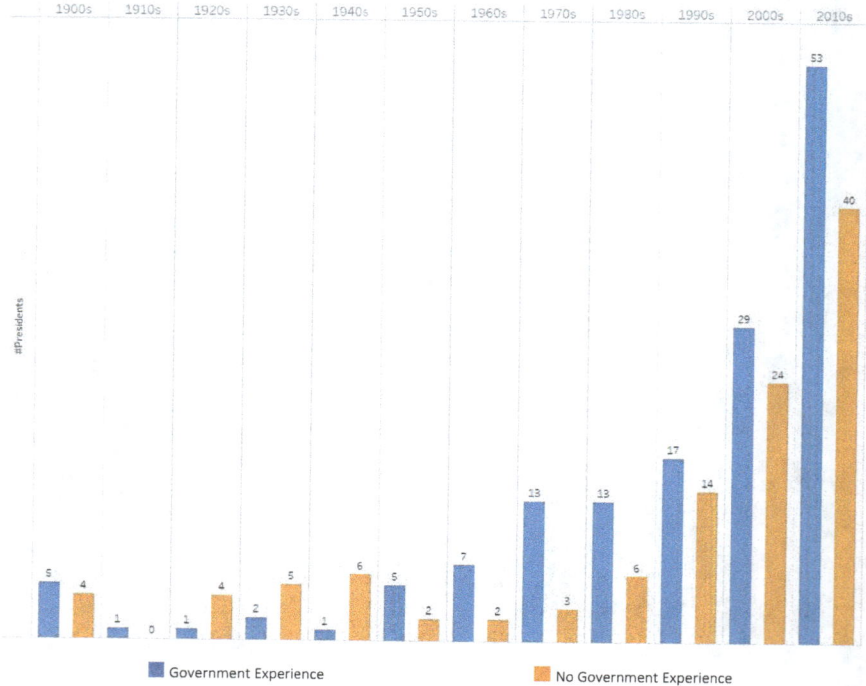

Notes
- Each appointment within a decade is counted by the start of a president's term.
- If a president was appointed twice in the same decade, they are only counted once.
- If a president was appointed in two different decades, they are counted in each decade.
- Appointments do not include presidents of private independent law schools.
- Appointments include presidents, chancellors, and CEOs.
- Interim positions are also included, and, if known, are generally considered as separate appointments from permanent positions.
- Presidents who started their appointment in 2020 and after are not included within this graph.
- Two current presidents have unidentified start dates for their terms. They are not included in this graph.

As illustrated in chart 4.20, in the 2010s the number of lawyer presidents with government experience at community colleges increased dramatically (by 30%) over the prior decade—from 27% to 57%. By raw numbers, overall, there were 50% fewer lawyer presidents in the 2000s as compared to the 2010s at these schools, but as the numbers increased, so did the percentage with government backgrounds. Interestingly, the percentage of lawyer presidents with government backgrounds in the 2010 is the same for public institutions and for

Chart 4.19. Lawyer Presidents at Private Institutions with Prior Government Experience (1900–2019)

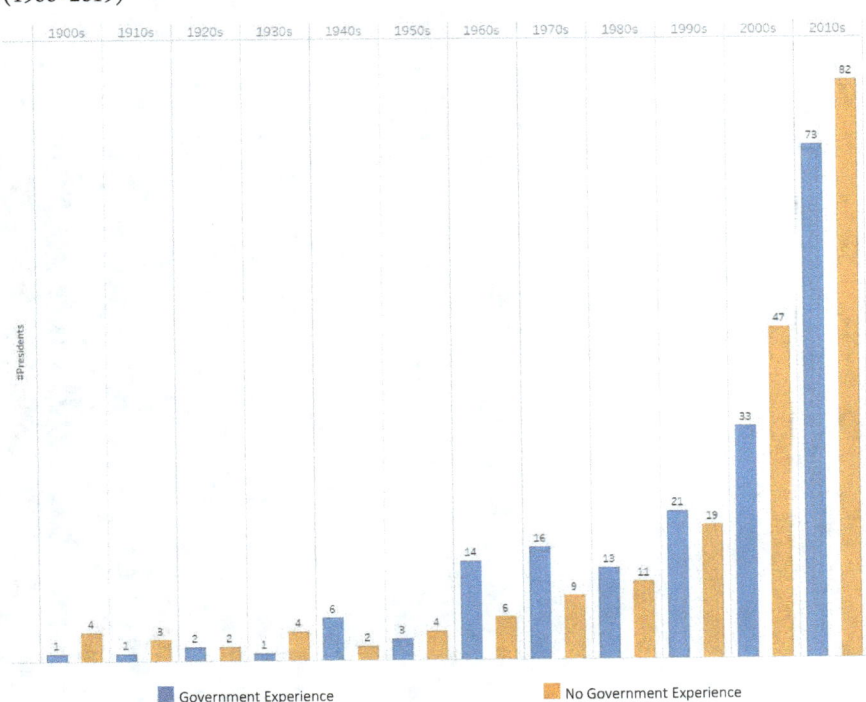

Notes
- Each appointment within a decade is counted by the start of a president's term.
- If a president was appointed twice in the same decade, they are only counted once.
- If a president was appointed in two different decades, they are counted in each decade.
- Appointments do not include presidents of private independent law schools.
- Appointments include presidents, chancellors, and CEOs.
- Interim positions are also included, and, if known, are generally considered as separate appointments from permanent positions.
- Presidents who started their appointment in 2020 and after are not included within this graph.
- Two current presidents have unidentified start dates for their terms. They are not included in this graph.

community colleges (many of which, but not all, are public). There may be many theories to explain the increase in number at community colleges, but among them could be the relationship between government and the support for career training that takes place at these two-year schools, the government funding for public community colleges and the need for strategic relationships with public partners, and the recent political agenda advancing the notion of a free community college education for all.

Chart 4.20. Lawyer Presidents at Community Colleges with Prior Government Experience (1900–2019)

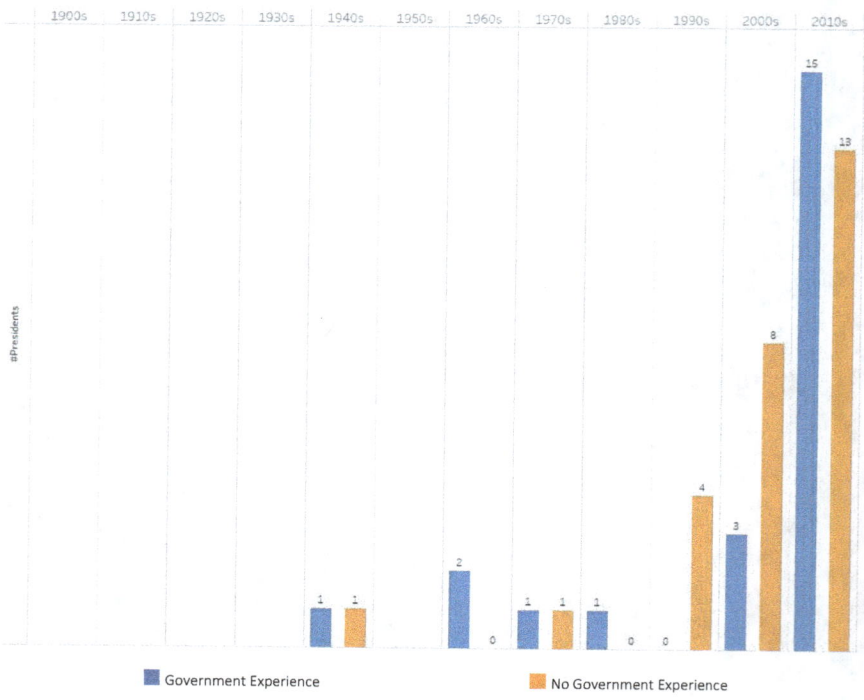

Notes
- Each appointment within a decade is counted by the start of a president's term.
- If a president was appointed twice in the same decade, they are only counted once.
- If a president was appointed in two different decades, they are counted in each decade.
- Appointments do not include presidents of private independent law schools.
- Appointments include presidents, chancellors, and CEOs.
- Interim positions are also included, and, if known, are generally considered as separate appointments from permanent positions.
- Presidents who started their appointment in 2020 and after are not included within this graph.
- Two current presidents have unidentified start dates for their terms. They are not included in this graph.

The number of lawyer presidents with some government experience at religiously affiliated institutions increased dramatically in the 2010s, consistent with the trend. Chart 4.21 shows an 18% increase in the number from the 2000s to the 2010s. Given some of the regulatory challenges, one might expect the number to be higher, but considering that religiously affiliated schools are less

Chart 4.21. Lawyer Presidents at Religiously Affiliated Institutions with Prior Government Experience (1900–2019)

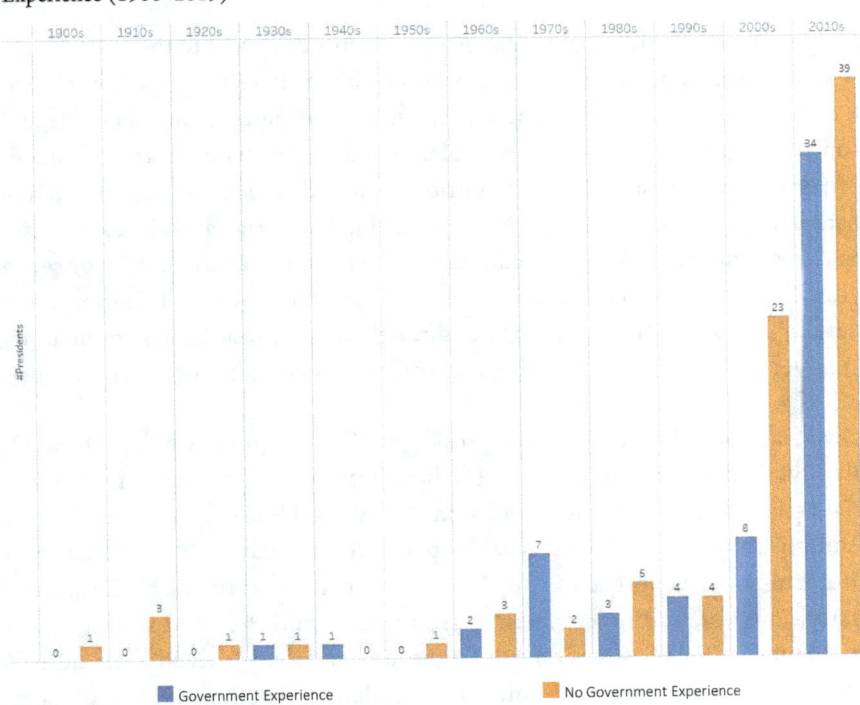

Notes
- Each appointment within a decade is counted by the start of a president's term.
- If a president was appointed twice in the same decade, they are only counted once.
- If a president was appointed in two different decades, they are counted in each decade.
- Appointments do not include presidents of private independent law schools.
- Appointments include presidents, chancellors, and CEOs.
- Interim positions are also included, and, if known, are generally considered as separate appointments from permanent positions.
- Presidents who started their appointment in 2020 and after are not included within this graph.
- Two current presidents have unidentified start dates for their terms. They are not included in this graph.

likely to receive special government funding and more likely to look for presidents who first and foremost are committed to the mission of the institution, this may further limit the pool of applicants (although there is no suggestion made that there are not devout lawyers with government experience who may be interested in higher education leadership).

Not All Lawyer Presidents Come from Academia

Despite the skills and insights that new presidents can bring to the table having served in academia, a number of lawyer presidents have been appointed who have had no prior academic experience, but rather experience in the private and sometimes public sectors. For example, Jennifer Raab, who became president of Hunter College in 2001, lacked prior higher education experience but she had practice experience in two Manhattan "big law" firms and she also served as chair of the New York City Landmarks Preservation Commission for seven years.[39] In a recent interview, Raab points to the negotiation skills lawyers must develop as instrumental in aiding her throughout her presidency, commenting, "Lawyers are brought up knowing that you are not going to succeed unless you can negotiate to a solution."[40]

Michael Sorrell, who became president of Paul Quinn College in 2007, also worked in private practice (Dallas, Texas) and in government (special assistant to the executive office in the White House during the Clinton Administration).[41] Sorrell's legal experience helped with his analytical problem-solving approach as president, particularly as it relates to the accreditation process, and he comments, "You understand the need to just take a moment, analyze the situation, look at the facts and then proceed from there."[42] Other lawyer presidents without prior academic experience include Harry Davros, who has served as president and CEO of the private Wade College for twenty-four years,[43] James Barba, former President of Albany Medical College,[44] and Howard Horton, when he was appointed to his first presidency

---

39 Hunter College, "Office of the President, Biography: About President Raab, the 13th President of Hunter College," *Hunter*, https://hunter.cuny.edu/about/leadership/president/bio/.
40 Moran, "Lawyers Find Their Skill Sets," 60.
41 Glen Hunter, "Lunch with D CEO: Michael J. Sorrell, The President of Paul Quinn College Talks Innovation in Education," Business, *D Magazine*, November 2016, accessed November 14, 2021, https://www.dmagazine.com/publications/d-ceo/2016/november/lunch-with-d-ceo-michael-j-sorrell/.
42 Moran, "Lawyers Find Their Skill Sets," 60.
43 "Faculty and Staff: Harry Davros," *Wade College*, accessed September 22, 2021, https://www.wadecollege.edu/about/faculty_and_staff.
44 See, for example, Casey Quinlan, "Universities Run into Problems When They Hire Presidents from the Business World," *Think Progress*, last modified March 7, 2016, accessed September 29, 2021, https://archive.thinkprogress.org/universities-run-into-problems-when-they-hire-presidents-from-the-business-world-a66b2739c1a/.

in 1988 at the Massachusetts Communications College/New England Institute of Art (he has since gone on to three additional presidencies—Bay State College, New England College of Business and Finance, and Cambridge College).[45] Despite the fact that some commentators have expressed caution about the appointment of college presidents in general who come completely from outside of the academy,[46] each of these lawyer presidents have enjoyed long successful careers in this role.

Fundraising Skills

Seasoned fundraisers are needed now more than ever in higher education. There is a desperate need for non-government revenue sources to fill the widening gap created by staggering decreases in usual revenue sources and from COVID-caused impediments to traditional campus-based and in-person "friend raising" cultivation programs including reunions and face-to-face fundraising events. High revenue losses coupled with the added costs of delivering quality education in a COVID environment—such as technology hardware and software, training, the growing facilities budgets to re-outfit rooms, provide for the increased use of cleaning agents and personnel to do the work, and the expense of campus-provided COVID tests for students, faculty, and staff—are budget busters. Academic administrators also are scrambling to identify new revenue streams for needed scholarship support for a growing number of students who find themselves and their families' victims of the economic havoc wrought by the pandemic.

A growing subset of lawyer presidents possess specific higher education fundraising experience, having served as vice presidents for institutional advancement, trustees, and alumni leaders. Data reveal that recent appointments include more than three dozen lawyer leaders, whose full-time job prior to assuming the campus presidency was in higher education philanthropy. Looking at the track record of various campus lawyer leaders with fundraising experience, there is a consistent pattern of dramatic growth in philanthropic, foundation, and public support, with evidence in some cases of a tripling of annual and endowment accounts.

---

45 Ibid.
46 Ibid.

Chart 4.22 illustrates that over the last three decades the number of lawyer presidents with fundraising experience has increased from three in the 1990s to twelve in the 2000s and to twenty-six in the 2010s. Charts 4.23 and 4.24 compare the number of lawyer presidents with previous fundraising experience at public and private institutions. Looking just at the last decade, at public institutions 6.4% of all lawyer presidents had prior professional fundraising experience as compared to 12% at private institutions. This is not surprising considering that historically private institutions have had to be more aggressive in pursuing philanthropy because they did not benefit from the same level of government support as public institutions. However, as most state governments have reduced support for public colleges in the last decade on average of 21%, going forward the ability of all presidents to successfully fundraise will be even more important.[47]

Notably, perhaps because of constraints on accessing certain public funds to support the institutions, religiously affiliated schools seem to place great value on prior fundraising experience for their lawyer presidents with a noticeable number of such appointments. Chart 4.26 shows that, from the 2000s to the 2010s, the number of lawyer presidents with fundraising experience at religiously affiliated schools tripled from five to sixteen. Turning to community colleges in chart 4.25, prior to the 2010s there were no lawyer presidents with fundraising backgrounds, but by the 2010s the first three were hired.

---

[47] Jillian Berman, "Why States Are Cutting Back on Higher Education Funding," *MarketWatch*, last modified January 7, 2017, accessed September 22, 2021, https://www.marketwatch.com/story/why-states-are-cutting-back-on-higher-education-funding-2016-01-07; Michael Mitchell, Michael Leachman, and Kathleen Masterson, "A Lost Decade in Higher Education Funding: State Cuts Have Driven Up Tuition and Reduced Quality," *Center on Budget and Policy Priorities*, last modified August 23, 2017, accessed September 22, 2021, https://www.cbpp.org/research/state-budget-and-tax/a-lost-decade-in-higher-education-funding.

Characteristics of Lawyer Presidents | 129

Chart 4.22. Lawyer Presidents with Prior Fundraiser Experience (1900–2019)

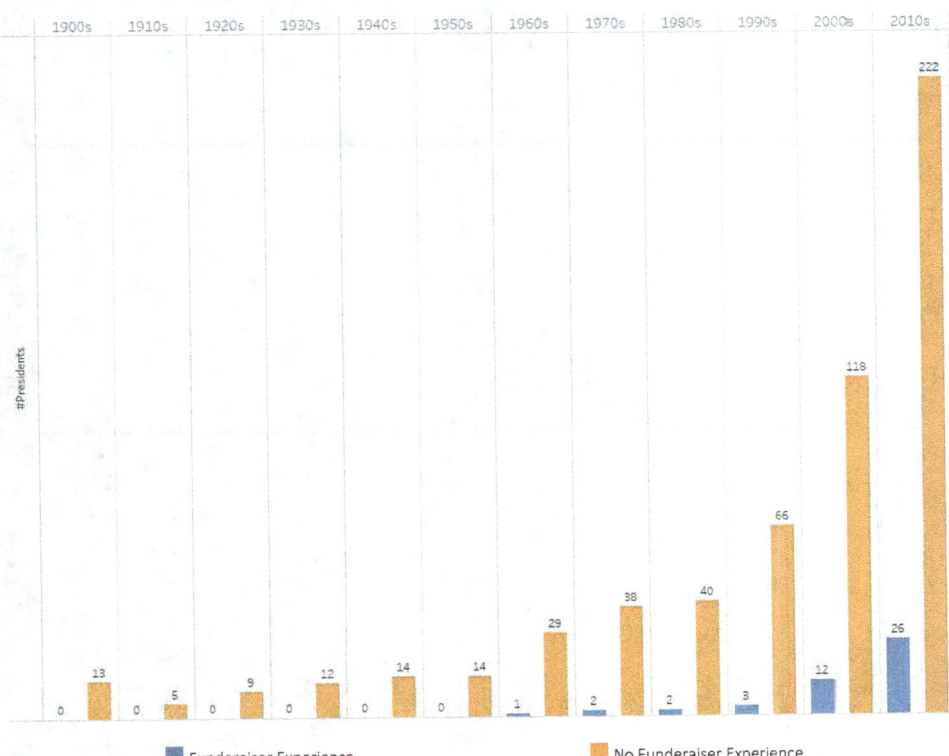

Notes
- Each appointment within a decade is counted by the start of a president's term.
- If a president was appointed twice in the same decade, they are only counted once.
- If a president was appointed in two different decades, they are counted in each decade.
- Appointments do not include presidents of private independent law schools.
- Appointments include presidents, chancellors, and CEOs.
- Interim positions are also included, and, if known, are generally considered as separate appointments from permanent positions.
- Presidents who started their appointment in 2020 and after are not included within this graph.
- Two current presidents have unidentified start dates for their terms. They are not included in this graph.

Chart 4.23. Lawyer Presidents at Public Institutions with Prior Fundraiser Experience (1900–2019)

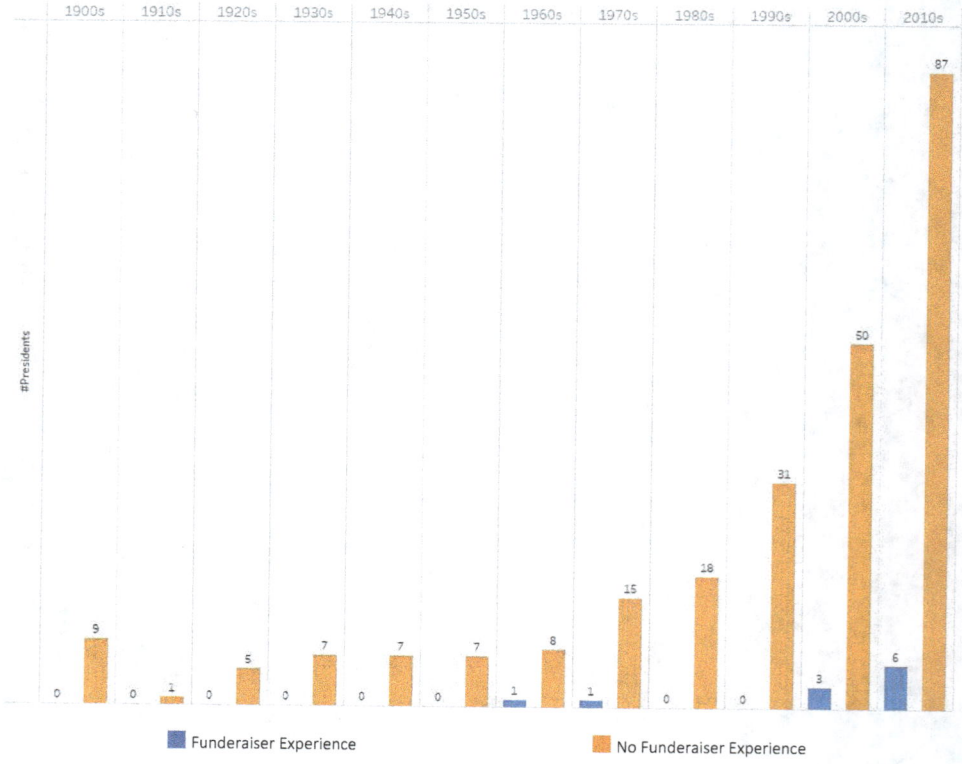

Notes
- Each appointment within a decade is counted by the start of a president's term.
- If a president was appointed twice in the same decade, they are only counted once.
- If a president was appointed in two different decades, they are counted in each decade.
- Appointments do not include presidents of private independent law schools.
- Appointments include presidents, chancellors, and CEOs.
- Interim positions are also included, and, if known, are generally considered as separate appointments from permanent positions.
- Presidents who started their appointment in 2020 and after are not included within this graph.
- Two current presidents have unidentified start dates for their terms. They are not included in this graph.

Chart 4.24. Lawyer Presidents at Private Institutions with Prior Fundraiser Experience (1900–2019)

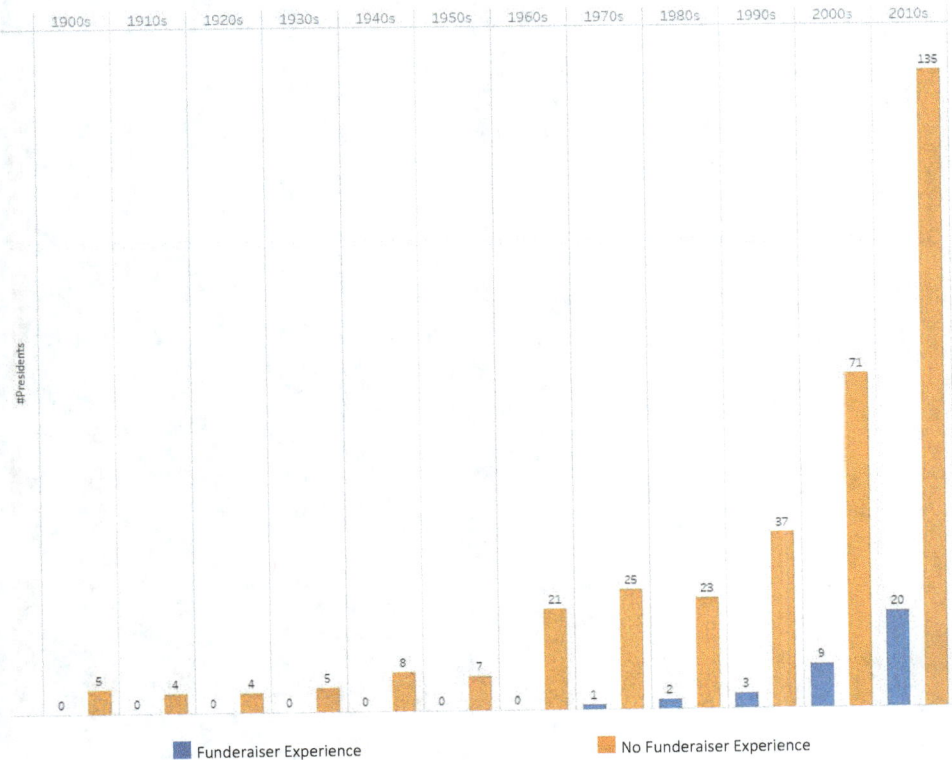

Notes
- Each appointment within a decade is counted by the start of a president's term.
- If a president was appointed twice in the same decade, they are only counted once.
- If a president was appointed in two different decades, they are counted in each decade.
- Appointments do not include presidents of private independent law schools.
- Appointments include presidents, chancellors, and CEOs.
- Interim positions are also included, and, if known, are generally considered as separate appointments from permanent positions.
- Presidents who started their appointment in 2020 and after are not included within this graph.
- Two current presidents have unidentified start dates for their terms. They are not included in this graph.

Chart 4.25. Lawyer Presidents at Community Colleges with Prior Fundraiser Experience (1900–2019)

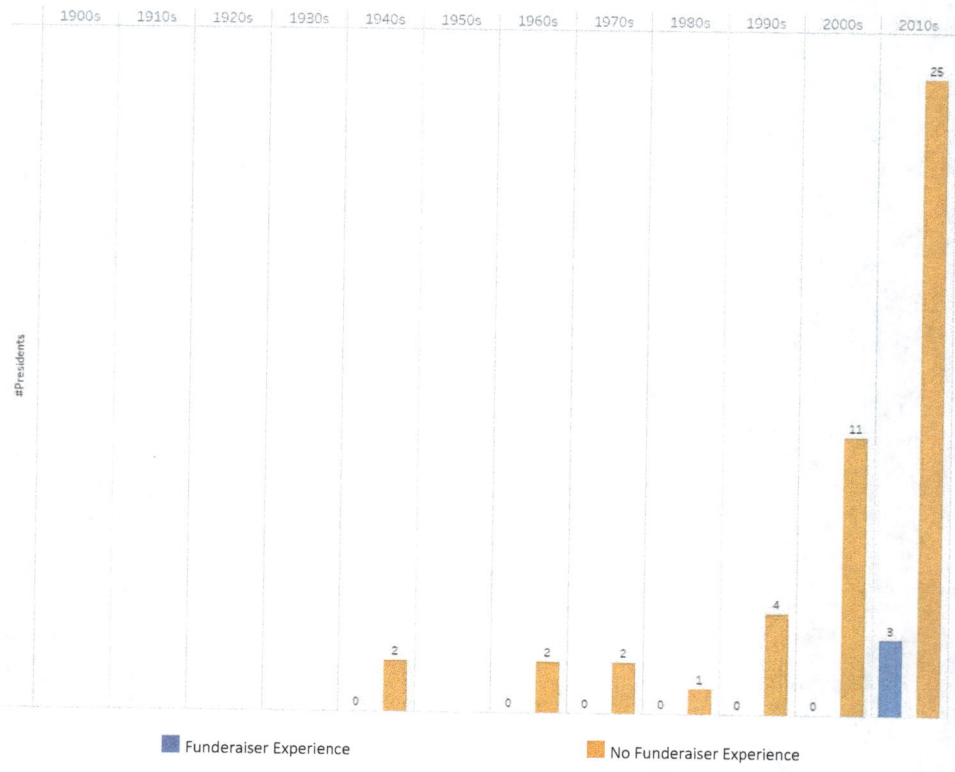

Notes
- Each appointment within a decade is counted by the start of a president's term.
- If a president was appointed twice in the same decade, they are only counted once.
- If a president was appointed in two different decades, they are counted in each decade.
- Appointments do not include presidents of private independent law schools.
- Appointments include presidents, chancellors, and CEOs.
- Interim positions are also included, and, if known, are generally considered as separate appointments from permanent positions.
- Presidents who started their appointment in 2020 and after are not included within this graph.
- Two current presidents have unidentified start dates for their terms. They are not included in this graph.

Chart 4.26. Lawyer Presidents at Religiously Affiliated Institutions with Prior Fundraiser Experience (1900–2019)

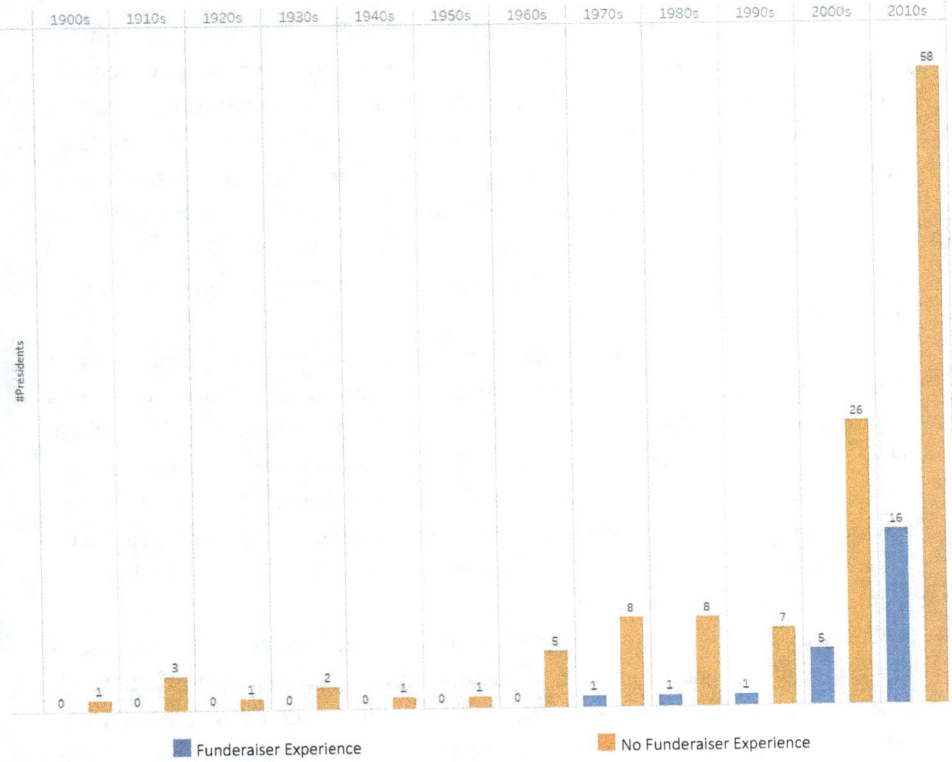

Notes
- Each appointment within a decade is counted by the start of a president's term.
- If a president was appointed twice in the same decade, they are only counted once.
- If a president was appointed in two different decades, they are counted in each decade.
- Appointments do not include presidents of private independent law schools.
- Appointments include presidents, chancellors, and CEOs.
- Interim positions are also included, and, if known, are generally considered as separate appointments from permanent positions.
- Presidents who started their appointment in 2020 and after are not included within this graph.
- Two current presidents have unidentified start dates for their terms. They are not included in this graph.

General Counsels Bring Seasoned Experience to the C-Suite

Search committees seeking their next campus president should not discount the value of a campus general counsel given the proliferation of statutory requirements, regulatory regimes, legal claims, and risks, not to mention the current challenges presented with campus responses to COVID-19 and racism. Over the last twenty years the number of former general counsel leading colleges and universities has increased sevenfold, and more than half of that number took the top job in the last five years (see chart 4.27). Between 2010 and 2019 there were roughly 250 lawyer presidents, and former general counsel accounted for almost 19% of that number.

When Laurie A. Carter became president of Shippensburg University in Pennsylvania, she brought with her more than twenty-five years of experience as inside counsel to higher education, first at the Juilliard School in New York where she was the school's inaugural chief legal officer, and then as university counsel and executive vice president at Eastern Kentucky University.[48] President Carter told the ABA Journal in the spring of 2021 that she used her legal background on a daily basis, specifically citing compliance with Title IX as one area where her legal experience was put to use.[49]

Compared to those who have worked in the public specter, the emergence of the Office of General Counsel in higher education is a relatively modern development. The earliest college counsel's office can be traced to the University of Alabama in 1925. By the 1960s there were 50 in-house general counsel. Today the National Association of College and University Attorneys (NACUA) membership includes more than 1,850 campuses and more than 5,000 lawyers. Without doubt, this dramatic increase was fueled by the social, political, and cultural disruption of the 1960s and 1970s. In those turbulent times, which many observers compare to our current circumstances, higher education was both deeply involved and dramatically affected by transformational legal change brought by courts, legislators, and regulatory bodies.

A 2019 report from the *Chronicle of Higher Education*, "The Successful President of Tomorrow: The Five Skills Future Leaders Will Need," posits that presidents of the future must be people "who will make difficult, data-driven decisions . . . an innovator and risk-taker who will reinvent the business model while staying true to institutional mission."[50] The report emphasizes that schools

---

48   Moran, "Lawyers Find Their Skill Sets," 57.
49   Ibid.
50   Field, "The Successful President of Tomorrow."

will "... require an expert communicator—someone who can make the case for change, calm the campus culture wars, and convince the public that college is indeed worth it."[51] The report offers the following five essential skills distilled from interviews with more than three dozen presidents and leadership experts: "analyzing the business; innovating; building relationships; careful communicating; and managing a crisis." These are all core skills that successful lawyers possess.

Law schools are increasingly offering courses in leadership, finance, and management, and lawyers acquire on-the-job training business experience. Most lawyers work in solo or small law firms where they are the managing partners and/or firm owners. They must run all aspects of the operation from business development (not unlike enrollment, branding, and resource development) to human resource management (such as hiring and firing, payroll, and accommodations). In 2012, almost 10% of the Fortune 500 CEOs held juris doctorate degrees (JDs). Forbes reported in 2019 that of the Fortune 100 CEOs who held graduate degrees 16% had earned law degrees. Considering that a growing number of general counsel of Fortune 50 companies have moved into the CEO role, David Steiner, a law firm partner turned CEO of Waste Management, Inc. commented that lawyers "... learn how to break down an issue and to analyze it ... are taught how to look and understand both sides of an issue because it helps you make a better decision ... are trained to think."[52] Steiner believes that boards of directors are turning to lawyers because they are very good businesspeople who must produce results in terms of solutions to problems.[53] Higher education is a business and lawyers possessing business acumen who also understand and can be true to an academic institutions culture and mission represent perhaps the fastest growing cohort of campus leaders.

Legal talent is not a requirement for an academic president. Yet, it doesn't hurt and it certainly can help. The increasing number of lawyers assuming the top campus leadership position is not likely to slow down. First, the intensity of the regulatory environment generates dozens of constantly evolving federal, state, and local laws as well as agency rulemaking. This poses complex compliance challenges for myriad everyday campus business issues. Second, in a litigious society, higher education has become both the subject and the target of investigations, enforcement actions and high visibility cases.

---

51 Ibid.
52 Curriden, "CEO, Esq."
53 Ibid.

Dealing with longstanding controversial legal issues such as affirmative action, free speech, tenure, and academic discipline has long been part of the job. The legal and economic challenges surrounding the impacts of COVID-19 for higher education (such as health and safety and class action law suits), combined with growing significant issues involving constitutional free speech, racism, civil rights, and diversity and inclusion, demand skilled leaders who have the educational and practical training to effectively respond to these issues. If not properly managed, any of these issues could overwhelm and have serious consequences for an institution's educational mission. Indeed, at least one scholar even recommends law-related training and education for faculty and academic administrators.

The legal demands facing higher education pose serious threats that can tear the fabric of an academic community and severely damage the reputation and sustainability of campuses. This is driven by increasing consumer-driven expectations of students and their parents, increasing transparency, a perception that higher education has deep pockets, and sadly growing skepticism about the value of higher education. Swift, decisive, and legally grounded responses are often required within hours of issues arising thanks to the Internet and social media, which are unforgiving to those who delay. Lawyers must be exceptional communicators to frame their cases to jurors and judges, to speak with clients and witnesses, and to work collaboratively with stakeholders who see things from different perspectives, much akin to the style of communication skills demanded of campus leaders.

Search committees should not overlook lawyer candidates as they cast their nets to recruit the best match to meet the needs of their campus community. Not every lawyer has what it takes to serve as president, but many including college and university general counsel may just be the right leader at the right time. Dennis Barden, a senior partner at WittKieffer, an executive search firm that engages in campus presidency searches, notes that, as general counsels also work closely with college and university boards, they gain insight into the importance of shared governance in higher education, and the experience also provides boards of trustees with some comfort in terms of candidates with whom they must build a partnership.[54]

When former general counsel to Rutgers University in New Jersey and the University of Michigan, Jonathan Alger, was appointed as president of James Madison University in Virginia in July 2012, he noted that while he intended to

---

54   Moran, "Lawyers Find Their Skill Sets," 58.

Chart 4.27. Lawyer Presidents with Prior General Counsel Experience (1900–2019)

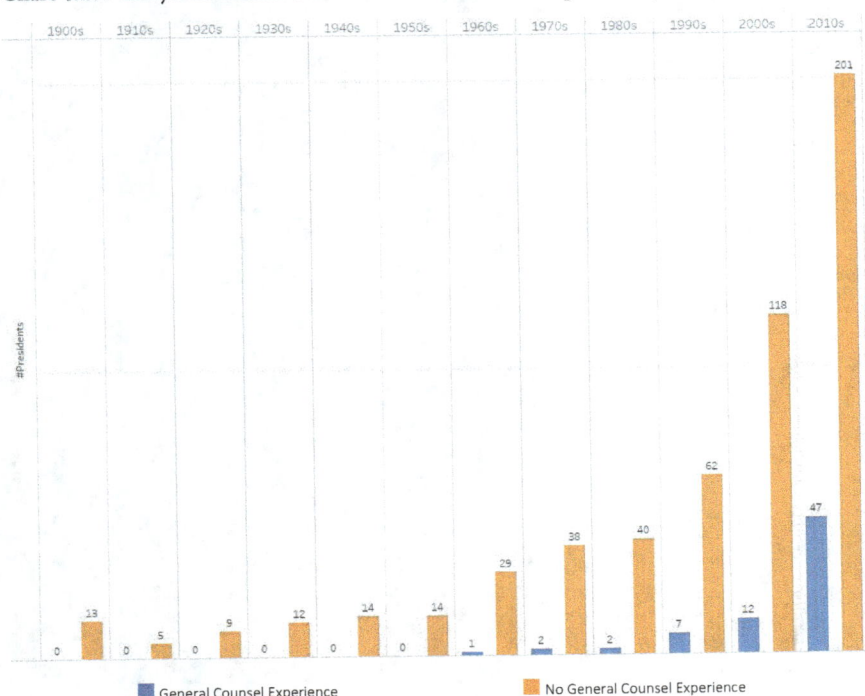

Notes
- Each appointment within a decade is counted by the start of a president's term.
- If a president was appointed twice in the same decade, they are only counted once.
- If a president was appointed in two different decades, they are counted in each decade.
- Appointments do not include presidents of private independent law schools.
- Appointments include presidents, chancellors, and CEOs.
- Interim positions are also included, and, if known, are generally considered as separate appointments from permanent positions.
- Presidents who started their appointment in 2020 and after are not included within this graph.
- Two current presidents have unidentified start dates for their terms. They are not included in this graph.

rely on University Counsel to give him advice in his new role as president, the skill he brought to the office as a lawyer included being a good advocate for the institution and "being able to hear and understand different points of view."[55] In reflecting on his presidency and how his time as general counsel prepared him for the role, Alger commented that serving as general counsel prepared him for the new role because, "it is one of the few jobs where you interact with everybody at the institution, both on the administrative side and the academic side."[56]

---

55 Schmidt, "A Lawyer Takes an Uncommon Path."
56 Moran, "Lawyers Find Their Skill Sets," 60.

Chart 4.28. Lawyer Presidents at Public Institutions with Prior General Counsel Experience (1900–2019)

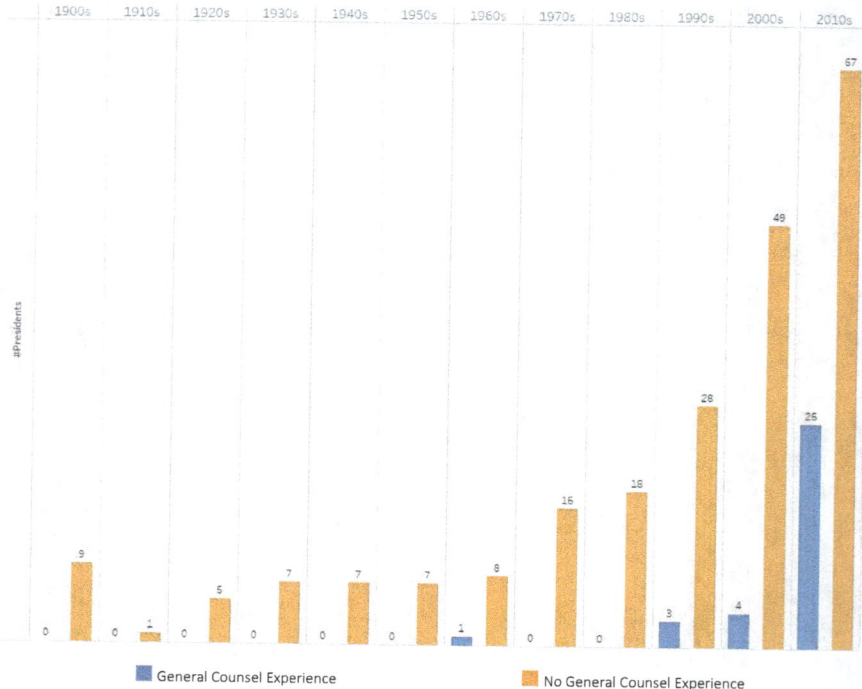

Notes
- Each appointment within a decade is counted by the start of a president's term.
- If a president was appointed twice in the same decade, they are only counted once.
- If a president was appointed in two different decades, they are counted in each decade.
- Appointments do not include presidents of private independent law schools.
- Appointments include presidents, chancellors, and CEOs.
- Interim positions are also included, and, if known, are generally considered as separate appointments from permanent positions.
- Presidents who started their appointment in 2020 and after are not included within this graph.
- Two current presidents have unidentified start dates for their terms. They are not included in this graph.

Marvin Krislov, current president of Pace University in New York and former president of Oberlin College in Ohio, also served as general counsel at University of Michigan (as well as for the U. S. Department of Labor during the Clinton administration).[57] He credits his legal training for helping him to

---

57 "Office of the President, Meet President Krisolv," *Pace University*, accessed September 9, 2021, https://www.pace.edu/president/meet-president-krislov.

Chart 4.29. Lawyer Presidents at Private Institutions with Prior General Counsel Experience (1900–2019)

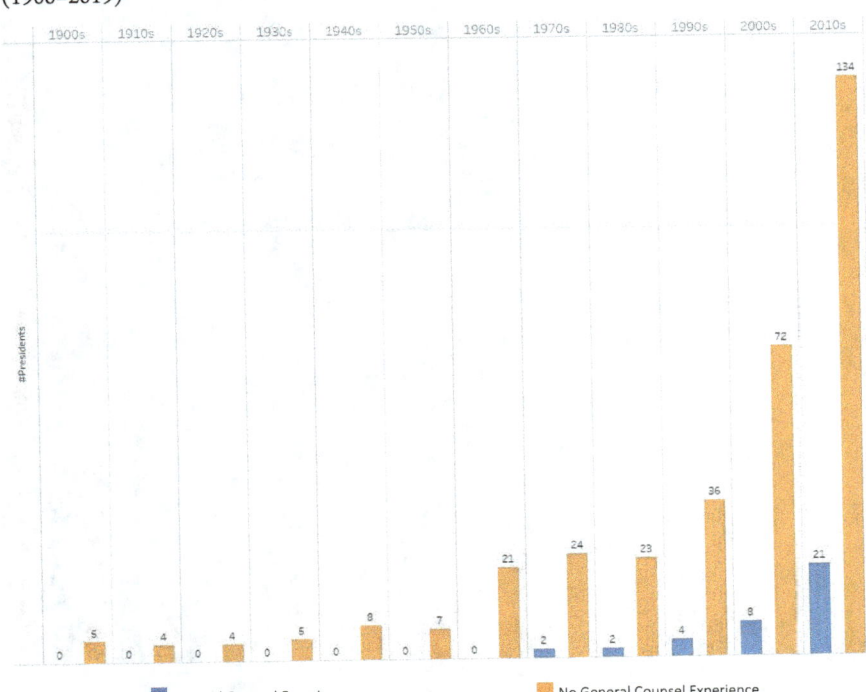

Notes
- Each appointment within a decade is counted by the start of a president's term.
- If a president was appointed twice in the same decade, they are only counted once.
- If a president was appointed in two different decades, they are counted in each decade.
- Appointments do not include presidents of private independent law schools.
- Appointments include presidents, chancellors, and CEOs.
- Interim positions are also included, and, if known, are generally considered as separate appointments from permanent positions.
- Presidents who started their appointment in 2020 and after are not included within this graph.
- Two current presidents have unidentified start dates for their terms. They are not included in this graph.

navigate difficult issues at Oberlin involving the local police and discriminatory behavior towards students of color.[58]

Charts 4.28 and 4.29 explore whether there is any discernable difference in the hiring of candidates with prior general counsel experience between public

---

58   Moran, "Lawyers Find Their Skill Sets," 60.

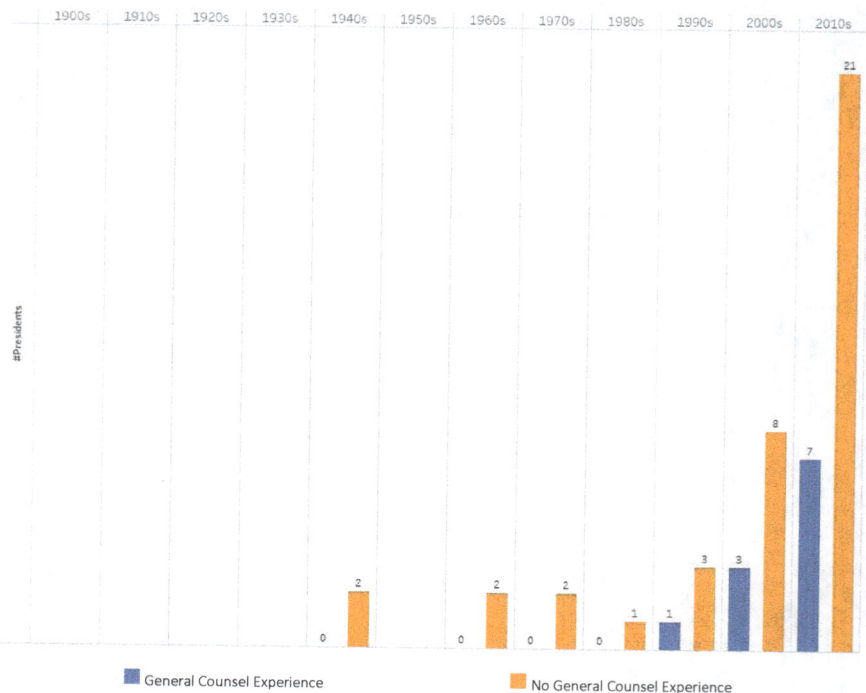

Chart 4.30. Lawyer Presidents at Community Colleges with Prior General Counsel Experience (1900–2019)

Notes
- Each appointment within a decade is counted by the start of a president's term.
- If a president was appointed twice in the same decade, they are only counted once.
- If a president was appointed in two different decades, they are counted in each decade.
- Appointments do not include presidents of private independent law schools.
- Appointments include presidents, chancellors, and CEOs.
- Interim positions are also included, and, if known, are generally considered as separate appointments from permanent positions.
- Presidents who started their appointment in 2020 and after are not included within this graph.
- Two current presidents have unidentified start dates for their terms. They are not included in this graph.

and private schools. During the last decade, almost 28% of the lawyer presidents at public schools had prior general counsel experience as compared to 13.5% at private institutions. Chart 4.30 shows that in the last decade 25% of the community college lawyer presidents had general counsel experience, and this number drops for religiously affiliated institutions to 12% (see chart 4.31). While this

Chart 4.31. Lawyer Presidents at Religiously Affiliated Institutions with Prior General Counsel Experience (1900–2019)

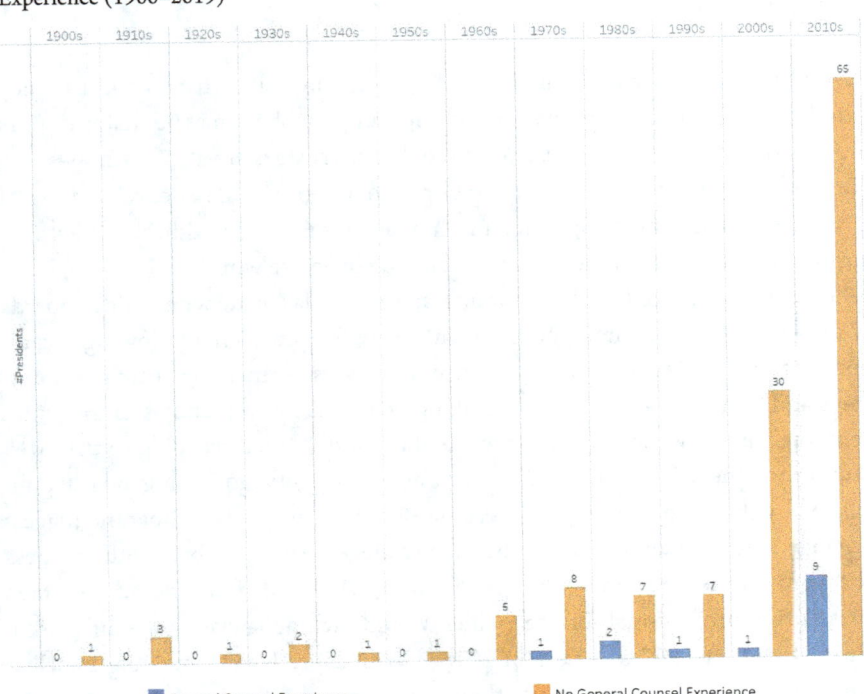

Notes
- Each appointment within a decade is counted by the start of a president's term.
- If a president was appointed twice in the same decade, they are only counted once.
- If a president was appointed in two different decades, they are counted in each decade.
- Appointments do not include presidents of private independent law schools.
- Appointments include presidents, chancellors, and CEOs.
- Interim positions are also included, and, if known, are generally considered as separate appointments from permanent positions.
- Presidents who started their appointment in 2020 and after are not included within this graph.
- Two current presidents have unidentified start dates for their terms. They are not included in this graph.

number is surprisingly low given the added legal challenges of religiously affiliated schools, chart 4.31 illustrates that the actual number of lawyer presidents with general counsel experience at these schools has increased from one or two in each of the four preceding decades to a jump of nine in the 2010s.

Governing Board Lawyers Increasingly Tapped to Lead Campuses

Typically, people are appointed as college and university trustees because they are leaders in the community around the campus. They may be major donors to the institution or have the capacity to do so. Trustees are also business-savvy individuals who can advise the campus president on critical issues related to real estate, financing and budgeting, and human resources. In addition, they have important networks in the public sector and corporate worlds.

Noteworthy is the fact that lawyers also serve as lay leaders on college boards of trustees, the ultimate appointing authority for presidents following a campus search process. The mere presence of lawyers permeating search committees and/or on the final decision-making board, likely contributes to the wider acceptance of lawyers as viable presidential candidates. According to the 2015 survey of the composition of college and university governing board published by the Association on Governing Boards in 2016, data show the biggest change in the percentage of independent college board members with business backgrounds is up from 47.9% in 1997 to 54.9% in 2015 and board members with other professional service (which would include lawyers) also increased, from 16.7% in 1997 to 21.8% in 2015.[59] With more lawyers helping to select the future of campus leadership, their presence and influence in validating the skills that lawyers possess as beneficial, overlapping, and essential for successful presidencies certainly helps to explain why more lawyers and legal educators are assuming these top campus leadership spots.

In such tumultuous times governing bodies may understandably have a comfort level about their trustee colleagues who are already intimately knowledgeable about the operation of the school, especially when the school may be facing serious challenges.[60] In May 2021, Dickinson College in Carlisle, PA announced that the chair of its Board of Trustees, the Hon. John E. Jones, III, who was stepping down as chief judge of the federal Middle District of Pennsylvania Court, would take over as interim president, as the sitting president announced plans to

---

[59] Association of Governing Boards of Universities and Colleges, *Policies, Practices, and Composition of Governing and Foundation Boards 2016* (AGB Press, 2016).

[60] Patricia E. Salkin, "In Tough Times, Schools Look to Lawyers to Lead," *Trusteeship*, May/June 2021, 28.

go back to her prior school.⁶¹ Jones has been on the Board for thirteen years and understandably has a close working relationship with the departing president. Richard Ekman, president of the Council of Independent Colleges, noted, "I see all these changes in a long-term pattern of greater variation in the kinds of experiences and credentials that colleges and universities are willing to consider and sometimes inclined to favor as they choose a president."⁶²

Inside Higher Education reported that "Leadership experts cite reasons why a board chair might be a qualified candidate for president or interim president. A chair who has been doing his or her job will be up to date on the challenges and opportunities an institution faces, and he or she is likely familiar with the institution's values and operations. At this moment, when the global pandemic has upended everything from traditional search processes to the recruiting market, institutions might prioritize the stability a board member represents—especially in cases where a transition has not been planned for an extensive period of time."⁶³

Boards may similarly look favorably upon candidates who have experience as trustees at other institutions. This is because effective board members must work in partnership with the campus president and truly have a handle on major economic, policy, and business operations of the school, more so that anyone else outside of the enterprise. Henry Stover, president and CEO of the Association of Governing Boards (AGB), described that "As fiduciaries, board members are accountable for everything that happens or fails to happen within the institution or foundation. It is important to know that from a technical leadership perspective, while accountability cannot be delegated, responsibility can be delegated. Ultimately, board members' primary and ultimate fiduciary duty is to be accountable for the institution's long-term reputation and vitality spanning reputation, financial health, academic quality, student success, workforce preparation, risk oversight, and much more."

---

61   Rick Seltzer, "Dickinson Plans Unique Presidential Transition," *Inside Higher Ed*, last modified May 17, 2021, accessed September 9, 2021, https://www.insidehighered.com/news/2021/05/17/board-chair-plans-two-year-interim-presidency-dickinson-college?utm_source=Inside+Higher+Ed&utm_campaign=00369dca8f-DNU_2021_COPY_02&utm_medium=email&utm_term=0_1fcbc04421-00369dca8f-19850 1589&mc_cid=00369dca8f&mc_eid=3e858f3f7a.

62   Ibid.

63   Ibid.

In the last ten years more than 10% of lawyer trustees have claimed this post. Since the 1970s, fifty-three lawyer trustees were appointed to lead a college campus with more than half of these appointments occurring between 2010 to present (see chart 4.32). Charts 4.33, 4.34, and 4.36 look at the number of lawyer presidents who were trustees and public, private and religiously affiliated schools. The highest percentage of lawyer presidents who were trustees is found in religiously affiliated schools (11%). Community college lawyer trustees were least likely to either seek out or be appointed to the presidency (see chart 4.35, which indicates there have only been two such presidents).

In 2001, Bowdoin College looked no farther than trustee lawyer Barry Mills, who ironically started out as chair of the search committee for a new campus leader.[64] Mills left a partnership at the prestigious Manhattan law firm of Debevoise & Plimpton, LLC for higher education, and the Bowdoin newspaper reported, "Mills demonstrated what many describe as a shrewd analytical prowess, honed by his time in corporate law. But Mills was no longer catering to clients and their problems; he was solving the problems of the College, ones he truly cared about."[65] Even though lawyer presidents were slowly increasing in number by the early 2000s, the newspaper noted, "His appointment was an unorthodox one. Colleges don't usually pull their leaders from outside the realm of higher education, and though he had a Ph.D., Mill's background in business and law was potentially polarizing."[66]

In 2013, former Isothermal Community College Board of Trustees Chair and lawyer, Walter Dalton, was named President of the College.[67] Dalton had another common characteristic of lawyer presidents—he has extensive background as a government lawyer having served most recently as lieutenant governor and prior to that as a state senator where he chaired the senate education and appropriations committee. Such was the case at Chicago State University when they appointed former Board vice chair Zaldwaynaka "Z" Scott as president in

---

64 "Office of the President, Barry Mills (2001–2015)," *Bowdoin*, accessed October 22, 2022, https://www.bowdoin.edu/president/past-presidents/mills.html.
65 Nick Daniels and Zoe Lescaze, "The Evolution of a Leader: Barry Mills as President," *The Bowdoin Orient*, December 10, 2010, accessed October 22, 2022, https://bowdoinorient.com/bonus/article/5878.
66 Ibid.
67 "Dalton Selected as Isothermal's Next President," *Tryon Daily Bulletin*, March 15, 2013, accessed October 10, 2022, https://www.tryondailybulletin.com/2013/03/15/dalton-selected-as-isothermals-next-president/.

2018 who had served as an assistant U. S. attorney and the first inspector general in Illinois for the Agencies of the Governor and Public Universities.[68]

Following ten years of service on the Board of Trustees, the Board of Lesley University appointed lawyer Janet Steinmayer as campus president in 2019.[69] While Steinmayer had experience as the president of Mitchell College immediately prior to the appointment, the Board Chair noted, among her many other qualifications, "Janet's extensive knowledge of and devotion to Lesley. . . ."[70] The following year, Miles College Trustee Bobbie Knight was tapped to lead the campus after first being named interim president in 2019.[71] Another characteristic common in lawyer presidents is also shared by Steinmayer and Knight—they both had prominent successful careers in the corporate sector, typically another desired qualification for Board service.

Some lawyer trustees, like Steinmayer, have extensive non-board related experience in higher education. For example, Paul Lowell Haines, who served on Taylor University's Board of Trustees for thirteen years prior to his appointment, also served as a vice president for student development prior to his fifteen-year career as an education lawyer in the private sector.[72] When Haines stepped down as president, the Board of Trustees again looked to their own and appointed trustee lawyer Paige Comstock Cunningham as interim president in 2019.[73]

Following service as chair of the University Council at the State University of New York at Albany (the body charged with recommending a new campus president) lawyer George Philip was appointed as interim president,[74] and then,

---

68 Dawn Rhodes, "Chicago State Picks Zaldwaynaka 'Z' Scott as New President," *Chicago Tribune*, May 9, 2018, accessed October 10, 2022, https://www.chicagotribune.com/news/ct-met-chicago-state-university-z-scott-president-20180509-story.html.

69 Lesley University, "Janet L. Steinmayer, Lesley University's Seventh President," April 23, 2019, accessed October 20, 2022, https://lesley.edu/news/janet-l-steinmayer.

70 Harvard Square, "Janet L. Steinmayer Named Lesley University's Seventh President," July 10, 2019, accessed October 20, 2022, https://www.harvardsquare.com/janet-l-steinmayer-named-lesley-universitys-seventh-president/.

71 WVTM 13 Digital, "Dr. Bobbie Knight Names Permanent President of Miles College," updated March 8, 2020, accessed October 21, 2022, https://www.wvtm13.com/article/interim-president-selected-for-miles-college/28441645#.

72 FaegreDrinker, "Partner Lowell Haines to Become President of Taylor University," January 21, 2016, accessed October 20, 2022, https://www.faegredrinker.com/en/about/news/2016/1/partner-lowell-haines-to-become-president-of-taylor-university.

73 Reed Parker, "Taylor University Appoints Interim President," August 2, 2019, accessed October 2022, https://www.insideindianabusiness.com/articles/taylor-university-appoints-interim-president.

74 David Henahan, "SUNY Interim Chancellor Clark Appoints George M. Philip as University at Albany Officer in Charge: Clark to Recommend Philip as Interim President to SUNY

Chart 4.32. Lawyer Presidents Who Were Prior Board of Trustees Members (1900–2019)

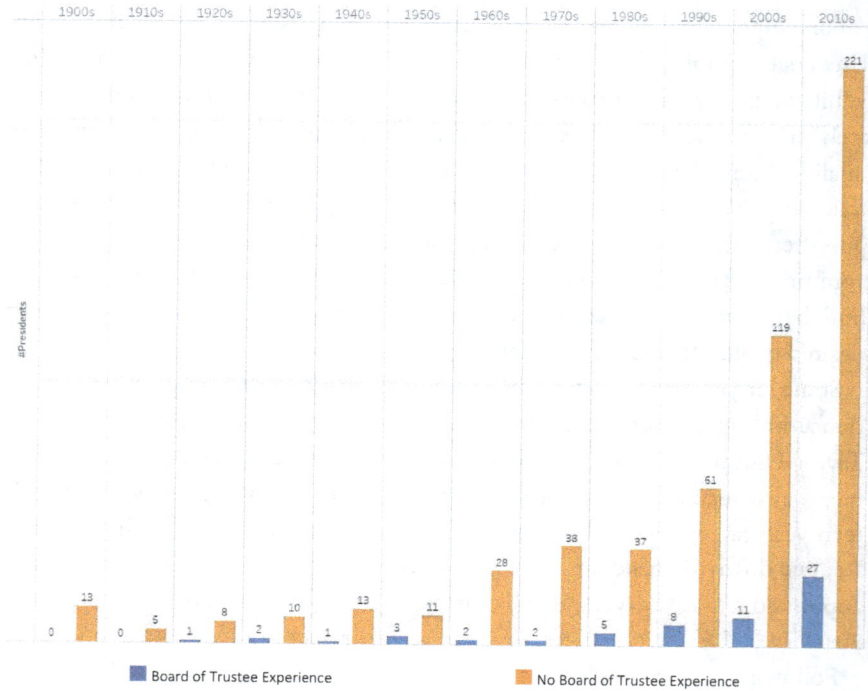

Notes
- Each appointment within a decade is counted by the start of a president's term.
- If a president was appointed twice in the same decade, they are only counted once.
- If a president was appointed in two different decades, they are counted in each decade.
- Appointments do not include presidents of private independent law schools.
- Appointments include presidents, chancellors, and CEOs.
- Interim positions are also included, and, if known, are generally considered as separate appointments from permanent positions.
- Presidents who started their appointment in 2020 and after are not included within this graph.
- Two current presidents have unidentified start dates for their terms. They are not included in this graph.

following a multi-year search estimated to cost $300,000,[75] he was appointed campus president. Like other lawyer trustees turned president, he previously

---

Board," *University at Albany*, October 3, 2007, accessed October 22, 2022, https://www.albany.edu/campusnews/releases_414.htm.

75   Bethany Bump, "UAlbany Pays Over $200k for Presidential Search Consultant," *Times Union*, February 22, 2017, accessed October 22, 2022, https://www.timesunion.com/local/article/UAlbany-pays-over-200K-for-presidential-search-10951363.php.

Chart 4.33. Lawyer Presidents at Public Institutions Who Were Prior Board of Trustees Members (1900–2019)

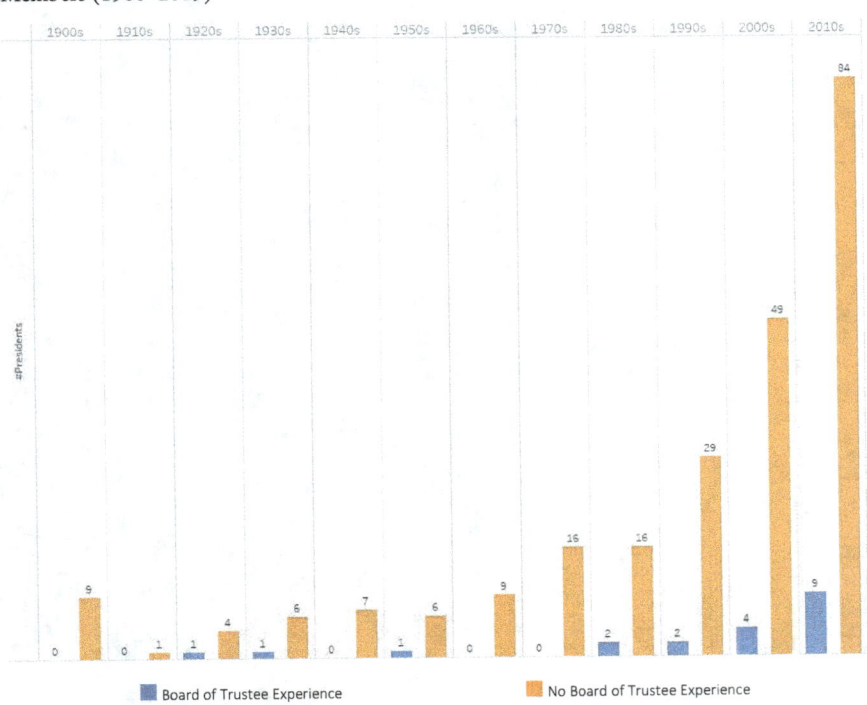

Notes
- Each appointment within a decade is counted by the start of a president's term.
- If a president was appointed twice in the same decade, they are only counted once.
- If a president was appointed in two different decades, they are counted in each decade.
- Appointments do not include presidents of private independent law schools.
- Appointments include presidents, chancellors, and CEOs.
- Interim positions are also included, and, if known, are generally considered as separate appointments from permanent positions.
- Presidents who started their appointment in 2020 and after are not included within this graph.
- Two current presidents have unidentified start dates for their terms. They are not included in this graph.

served in government as executive director of the New York State Teachers' Retirement System and as chief financial officer.

When the Board of Valparaiso University announced that effective January 1, 2021 José D. Padilla would be its next president, the press release pointed to, among other things, his superior business acumen, his prior board service (not at Valpo but at St. Thomas Aquinas) and that he is a dynamic innovator, thinker, and natural leader, bringing "many skills, experiences and accomplishments in higher education which are ideally suited to the University's needs today and in

Chart 4.34. Lawyer Presidents at Private Institutions Who Were Prior Board of Trustees Members (1900–2019)

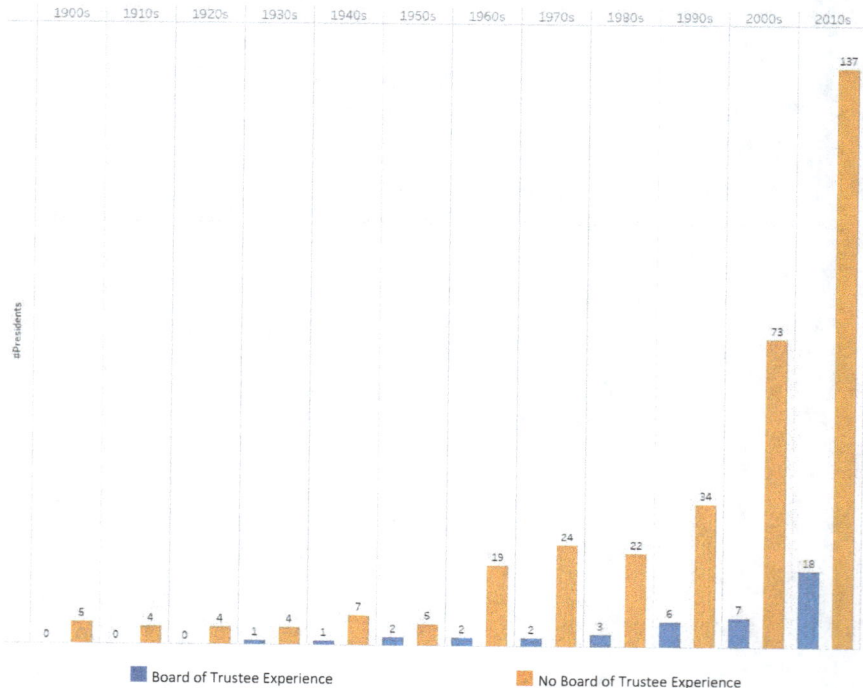

Notes
- Each appointment within a decade is counted by the start of a president's term.
- If a president was appointed twice in the same decade, they are only counted once.
- If a president was appointed in two different decades, they are counted in each decade.
- Appointments do not include presidents of private independent law schools.
- Appointments include presidents, chancellors, and CEOs.
- Interim positions are also included, and, if known, are generally considered as separate appointments from permanent positions.
- Presidents who started their appointment in 2020 and after are not included within this graph.
- Two current presidents have unidentified start dates for their terms. They are not included in this graph.

the future."[76] In his last two roles in higher education, his responsibilities including service as general counsel.

Despite the appearance of a potential conflict when a board of trustees appoints one of their own to the top campus post, nearly every time the selection occurs

[76] Valparaiso University, "Valparaiso University Names New President," December 2, 2020, accessed October 10, 2022, https://www.valpo.edu/news/2020/12/02/valparaiso-university-names-new-president/.

Chart 4.35. Lawyer Presidents at Community Colleges Who Were Prior Board of Trustees Members (1900–2019)

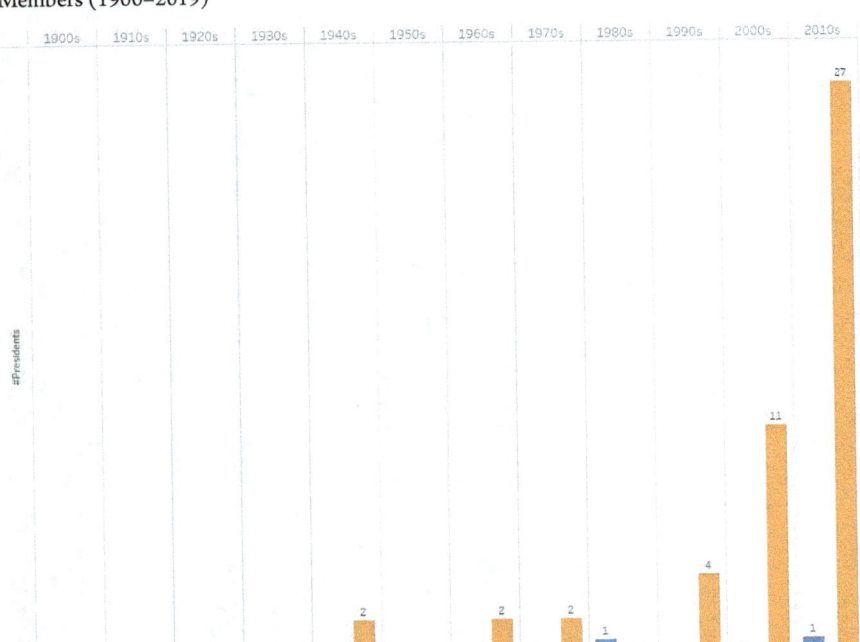

Notes
- Each appointment within a decade is counted by the start of a president's term.
- If a president was appointed twice in the same decade, they are only counted once.
- If a president was appointed in two different decades, they are counted in each decade.
- Appointments do not include presidents of private independent law schools.
- Appointments include presidents, chancellors, and CEOs.
- Interim positions are also included, and, if known, are generally considered as separate appointments from permanent positions.
- Presidents who started their appointment in 2020 and after are not included within this graph.
- Two current presidents have unidentified start dates for their terms. They are not included in this graph.

through a competitive national search or after the appointment of the lawyer trustee to the role on an interim basis for stability pending the comprehensive search. Lawyer trustees appointed at first blush as an interim president, may be in effect auditioning for the role. There has been little public criticism in these appointments, as the reality has been that nearly all of these former lawyer trustees have, and continue to, serve their institutions well.

Chart 4.36. Lawyer Presidents at Religiously Affiliated Institutions Who Were Prior Board of Trustees Members (1900–2019)

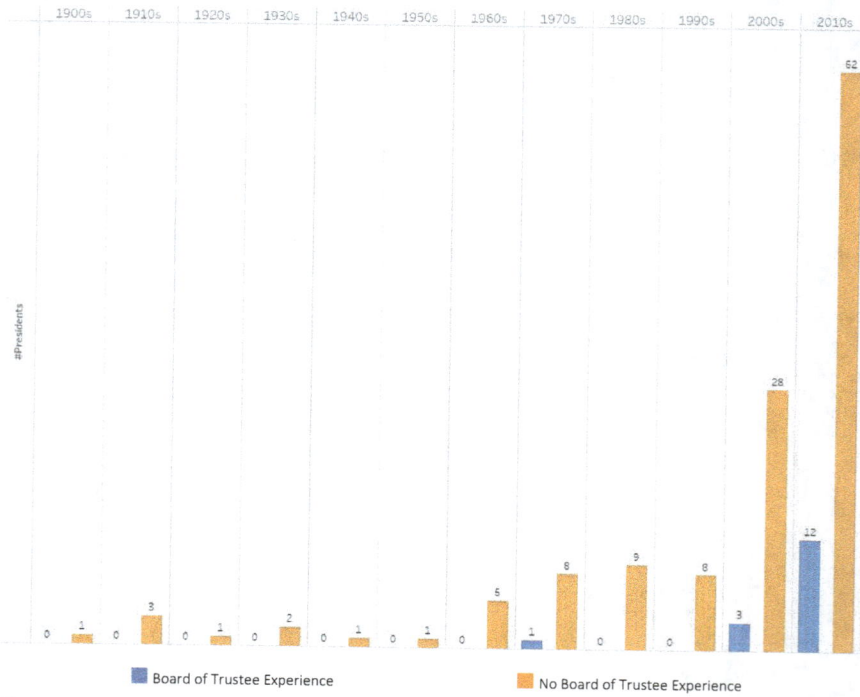

Notes
- Each appointment within a decade is counted by the start of a president's term.
- If a president was appointed twice in the same decade, they are only counted once.
- If a president was appointed in two different decades, they are counted in each decade.
- Appointments do not include presidents of private independent law schools.
- Appointments include presidents, chancellors, and CEOs.
- Interim positions are also included, and, if known, are generally considered as separate appointments from permanent positions.
- Presidents who started their appointment in 2020 and after are not included within this graph.
- Two current presidents have unidentified start dates for their terms. They are not included in this graph.

Lawyer Presidents and Race

As noted in the methodology at the beginning of this research, for purposes of the independent empirical research collected for this study, race is not being evaluated based on the new data collection since individuals were not surveyed and therefore had no opportunity to self-identify. The two tables below were prepared by Dr. Jonathan M. Turk of ACE in response to a data inquiry based upon the last four American College President Studies conducted by the American Council on Education.[77]

---

77 Turk, "ACPS Data Request," February 21, 2020.

The data in the two tables below reveals that through 2017 campuses have been led by predominantly white individuals and the percentage of white lawyers as compared to the non-lawyer presidents was pretty close. An examination of the American Bar Association's National Lawyer Population Survey reports that in 2017 85% of all lawyers were Caucasian, 5% were African American, 2% were Asian, 5% were Hispanic, 2% were multiracial, and 1% was Native American.[78]

Table 4.8. Distribution of Race among JD Holding Presidents, by Survey Year

Race	2002	2007	2012	2017
White	86.44%	92.24%	86.96%	83.61%
Black	6.78%	5.17%	5.22%	9.02%
Hispanic	2.54%	0.86%	1.74%	3.28%
Asian	1.69%	0.86%	0.87%	3.28%
American Indian	0.85%	0.00%	1.74%	0.00%
More than One Race	0.00%	0.86%	3.48%	0.00%
Middle Eastern	N/A	N/A	N/A	0.82%
Other	1.69%	0.00%	0.00%	0.00%
Total	100%	100%	100%	100%

Note: N/A indicates response category was not an option in the given survey year.

Table 4.9. Distribution of Race among All Presidents, by Survey Year

Race	2002	2007	2012	2017
White	87.27%	86.41%	87.18%	83.16%
Black	6.26%	5.94%	5.92%	7.93%
Hispanic	3.62%	4.48%	3.79%	3.93%
Asian	1.11%	0.93%	1.53%	2.29%
American Indian	0.60%	0.73%	0.79%	0.66%
More than One Race	0.00%	1.51%	0.79%	1.44%
Middle Eastern	N/A	N/A	N/A	0.59%
Other	1.15%	0.00%	0.00%	0.00%
Total	100%	100%	100%	100%

Note: N/A indicates response category was not an option in the given survey year.

---

78 "ABA National Lawyer Population Survey: Lawyer Population by State," *American Bar Association*, last modified 2021, accessed September 22, 2021, https://www.americanbar.org/content/dam/aba/administrative/market_research/2021-national-lawyer-population-survey.pdf.

Table 4.10. American Bar Association, National Lawyer Population Survey, Resident Active Attorney Demographics, Race/Ethnicity, 2011–2021

	Resident Active Attorney Demographics: Race/Ethnicitiy											
	2011	2012	2013	2014	2015	2016	2017	2018	2019	2020	2021	Change from 2011
Race/Ethnicity (2)												
African-American	5%	5%	5%	5%	5%	5%	5%	5%	5%	5%	5%	–0.2 pp
Asian	2%	2%	2%	2%	2%	3%	2%	3%	2%	2%	2%	0.8 pp
Caucasian/White	88%	88%	89%	88%	86%	85%	85%	85%	85%	86%	85%	–2.9 pp
Hawaiian/Pacific Islander	0%	1%	0%	0%	1%	0%	0%	0%	0%	0%	0%	0.0 pp
Hispanic	4%	3%	4%	4%	5%	5%	5%	5%	5%	5%	5%	0.9 pp
Multiracial (1)	N/A	N/A	N/A	0%	0%	1%	2%	1%	2%	2%	2%	2.0 pp
Native American	1%	1%	1%	1%	1%	0%	1%	1%	1%	0%	0%	–0.8 pp
Court of States Reporting Statistic	17	16	16	17	18	19	22	21	20	21	25	8
% of Lawers with Reported Statistics	21%	21%	21%	21%	25%	30%	29%	28%	35%	31%	36%	15.0 pp

Data source: American Bar Association's National Lawyer Population Survey.
*Individual state bar associations or licensing agencies are asked to provide demographics data for resident and active attorneys as of December 31st of the prior year, e.g. 2021 data is as of 12/31/2020. The numbers reflected here are the best available data provided to the ABA from the respective associations or agencies.
Notes: In 2018, Indiana corrected the resident active figures for 2016; this report has been updated to reflect the new total attorney count for 2016 than was previously reported. In 2019, Maryland, Nevada, and New York provided corrected 2018 lawyer counts; this report reflects the corrected 2018 total attorney count.

(1) Beginning with the 2020 survey, choices included "Multiracial" as an option for race/ethnicity and "Other" as an option for gender.
(2) Race/ethnicity percentages may total to more than 100% as many states allow responders to choose more than one option for race/ethnicity.

Beginning with the 2020 survey, two new questions about attorneys who identify as LGBTQ+ and as persons with disability wew asked. Results are not included in the 2021 report due to insufficient response.
Copyright © 2021 American Bar Association, All Rights Reserved.
The ABA hereby grants permission for copies of the materials herein to be made, in whole or in part, for classroom use in an institution of higher learning or for use by not-for-profit organizations, provided that the use is for informational, educational, non-commercial purposes only and any copy of the materials or portion thereof acknowledges original publication by the ABA, including the title of the publication, the name of the author, and the legend "Reprinted with permission of the American Bar Association. All rights reserved." Requests to reproduce portions of this publication in any other manner should be sent to ABA Reprints, Licensing & Permissions at www.americanbar.org/reprint.

When comparing the lawyer demographics to the lawyer president demographics, there are similarities between the percentage of white lawyer presidents and the percentage nationally of white lawyers in the profession. The percentage of Black lawyer presidents in 2017 (9.02%) outpaces the percentage of Black lawyers in the profession. However, the percentage of Hispanic lawyer presidents (3.28%) is lower than the number of Hispanic lawyers in the profession. The percentage of Asian lawyer presidents (3.28%) is about equal to the number of Asian lawyers in the profession. While the legal profession works to better diversify itself, higher education is making strides more quickly based upon the daily updates of new hires reported in the *Chronicle of Higher Education* and in *Inside Higher Education*.

While, as mentioned at the end of the last chapter, the overall trend for higher educational institutions to employ lawyer presidents appears to be influenced largely by external factors, the desired backgrounds these candidates bring appear to be quite specific to the schools. While some need leaders who know the government well, so they can deal with changing regulations, others need a president whose past gives them unrestricted fundraising abilities. Others, perhaps in seeking comfort of candidates who know the institution well in terms of finance, compliance and routine business matters may lean towards those who have been responsible for governance and oversight. No matter who they choose, an institution must be cognizant of the skills the candidates have obtained in previous positions inside and/or outside of the academy.

CHAPTER 5

Women Lawyers Emerging as Campus Presidents

The single fastest growing demographic subset of lawyer presidents is women (as compared to demographic categories based on race and ethnicity). Despite the strides that are being made, particularly in the last decade, there is still a long way to go to balance the number of actual appointments more equally. However, as the discussion below will demonstrate, set in the context of the rise of women in the legal profession, and as compared to the number of all women college presidents, the number of women lawyer presidents still falls behind.

The most recent 2017 American Council on Education (ACE) American College Presidents Study confirmed that the occupants of the office of president are disproportionately white males with only one-third being women.[1] With respect to the data specific to lawyer presidents, the representation is less than one-third. Tables 5.1 and 5.2 below from the ACE based on data culled from their American College Presidents studies illustrates the (slow) growing number of women among the lawyer presidents.

Table 5.1. Distribution of JD Holding Presidents Each Year, by Sex

	2002	2007	2012	2017
Female	14.29%	16.95%	13.04%	20.00%
Male	85.71%	83.05%	86.96%	80.00%
Total	**100%**	**100%**	**100%**	**100%**

---

1   Gagliardi et al., *American College President Study 2017*.

Table 5.2. Distribution of Presidents Each Year, by Sex

	2002	2007	2012	2017
Female	21.06%	22.95%	26.40%	30.12%
Male	78.94%	77.05%	73.60%	69.88%
Total	100%	100%	100%	100%

Chart 5.1 below derived from the empirical data collected for this study contains more comprehensive data on lawyer presidents between 2010 and 2019, and shows roughly 2% more women lawyer presidents than the ACE data through 2017. Chart 5.2 illustrates the growth in the number of women lawyer presidents as compared to male lawyer presidents since the 1970s, and chart 5.3 shows the actual number of women lawyer presidents by decade from the 1970s through the 2010s, illustrating the most significant increase from eighteen in the 2000s to sixty-four in the 2010s. Chart 5.4 examines just the last decade and indicates the number of women lawyers who were appointed as president in each year of the decade. The numbers are low at the start of the decade but they increase in 2013–2015 and increase again at the end of the decade.

Chart 5.1. Lawyer Presidents—Gender (2010–2019)

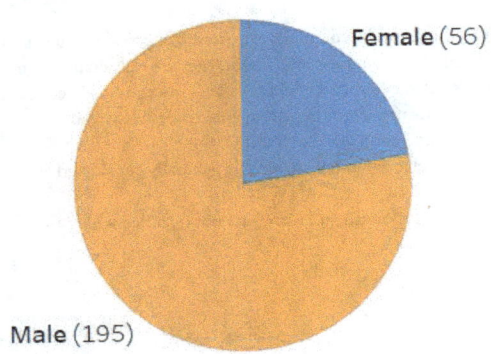

Notes
- This chart represents each president once, even if they have multiple appointments.
- Appointments do not include presidents of private independent law schools.
- Appointments include presidents, chancellors, and CEOs.
- Interim positions are also included, and, if known, are generally considered as separate appointments from permanent positions.
- Presidents who started their appointment in 2020 are not included within this chart.

Chart 5.2. Lawyer Presidents—Gender (1900–2019)

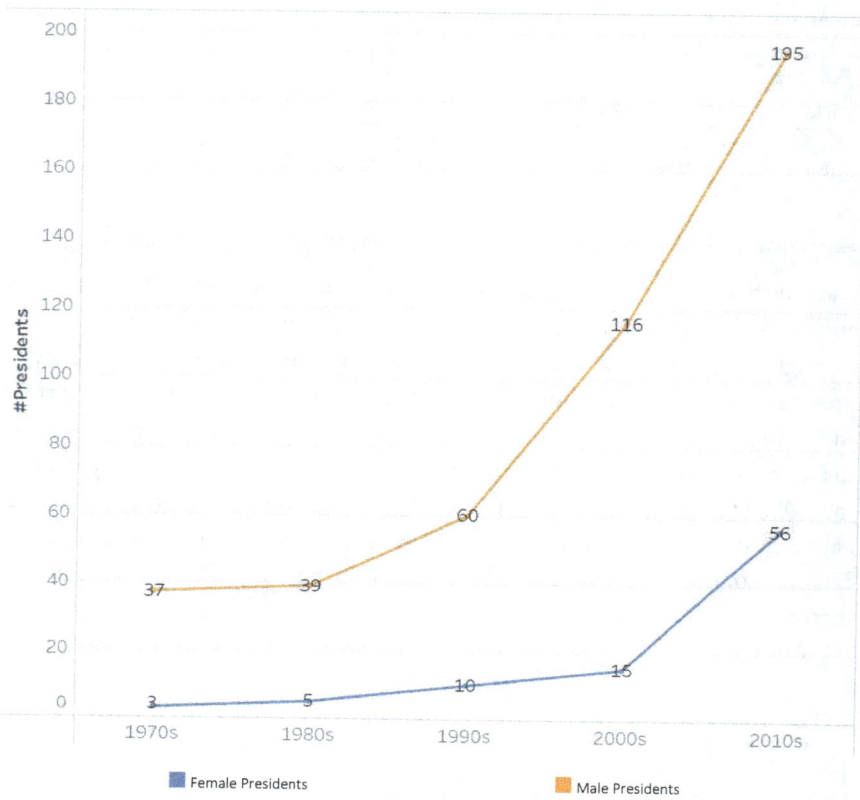

Notes
- Each appointment within a decade is counted by the start of a president's term.
- If a president was appointed twice in the same decade, they are only counted once.
- If a president was appointed in two different decades, they are counted in each decade.
- Appointments do not include presidents of private independent law schools.
- Appointments include presidents, chancellors, and CEOs.
- Interim positions are also included, and, if known, are generally considered as separate appointments from permanent positions.
- Presidents who started their appointment in 2020 are not included within this chart.

Chart 5.3. Appointments of Female Lawyer Presidents (by Decade)

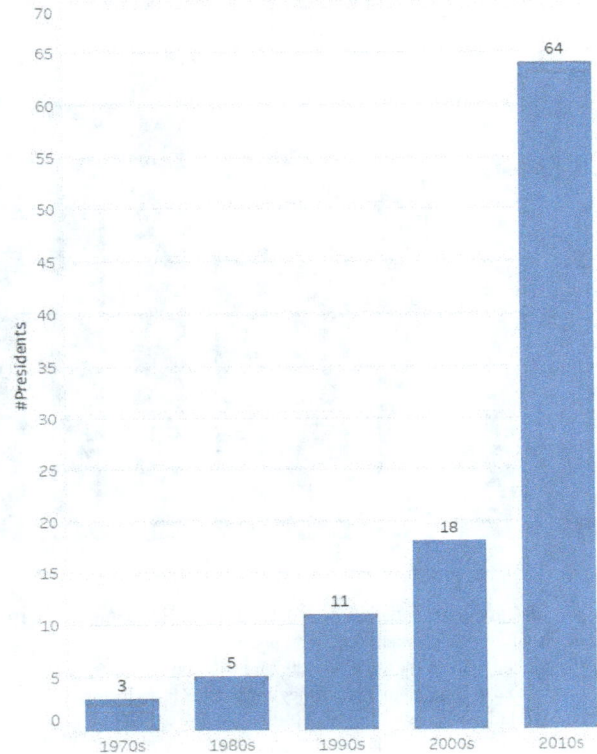

Notes
- This graph only goes back to the 1970s, beginning with the first female appointment in 1976.
- Each appointment within a decade is counted by the start of a president's term.
- If a president was appointed twice in the same decade, they are counted for each appointment.
- If a president was appointed in two different decades, they are counted in each decade.
- Appointments do not include presidents of private independent law schools.
- Appointments include presidents, chancellors, and CEOs.
- Interim positions are also included, and, if known, are generally considered as separate appointments from permanent positions.
- Presidents who started their appointment in 2020 and after are not included within this graph.

Chart 5.4. Female Lawyer Presidents (Last Decade)

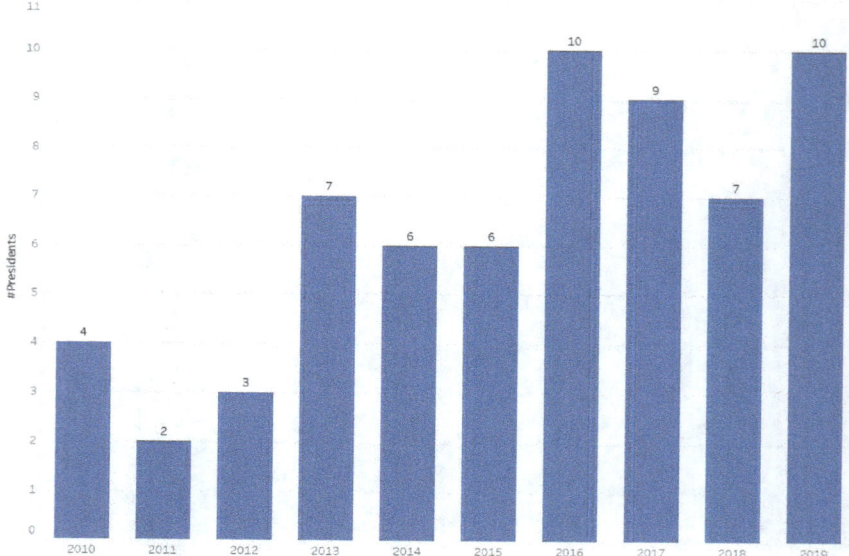

Notes
- This graph only goes back to the 1970s, beginning with the first female appointment in 1976.
- Each appointment within a year is counted by the start of a president's term.
- If a president was appointed twice in the same year, they are only counted once.
- If a president was appointed in two different years, they are counted in each year.
- Appointments do not include presidents of private independent law schools.
- Appointments include presidents, chancellors, and CEOs.
- Interim positions are also included, and, if known, are generally considered as separate appointments from permanent positions.
- Presidents who started their appointment in 2020 and after are not included within this graph.

Chart 5.5. Female Lawyer Presidents (by Decade)

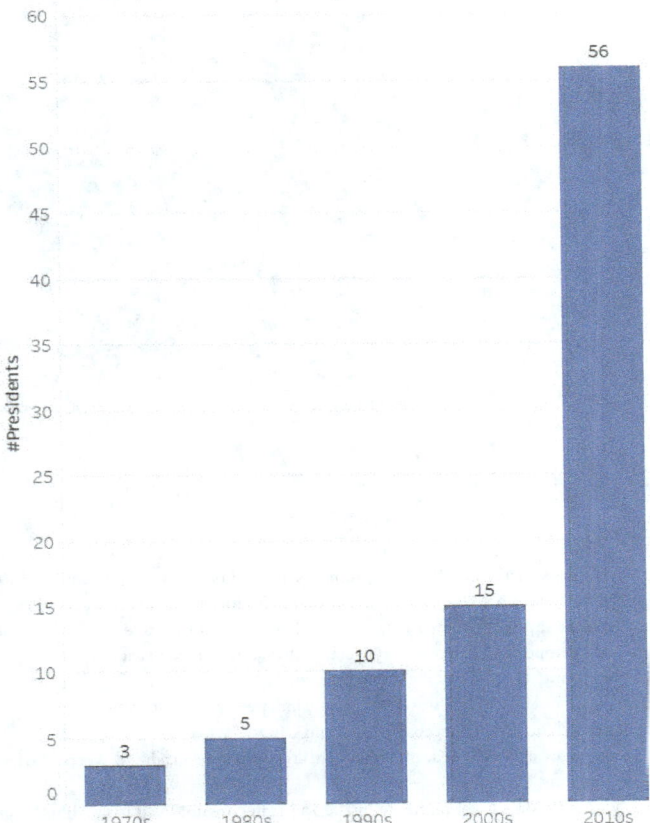

Notes
- This graph only goes back to the 1970s, beginning with the first female appointment in 1976.
- Each appointment within a decade is counted by the start of a president's term.
- If a president was appointed twice in the same decade, they are only counted once.
- If a president was appointed in two different decades, they are counted in each decade.
- Appointments do not include presidents of private independent law schools.
- Appointments include presidents, chancellors, and CEOs.
- Interim positions are also included, and, if known, are generally considered as separate appointments from permanent positions.
- Presidents who started their appointment in 2020 and after are not included within this graph.

Map 5.1. Schools with Female Lawyer Presidents by State (1970–2019)

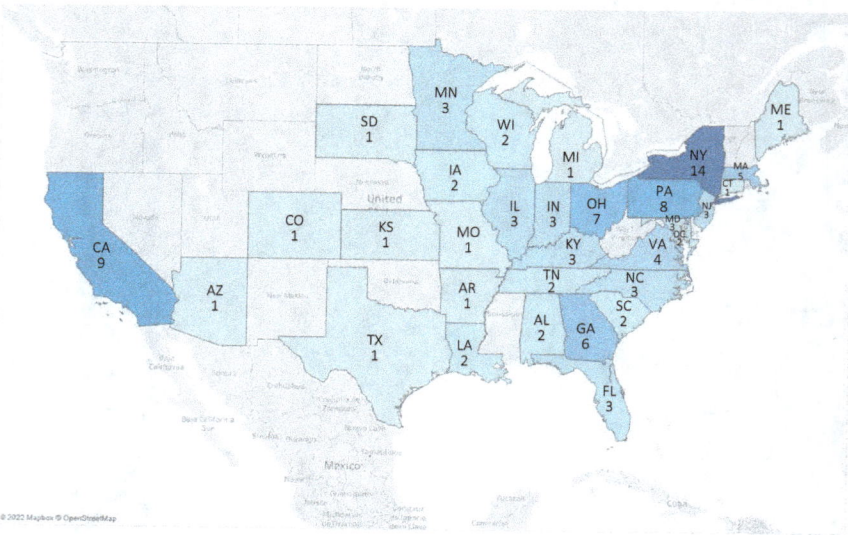

Notes
- This graph only goes back to the 1970s, beginning with the first female appointment in 1976.
- Each appointment is counted by the start of a president's term.
- A president can be appointed more than once in a state, at either the same school or a different one.
- If a president was appointed in two different states, they are counted in each state.
- Presidents are counted for each of their appointments.
- Appointments do not include presidents of private independent law schools.
- Appointments include presidents, chancellors, and CEOs.
- Interim positions are also included, and, if known, are generally considered as separate appointments from permanent positions.
- Presidents who started their appointment in 2020 and after are not included within this graph.
- Appointments in fifty U. S. states are included.
- Darker shades of colors represent a higher number of appointments.

Geography and Women Lawyer Presidents

Map 5.1 shows the geographic location of colleges and universities with female lawyer presidents over the last fifty years. New York had the most with 14 appointments, followed by California with 9, Pennsylvania with 8, Ohio with 7, and Georgia with 6. This map, compared to the data in chart 3.1 that illustrated the top states for lawyer presidents over the last 100 years (as opposed to only 50 years of women lawyer presidents) shows fairly consistent results as

New York (64), California (46), and Pennsylvania (41) were the top three states for lawyer presidents, in that order. Interestingly, Georgia did not make the list of the top nine states for appointing lawyer presidents (see chart 3.1) and Ohio tied with Texas for the sixth spot. When it came to women lawyer presidents, Texas boasts only one.

Women Lawyer Presidents and Types of Schools

Charts 5.6 and 5.7 give more detail on the number of women presidents at various categories of colleges and universities over the last fifty years. Women lawyers have been more likely to be selected to lead private institutions (60) as opposed to public institutions (34). The data in chart 5.7 reveals that for public schools that appointed a lawyer president, only just over 1% of those appointments were women.

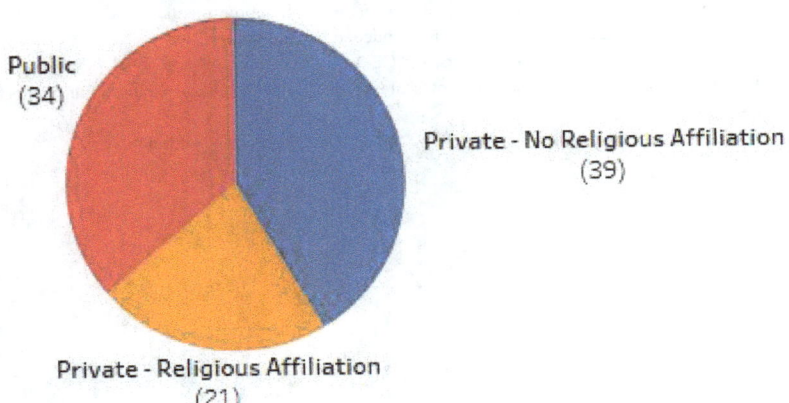

Chart 5.6. Institutions with Female Lawyer Presidents (1970–2019)

Notes
- This graph only goes back to the 1970s, beginning with the first female appointment in 1976.
- This graph counts each school only once, even if there are multiple appointments.
- Appointments do not include presidents of private independent law schools.
- Appointments include presidents, chancellors, and CEOs.
- Interim positions are also included, and, if known, are generally considered as separate appointments from permanent positions.
- Presidents who started their appointment in 2020 and after are not included within this graph.

Chart 5.7. Institutions with Lawyer Presidents (1970–2019)

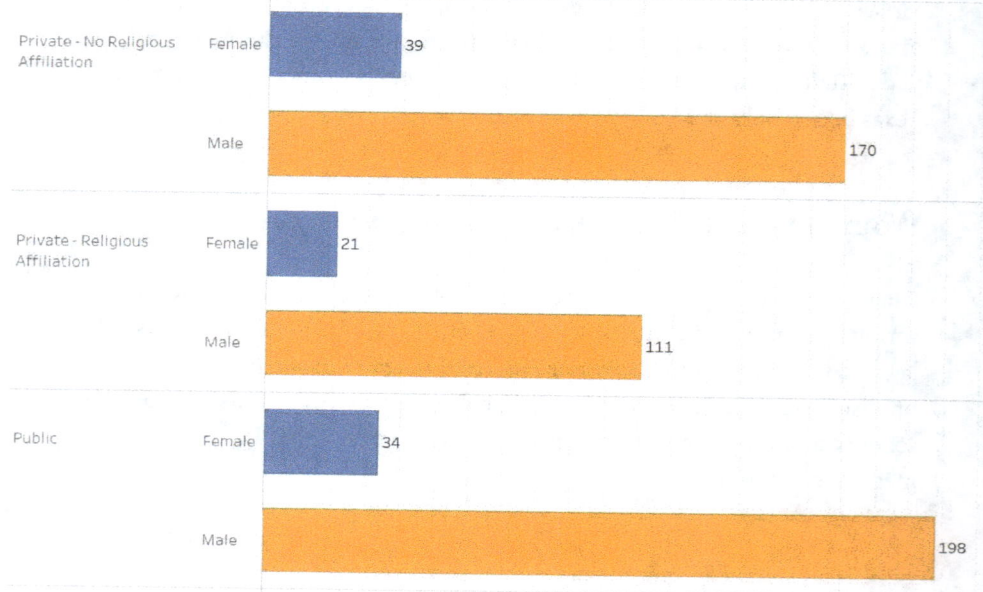

Notes
- This graph only goes back to the 1970s, beginning with the first female appointment in 1976.
- This graph counts each school only once, even if there are multiple appointments.
- Appointments do not include presidents of private independent law schools.
- Appointments include presidents, chancellors, and CEOs.
- Interim positions are also included, and, if known, are generally considered as separate appointments from permanent positions.
- Presidents who started their appointment in 2020 and after are not included within this graph.

Women Lawyer Presidents and Prior Academic Experience

Charts 5.8, 5.9, and 5.10 examine more broadly the prior academic experience female lawyer presidents have brought to the office, as compared with their male counterparts. Chart 5.8 shows that in every decade the number of women lawyer presidents with prior academic experience was significantly higher than the

Chart 5.8. Female Lawyer Presidents with Prior Academic Experience (by Decade)

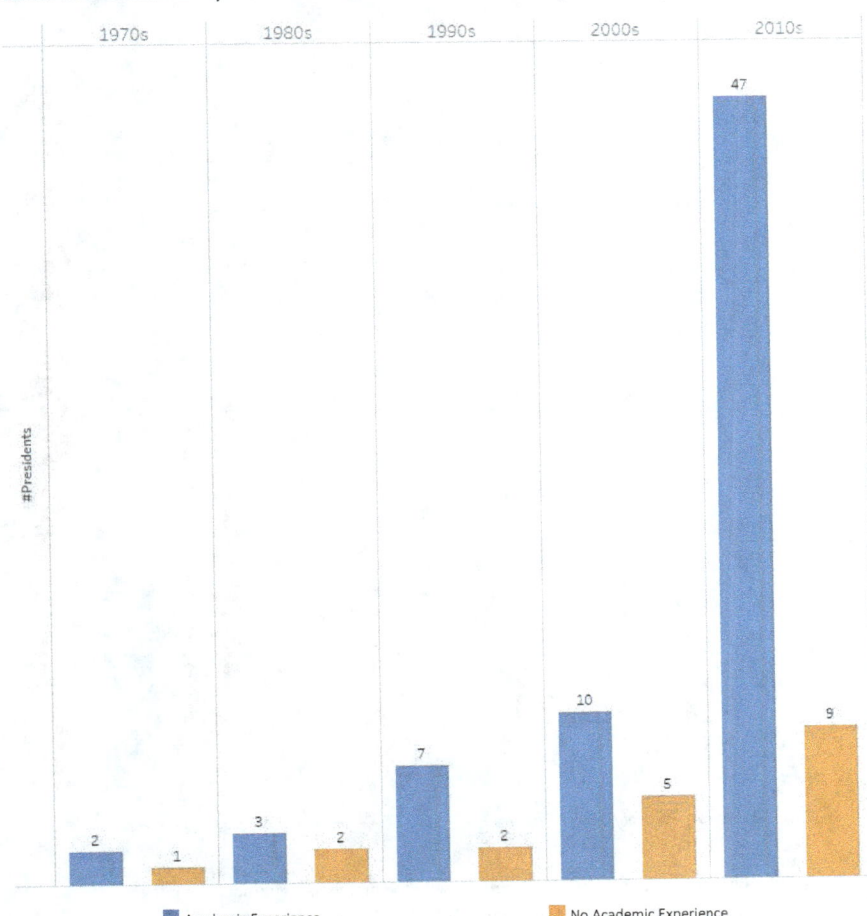

Notes
- This graph only goes back to the 1970s, beginning with the first female appointment in 1976.
- Each appointment within a decade is counted by the start of a president's term.
- If a president was appointed twice in the same decade, they are only counted once.
- If a president was appointed in two different decades, they are counted in each decade.
- Appointments do not include presidents of private independent law schools.
- Appointments include presidents, chancellors, and CEOs.
- Interim positions are also included, and, if known, are generally considered as separate appointments from permanent positions.
- Presidents who started their appointment in 2020 and after are not included within this graph.

number of women lawyer presidents without such credentials. Chart 5.9 shows that of the eighty female lawyer presidents over the last fifty years, 77.5% had prior academic experience. In examining chart 4.2, which looks at all lawyer

Chart 5.9. Lawyer Presidents with Prior Academic Experience (by Decade and Gender)

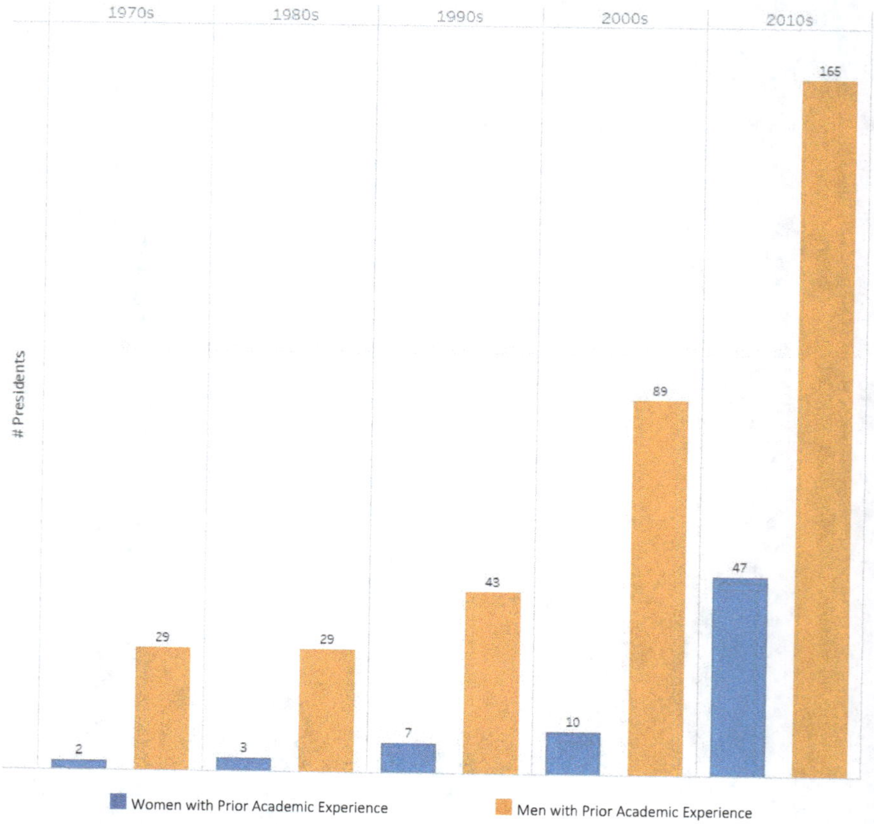

Decade	Women with Prior Academic Experience	Men with Prior Academic Experience
1970s	2	29
1980s	3	29
1990s	7	43
2000s	10	89
2010s	47	165

Notes
- This graph only goes back to the 1970s, beginning with the first female appointment in 1976.
- Each appointment within a decade is counted by the start of a President's term.
- If a president was appointed twice in the same decade, they are only counted once.
- If a president was appointed in two different decades, they are counted in each decade.
- Appointments do not include presidents of private independent law schools.
- Appointments include presidents, chancellors, and CEOs.
- Interim positions are also included, and, if known, are generally considered as separate appointments from permanent positions.
- Presidents who started their appointment in 2020 and after are not included within this graph.
- Two current presidents have unidentified start dates for their terms. They are not included in this graph.

presidents with prior academic experience by the decade, as compared to chart 5.10, which focuses solely on the prior academic experience of women lawyer presidents, there is no real difference in the 2010s with respect to the percentage of lawyer presidents with prior academic experience.

Chart 5.10. Female Lawyer Presidents with Prior Academic Experience (1970–2019)

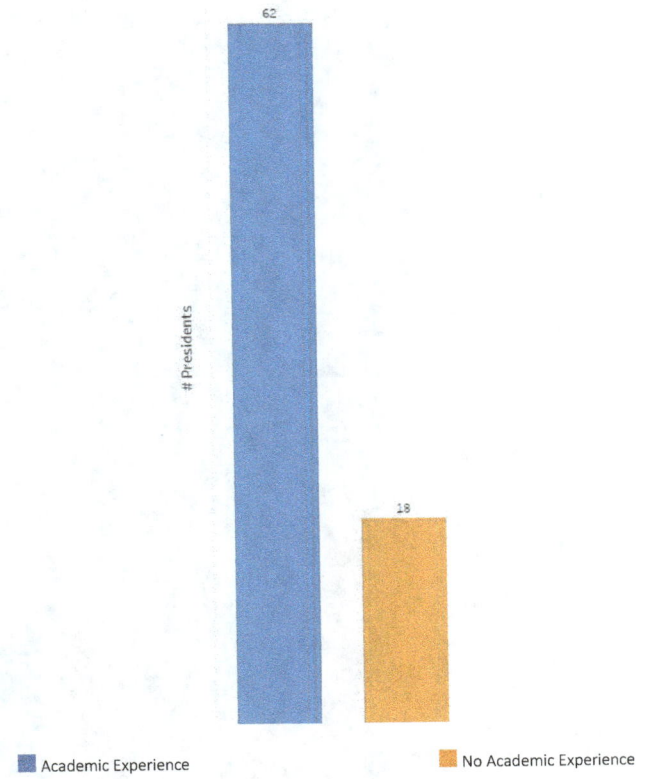

Notes
- This graph only goes back to the 1970s, beginning with the first female appointment in 1976.
- This graph represents each president once, even if they have multiple appointments.
- Appointments do not include presidents of private independent law schools.
- Appointments include presidents, chancellors, and CEOs.
- Interim positions are also included, and, if known, are generally considered as separate appointments from permanent positions.
- Presidents who started their appointment in 2020 and after are not included within this graph.

Chart 5.11. Female Lawyer Presidents with Prior Law Professor Experience (by Decade)

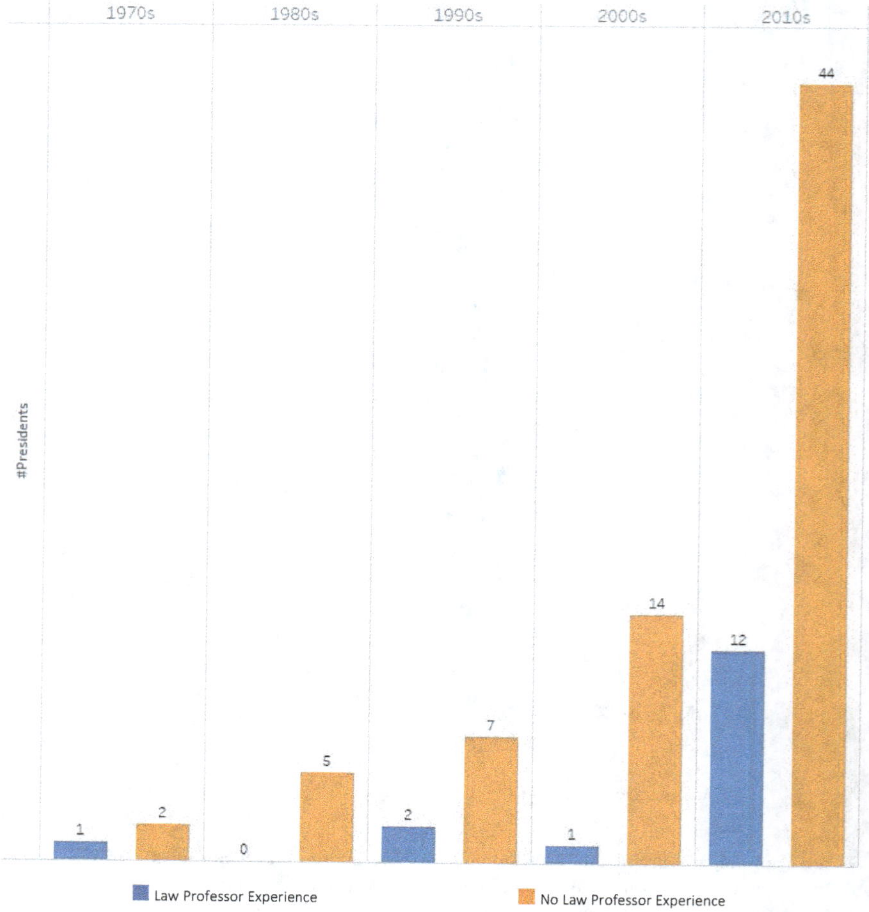

Decade	Law Professor Experience	No Law Professor Experience
1970s	1	2
1980s	0	5
1990s	2	7
2000s	1	14
2010s	12	44

Notes
- This graph only goes back to the 1970s, beginning with the first female appointment in 1976.
- Each appointment within a decade is counted by the start of a president's term.
- If a president was appointed twice in the same decade, they are only counted once.
- If a president was appointed in two different decades, they are counted in each decade.
- Appointments do not include presidents of private independent law schools.
- Appointments include presidents, chancellors, and CEOs.
- Interim positions are also included, and, if known, are generally considered as separate appointments from permanent positions.
- Presidents who started their appointment in 2020 and after are not included within this graph.

Charts 5.11, 5.12, and 5.13 examine the data regarding female lawyer presidents who had prior experience as law professors. Chart 5.11 shows cumulatively over the last fifty years that most women lawyer presidents did not have law professor

Chart 5.12. Lawyer Presidents with Prior Law Professor Experience (by Decade)

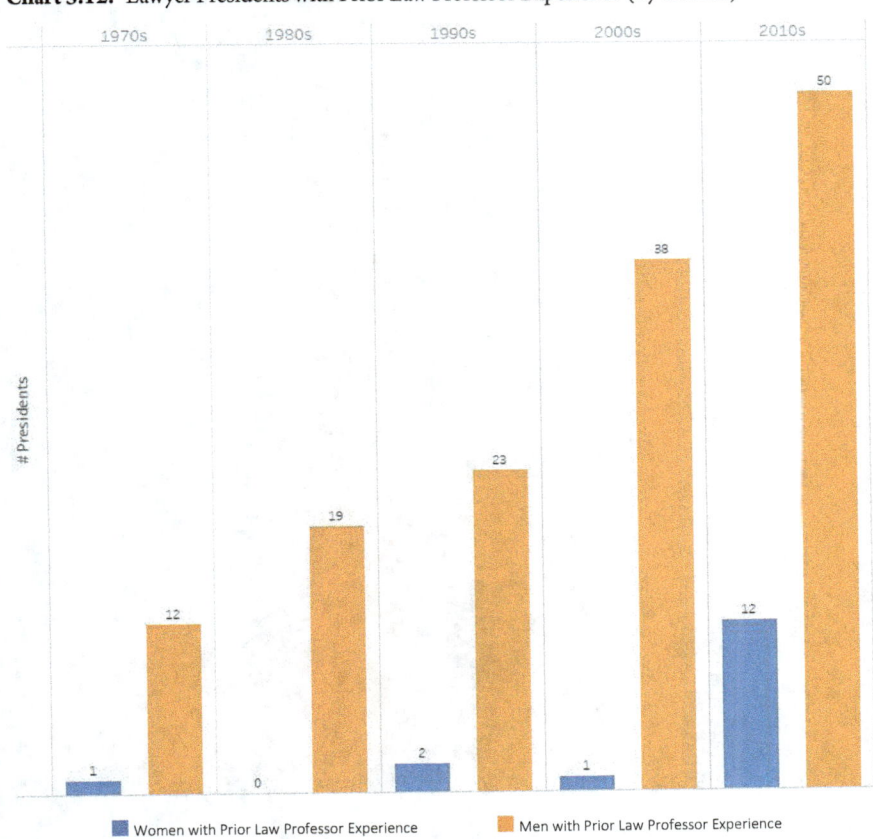

Notes
- This graph only goes back to the 1970s, beginning with the first female appointment in 1976.
- Each appointment within a decade is counted by the start of a president's term.
- If a president was appointed twice in the same decade, they are only counted once.
- If a president was appointed in two different decades, they are counted in each decade.
- Appointments do not include presidents of private independent law schools.
- Appointments include presidents, chancellors, and CEOs.
- Interim positions are also included, and, if known, are generally considered as separate appointments from permanent positions.
- Presidents who started their appointment in 2020 and after are not included within this graph.
- Two current presidents have unidentified start dates for their terms. They are not included in this graph.

experience (80%). Chart 5.12 illustrates that in the last decade the number of women lawyer presidents who did have law professor experience increased substantially.

Chart 5.13. Female Lawyer Presidents with Prior Law Professor Experience (1970–2019)

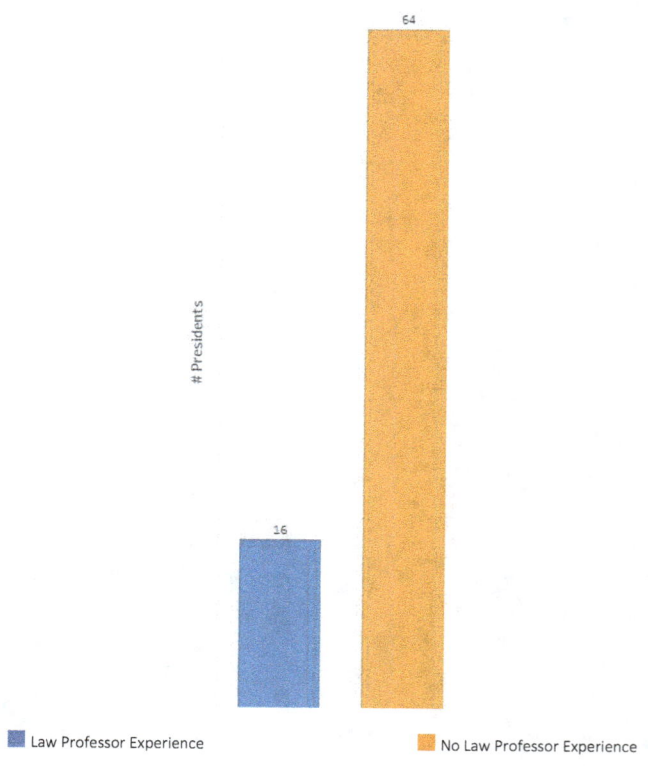

Notes
- This graph only goes back to the 1970s, beginning with the first female appointment in 1976.
- This graph represents each president once, even if they have multiple appointments.
- Appointments do not include presidents of private independent law schools.
- Appointments include presidents, chancellors, and CEOs.
- Interim positions are also included, and, if known, are generally considered as separate appointments from permanent positions.
- Presidents who started their appointment in 2020 and after are not included within this graph.

Chart 5.14. Female Lawyer Presidents with Prior Law Dean Experience (by Decade)

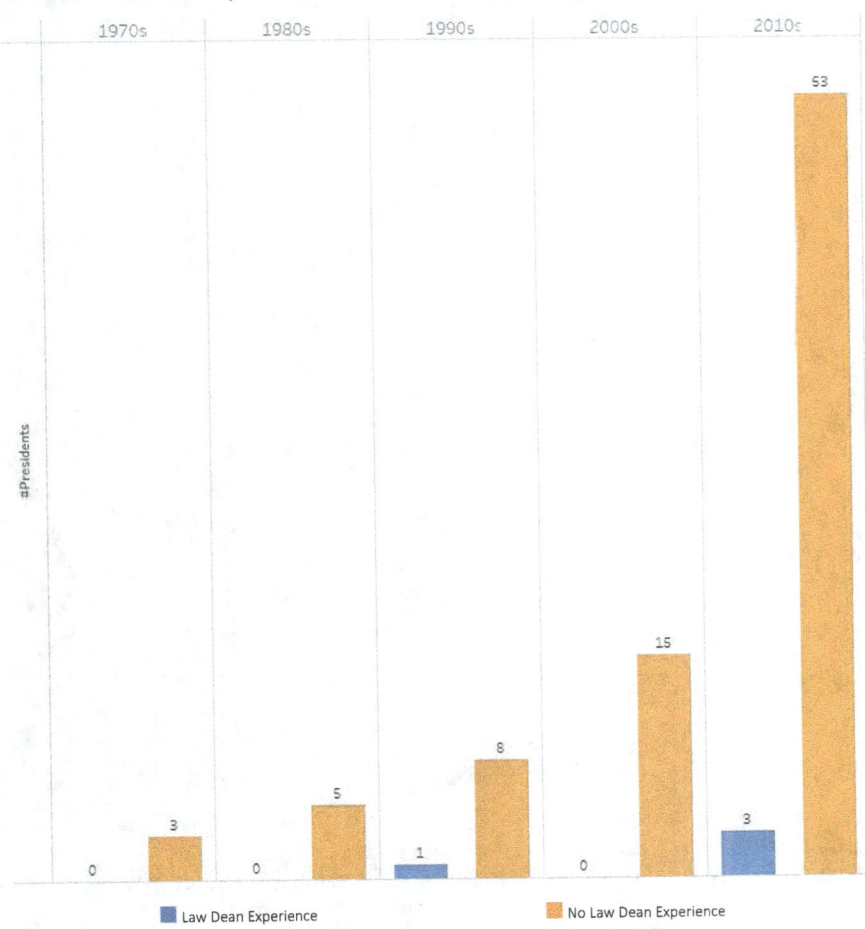

Notes
- This graph only goes back to the 1970s, beginning with the first female appointment in 1976.
- Each appointment within a decade is counted by the start of a president's term.
- If a president was appointed twice in the same decade, they are only counted once.
- If a president was appointed in two different decades, they are counted in each decade.
- Appointments do not include presidents of private independent law schools.
- Appointments include presidents, chancellors, and CEOs.
- Interim positions are also included, and, if known, are generally considered as separate appointments from permanent positions.
- Presidents who started their appointment in 2020 and after are not included within this graph.

Exploring the data regarding women lawyer presidents and their prior experience as a law dean, charts 5.14, 5.15, and 5.16 show that the number is very small as compared with their male counterparts. The charts reveal that over the last fifty years only four female lawyer presidents were law deans, yet chart 5.14 shows the by the 2010s, when the count for women was three, the count for men

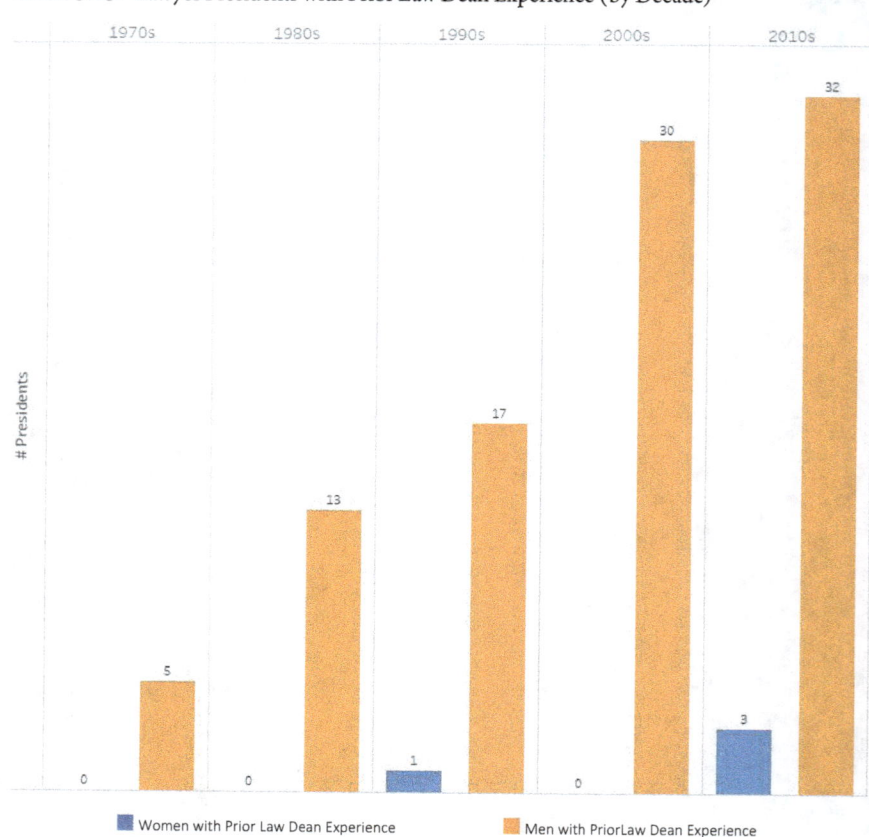

Chart 5.15. Lawyer Presidents with Prior Law Dean Experience (by Decade)

Notes
- This graph only goes back to the 1970s, beginning with the first female appointment in 1976.
- Each appointment within a decade is counted by the start of a president's term.
- If a president was appointed twice in the same decade, they are only counted once.
- If a president was appointed in two different decades, they are counted in each decade.
- Appointments do not include presidents of private independent law schools.
- Appointments include presidents, chancellors, and CEOs.
- Interim positions are also included, and, if known, are generally considered as separate appointments from permanent positions.
- Presidents who started their appointment in 2020 and after are not included within this graph.
- Two current presidents have unidentified start dates for their terms. They are not included in this graph.

was thirty-two. This is a good trend as it shows that women lawyers did not have to serve as a law dean to demonstrate qualifications for the presidency, and this is important because of the historically low number of female law deans. In 1998 there were a mere fourteen women law deans, which had more than doubled to the low thirties by 2006.[2] By 2017 the number of women law deans increased

---

[2] Laura M. Padilla, "A Gendered Update on Women Law Deans: Who, Where, Why, and Why Not?" *Journal of Gender, Social Policy & the Law* 15, no. 3 (2007): 443–546, accessed

Chart 5.16. Female Lawyer Presidents with Prior Law Dean Experience (1970–2019)

Notes
- This graph only goes back to the 1970s, beginning with the first female appointment in 1976.
- This graph represents each president once, even if they have multiple appointments.
- Appointments do not include presidents of private independent law schools.
- Appointments include presidents, chancellors, and CEOs.
- Interim positions are also included, and, if known, are generally considered as separate appointments from permanent positions.
- Presidents who started their appointment in 2020 and after are not included within this graph.

to about 30% of all law deans,[3] making it possible to see more women lawyer presidents with law dean experience in the future.

September 22, 2021, https://digitalcommons.wcl.american.edu/cgi/viewcontent.cgi?referer=https://www.google.com/&httpsredir=1&article=1253&context=jgspl

3 "If It's a New Law Dean, It's Likely and Woman," *Law.com*, March 30, 2017, accessed September 22, 2021, https://www.law.com/sites/almstaff/2017/03/30/if-its-a-new-law-dean-its-likely-a-woman/.

Chart 5.17. Female Lawyer Presidents with Prior Provost Experience (by Decade)

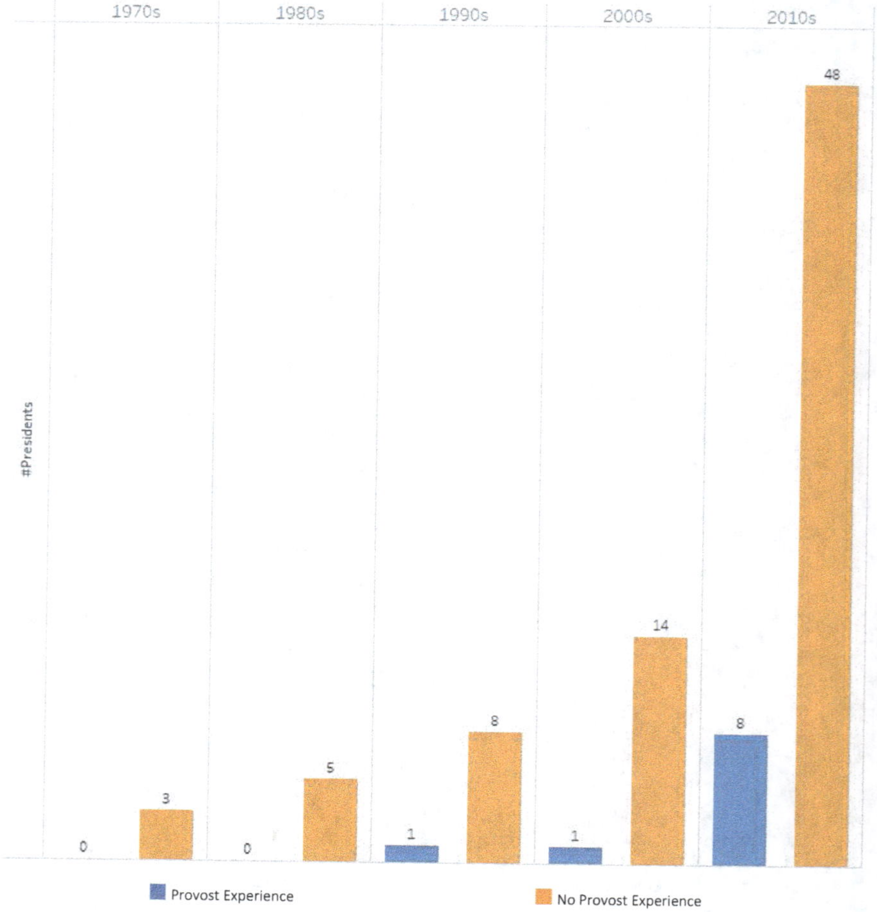

Decade	Provost Experience	No Provost Experience
1970s	0	3
1980s	0	5
1990s	1	8
2000s	1	14
2010s	8	48

Notes
- This graph only goes back to the 1970s, beginning with the first female appointment in 1976.
- Each appointment within a decade is counted by the start of a president's term.
- If a president was appointed twice in the same decade, they are only counted once.
- If a president was appointed in two different decades, they are counted in each decade.
- Appointments do not include presidents of private independent law schools.
- Appointments include presidents, chancellors, and CEOs.
- Interim positions are also included, and, if known, are generally considered as separate appointments from permanent positions.
- Presidents who started their appointment in 2020 and after are not included within this graph.

The next three charts focus on the number of female lawyer presidents who have had prior experience serving as a college or university provost. Chart 5.17 shows that only ten women lawyer presidents have served in this capacity over the last fifty years (12.5%). Most of the women presidents with provost

Chart 5.18. Lawyer Presidents with Prior Provost Experience (by Decade)

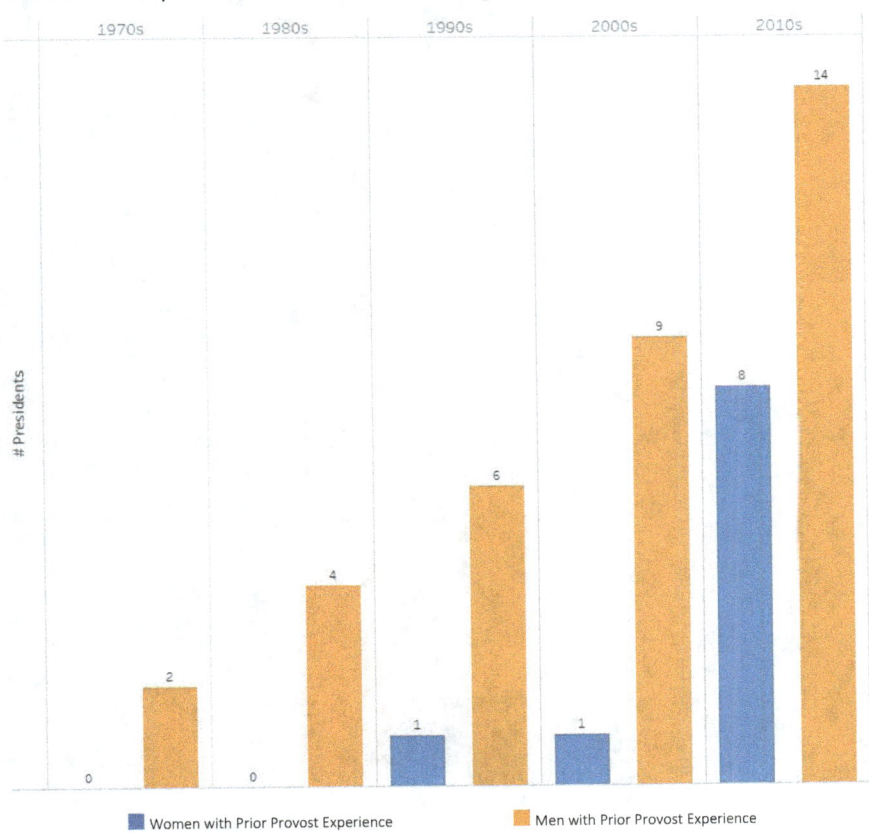

Notes
- This graph only goes back to the 1970s, beginning with the first female appointment in 1976.
- Each appointment within a decade is counted by the start of a president's term.
- If a president was appointed twice in the same decade, they are only counted once.
- If a president was appointed in two different decades, they are counted in each decade.
- Appointments do not include presidents of private independent law schools.
- Appointments include presidents, chancellors, and CEOs.
- Interim positions are also included, and, if known, are generally considered as separate appointments from permanent positions.
- Presidents who started their appointment in 2020 and after are not included within this graph.
- Two current presidents have unidentified start dates for their terms. They are not included in this graph.

experience have been appointed in the last decade (eight out of the ten) as shown on chart 5.18. Although as previously discussed, the number of lawyer presidents with prior provost experience in general is relatively low, chart 5.18 shows that men outnumber women in having served in this role. This data diverges from the 2017 ACE Demographic Profile of America's College and

Chart 5.19. Female Lawyer Presidents with Prior Provost Experience (1970–2019)

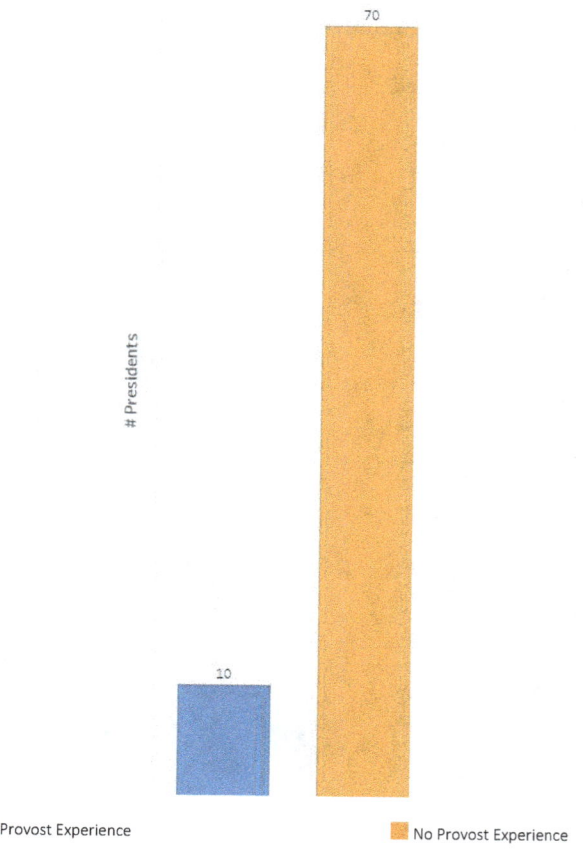

Notes
- This graph only goes back to the 1970s, beginning with the first female appointment in 1976.
- This graph represents each president once, even if they have multiple appointments.
- Appointments do not include presidents of private independent law schools.
- Appointments include presidents, chancellors, and CEOs.
- Interim positions are also included, and, if known, are generally considered as separate appointments from permanent positions.
- Presidents who started their appointment in 2020 and after are not included within this graph.

University Presidents, which reports that 35% of all women presidents served as provost/chief academic officer prior to the appointment as president.[4] It shows that women lawyers are entering the presidency from more nonconventional pathways.

---

4   "2017 Overview, Women Presidents," *American Council on Education*, accessed August 29, 2021, https://www.aceacps.org/women-presidents/, noting that women were more likely than men to have served in this role.

Women Lawyer Presidents and Prior Experience in Government, as General Counsel, Trustee, and Fundraiser

Prior government experience, as previously discussed, is a significant common background shared by many lawyer presidents. Chart 5.20 illustrates that

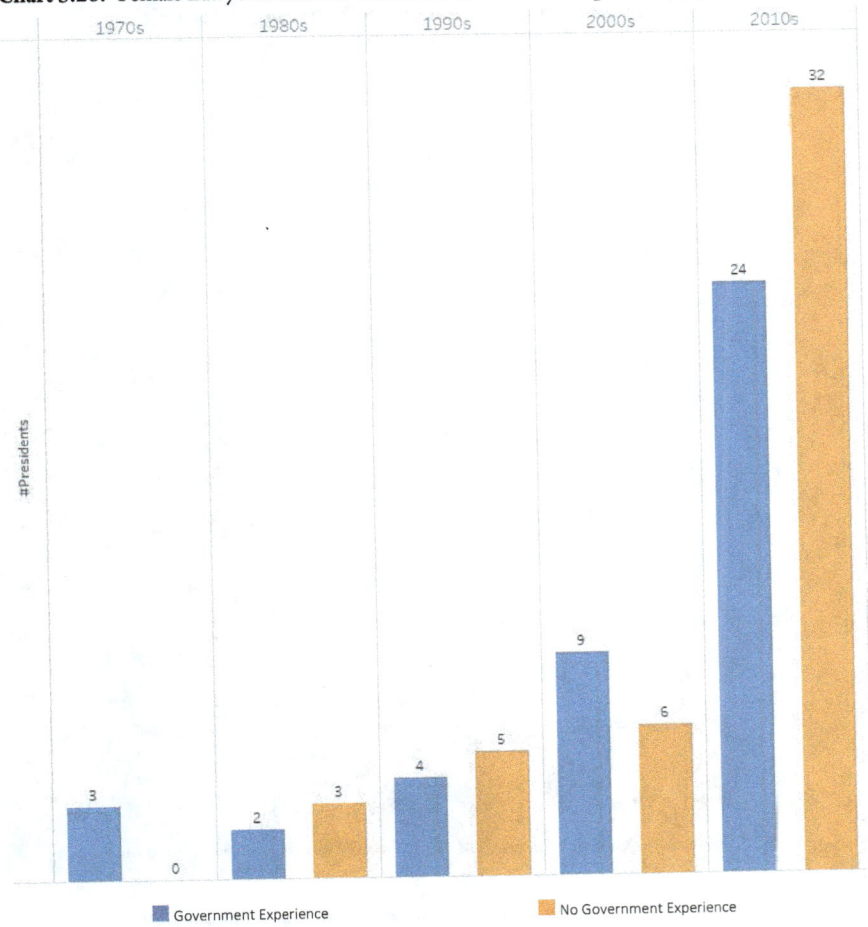

Chart 5.20. Female Lawyer Presidents with Prior Government Experience (by Decade)

Notes
- This graph only goes back to the 1970s, beginning with the first female appointment in 1976.
- Each appointment within a decade is counted by the start of a president's term.
- If a president was appointed twice in the same decade, they are only counted once.
- If a president was appointed in two different decades, they are counted in each decade.
- Appointments do not include presidents of private independent law schools.
- Appointments include presidents, chancellors, and CEOs.
- Interim positions are also included, and, if known, are generally considered as separate appointments from permanent positions.
- Presidents who started their appointment in 2020 and after are not included within this graph.

less than 50% of women lawyer presidents had prior government experience (47.5%). While chart 5.21 shows that the number of female lawyer presidents with prior government experience has been increasing in the last three decades, chart 5.21 demonstrates the significant lag behind their male counterparts. In looking at the last decade, of all of the lawyer presidents with prior government

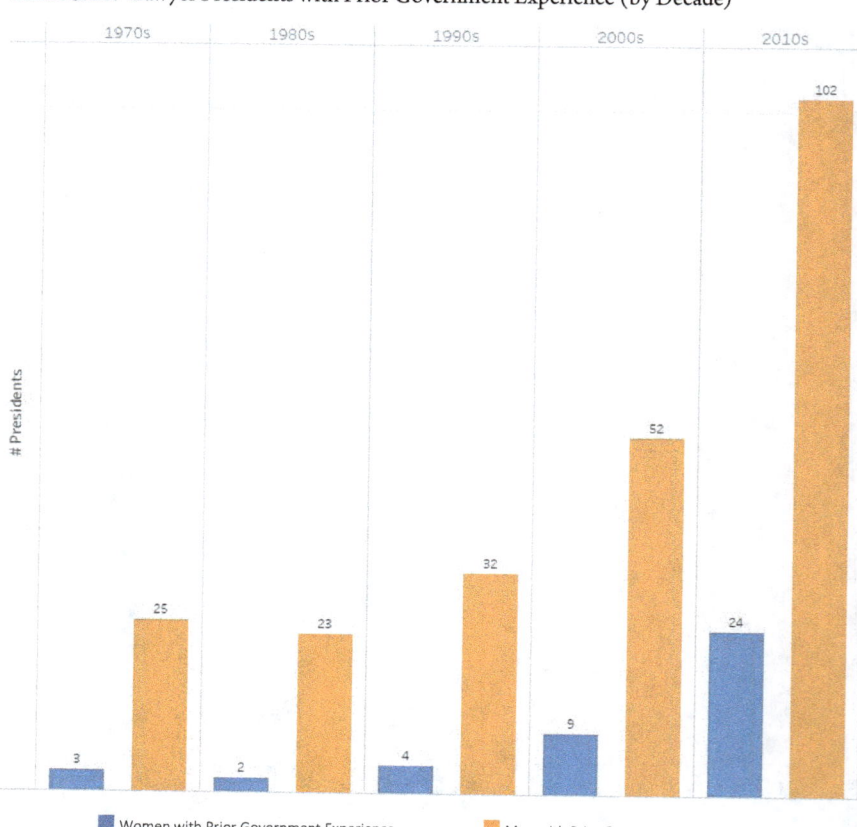

Chart 5.21. Lawyer Presidents with Prior Government Experience (by Decade)

Notes
- This graph only goes back to the 1970s, beginning with the first female appointment in 1976.
- Each appointment within a decade is counted by the start of a president's term.
- If a president was appointed twice in the same decade, they are only counted once.
- If a president was appointed in two different decades, they are counted in each decade.
- Appointments do not include presidents of private independent law schools.
- Appointments include presidents, chancellors, and CEOs.
- Interim positions are also included, and, if known, are generally considered as separate appointments from permanent positions.
- Presidents who started their appointment in 2020 and after are not included within this graph.
- Two current presidents have unidentified start dates for their terms. They are not included in this graph.

Chart 5.22. Female Lawyer Presidents with Prior Government Experience (1970–2019)

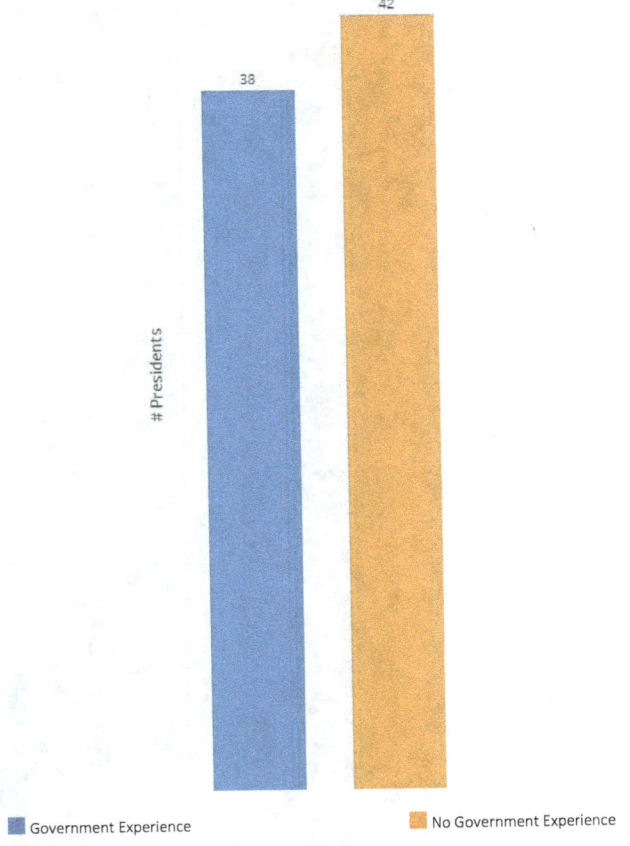

Notes
- This graph only goes back to the 1970s, beginning with the first female appointment in 1976.
- This graph represents each president once, even if they have multiple appointments.
- Appointments do not include presidents of private independent law schools.
- Appointments include presidents, chancellors, and CEOs.
- Interim positions are also included, and, if known, are generally considered as separate appointments from permanent positions.
- Presidents who started their appointment in 2020 and after are not included within this graph.

experience, women represented 19.2% of this demographic, which is an increase from 15% in the 2000s.

Exploring the more recent trend of higher education general counsel being desirable candidates for institutional leadership, charts 5.23, 5.24, and 5.25 look at the number of female lawyer presidents with this background. Chart 5.23 show that over the last fifty years only 12.5% of women lawyer presidents

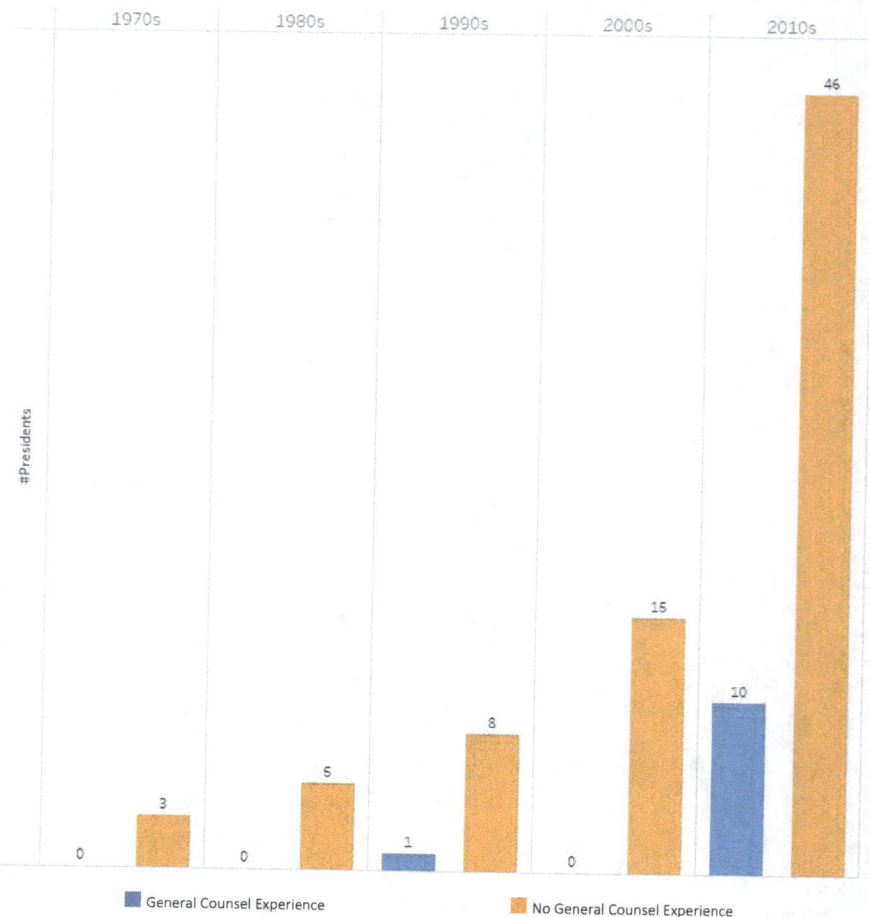

Chart 5.23. Female Lawyer Presidents with Prior General Counsel Experience (by Decade)

Notes
- This graph only goes back to the 1970s, beginning with the first female appointment in 1976.
- Each appointment within a decade is counted by the start of a president's term.
- If a president was appointed twice in the same decade, they are only counted once.
- If a president was appointed in two different decades, they are counted in each decade.
- Appointments do not include presidents of private independent law schools.
- Appointments include presidents, chancellors, and CEOs.
- Interim positions are also included, and, if known, are generally considered as separate appointments from permanent positions.
- Presidents who started their appointment in 2020 and after are not included within this graph.

had previously served as general counsel to a college or university. However, chart 5.24 reveals that this number has grown from zero in the 2000s to over 20% in the 2010s. As chart 5.24 shows, there was only one female lawyer

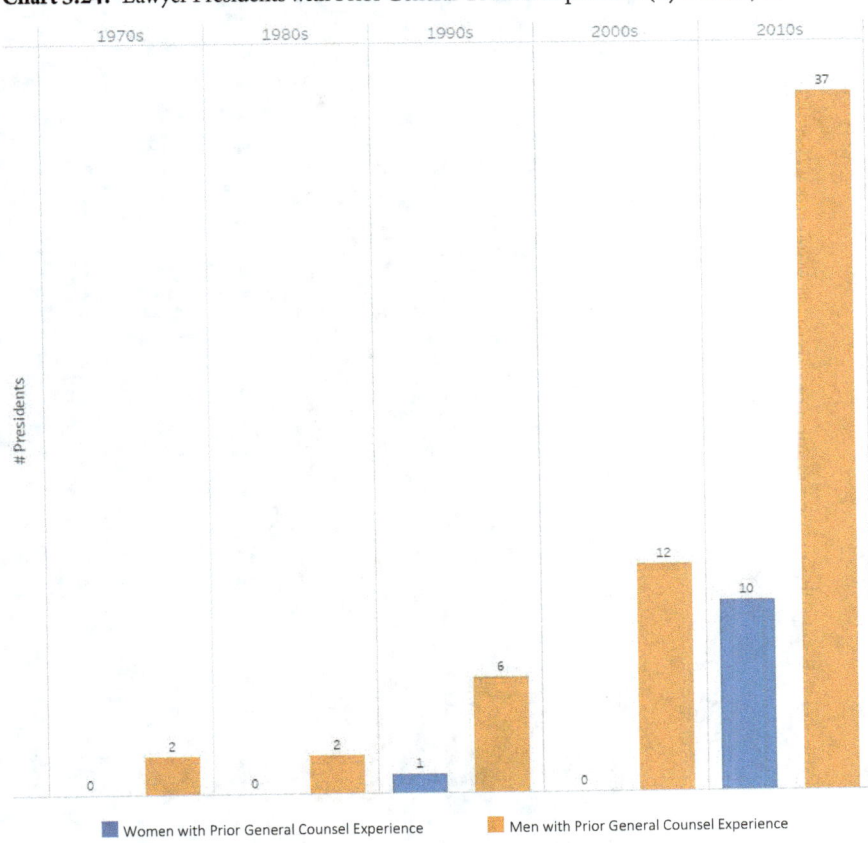

Chart 5.24. Lawyer Presidents with Prior General Counsel Experience (by Decade)

Notes
- This graph only goes back to the 1970s, beginning with the first female appointment in 1976.
- Each appointment within a decade is counted by the start of a president's term.
- If a president was appointed twice in the same decade, they are only counted once.
- If a president was appointed in two different decades, they are counted in each decade.
- Appointments do not include presidents of private independent law schools.
- Appointments include presidents, chancellors, and CEOs.
- Interim positions are also included, and, if known, are generally considered as separate appointments from permanent positions.
- Presidents who started their appointment in 2020 and after are not included within this graph.
- Two current presidents have unidentified start dates for their terms. They are not included in this graph.

president with prior general counsel experience in the 1990s, and other than that decade and the 2010s, the number was zero.

As all campus leaders today are engaged in non-tuition resource generation for their institutions, it is not only common, but it is essential for presidents to have some prior experience in fundraising. This experience can come from prior

Chart 5.25. Female Lawyer Presidents with Prior General Counsel Experience (1970–2019)

Notes
- This graph only goes back to the 1970s, beginning with the first female appointment in 1976.
- This graph represents each president once, even if they have multiple appointments.
- Appointments do not include presidents of private independent law schools.
- Appointments include presidents, chancellors, and CEOs.
- Interim positions are also included, and, if known, are generally considered as separate appointments from permanent positions.
- Presidents who started their appointment in 2020 and after are not included within this graph.

academic roles, such as a dean who raises funds for their departments, from prior government experience since many had to directly raise campaign funds for themselves or others, or from formal experience as a development/institutional advancement officer in higher education. For purposes of the data below, the lawyer presidents identified as having prior fundraising experience where those who had paid employment as a professional fundraiser.

The data in chart 5.26 reveals that women lawyer presidents have not had formal higher education fundraising as prior work experience. As chart 5.26 shows, over the last fifty years only a total of four out of eighty or 5% of all women lawyer presidents fit this profile. However, when compared to the male lawyer

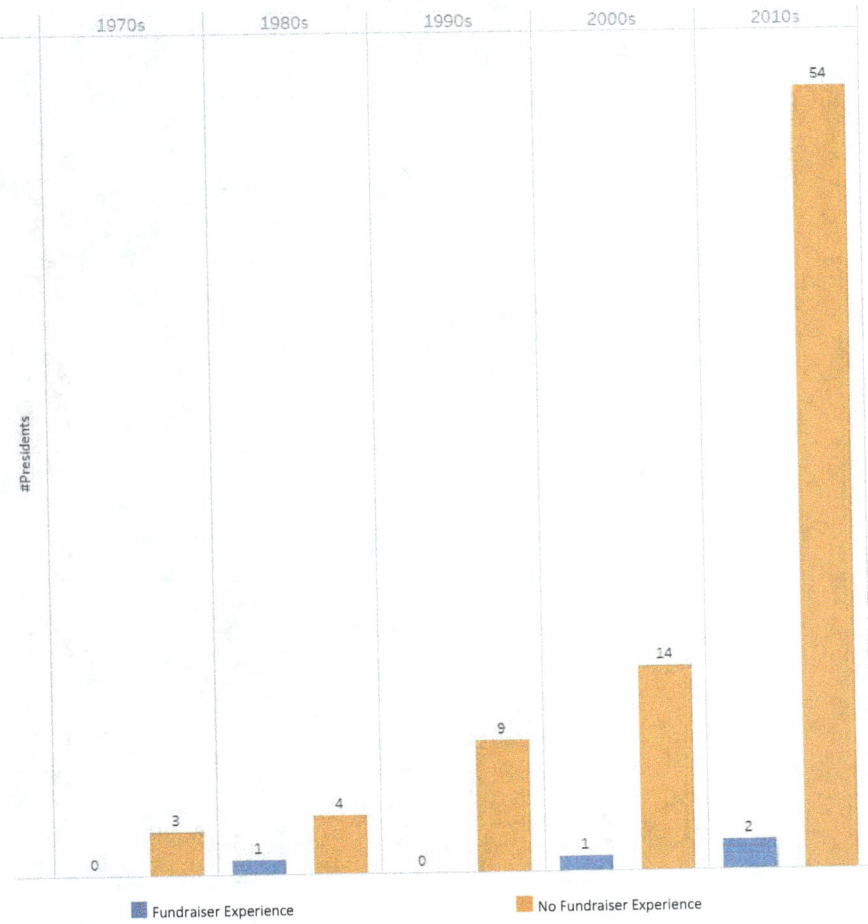

Chart 5.26. Female Lawyer Presidents with Prior Fundraiser Experience (by Decade)

Notes
- This graph only goes back to the 1970s, beginning with the first female appointment in 1976.
- Each appointment within a decade is counted by the start of a president's term.
- If a president was appointed twice in the same decade, they are only counted once.
- If a president was appointed in two different decades, they are counted in each decade.
- Appointments do not include presidents of private independent law schools.
- Appointments include presidents, chancellors, and CEOs.
- Interim positions are also included, and, if known, are generally considered as separate appointments from permanent positions.
- Presidents who started their appointment in 2020 and after are not included within this graph.

presidents in chart 5.27, despite the small numbers, women seemed to keep pace with the men in the last two decades with the percentage increase from the 2000s (8.3%) to the 2010s (7.6%).

Another recent trend has been the appointment of members of higher education boards of trustees to lead institutions (regardless of whether they are tapped

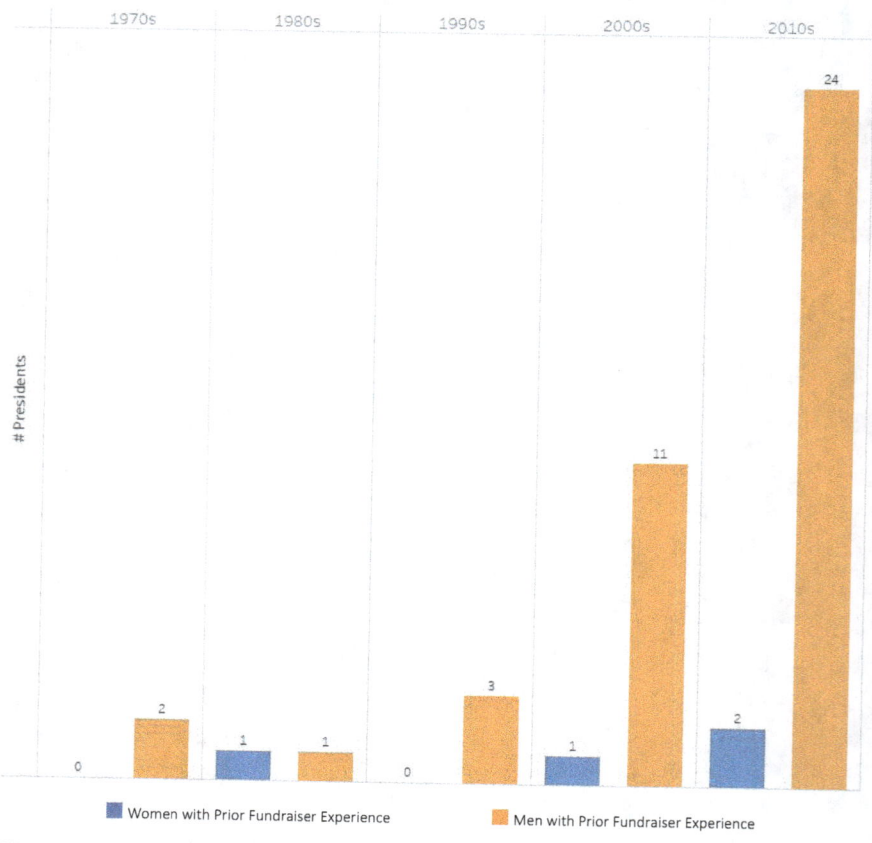

Chart 5.27. Lawyer Presidents with Prior Fundraiser Experience (by Decade)

Notes
- This graph only goes back to the 1970s, beginning with the first female appointment in 1976.
- Each appointment within a decade is counted by the start of a president's term.
- If a president was appointed twice in the same decade, they are only counted once.
- If a president was appointed in two different decades, they are counted in each decade.
- Appointments do not include presidents of private independent law schools.
- Appointments include presidents, chancellors, and CEOs.
- Interim positions are also included, and, if known, are generally considered as separate appointments from permanent positions.
- Presidents who started their appointment in 2020 and after are not included within this graph.
- Two current presidents have unidentified start dates for their terms. They are not included in this graph.

Chart 5.28. Female Lawyer Presidents with Prior Fundraiser Experience (1970–2019)

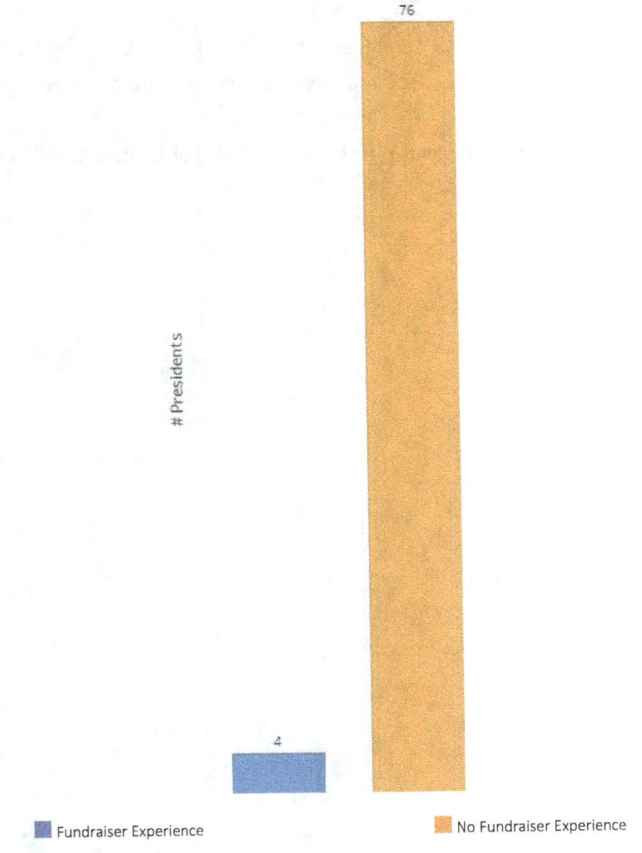

Notes
- This graph only goes back to the 1970s, beginning with the first female appointment in 1976.
- This graph represents each president once, even if they have multiple appointments.
- Appointments do not include presidents of private independent law schools.
- Appointments include presidents, chancellors, and CEOs.
- Interim positions are also included, and, if known, are generally considered as separate appointments from permanent positions.
- Presidents who started their appointment in 2020 and after are not included within this graph.

to serve the institution on whose board they sat or a different college or university. Interestingly, more women lawyers were tapped as president from this experience than from prior work as a law dean, a provost, general counsel, or as a fundraiser. One plausible explanation is that the boards of trustees are typically the appointing authority for the campus president, and board members have the longitudinal experience working with the (female) board candidates and may have developed a sense of trust and belief of shared vision and experience that does not exist with non-board candidates who are typically otherwise unknown to the Board.

The data below in chart 5.29 shows that 17.5% of all women lawyer presidents previously served on a board of trustees (fourteen out of eighty presidents).

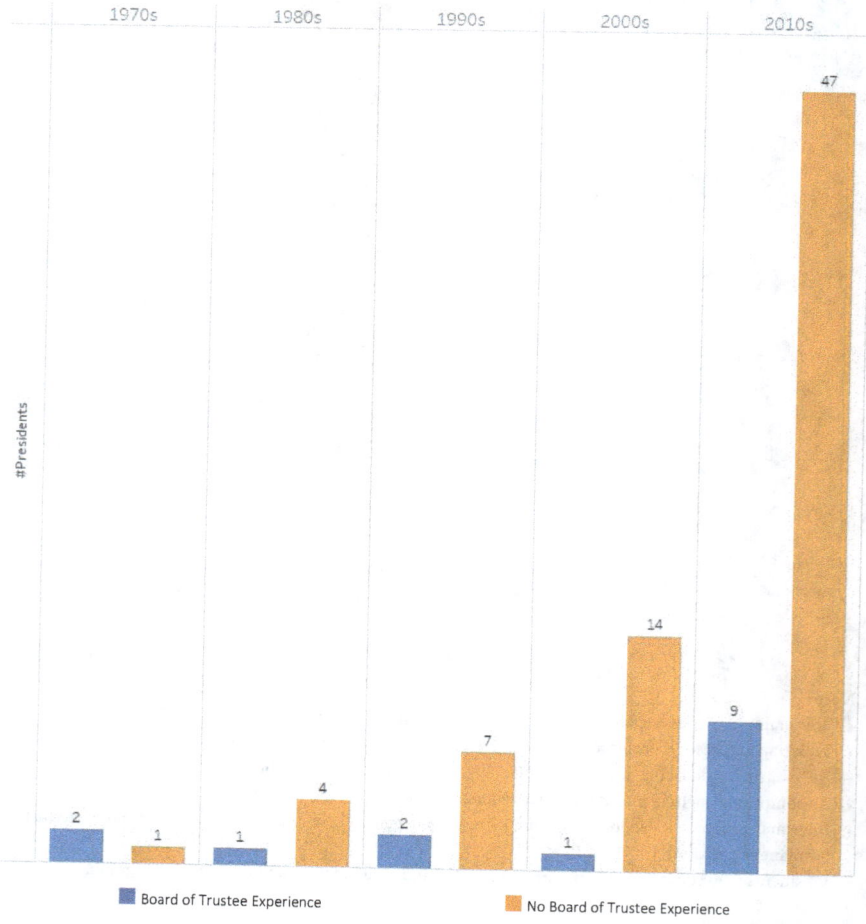

Chart 5.29. Female Lawyer Presidents Who Were Prior Board of Trustees Members (by Decade)

Notes
- This graph only goes back to the 1970s, beginning with the first female appointment in 1976.
- Each appointment within a decade is counted by the start of a president's term.
- If a president was appointed twice in the same decade, they are only counted once.
- If a president was appointed in two different decades, they are counted in each decade.
- Appointments do not include presidents of private independent law schools.
- Appointments include presidents, chancellors, and CEOs.
- Interim positions are also included, and, if known, are generally considered as separate appointments from permanent positions.
- Presidents who started their appointment in 2020 and after are not included within this graph.

Chart 5.30. Lawyer Presidents Who Were Prior Board of Trustees Members (by Decade)

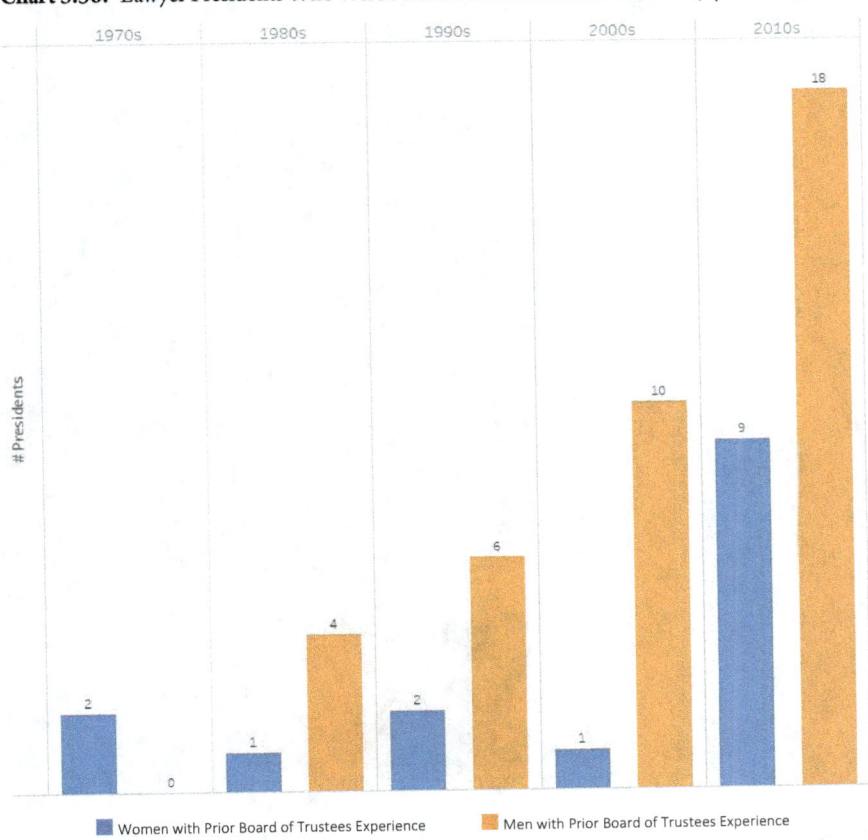

Notes
- This graph only goes back to the 1970s, beginning with the first female appointment in 1976.
- Each appointment within a decade is counted by the start of a president's term.
- If a president was appointed twice in the same decade, they are only counted once.
- If a president was appointed in two different decades, they are counted in each decade.
- Appointments do not include presidents of private independent law schools.
- Appointments include presidents, chancellors, and CEOs.
- Interim positions are also included, and, if known, are generally considered as separate appointments from permanent positions.
- Presidents who started their appointment in 2020 and after are not included within this graph.
- Two current presidents have unidentified start dates for their terms. They are not included in this graph.

There was a large jump in numbers in the 2010s as nine of the fourteen were appointed in the last decade (see chart 5.29) representing 33% of all lawyer presidents who previously served on a board of trustees. With small numbers in the preceding decades, it is difficult to draw conclusions based on the data in chart 5.30 other than appointing boards were more open to selecting women lawyer board members as campus leaders in the last decade.

Chart 5.31. Female Lawyer Presidents Who Were Prior Board of Trustees Members (by Decade)

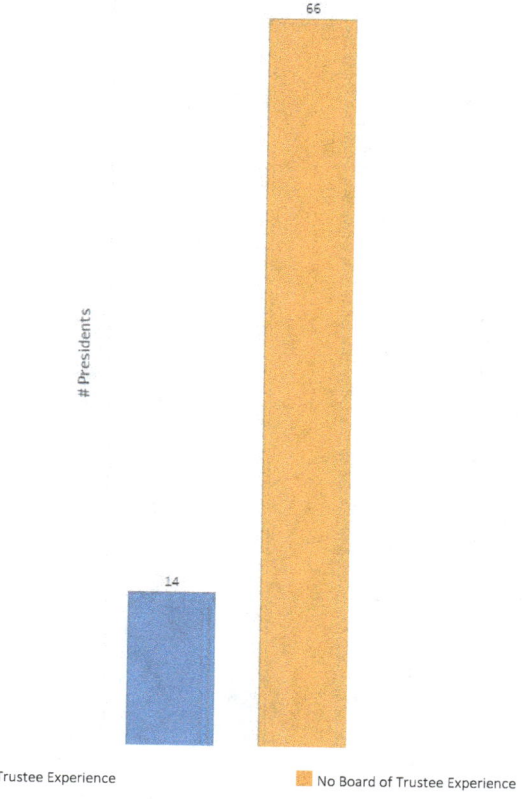

Notes
- This graph only goes back to the 1970s, beginning with the first female appointment in 1976.
- This graph represents each president once, even if they have multiple appointments.
- Appointments do not include presidents of private independent law schools.
- Appointments include presidents, chancellors, and CEOs.
- Interim positions are also included, and, if known, are generally considered as separate appointments from permanent positions.
- Presidents who started their appointment in 2020 and after are not included within this graph.

Women Leading Higher Education—Public Opinion

The White House Project in 2007 reported that 94% of those surveyed were comfortable with a woman leading an institution of higher education,[5] yet

---

5   *The White House Project Report: Benchmarking Women's Leadership* (New York: White House Project, 2009), 8, accessed September 9, 2021, https://www.in.gov/icw/files/benchmark_wom_leadership.pdf.

women held only 23% of the leadership positions in education.[6] The report noted the following.

- Nationally, women are 57% of all college students but only 26% of full professors, 23% of university presidents and 14% of presidents at the doctoral degree-granting institutions.
- The number of female presidents has not changed in the last ten years.
- Women account for less than 30% of the board members on college and university boards.
- Female faculty have not made any progress in closing the salary gap with their male counterparts. In 1972, they made 83% of what male faculty made; today they make 82% of what male faculty make.[7]

The report continued, "About two decades ago, women started making important strides toward the top at institutions of higher learning—the presidency. Women currently make up 23 percent of the presidents at colleges and universities, up from only 9.5 percent two decades ago. But for the last 10 years the number of female presidents has held steady at about 500. Unchanged, too, is the pattern that, as the degree-level awarded by the institution rises, women's representation at the top declines. Women today account for 29 percent of presidents at two-year colleges, compared with 14 percent at universities that grant doctoral degrees."[8]

The White House Project closed in 2012, and in 2013 the Colorado Women's College of the University of Denver filled the void and issued an updated report, *Benchmarking Women's Leadership in the United States*.[9] Key findings in this study regarding women in higher education included the fact that "women led five of the eight Ivy League institutions,"[10] and that "women comprise an average of 24.53 of positional leaders in academia."[11] The report pointed out though that all of the five Ivy League schools were chartered before the American Revolution

---

6   Ibid., 9.
7   Ibid., 10.
8   Ibid., 19.
9   Tiffani Lennon, *Benchmarking Women's Leadership in the United States* (Denver, CO: Colorado Women's College, University of Denver, 2013), https://www.issuelab.org/resources/26706/26706.pdf.
10 The five Ivy League institutions are: Brown, Dartmouth, Harvard, Princeton, and the University of Pennsylvania. See ibid., 19.
11 Ibid., 8.

but it took 200 years to appoint a woman president, with the University of Pennsylvania being the first.[12]

Women Campus Presidents Matter

It matters that women are appointed to leadership roles in higher education. For one reason, they serve as important role models to younger female students and they are role models for other women in all levels and positions in academia. Despite the fact that the number of women earning higher education degrees has significantly increased, and in fact 56% of all undergraduate degrees are earned by women,[13] they still lag behind men in leadership positions in the academy.

As previously discussed, the American Council on Education (ACE) noted in their 2017 American College Presidents Study that there is still a wide long-standing gender gap within the ranks of the campus presidency.[14] Although the ACE report documents that since the first Presidents survey in 1986 the number of women presidents has tripled, the percentage of women presidents only grew by 4% between 2011 and 2016.[15] In exploring the journey to the presidency for women, the ACE 2017 study reported on familial status noting that 74.7% of the women presidents were currently married while 89.8% of their male counterparts were married, and that 73.7% of the women presidents had children yet 88.6% of the male presidents had children.[16] 10% of women presidents had never been married.[17]

These data points compel the question of whether women have felt at some level they had to forgo marriage and children to rise within their chosen field. In terms of career history, fewer women than men were appointed as president from outside of the academy (15.9% of men and 13.6% of women) and women presidents were more likely than their male counterparts to have served in the role of provost or chief academic officer (46.1% of women compared to 41.1% of men).[18] Women presidents are also more likely than male presidents to hold a PhD or an EdD (86% of women as compared to 77% of men).[19]

---

12 Ibid., 19.
13 Gagliardi et al., *American College President Study 2017*, 29.
14 Ibid.
15 Ibid.
16 Ibid., 30.
17 Ibid., 30.
18 Ibid., 32.
19 Ibid.

Although the first woman president was appointed in 1871 (albeit of an all-women's school and when it merged with a university, she was simply appointed dean of women and not president), it was not until 1925 that a woman was appointed to lead a coeducational institution, after her husband, who was president, died. It was not until the 1980s that women lawyers were first appointed as college and university presidents. Still, between 1980 and 2001 only eight women lawyers were appointed as College Presidents: 1980—Ellen V. Futter, acting president and president of Barnard College (NY), now president of the American Museum of Natural History; 1986—Linda Lorimer, president of Randolph College (formerly Randolph-Macon Woman's College) (VA), who retired in April 2015 and was Yale's longest serving officer; 1986—Nancy Y. Bekavac, president of Scripps College (CA), now a consultant in higher education; 1989—Patricia McGuire, Trinity University (DC), still serving; 1990—Jamie Studley, president of Skidmore (NY), now president of WASC; 1995—Deborah Stanley, interim president and then president of SUNY Oswego (NY), still serving; 1999—Jennifer Raab, president of Hunter College, CUNY (NY), still serving; and from 1999 to 2013—Pamela Gann, Claremont McKenna College (CA).

The fact that it took until the 1980s for women lawyers to ascend to the campus presidency is not surprising since it was not until 1987 that the American Bar Association announced the Commission on Women in the Profession, chaired by Hillary Rodham Clinton, to "assess the status of women in the legal profession, identify barriers to advancement, and recommend to the ABA actions to address problems identified."[20]

---

20 "Commission on Women in the Profession," *American Bar Association*, accessed September 9, 2021, https://www.americanbar.org/groups/diversty/women/about_us/.

CHAPTER 6

Lawyers Will Continue to Lead Campuses: What Does That Mean for the Future of Higher Education?

In the context of all of higher education, the actual number of lawyer presidents is relatively small and unlikely to produce seismic shifts in higher education as a whole. However, as the data indicates, the number of lawyer presidents has doubled in each of the last three decades, and early indications in Appendix 2, which lists lawyer presidents appointed from the start of the 2020s (through August of 2021) suggests that this trend will continue. Based on the data from the last thirty years, it is likely that by 2029 lawyers will account for 300 to 400 presidents—or more than 10% of all sitting presidents. For campuses who believe they can benefit from leaders who bring certain formal educational training and skill sets to the table, the appointment of a lawyer president can shift the campus culture and can produce desired different results.

Nonetheless, while there will always be "non-traditional" presidents, similar to the non-traditional law deans who are selected from outside of the academy, the data still shows that the majority of college and university presidents who are lawyers come from legal education and from higher education in general. This will continue to be a career path for lawyers who work as professors, law school administrators and lawyers in the central college/university administration who desire to serve the larger campus community and a broader higher education constituency.

Search Firms Are Buzzing about Lawyer Presidents

William Howard, vice president and senior consultant at Academic Search, posted an article on LinkedIn in 2019 noting the appeal of law school deans as college presidents. Robin Mamlet, of Witt/Kiefer, reported that more chief diversity officers, directors of student affairs, and enrollment managers are being considered for presidencies, and in fact some of the lawyer presidents have served in these campus roles. She also noted that many governing boards are now willing to consider candidates from outside of the academy, and this is consistent with a number of lawyer presidents who have emerged from the private sector (although they often had a connection to the particular campus they were tapped to lead). Lawyers by their nature are businesspeople, and, according to search firm experts, governing boards who are composed primarily of business leaders find the slow pace of academic decision making frustrating, so they are looking for candidates able to respect the culture but also to understand the business of higher education and make business-like decisions in quicker timeframes.

A recent study of non-traditional presidents in *Academic Leadership: The Online Journal* looked to the value of past leadership experiences of value to the institution and concluded that those who brought backgrounds in financial skills including fundraising, political sophistication, public policy experience, work with multiple and at times conflicting constituencies, and ability to work with high level governing boards were most desirable.[1]

Influencers and Appointing Authority

It stands to reason that with more college and universities who house law schools within their portfolio, it is likely that law faculty and administrators are tapped to serve on presidential search committees. According to the 2015 survey of the composition of college and university governing board published by the Association on Governing Boards in 2016, data show the biggest change in the percentage of independent college board members with business backgrounds is up from 47.9% in 1997 to 54.9% in 2015 and board members with other professional service (which would include lawyers) also increased, from 16.7% in 1997 to 21.8% in 2015. With more lawyers helping to select the future of campus leadership, their presence and influence in validating the skills that lawyers possess as beneficial, overlapping and essential for successful presidencies certainly helps to explain why more lawyers and legal educators are assuming these top campus leadership spots.

---

1 Delabbio and Palmer, "A 360° View of Non-Traditional University Presidents," 16.

Findings

The Role of Legal Education

The only common denominator that all lawyer presidents share is that they possess an earned juris doctorate degree. After that, as demonstrated in chapter four, they even differ in where they earned the degree and whether they received other formal post-BAccalaureate academic training. They also differ in the career paths that ultimately led them to the campus C-suite.

While legal education has certainly changed over time as the body of law has become more expansive, the American Bar Association's Council on Legal Education continuously adopts changes to the Standard of Legal Education, and law schools experiment with and adopt new experiential opportunities for students combined with curricular modernization, the question remains as to whether there is a foundational role that legal education plays in preparing students for positions of leadership.

Does Legal Education Teach Lawyers to be Leaders?

Lawyers are prone to describe themselves as creative problem solvers who possess necessary leadership skills for success as leaders in law firms, government, business, and increasingly in higher education. But are lawyers born leaders or do lawyers acquire leadership skills as part of their formal academic training? Until very recently, few if any law schools historically included leadership training as a distinct topic of study in the curriculum. In fact, Professor Deborah Rhode wrote in one of the first newsletters of the AALS Section on Leadership, "As you all know, it is a shameful irony that the occupation that produces the greatest number of American leaders has done so little to effectively and intentionally prepare them for that role. Although the legal profession accounts for only about .4 percent of the country's population, it has supplied a majority of American presidents, and innumerable leaders throughout the public and private sector. Few of these individuals receive any formal leadership training in law schools."[2] Rhodes reiterated this sentiment during an AALS interview calling on

---

2 Deborah Rhode, "Section on Leadership: Message from the Chair, 2018," *The Association of American Law Schools*, last modified November 1, 2018, accessed September 2, 2021, https://sectiononleadership.org/2018/11/.

law schools to embrace the need for more formal leadership training, which can and should be more intentionally learned.

The legal academy had paid little attention to this critical topic. Scattered posts on legal education blogs have focused on the addition of a new course at one school,[3] the establishment of the new AALS Section on Leadership and a workshop for law professors[4] interested in integrating leadership-related topics into classes, and the launch of the Leading as Lawyers Blog.[5] Yet, the call for more deliberate inclusion of leadership studies in legal education is rising. Thanks in large part of the efforts of Baylor Law Associate Dean Leah Teague, in 2017 the American Association of Law Schools charted the new Section on Leadership, "to promote scholarship, teaching and related activities that will help prepare lawyers and law students to serve in leadership roles."[6] A panel discussion moderated by Baylor Dean Bradley J. B. Toben on Leadership Programming in Law Schools at the 2020 Baylor Law School Vision for Leadership Conference noted that 80 of the 203 law schools now have some form of leadership development for students.[7] UIC John Marshall Dean Darby Dickerson posited that because of legal training, lawyers are well-positioned to be leaders in a VUCA world (volatility, uncertainty, complexity, and ambiguity).[8] She explained that lawyers are trained to: continuously ask hard questions; find the essence of the problem by breaking it down into subparts—taking it apart and putting it together again; use multiple perspectives; be problem solvers; analyze and cope with fact gaps

---

3   Rosemary Queenan and Mary Walsh, "Leadership Courses: Paving the Path for Future Attorneys," *Best Practices for Legal Education* (blog), entry posted January 30, 2019, accessed September 30, 2021, https://bestpracticeslegaled.com/2019/01/30/leadership-courses-paving-the-way-for-future-attorneys/.

4   Paul Schaefer, "Leadership Education in Law School: You're Already Providing It," *Best Practices for Legal Education* (blog), entry posted January 16, 2019, accessed September 30, 2021, https://bestpracticeslegaled.com/2019/01/16/leadership-education-in-law-school-youre-already-providing-it/.

5   *Leading as Lawyers* (blog), accessed September 30, 2021, https://leadingaslawyers.blog/posts/.

6   "Section on Leadership," *Association of American Law Schools*, accessed September 2, 2021, https://www.aals.org/sections/list/leadership/.

7   "2020 Vision for Leadership Conference at Baylor Law, Law School Deans Panel: Leadership Programing in Law Schools, Monday, September 14, 2020," transcript, *Baylor Law*, last modified September 22, 2020, accessed September 30, 2021, https://www.baylor.edu/law/doc.php/364678.pdf.

8   "2020 Vision for Leadership Conference at Baylor Law, Day 1—Session 1, Reflections on the Challenges Facing Legal Education and Leadership Lessons from the Challenges of 2020," transcript, *Baylor Law*, last modified September 22, 2020, accessed September 30, 2021, https://www.baylor.edu/law/doc.php/364677.pdf.

and ambiguity; understand agreements and honor commitments; communicate clearly and concisely; and be lifelong learners.[9]

In one of her seminal books, Deborah Rhode, writing about leadership traits of lawyers, noted that despite the robust literature on "trait theories" of leadership, the context and roles in which lawyers function are critically important. She explained that the widely accepted traits of successful leaders include:

- values (such as integrity, honesty, trust and an ethic of service);
- personal skills (such as self-awareness, self-control, and self-direction);
- interpersonal skills (such as social awareness, empathy, persuasion, and conflict management);
- vision (such as a forward-looking and inspirational one); and
- technical competence (such as knowledge, preparation, and judgment).[10]

The Center for Creative Leadership also identified ten core skills that effective leaders possess, only a few of which overlap with Rhode's list: integrity; ability to delegate; communication; self-awareness; gratitude; learning agility; influence; empathy; courage; and respect.[11] Two skills that lawyers pride themselves on, creativity (for example, being creative problem solvers) and innovation, are missing from this list.

The intersection between leadership and creativity has not been widely studied. Ben Heineman, Jr., in his essay on *Lawyers as Leaders*, called upon law schools to require students to create and not just critique as part of their education.[12] In a recently published article, University of Idaho College of Law professor John Dykstra made a compelling case for fostering and teaching creativity in the law school curriculum, and he suggested ways in which it can be incorporated into legal writing programs.[13]

---

9   Ibid.
10 Rhode, *Lawyers as Leaders*.
11 "What Are the Characteristics of a Good Leader?," *Center for Creative Leadership*, accessed November 15, 2021, https://www.ccl.org/articles/leading-effectively-articles/characteristics-good-leader/.
12 Ben W. Heineman, Jr, "Lawyers as Leaders," *Yale Law Journal Forum* 116, no. 30 (February 16, 2007), accessed September 30, 2021, https://www.yalelawjournal.org/forum/lawyers-as-leaders.
13 Jason G. Dykstra, "Teasing the Arc of Electric Spark: Fostering and Teaching Creativity in the Law School Curriculum," *Wyoming Law Review* 20, no. 1 (2020): 1–42, accessed September 30, 2021, https://scholarship.law.uwyo.edu/cgi/viewcontent.cgi?article=1427&context=wlr.

All of these identified traits and/or skills could be deliberately mapped through the curriculum in addition to offering focused seminars on leadership for lawyers. For example, Columbia Law School has developed a Leadership Competency Matrix that focuses on how lawyers lead self, lead others, and lead change through: vision and strategy, management and teamwork, problem solving, cultural literacy, and learning and improvement.[14]

The good news is that law schools are starting to heed the call for increased leadership training. In addition to the annual Baylor Law conferences, in November 2019 the Freedman Institute of Hofstra University's Maurice A. Deane School of Law hosted a conference at the Association of the Bar of the City of New York on training lawyers as leaders.[15] Formal programs on leadership for lawyers (that is, more than simply a course) exist at a number of schools including: Baylor Law School,[16] Santa Clara University School of Law,[17] University of Tennessee College of Law,[18] Cleveland-Marshall College of Law,[19] and the Moritz School of Law at Ohio State University.[20] The following is an illustrative but not exhaustive list of law school courses and programs on leadership: Albany Law; Baylor Law; Berkeley Law; Cleveland-Marshall School of Law; Columbia Law; Creighton University School of Law; Elon Law; George Mason University-Antonin Scalia Law School; New York University Law; Ohio State's Moritz College of Law School; Santa Clara Law School; Stanford Law School; Tennessee College of Law; Texas A&M School of law; University of Chicago Law School; University of the

---

14 "Leadership Competency Matrix," table, *Columbia University*, accessed September 28, 2021, https://leadership-initiative.law.columbia.edu/sites/default/files/content/FINAL_Leadership%20Competency%20Matrix.pdf.

15 "Leading Differently Across Difference: National Conference on Training Lawyers as Leaders," *Hofstra University Maurice A. Deane School of Law, Freedman Institute*, accessed September 29, 2021, https://freedmaninstitute.hofstra.edu/events/leading-differently-across-difference-a-national-conference-on-training-lawyers-as-leaders/#cle-materials.

16 "Leadership Development," *Baylor Law*, accessed September 29, 2021, https://www.baylor.edu/law/currentstudents/index.php?id=935914.

17 "Institute for Lawyer Leadership Education," *Santa Clara University School of Law*, accessed September 29, 2021, https://law.scu.edu/leadership/leadership-institute-info/.

18 "Institute for Professional Leadership Preparting," *University of Tennessee Knoxville College of Law*, accessed September 29, 2021, https://law.utk.edu/programs/leadership/.

19 "C|M|Law. P. Kelly Tompkins Leadership and the Law Program," *Cleveland-Marshall College of Law*, accessed September 29, 2021, https://www.law.csuohio.edu/academics/leadership.

20 "Program on Law and Leadership," *The Ohio State University Moritz College of Law*, accessed September 29, 2021, https://moritzlaw.osu.edu/faculty-and-research/program-law-and-leadership.

Pacific McGeorge School of Law and Pritzker School of Law Northwestern University; University of San Francisco School of Law; and Villanova University School of Law School.[21]

Will Lawyer Presidents Dramatically Change the Course of Higher Education?

While every college and university president brings their unique academic discipline training and leadership lens, lawyers also bring a different skill set and perspective to the presidency in terms of leadership style, communication style, business savvy and preventive law strategies. Not all lawyer presidents are the same. They have different backgrounds, different personalities and different experiences that they bring to the table, but as gleaned from the handful of interviews of and comments by lawyer presidents, they see their communication, team-building, decision-making, government savvy, and problem-solving skills as key components of their leadership styles.

As noted at the start of this concluding chapter, lawyers are not likely to single-handedly make dramatic changes in the administration of higher education. While lawyers are likely to approach higher education as a business, and today there is no doubt that is what it is, most lawyers have benefitted from a liberal arts education and appreciate the value proposition of higher education in its totality. It is unlikely that they will make economic decisions about low performing or underenrolled departments and majors that would generally produce results any different from their non-lawyer counterparts.

Lawyer presidents as a group have the leadership potential to aid individual campuses due to their: either innate or learned creative problem solving skills; collaborative teambuilding inclination; persuasive communication style typically tailored to the audience and the issue at hand; strategic communication experience in dealing with challenging public issues for clients (whether private or government); business acumen including human resources management and

---

21 Patricia E. Salkin, "Lawyers Are Leading Higher Education as Advocates Call for More Formal Leadership Training in Legal Education," *Best Practices for Legal Education* (blog), entry posted February 18, 2021, accessed September 29, 2021, https://bestpracticeslegaled.com/2021/02/18/lawyers-are-leading-higher-education-as-advocates-call-for-more-formal-leadership-training-in-legal-education/.

finances acquired through on-the-job training in running law offices, law departments, and government offices; and knowledge of the ever increasing complexity of legal and regulatory underpinnings of higher education.

Effective leadership in higher education today requires people who can manage all of the pieces of a large puzzle to create a complete and sustainable campus with sufficient stakeholder satisfaction and an economic future that effectively enables the institution to educate future generations. Campuses that select presidents with legal training can find comfort in the unique skill set these leaders can offer to meet the needs and challenges of the institution today and into the future.

Appendices

Appendix 1—Lawyer Presidents, 1700s to 2019

Name	Position	School	Term of Office
Abbott, James	President	University of South Dakota (SD)	1997–2018
Abdullah, Edythe	Campus President	Florida State College at Jacksonville (FL)	1985–2010
Abdullah, Edythe	President	Essex County College (NJ)	2010–2013
Abercrombie, John	President	University of Alabama (AL)	1902–1911
Abrams, Norman	President	University of California, Los Angeles (CA)	2006–2007
Achampong, Francis	Chancellor	Penn State Fayette (PA)	2010–2013
Achampong, Francis	Chancellor	Penn State Mont Alto (PA)	2013–Present
Adamany, David	President	Wayne State University (MI)	1982–1997
Adamany, David	President	Temple University (PA)	2000–2006
Adams, Ralph Wyatt	President	Troy University (AL)	1964–1989
Adelman, Michael	President	West Virginia School of Osteopathic Medicine (WV)	2010–2018
Alanis, Javier	President	Seminary of the Southwest (TX)	2009–Present
Alexander, Laurence	President	University of Arkansas at Pine Bluff (AK)	2013–Present
Alger, Jonathan	President	James Madison University (VA)	2012–Present
Ambar, Carmen Twillie	President	Douglass College (NJ)	2002–2008
Ambar, Carmen Twillie	President	Cedar Crest College (PA)	2008–2017
Ambar, Carmen Twillie	President	Oberlin College (OH)	2017–Present
Anderson, Hurst Robbins	President	Centenary College (NJ)	1943–1948
Anderson, Hurst Robbins	President	Hamline College (MN)	1948–1952
Anderson, Hurst Robbins	President	American University (DC)	1952–1968
Anderson, Michelle	President	Brooklyn College-CUNY (NY)	2016–Present
Appel, Anthony R.	President	Franklin and Marshall (PA)	1962–1962
Archer, Sr., Gleason	President	Suffolk University (MA)	1937–1948
Armbrister, Clarence	President	Johnson C. Smith University (NC)	2018–Present
Armstrong, David	President	Thomas More College (KY)	2013–2018
Armstrong, David	President	St. Thomas University (MN)	2018–Present
Armstrong, Richard H.	President	University of Southern Maine (ME)	1945–1961

Name	Position	School	Term of Office
Arnold, W. Ellis	President	Lambuth University (TN)	1996–1996
Arnold, W. Ellis	President	Hendrix College (AR)	2019–Present
Arthur, Virginia	President	Metropolitan State University (MN)	2016–Present
Aycock, William Brantley	Chancellor	University of North Carolina (NC)	1957–1964
Bacow, Lawrence	President	Tufts University (MA)	2001–2011
Bacow, Lawrence	President	Harvard University (MA)	2018–2023
Bahls, Steven	President	Augustana College (IL)	2003–Present
Bailey, Chris	President	Lower Columbia College (WA)	2011–Present
Bair, Sheila C.	President	Washington College (MD)	2015–Present
Baker, Bruce	President	Chippewa Valley Technical College (WI)	2007–Present
Baker, Simon Strousse	President	Washington and Jefferson College (PA)	1922–1931
Baldasare, Paul	President	St. Andrews University (NC)	2006–2020
Baldwin, Abraham	President	University of Georgia (GA)	1785–1801
Baldwin, James	President	Excelsior College (NY)	2016–2020
Ballard-Washington, Kimberly	Interim President	Albany State University (GA)	2013–2013
Ballard-Washington, Kimberly	Interim President	Fort Valley State University (GA)	2013–2013
Ballard-Washington, Kimberly	Interim President	Savannah State University (GA)	2019–2021
Baltodano, Josefina Castillo	President	Marian University (WI)	2006–2009
Barba, James	President	Albany Medical College (NY)	1995–2020
Barnwell, Robert Woodward	President	South Carolina College (SC)	1833–1841
Barry, Jeffrey	President	Walsh College (MI)	1971–1991
Bartle, Harold Roe	President	Missouri Valley College (MO)	1948–1950
Baston, Michael	President	Rockland County Community College (NY)	2017–2022
Battle, Kemp Plummer	President	University of North Carolina (NC)	1876–1891
Beauchamp, Rev. E. William	President	University of Portland (OR)	2004–2014
Becton, Charles L.	Interim Chancellor	North Carolina Central University (NC)	2012–2013
Becton, Charles L.	Interim Chancellor	Elizabeth City State University (NC)	2013–2014
Bekavac, Nancy Y.	President	Scripps College (CA)	1990–2007
Bennett, James Jefferson	President	Sewanee-The University of the South (TN)	1971–1977

Name	Position	School	Term of Office
Benton, Andrew K.	President	Pepperdine University (CA)	2000–2019
Bepko, Gerald	Chancellor	Indiana University-Purdue University Indianapolis (IN)	1986–2003
Bepko, Gerald	Interim President	Indiana University (IN)	2003–2003
Bernstine, Daniel	President	Portland State University (OR)	1997–2007
Beury, Charles Ezra	President	Temple University (PA)	1926–1941
Beutler, Randy	President	Southern Oklahoma State University (OK)	2010–Present
Bissell, Wilson Shannon	Chancellor	University at Buffalo (NY)	1902–1903
Black, James D.	President	Union College (KY)	1910–1912
Black, Robert	Interim President	Rocky Vista University (CO)	2009–2010
Bloustein, Edward J.	President	Bennington College (VT)	1965–1971
Bloustein, Edward J.	President	Rutgers University (NJ)	1971–1989
Boehmer, Bob	Interim President	East Georgia State College (GA)	2011–2011
Boehmer, Bob	President	East Georgia State College (GA)	2012–Present
Bogomolny, Robert	President	University of Baltimore (MD)	2002–2014
Bok, Derek	President	Harvard University (MA)	1971–1999
Bok, Derek	President	Harvard University (MA)	2006–2007
Bollinger, Lee	President	University of Michigan at Ann Arbor (MI)	1996–2002
Bollinger, Lee	President	Columbia University (NY)	2002–2023
Boren, David	President	University of Oklahoma (OK)	1994–2018
Bowman, John Bryan	President	Transylvania University (KY)	1865–1875
Bowman, Milo Jesse	Interim President	Valparaiso University (IN)	1922–1922
Bradford, James	President	Sattler College (MA)	2018–2019
Bragdon, Paul E.	President	Reed College (OR)	1971–1988
Bragdon, Paul E.	Interim President	Lewis and Clark College (OR)	2003–2004
Brainard, Mark	President	Delaware Technical Community College-Terry (DE)	2014–Present
Brand, Jonathan	President	Doane College (NE)	2005–2011
Brand, Jonathan	President	Cornell College (IA)	2011–Present
Braveman, Daan	President	Nazareth College (NY)	2005–2020
Brett, Sr., Philip Milledoler	Acting President	Rutgers University-Newark (NJ)	1930–1932
Brewster, Carroll	President	Hollins University (VA)	1975–1981

Name	Position	School	Term of Office
Brewster, Carroll	President	Hobart William Smith Colleges (NY)	1982–1991
Brewster, Jr Kingman	President	Yale University (CT)	1963–1977
Brickley, James H.	President	Eastern Michigan University (MI)	1975–1978
Brown II., John	President	John Brown University (AR)	1979–1993
Brown, Barry	Interim President	Suffolk University (MA)	2010–2012
Brown, Barry	President	Mount Ida College (MA)	2012–2018
Brown, Hank	President	University of Northern Colorado (CO)	1998–2002
Brown, Hank	President	University of Colorado-Boulder (CO)	2005–2008
Brown, Keith	President	Jefferson State Community College (AL)	2018–Present
Bruntmyer, Eric	President	Hardin-Simmons University (TX)	2016–Present
Bulger, William	President	University of Massachusetts (MA)	1995–2003
Burcham, David	Interim President	Loyola Marymount University (CA)	2010–2010
Burcham, David	President	Loyola Marymount University (CA)	2010–2015
Burse, Walter	President	Suffolk University (MA)	1948–1954
Butts, Alfred Benjamin	Chancellor	University of Mississippi (MS)	1935–1946
Byas, Renee	Acting Chancellor	Houston Community College (TX)	2013–2014
Campbell, Colin	President	Wesleyan University (CT)	1970–1988
Capehart, Robin	President	West Liberty University (WV)	2007–2015
Capehart, Robin	President	Bluefield State College-Bluefield Campus (WV)	2019–Present
Caroll, Brian J.	President	Community Christian College (CA)	2017–Present
Carothers, Robert L.	President	Southwest Minnesota State University (MN)	1983–1986
Carothers, Robert L.	Chancellor	Minnesota State University System (MN)	1986–1991
Carothers, Robert L.	President	University of Rhode Island (RI)	1991–2009
Carter, Laurie	President	Shippensburg University of Pennsylvania (PA)	2017–2021
Carter, Lisle C.	President	University of the District of Columbia (DC)	1977–1982
Casey, Brian	President	DePauw University (IN)	2008–2016
Casey, Brian	President	Colgate University (NY)	2016–Present
Casper, Gerhard	President	Stanford University (CA)	1992–2000
Cassidy, Joseph	President	Washington County Community College (ME)	2013–2018
Cassidy, Joseph	Interim President	Eastern Maine Community College (ME)	2015–2016

Name	Position	School	Term of Office
Cassidy, Joseph	President	Southern Maine Community College (ME)	2018–Present
Chambers, Julius L.	Chancellor	North Carolina Central University (NC)	1994–2001
Cheek, Jr., King V.	President	Shaw University (NC)	1969–1971
Cheek, Jr., King V.	President	Morgan State University (MD)	1971–1974
Cheek, Jr., King V.	President	Union Insitute and University (OH)	1976–1978
Cheek, Jr., King V.	Chancellor	New York College of Health Professionals (NY)	2001–2003
Chema, Thomas V.	President	Hiram College (OH)	2003–2014
Chodosh, Hiriam	President	Claremont McKenna College (CA)	2013–Present
Clark, Lawrence	President	Louisiana State University in Shreveport (LA)	2014–Present
Clark, Peter	President	Washington College (MD)	1829–1832
Clark-Artis, Roslyn	President	Florida Memorial University (FL)	2013–2017
Clark-Artis, Roslyn	President	Benedict College (SC)	2017–Present
Clayton, Henry Delamar	President	University of Alabama (AL)	1886–1889
Cline, Kimberly	President	Mercy College (NY)	2008–2013
Cline, Kimberly	President	Long Island University (NY)	2013–Present
Cobb, John Whitehouse	President	Naropa University (CO)	1993–2003
Cobb, John Whitehouse	Interim President	Naropa University (CO)	2011–2012
Cohen, David	President	Five Towns College (NY)	2016–Present
Collens, Lew	President	Illinois Institute of Technology (IL)	1990–2007
Cordana, Roberta	President	Gallaudet University (DC)	2016–Present
Cordes Larson, Gloria	President	Bentley (MA)	2007–2018
Courtway, Tom	Interim President	University of Central Arkansas (AR)	2011–2011
Courtway, Tom	President	University of Central Arkansas (AR)	2011–2016
Cox, Cathy	President	Young Harris College (GA)	2007–2017
Crawford, David	President	McCormack Theological Seminary (IL)	2018–Present
Criser, Marshall	President	University of Florida (FL)	1984–1989
Crosby, Harold B.	President	University of Florida (FL)	1964–1974
Crosby, Harold B.	Interim President	Florida International University (FL)	1975–1975
Crosby, Harold B.	President	Florida International University (FL)	1976–1979
Cummings, Joseph	President	Northwestern University (IL)	1881–1890
Cunningham, Paige Comstock	Interim President	Taylor University (IN)	2019–2021
Curan, Thomas	President	Rockhurst University (MO)	2006–Present

Name	Position	School	Term of Office
D'Emilio, Deaane Horner	President	Gwynedd Mercy University (PA)	2017–Present
D'Alembert, Talbert "Sandy"	President	Florida State University (FL)	1994–2003
Dalton, Walter	President	Isothermal Community College (NC)	2013–2021
Daniels, Ronald	President	Johns Hopkins (MD)	2009–Present
Daniels, Mitchell	President	Purdue (IN)	2013–2022
Darden, Jr., Colgate Whitehead	President	University of Virginia (VA)	1947–1959
Darrell, Barton	President	Kentucky Wesleyan College (KY)	2014–2019
Davenport, David	President	Pepperdine University (CA)	1985–2000
Davis, Bradley	President	West Valley College (CA)	2012–Present
Davis, Harwell Goodwin	President	Samford University (also known as Howard College) (AL)	1938–1958
Davis, Joan Y.	Interim President	Shelton State Community College (AL)	2013–2014
Davis, Joan Y.	Chancellor	Delgado Community College (LA)	2014–2018
Davis, John W.	President	West Virginia State University (WV)	1919–1953
Davros, Harry	President and CEO	Wade College (TX)	1997–Present
DeCoudreaux, Alecia A.	President	Mills College (CA)	2011–2016
Decatur, William	Interim President	University of Toledo (OH)	2000–2001
Degnan, Rev Daniel A.	President	Saint Peter's University (NJ)	1990–1995
Delaney, John	President	University of North Florida (FL)	2003–2018
Denson, Rob	President	Northeast Iowa Community College (IA)	1998–2003
Denson, Rob	President	Des Moines Area Community Colleges (IA)	2003–Present
Desteiguer, John	President	Oklahoma Christian University (OK)	2012–Present
Deur, William Alexander	President	Columbia University (NY)	1829–1842
Dimenna, Gary	President	Monmouth University (NJ)	2017–Present
Diver, Colin	President	Reed College (OR)	2002–2012
Dobson, William Davis	President	Truman State University (MO)	1891–1899
Dodge, Randall	President	Horizon University (IN)	2017–Present
Donner, Thomas	Interim President	Santa Monica College (CA)	1994–1995
Donner, Thomas	Interim President	Santa Monica College (CA)	2005–2005
Donovan, James	President	Pratt Institute (NY)	1968–1970
Doran, Sandra J.	President	American College of Education (IN)	2011–2014

Name	Position	School	Term of Office
Doran, Sandra J.	Interim President	Salem College (NC)	2018–Present
Drinker, Henry Sturgis	President	Lehigh University (PA)	1905–1920
Drinnon, James E.	Chancellor	University of Tennessee-Chattanooga (TN)	1973–1981
Dunagan, Nick	Chancellor	University of Tennessee-Martin (TN)	2001–2007
Dunkle, Rev. Kurt H.	President	The General Theological Seminary (NY)	2013–Present
Dunsworth, Richard	Interim President	Millikin University (IL)	2013–2013
Dunsworth, Richard	President	University of the Ozarks (AR)	2014–Present
Dybward, Peter	President	The Wright Institute (CA)	1982–Present
Dykstra, Kurt	President	Trinity Christian College (IL)	2015–Present
Easton, Stephen	Interim President	Dickinson State University (ND)	2019–2020
Eck, Daniel	President	Lakeland University (WI)	2013–2017
Ehrlich, Thomas	President	Indiana University (IN)	1987–1994
Eisgruber, Christopher	President	Princeton University (NJ)	2013–Present
Eliot, Thomas H.	Chancellor	Washington University in St. Louis (MO)	1962–1971
Elliott, David	President	Washington College (MD)	1830–1831
Ellis, David	Interim President	Lewis and Clark College (OR)	2017–2017
Emery, Alfred C.	President	University of Utah (UT)	1971–1973
Emory, Robert	Interim President	Dickinson College (PA)	1842–1843
Emory, Robert	President	Dickinson College (PA)	1845–1847
Engler, John	Interim President	Michigan State University (MI)	2018–2019
Ethierington, Edwin	President	Wesleyan University (CT)	1967–1979
Eyring, Henry Johnson	President	Brigham Young University-Idaho (ID)	2017–Present
Fagg, Jr., Fred D.	President	University of Southern California (CA)	1947–1957
Faison, Jr., Zachary	President	Edward Waters College (FL)	2018–Present
Falwell, Jr., Jerry Lamon	President	Liberty University (VA)	2007–2020
Farenthold, Frances Tarlton "Sissy"	President	Wells College (NY)	1976–1980
Farish, Donald	President	Rowan University (NJ)	1998–2011
Farish, Donald	President	Roger Williams University (RI)	2011–2018
Farnsworth, Charles Buchanan	President	Rhode Island School of Design (RI)	1877–1888
Farrell, Michael Jospeh	Interim President	Marshall University (WV)	2005–2005

Name	Position	School	Term of Office
Farris, Michael	President	Patrick Henry College (VA)	2000–2006
Farris, Michael	Chancellor	Patrick Henry College (VA)	2006–2017
Felton, Jr., Herman J.	President	Wilberforce University (OH)	2016–2017
Felton, Jr., Herman J.	President	Wiley College (TX)	2017–Present
Fenton, John E.	President	Suffolk University (MA)	1965–1970
Ferguson, Glenn	Chancellor	Long Island University (NY)	1969–1970
Ferguson, Glenn	President	Clark University (MA)	1970–1973
Ferguson, Glenn	President	University of Connecticut (CT)	1973–1978
Ferrentino, Robert	President	Montcalm Community College (MI)	2009–Present
Ferrero, Ray	CEO	Nova Southeastern University (FL)	1988–2010
Ferrero, Ray	Chancellor/CEO	Nova Southeastern University (FL)	2010–2011
Ferrero, Ray	Chancellor	Nova Southeastern University (FL)	2011–Present
Few, Ignatius Alphonso	President	Emory University (GA)	1836–1839
Fey, John T.	President	University of Vermont (VT)	1958–1964
Fey, John T.	President	University of Wyoming (WY)	1964–1966
Fillmore, Millard	Chancellor	University at Buffalo (NY)	1846–1874
Finnegan, Patrick	President	Longwood University (VA)	2010–2012
Fitts, Michael	President	Tulane University (LA)	2014–Present
Flanagan, David	President	University of Southern Maine (ME)	2014–2015
Flicker, John	President	Prescott College (AZ)	2014–Present
Floyd, John Anthony	President	Mars Hill University (NC)	2018–Present
Follick, Edwin	President	South Baylo University School of Oriental Medicine (CA)	2018–Present
Forsyth, James	President	Rensselaer Polytechnic Institute (NY)	1868–1886
Foster, Richard Clark	President	University of Alabama (AL)	1937–1941
Foster, Tim	President	Colorado Mesa Univeristy (CO)	2004–2021
Fowler, Charles Henry	President	Northwestern University (IL)	1873–1876
Francis, Norman C.	President	Xavier University of Louisiana (LA)	1968–2015
Freedman, James O.	President	University of Iowa (IA)	1982–1987
Freedman, James O.	President	Dartmouth College (NH)	1987–1998
Freidman, Stephen	President	Pace University (NY)	2007–2017
Frelinghuysen, Theodore	President	Rutgers University (NJ)	1850–1862
French, George	President	Miles College (AL)	2006–2019
French, George	President	Clark Atlanta University (GA)	2019–Present
Frisch, Randy	President	City University of Seattle (WA)	2016–Present
Frohnmayer, David	President	University of Oregon (OR)	1994–2000

Name	Position	School	Term of Office
Fulbright, J. William	President	University of Arkansas (AR)	1939–1941
Funk, Robert N.	President	Cornish College of the Arts (WA)	1985–1994
Funk, Robert N.	Interim President	Sierra Nevada College (NV)	1995–1997
Funk, Robert N.	Interim President	St. Edwards University (TX)	1998–1998
Funk, Robert N.	Interim President	Villa Julie College (now Stevenson University) (MD)	1999–2000
Funk, Robert N.	Interim President	Hood College (MD)	2000–2001
Fuster, Jamie	President	Pontifical Catholic University of Puerto Rico (PR)	1981–1984
Futter, Ellen V.	Acting President/President	Barnard College (NY)	1980–1993
Gabel, Joan T.A.	President	University of Minnesota (MN)	2019–Present
Galligan, Jr., Thomas	President	Colby-Sawyer College (NH)	2006–2016
Gallot, Jr., Richard Joseph	President	Grambling State University (LA)	2019–Present
Gann, Pamela B.	President	Claremont McKenna College (CA)	1993–2013
Garcia, Joseph A.	President	Pikes Peak Community College (CO)	2001–2006
Garcia, Joseph A.	President	Colorado State University-Pueblo (CO)	2006–2010
Gardner, James A.	President	Lewis and Clark College (OR)	1989–2003
Garfield, Henry Augustus	President	Williams College (MA)	1908–1934
Garrett, Allison	President	Emporia State University (KS)	2016–2021
Garrett, Elizabeth	President	Cornell University (NY)	2015–2016
Garrison, Michael	President	West Virginia University (WV)	2007–2008
Garside, Charles	Acting President	State University of New York (NY)	1951–1952
Garvey, John	President	Catholic University of America (DC)	2010–2022
Gash, Jim	President	Pepperdine University (CA)	2019–Present
Gates, Thomas Sovereign	President	University of Pennsylvania (PA)	1930–1944
Gee Gordon, E	President	West Virginia University (WV)	1981–1985
Gee Gordon, E	President	University of Colorado System (CO)	1985–1990
Gee Gordon, E	President	Ohio State University (OH)	1990–1998
Gee Gordon, E	President	Brown University (RI)	1998–2000
Gee Gordon, E	President	Vanderbilt University (TN)	2000–2007
Gee Gordon, E	President	Ohio State University (OH)	2007–2013
Gee Gordon, E	President	West Virginia University (WV)	2014–Present

Name	Position	School	Term of Office
Gerety, Tom	President	Trinity College (CT)	1989–1994
Gerety, Tom	President	Amherst College (MA)	1994–2003
Gerhart, Peter	President	Lake Erie College (OH)	2015–2016
Glover, Glenda Baskin	President	TN State University (TN)	2013–Present
Godfrey III, Edward S.	President	University of Southern Maine (ME)	1962–1973
Godwin, Angeline	President	Ashland Community and Technical College (KY)	1997–2000
Godwin, Angeline	President	Patrick Henry College (VA)	2012–Present
Goodnow, Frank Johnson	President	Johns Hopkins (MD)	1914–1929
Gormley, Ken	President	Duquesne (PA)	2015–Present
Gotanda, John	President	Hawaii Pacific University (HI)	2016–Present
Green, O. Jerome	President	Shorter College (AR)	2012–Present
Greenberg, Erwin	President	Worsham College of Mortuary Science (IL)	1961–1979
Greenwald, Stephen	President	Metropolitan College of New York (NY)	1999–2008
Gregg, John R.	Interim President	Vincennes University (IN)	2003–2004
Greiner, William R.	President	University of Buffalo (NY)	1991–2004
Groves, William P	Chancellor	Antioch University (NH)	2017–Present
Guerry, Alexander	President	University of Chattanooga (TN)	1929–1938
Guerry, Alexander	President	Sewanee-The University of the South (TN)	1938–1948
Habecker, Eugene	President	Huntington University (IN)	1981–1991
Habecker, Eugene	President	Taylor University (IN)	2005–2019
Haddon, Phoebe	Chancellor	Rutgers University-Camden (NJ)	2014–2020
Hadley, Herbert S.	President	Washington University in St. Louis (MO)	1923–1927
Haile, Gregory	President	Broward College (FL)	2018–Present
Haines, Paul Lowell	President	Taylor University (IN)	2016–2019
Hale, Horace M.	President	University of Colorado-Boulder (CO)	1887–1892
Hall, Arnold Bennett	President	University of Oregon (OR)	1926–1932
Hall, David	President	University Virgin Islands (VI)	2009–Present
Hall, Timothy	President	Austin Peay State University (TN)	2007–2014
Hall, Timothy	President	Mercy College (NY)	2014–Present
Hamen, Laurie M.	President	Mount Mercy University (IA)	2014–2020
Hanley, Dexter L.	President	University of Scranton (PA)	1970–1975
Hanycz, Colleen	President	LaSalle Univeristy (PA)	2015–2021
Hardaway, Patricia	President	Wilberforce University (OH)	2007–2013
Hardesty, Jr., David S.	President	West Virginia State University (WV)	1995–2007

Name	Position	School	Term of Office
Hardin III, Paul	President	Wofford College (SC)	1968–1972
Hardin III, Paul	President	Southern Methodist University (TX)	1972–1974
Hardin III, Paul	President	Drew University (NJ)	1974–1988
Hardin III, Paul	Chancellor	University of North Carolina (NC)	1988–1995
Hardin, Lu	President	University of Central Arkansas (AR)	2002–2008
Hardy, John Crumpton	President	Mississippi State University (MS)	1900–1912
Hardy, John Crumpton	President	University of Mary Hardin-Baylor (TX)	1912–1937
Harpool, David	President	North Central University (Online) (CA)	2015–Present
Harris, Rufus Carrollton	President	Tulane University (LA)	1939–1960
Harris, Rufus Carrollton	President	Mercer University (GA)	1960–1979
Harrison, Valerie	President	Lincoln University (PA)	2014–Present
Harroz, Joseph	Interim President	University of Oklahoma (OK)	2019–2020
Hartzog, Henry	President	Clemson University (SC)	1897–1902
Hartzog, Henry	President	University of Arkansas (AR)	1902–1905
Hartzog, Henry	President	Ouachita Baptist University (AR)	1907–1911
Hasbrouck, Abraham Bruyn	President	Rutgers University (NJ)	1840–1850
Hawk, Rupert A.	Acting President	Grinnell College (IA)	1954–1955
Haynes, David S.	President	Northern Michigan University (MI)	2012–2014
Haynes, Ulric	Acting President	SUNY College at Old Westbury (NY)	1981–1981
Helfferich, Donald L. "Ty"	President	Ursinus College (PA)	1958–1970
Helmer, Robert	President	Lourdes University (OH)	2003–2012
Helmer, Robert	President	Baldwin Wallace University (OH)	2012–Present
Herseth Sandlin, Stephanie	President	Augustana University (SD)	2017–Present
Hespe, David	President	Rowan College at Burlington County (NJ)	2012–2015
Heyman, Ira Michael	Chancellor	University of California, Berkeley (CA)	1980–1990
Hill, John H.	President	West Virginia State University (WV)	1894–1898
Hill, Sister Elizabeth A.	President	St. Joseph's College (NY)	1997–2014
Hill, Walter Barnard	Chancellor	University of Georgia (GA)	1899–1905
Hill-Kennedy, Scott	Interim President	Ferris State University (MI)	2003–2003
Hillman, Elizabeth	President	Mills College (CA)	2016–Present
Hoi, Samuel	President	Otis College of Art and Design (CA)	2000–2014
Hoi, Samuel	President	Maryland Institute College of Art (MD)	2014–Present

Name	Position	School	Term of Office
Holmes, Barbara A.	President	United Theological Seminary of the Twin Cities (MN)	2012–2016
Holton, Anne	Interim President	George Mason University (VA)	2019–Present
Horton, Howard E.	President	Massachusetts Communications College/ New England Institute of Art (MA)	1988–2000
Horton, Howard E.	President	Bay State College (MA)	2000–2006
Horton, Howard E.	President	New England College of Business and Finance (MA)	2006–2020
Hull, Roger	President	Beloit College (WI)	1981–1990
Hull, Roger	President	Union College (NY)	1990–2005
Hunter, James	President	Point Park University (PA)	1995–1997
Huntley, Robert E. R.	President	Washington and Lee University (VA)	1968–1983
Hurley, John J.	President	Canisius College (NY)	2010–2022
Hutchins, Robert Maynard	President	University of Chicago (IL)	1929–1945
Hutchins, Robert Maynard	Chancellor	University of Chicago (IL)	1945–1951
Hyde, Kevin	Interim President	Florida State College at Jacksonville (FL)	2019–Present
Iacullo, Steven	President	Health Care Institute (FL)	2014–Present
Iseman, Joseph S.	Acting President	Bennington College (VT)	1976–1976
Iuliano, Robert	President	Gettysburg College (PA)	2019–Present
Jackson, Thomas H.	President	University of Rochester (NY)	1994–2005
Jacobs, Albert C.	Chancellor	University of Denver (CO)	1949–1953
Jacobs, Albert C.	President	Trinity College (CT)	1953–1968
Jeffcoat, Harold	President	Texas Wesleyan University (TX)	2000–2010
Jeffcoat, Harold	President	Millikin University (IL)	2011–2012
Jerome, March	President	Monroe College (NY)	2017–Present
Jewell, Richard G.	President	Grove City College (PA)	2003–2014
Joel, Richard	President	Yeshiva University (NY)	2003–2017
Johnson, Ed	President	Sterling College-Kansas (KS)	1997–2003
Johnson, Ed	President	Everest College Phoenix and Everest Univeristy Online (AZ)	2011–2015
Johnson, George R.	President	Lemoyne-Owen College (TN)	1996–2002
Johnson, Jr., Glen D.	President	Southeastern Oklahoma State University (OK)	1997–2006
Johnson, Jr., Glen D.	Chancellor	Oklahoma System of Higher Education (OK)	2007–Present

Name	Position	School	Term of Office
Johnson, William Samuel	President	Columbia University (NY)	1787–1800
Johnston, Bryan M.	Interim President	Willamette University (OR)	1997–1998
Johnston, Bryan M.	President	Saint Martin's University (OR)	2008–2008
Jones, Brian	President	Strayer University (VA)	2015–Present
Jones, Jr., Glendell	President	Henderson State University (AR)	2012–2019
Kauffman, Bill	Interim President	St. Louis University (MO)	2013–2014
Kavalhuna, Russell	President	Henry Ford College (MI)	2018–2022
Keck, Rachelle (Karstens)	President	Briar Cliff University (IA)	2018–Present
Keenan, John D.	President	Salem State University (MA)	2017–Present
Keith, Kent M.	President	Chaminade University of Honolulu (HI)	1989–1995
Keith, Kent M.	President	Pacific Rim Christian University (HI)	2015–Present
Kelliher, Marsha	President	Walsh College (MI)	2017–2020
Kerr, David	President	University of North Carolina (NC)	1794–1796
Khaytat, Robert	President	University of Mississippi (MS)	1995–2009
Kinney, RADM, Sheldon H.	President	SUNY Maritime College (NY)	1972–1982
Kirk, John Robert	President	Truman State University (MO)	1899–1925
Klauber, James S.	President	Ownesboro Community and Tech College (KY)	2010–2015
Klauber, James S.	President	John C. Calhoun State Community College (AL)	2015–2018
Klauber, James S.	President	Hagerstown Community College (MD)	2018–Present
Klein, John E.	President	Randolph College (VA)	2007–2013
Knapp, Bradford	President	Texas Tech University (TX)	1932–1938
Kneebone, Elaine	Acting President	Henderson State University (AR)	2019–Present
Knight, Bobbie	President	Miles College (AL)	2019–Present
Krislov, Marvin	President	Oberlin College (OH)	2007–2017
Krislov, Marvin	President	Pace University (NY)	2017–Present
Kroger, John	President	Reed College (OR)	2012–2018
Kuttler, Jr., Carl M.	President	St. Petersburg College (FL)	1978–2009
Kyle, Penelope Ward	President	Radford University (VA)	2005–2016
La Lumiere, Stanislaus	President	Marquette University (WI)	1887–1889
LaForge, William N.	President	Delta State University (MS)	2013–2022
LaGree, Kevin	President	Simpson College (IA)	1999–2005
Lader, Philip	President	Winthrop University (SC)	1983–1985

Name	Position	School	Term of Office
Lambert, Lee D.	President	Shoreline Community College (WA)	2006–2013
Lambert, Lee D.	Chancellor	Pima County Community College (AZ)	2013–Present
Lamberton, Robert Alexander	President	Lehigh University (PA)	1880–1893
Landsmark, Ted	President	Boston Architectural College (MA)	1997–2004
Langston, John Mercer	Acting President	Howard University (DC)	1872–1872
Langston, John Mercer	President	Virginia State University (VA)	1882–1882
Lapp, Joseph	President	Eastern Memmonite University (PA)	1987–2003
Lash, Jonathan	President	Hampshire College (MA)	2011–2018
Lawrence, Fred	President	Brandeis (MA)	2011–2015
Laws, Samuel	President	Westminster College (MO)	1854–1861
Laws, Samuel	President	University of Missouri (MO)	1876–1889
Lee, Calvin B.T.	Acting President	Boston University (MA)	1970–1971
Lee, Calvin B.T.	Chancellor	University of Maryland, Baltimore (MD)	1971–1976
Lee, Douglas	President	Waynesburg University (PA)	2013–Present
Lee, Jay	President	Northeastern Junior College (CO)	2012–Present
Leebron, David	President	Rice University (TX)	2004–2022
Lehman, Jeffrey S.	President	Cornell University (NY)	2003–2005
Lesar, Hiram	Interim President	Southern Illinois University-Carbondale (IL)	1974–1974
Lesar, Hiram	Interim President	Southern Illinois University-Carbondale (IL)	1979–1980
Leverett, John	President	Harvard University (MA)	1708–1724
Levi, Edward H.	President	University of Chicago (IL)	1968–1975
Lewis, Brien	President	Catwaba College (NC)	2012–2020
Lewis, Burwell Boykin	President	University of Alabama (AL)	1880–1885
Lewis, Ovid C.	President	Nova Southeastern University (FL)	1994–1997
Liacouras, Peter	President	Temple University (PA)	1981–2000
Liacouras, Peter	Chancellor	Temple University (PA)	2000–2016
Lief, Charles	President	Naropa University (CO)	2012–Present
Lindgren, Robert	President	Randolph College (VA)	2006–Present
Linsley, Joel Harvey	President	Marietta College (OH)	1835–1846
Lockmiller, David A.	President	University of Chattanooga (TN)	1942–1959
Loh, Wallace	President	University of Maryland, College Park (MD)	2010–2020
Longstreet, Augustis Baldwin	President	Emory University (GA)	1839–1839

Name	Position	School	Term of Office
Longstreet, Augustis Baldwin	President	Emory University (GA)	1840–1848
Longstreet, Augustis Baldwin	President	Centenary College (LA)	1849–1849
Longstreet, Augustis Baldwin	President	University of Mississippi (MS)	1850–1850
Longstreet, Augustis Baldwin	President	South Carolina College (SC)	1856–1856
Looney, Susan	President	Reading Area Community College (PA)	2018–Present
Lorimer, Linda	President	Randolph College (VA)	1986–1993
Lowell, Lawrence	President	Harvard University (MA)	1909–1933
Lowry III, L. Randolph	President	Lipscomb University (TN)	2005–2021
Ludwick, Richard	President	University of St. Thomas (MN)	2017–Present
Lugo, Daniel	President	Queens College of Charlotte (NC)	2019–Present
Macchiarola, Frank	President	St. Francis College (NY)	1996–2008
Macchiarola, Frank	Chancellor	St. Francis College (NY)	2008–2012
Machtley, Ronald	President	Bryant University (RI)	1996–2020
Mackey, M. Cecil	President	University of South Florida (FL)	1971–1976
Mackey, M. Cecil	President	Texas Tech University (TX)	1976–1979
Mackey, M. Cecil	President	Michigan State University (MI)	1979–1985
Madison, Bishop James	President	College of William and Mary (VA)	1777–1812
Magoun, George	President	Grinnell College (IA)	1865–1884
Malloy, Dannel	Chancellor	University of Maine (ME)	2019–Present
Maniaci, Vincent	President	American International College (MA)	2005–Present
Marcy, Oliver	President	Northwestern University (IL)	1876–1881
Marcy, Oliver	President	Northwestern University (IL)	1890–1890
Martin, Jr., Harold	President	Morehouse College (GA)	2017–Present
Martin, Daniel	President	Mount Vernon Nazarene University (OH)	2007–2012
Martin, Daniel	President	Seattle Pacific University (WA)	2012–2021
Martin, Earl F.	President	Drake University (IA)	2015–Present
Mason, Karol	President	John Jay (NY)	2017–Present
Mason, Ronald	President	Jackson State University (MS)	2000–2010
Mason, Ronald	President	Southern University System (LA)	2010–2015
Mason, Ronald	President	University of the District of Columbia (DC)	2015–Present
Mautz, Robert	Chancellor	State University System of Florida (FL)	1968–1975
Maxwell, William	President	Hampden-Sydney College (VA)	1838–1844
McClure, Tori Murden	President	Spalding University (KY)	2010–Present

Name	Position	School	Term of Office
McConnell, Glenn F.	President	College of Charleston (SC)	2014–2018
McConnell, Joyce	President	Colorado State (CO)	2019–2022
McCormick, Cecilia	President	Elizabethtown College (PA)	2019–Present
McCormick, James Byron	President	University of Arizona (AZ)	1947–1951
McCormick, Mark	President	Middlesex County College (NJ)	2019–Present
McCormick, Samuel	Chancellor	University of Pittsburgh (PA)	1904–1921
McCormick, Samuel	President	Coe College (IA)	1897–1904
McDaniel, Tom J.	President	Northwestern Oklahoma State University (OK)	2000–2001
McDaniel, Tom J.	President	Oklahoma City University (OK)	2001–2004
McDonald, Clay	President	Logan University (MO)	2013–Present
McDonald, J. Clay	President	Logan University (MO)	2003–Present
McFarland, Carl	President	University of Montana (MT)	1951–1958
McGlothlin, Michael	Interim President	Appalachian College of Pharmacy (VA)	2005–2006
McGlothlin, Michael	President	Appalachian College of Pharmacy (VA)	2008–2008
McGlothlin, Michael	President and CEO	Appalachian College of Pharmacy (VA)	2009–Present
McGuire, Patricia	President	Trinity Washington University (DC)	1989–Present
McKenna, Margaret	President	Lesley University (MA)	1985–2007
McKenna, Margaret	President	Suffolk University (MA)	2015–2016
McNulty, Paul	President	Grove City College (PA)	2014–Present
McPherson, M. Peter	President	Michigan State University (MI)	1993–2004
Meador, Earl W.	Chancellor	South Central Louisiana Technical College (LA)	2012–2017
Meador, Earl W.	Interim Chancellor	Fletcher Technical Community College (LA)	2014–2015
Meador, Earl W.	Chancellor	Northwest Louisiana Technical Community College (LA)	2017–Present
Mearns, Geoffrey S.	President	Northern Kentucky University (KY)	2012–2017
Mearns, Geoffrey S.	President	Ball State University (IN)	2017–Present
Meehan, Martin	Chancellor	University of Massachusetts Lowell (MA)	1995–2003
Meehan, Martin	President	University of Massachusetts System (MA)	2015–Present
Meigs, Josiah	President	University of Georgia (GA)	1801–1810
Mengler, Thomas	President	St. Mary's University (TX) (TX)	2012–Present
Mercer, Peter	President	Ramapo College (NJ)	2005–Present
Messer, Asa	President	Brown University (RI)	1802–1826
Miller, Michael	President	Pfeiffer University (NC)	2010–2014

Appendices

Name	Position	School	Term of Office
Milliken, James	President	University of Nebraska (NE)	2004–2014
Milliken, James	President	City University of New York (NY)	2014–2018
Milliken, James	Chancellor	University of Texas System (TX)	2018–Present
Mills, Barry	President	Bowdoin College (ME)	2001–2015
Mills, Barry	Interim Chancellor	University of Massachusetts Boston (MA)	2017–2018
Montgomery, Douglas	President	Blue Ridge Community College (VA)	1966–1968
Montgomery, Douglas	President	Tidewater Community College (VA)	1968–1972
Mooney, Carol Ann	President	Saint Mary's College (IN)	2004–2016
Mooney, Christopher F.	President	Woodstock College (NY)	1969–1974
Moore, Ernest Carroll	President	University of California, Los Angeles (CA)	1927–1929
Moore, Nathaniel Fish	President	Columbia University (NY)	1842–1849
Morales, Jose Alberto	President	Pontifical Catholic University of Puerto Rico (PR)	2001–2006
Morehead, Jere W.	President	University of Georgia (GA)	2013–Present
Moron, Alonzo Graseano	Acting President	Hampton University (VA)	1948–1948
Moron, Alonzo Graseano	President	Hampton University (VA)	1949–1959
Moseley, John Ohleyer	President	University of Central Oklahoma (OK)	1935–1939
Moseley, John Ohleyer	President	University of Nevada, Reno (NV)	1944–1949
Munsil, Len	President	Arizona Christian University (AZ)	2010–Present
Murrh, William Belton	President	Millsaps College (MS)	1890–1910
Musterman, Cynthia	President	Stevens-The Institute of Business and Arts (MO)	1999–Present
Nabrit, James	President	Howard University (DC)	1960–1969
Napolitano, Janet	President	UC system (CA)	2013–2020
Neimic, Catherine	President and Founder	Phoenix Institute of Herbal Medicine and Accupuncture (AZ)	1996–Present
Nelson, Christopher B.	President	St. John's College-Annapolis (MD)	1991–2017
Newkirk, Krista	President	Converse College (SC)	2016–Present
Newton, J. Quigg	President	University of Colorado-Boulder (CO)	1956–1963
Nguyen, Thuy Thi	President	Foothills College (CA)	2016–Present
Nichol, Gene R.	President	College of William and Mary (VA)	2005–2008
Nordenberg, Mark	Interim Chancellor	University of Pittsburgh (PA)	1995–1995
Nordenberg, Mark	Chancellor	University of Pittsburgh (PA)	1996–2014
Northrop, Cyrus	President	University of Minnesota (MN)	1884–1911

Name	Position	School	Term of Office
Norton, Charles Phelps	Chancellor	University at Buffalo (NY)	1909–1920
O'Brien, Kevin	President	Santa Clara University (CA)	2019–Present
O'Connor, Maureen	President	Palo Alto University (CA)	2016–Present
O'Day, Steven	President	Austin College (TX)	2017–Present
O'Hara, William T.	President	Mounty Saint Mary College (NY)	1972–1976
O'Hara, William T.	President	Bryant University (RI)	1976–1989
O'Leary, Hazel	President	Fisk University (TN)	2005–2013
O'Neil, Robert Marchant	President	University of Wisconsin (WI)	1980–1985
O'Neil, Robert Marchant	President	University of Virginia (VA)	1985–1990
Olsen, James Karge	President	William Paterson University of New Jersey (NJ)	1968–1972
Onders, Bob	President	Alaska Pacific University (AK)	2017–Present
Osgood, Russell K.	President	Grinnell College (IA)	1998–2010
Owens, Steven	Interim President	University of Missouri (MO)	2011–2021
Oxholm, Carl	President	Arcadia (PA)	2011–2013
Padilla, Antonio Garcia	President	University of Puerto Rico (PR)	2001–2009
Pantzer, Robert T.	President	University of Montana (MT)	1966–1974
Parish, Michael C.	President	Bay Mills Community College (MI)	2002–Present
Parker, Ava	President	Palm Beach State College (FL)	2015–Present
Patterson, Bart	President	Nevada State College (NV)	2011–Present
Pearce, Richard	President	Methodist University (NC)	1973–1983
Pearsall, Joel K.	Interim President	Northwest Nazarene University (ID)	2015–2015
Pearsall, Joel K.	President	Northwest Nazarene University (ID)	2016–Present
Peck, John Hudson	President	Rensselaer Polytechnic Institute (NY)	1888–1901
Peri, Jonathan	President	Manor College (PA)	2015–Present
Perlman, Harvey	Chancellor	University of Nebraska (NE)	2001–2016
Perrin, Larry Timothy	President	Lubbock Christian University (TX)	2012–Present
Perry, Audy Michael	Interim President	Marshall University (WV)	1999–2000
Perry, Audy Michael	President	Marshall University (WV)	2000–2005
Peterson, Shirely	President	Hood College (MD)	1995–2000
Petrizzo, Louis	Interim President	Suffolk County Community College (NY)	2019–2021
Phillip, George	Interim President	University at Albany (NY)	2007–2009
Phillip, George	President	University at Albany (NY)	2009–2012
Pickens, Joe	President	St. John's River State College (FL)	2008–Present

Appendices | 217

Name	Position	School	Term of Office
Pierce, George Foster	President	Georgian Female College (later Wesleyan) (GA)	1838–1840
Pierce, George Foster	President	Emory University (GA)	1848–1854
Pietruszkiewicz, Christopher	President	University of Evansville (IN)	2018–Present
Pistole, John	President	Anderson University (IN)	2015–Present
Pollard, Chip	President	John Brown University (AR)	2004–Present
Poskanzer, Steven	President	SUNY New Paltz (NY)	2001–2010
Poskanzer, Steven	President	Carlton College (MN)	2010–Present
Powers, Jr., William	President	University of Texas at Austin (TX)	2006–2015
Preston, William C.	President	South Carolina College (SC)	1845–1851
Pretty, Keith	President	Walsh College (MI)	1999–2006
Pretty, Keith	President	Northwood University (MI)	2006–2019
Price, Alan	President	Ealham College (IN)	2017–2018
Price, James F.	President	Kansas State Teachers College/Emporia College (KS)	1943–1945
Price, James F.	Chancellor	University of Denver (CO)	1948–1948
Purnell, William Henry	President	University of Delaware (DE)	1870–1875
Pye, A. Kenneth	Chancellor	Duke University (NC)	1970–1971
Pye, A. Kenneth	Chancellor	Duke University (NC)	1976–1982
Pye, A. Kenneth	President	Southern Methodist University (TX)	1987–1994
Quigley, Jr., Kenneth	President	Curry College (MA)	1996–Present
Quincy III., Josiah	President	Harvard University (MA)	1829–1845
Quinn, Kevin	President	University of Scranton (PA)	2011–2017
Raab, Jennifer	President	Hunter College, CUNY (NY)	2001–Present
Rabinowitz, Stuart	President	Hofstra (NY)	2001–2021
Rainsford, George Nichols	President	Kalamzoo College (MI)	1972–1983
Rainsford, George Nichols	President	Lynchburg College (VA)	1983–1993
Rallo, Joseph	President	Angelo State University (TX)	2007–2015
Ray, Alan	President	Elmhurst College (IL)	2003–2015
Ray, Alan	President	Fisher College (MA)	2017–Present
Reiss, Mitchell B.	President	Washington College (MD)	2010–2014
Rendelman, John S.	President	Southern Illinois University-Edwardsville (IL)	1968–1976
Reveley III, Walter Taylor	President	College of William and Mary (VA)	2008–2018
Reveley, IV, W. Taylor	President	Longwood University (VA)	2013–Present

Name	Position	School	Term of Office
Rexach, Jamie Benitez	President	University of Puerto Rico (PR)	1966–1970
Richey, James H.	President	Eastern Florida State College (FL)	2012–Present
Rimai, Monica	Interim President	University of Cincinnati (OH)	2009–2009
Rinehart, Kathleen	President	Cardinal Stritch University (WI)	2018–Present
Roberts, Gary	President	Bradley University (IL)	2016–Present
Rodriguez, Jorge E. Mojica	President	Humacao Community College (PR)	2003–Present
Rogers, Henry Wade	President	Northwestern University (IL)	1890–1900
Rooney, Jo Ann	President	Spalding University (KY)	2002–2010
Rooney, Jo Ann	President	Mount Ida College (MA)	2010–2010
Rooney, Jo Ann	President	Loyola University Chicago (IL)	2016–2022
Roosevelt, Mark	President	St. John's College (NM)	2016–Present
Rosen, Andrew	President	Kaplan University (IA)	2002–2008
Rosen, Andrew	CEO and Chairman	Kaplan University (IA)	2008–Present
Rosenblum, Victor	President	Reed College (OR)	1968–1970
Rothkopf, Arthur	President	Lafayette College (PA)	1993–2005
Russell, Donald S.	President	University of South Carolina (SC)	1952–1957
Ryan, Barry	President	Agrosy University, Southern CA campuses (CA)	2007–2009
Ryan, Barry	President and CEO	West Coast University (CA)	2009–2014
Ryan, Barry	Chancellor	Agrosy University (CA)	2014–2015
Ryan, Barry	President and CEO	United States University (CA)	2015–2016
Ryan, Barry	President	Sofia University (CA)	2018–2020
Ryan, James	President	University of Virginia (VA)	2018–Present
Salmon, Thomas P.	President	University of Vermont (VT)	1991–1997
Sam, David	President	North Harris College (TX)	2000–2007
Sam, David	President	Elgin Community College (IL)	2007–Present
Sanchez, Luis	President	Moorpark College (CA)	2015–2019
Sanchez, Luis	Interim President	Oxnard College (CA)	2019–Present
Sands, Harlan	President	Cleveland State University (OH)	2018–Present
Sargent, David	President	Suffolk University (MA)	1989–2010
Satterlee, Kevin	President	Idaho State University (ID)	2018–Present
Scanlon, Michael	President	Franciscan University of Steubenville (OH)	1974–2000

Name	Position	School	Term of Office
Scanlon, Michael	Chancellor	Franciscan University of Steubenville (OH)	2000–2011
Schall, Lawrence M. (Larry)	President	Oglethorpe University (GA)	2005–2020
Scherrens, Maurice William	President	Newbury College (MA)	2012–Present
Schill, Michael	President	University of Oregon (OR)	2015–Present
Schmidt, Benno	President	Yale University (CT)	1986–1992
Schmoke, Kurt	President	University of Baltimore (MD)	2014–Present
Schwarz, Thomas	Acting President	Hamilton College (NY)	1999–1999
Schwarz, Thomas	President	Purchase College-State University of New York (NY)	2013–2019
Scott, Zaldwaynaka 'Z'	President	Chicago State University (IL)	2018–Present
Sea, Brooks	Interim President	Young Harris College (GA)	2017–2017
Seligman, Joel	President	University of Rochester (NY)	2005–2018
Sexton, John	President	New York University (NY)	2002–2015
Shafer, Raymond P.	Interim President	Allegheny Community College (PA)	1985–1986
Shannon, Jack	President	Christian Brothers University (TN)	2019–Present
Shaw, Manford A.	President	Westminster College (UT)	1968–1976
Sheilds, Dennis	Chancellor	University of Wisconsin Platteville (WI)	2010–Present
Shepley, Ethan A. H.	Chancellor	Washington University in St. Louis (MO)	1953–1961
Sheridan, Sean	President	Franciscan University of Steubenville (OH)	2013–2019
Sherman, Max	President	West Texas A&M University (TX)	1977–1982
Shutkin, William	President	Presidio Graduate School (CA)	2011–2016
Shutt, Steven	President	Lake Forest College (IL)	2001–Present
Siemens, Cornelius Henry	President	Compton College (CA)	1946–1950
Siemens, Cornelius Henry	President	Humboldt State University (CA)	1950–1973
Sikorsky, Fr. Charles	President	Divine Mercy University (VA)	2007–Present
Slabach, Frederick G.	President	Texas Wesleyan University (TX)	2011–Present
Sloan, Albert J.	Interim President	Miles College (AL)	1989–1989
Sloan, Albert J.	President	Miles College (AL)	1989–2006
Smart, Clifton	Interim President	Missouri State University-Springfield (MO)	2011–2012

Name	Position	School	Term of Office
Smart, Clifton	President	Missouri State University-Springfield (MO)	2012–Present
Smith, Hildreth	President	Catawba College (NC)	1853–1856
Smith, Hildreth	President	Sam Houston State University (TX)	1879–1881
Smith, Luther M.	President	Emory University (GA)	1867–1871
Smith, Rodney	President	Southern Virginia University (VA)	2004–2011
Smith, Virginia B.	President	Vassar College (NY)	1977–1986
Smith, Virginia B.	Acting President	Mills College (CA)	1990–1990
Smith, William Russell	President	University of Alabama (AL)	1869–1871
Smolla, Rodney	President	Furman College (SC)	2010–2013
Snyder, Barbara	President	Case Western Reserve (OH)	2007–Present
Sorell, Michael	President	Paul Quinn College (TX)	2007–Present
Sovern, Michael	President	Columbia University (NY)	1980–1993
Spangler, James	President	Worsham College of Mortuary Science (IL)	1961–1979
Spaniolo, James	President	University of Texas at Arlington (TX)	2004–2013
Sparks, Laura	President	Cooper Union (NY)	2017–Present
Spectar, Jem	President	University of Pittsburgh-Johnstown (PA)	2007–Present
Spencer, Clayton	President	Bates College (ME)	2012–Present
Sprague, Carleton	Chancellor	University at Buffalo (NY)	1885–1895
Sprague, Homer	President	Mills College (CA)	1885–1887
Sprague, Homer	President	University of North Dakota (ND)	1887–1891
St. Amand, Gerry	Interim President	Northern Kentucky University (KY)	2017–Present
Stanley, Deborah F.	Interim President	SUNY Oswego (NY)	1995–1997
Stanley, Deborah F.	President	SUNY Oswego (NY)	1997–2021
Starcher, Jr., John M.	President	Southside Regional Medical Center-Professional Schools (VA)	2018–Present
Stargardter, Steven	President	John F. Kennedy University (CA)	2004–Present
Starr, Kenneth	President	Baylor University (TX)	2010–2016
Stassen, Harold	President	University of Pennsylvania (PA)	1948–1953
Staton, Robert	President	Presbyterian College (SC)	2015–Present
Stearns, Robert	President	University of Colorado-Boulder (CO)	1939–1953
Steiner, Stuart	President	Genesee Community College (KY)	1975–2011
Steinmayer, Janet	President	Mitchell College (CT)	2014–2019
Steinmayer, Janet	President	Lesley University (MA)	2019–Present
Stern, Eliot	President	Saddleback College (CA)	2019–Present

Name	Position	School	Term of Office
Stevens, Robert	President	Haverford College (PA)	1978–1987
Stevens, Robert	Chancellor	University of California, Santa Cruz (CA)	1987–1991
Stith, Jr., Millard "Pete"	President	Saint Paul College (MN)	2013–2016
Stoepler, John W.	Interim President	University of Toledo (OH)	1988–1989
Stone, Jesse N.	President	Southern University and A&M College (LA)	1974–1985
Stone, Philip	President	Bridgewater College (VA)	1994–2010
Stone, Philip	President	Sweet Briar College (VA)	2015–2017
Studley, Jamie	President	Skidmore (NY)	1999–2003
Sullivan, Thomas, E.	President	University of Vermont (VT)	2012–Present
Sullivan, Timothy J.	President	College of William and Mary (VA)	1992–2005
Sutton, Andrew J.	President	Washington College (MD)	1860–1867
Swain, David Lowry	President	University of North Carolina (NC)	1835–1868
Sweavingen, Tilford	President	William Woods College (MI)	1951–1961
Swygert, H. Patrick	President	University at Albany (NY)	1990–1995
Swygert, H. Patrick	President	Howard University (DC)	1995–2008
Sylvester, Esther R.	Interim President	Rosemont College (PA)	1978–1979
Syverud, Kent	President	Syracuse University (NY)	2014–Present
Taylor, A. N.	President	Northern Arizona University (AZ)	1899–1909
Tetlow, Tania	President	Loyola University (LA)	2018–2022
Thierstein, Joel	Interim President	Mount St. Joseph University (OH)	2014–2014
Thierstein, Joel	President	West Virginia Wesleyan College (WV)	2017–Present
Thomason, Chris	Chancellor	University of Arkansas Community College at Hope-Texarcana (AR)	2008–Present
Thompson, Larry	President	Ringling College of Art and Design (FL)	1999–Present
Thompson, Winfred	President	American University of Kuwait (Kuwait)	2013–2013
Thompson, Winfred	President	American University in Kosovo (Kosovo)	2014–Present
Thornton, Ray	President	Arkansas State University (AR)	1981–1984
Thornton, Ray	President	University of Arkansas (AR)	1984–1990
Thrasher, John E.	President	Florida State University (FL)	2014–2020
Tillman, John N.	President	University of Arkansas (AR)	1905–1912
Titus, Steven	President	Midland University (NE)	2002–2007
Titus, Steven	President	Iowa Wesleyan University (IA)	2013–Present
Towey, Jim	President	Saint Vincent College (PA)	2006–2010

Name	Position	School	Term of Office
Trachtenberg, Steven	President	Univeristy of Hartford (CT)	1977–1998
Trachtenberg, Steven	President	George Washington University (DC)	1988–2007
Traer, James	President	Westminster College (MO)	1993–1999
Trible, Paul	President	Christopher Newport University (VA)	1996–2022
Tucker, Thomas DeSaille	President	Florida Agricultural and Mechanical University (FL)	1887–1901
Tweed, Harrison	Acting President	Sarah Lawrence College (NY)	1959–1960
Tyler, Lyon Gardiner	President	College of William and Mary (VA)	1888–1919
Ulmer, Frances	Chancellor	University of Alaska-Anchorage (AK)	2007–2011
Underwood, William	Interim President	Baylor University (TX)	2005–2006
Underwood, William	President	Mercer University (GA)	2006–Present
Van Zandt, David	President	The New School (NY)	2011–2020
Verkuil, Paul Robert	President	College of William and Mary (VA)	1985–1992
Vestal, Theodore M. "Ted"	President	California Institute of Integrated Studies (CA)	1979–1983
Viar, David	President	American River College (CA)	1995–2013
Viar, David	President	Glendale Community College (CA)	2013–Present
Victor, Michael	President	Lake Erie College (OH)	2006–2015
Victor, Michael	President	Mercyhurst University (PA)	2015–2021
Vincent, Gregory	President	Hobart William Smith Colleges (NY)	2017–2018
Virjee, Framroze	President	California State University Fullerton (CA)	2017–Present
Vogt, Carl	President	Williams College (MA)	1999–2000
Walker, Francis Amasa	President	Massachusetts Institute of Technology (MA)	1881–1897
Walsh, Suzannne	President	Bennett College (NC)	2019–Present
Ward, George Morgan	President	Rollins College (FL)	1886–1902
Warfield, Ethelbert Dudley	President	Miami University (OH)	1888–1891
Warfield, Ethelbert Dudley	President	Lafayette College (PA)	1891–1914
Warfield, Ethelbert Dudley	President	Wilson College (PA)	1915–1936
Webb, W. Roger	President	Northeastern State University (OK)	1978–1997
Webb, W. Roger	President	University of Central Oklahoma (OK)	1997–2011
Weiss, Jeff A.	President	Lesley University (MA)	2016–2018
Welch, Adoniah Strong	President	Eastern Michigan University (MI)	1851–1865

Name	Position	School	Term of Office
Welch, Adoniah Strong	President	Iowa State University (IA)	1869–1883
Weld, Frank	President	Minnesota State University Moorhead (MN)	1899–1920
Wells, Rainey T.	President	Murray State University (KY)	1926–1932
Whaley, Chris	President	Roane State Community College (TN)	2012–Present
Whitaker, Alexander	President	King University (TN)	2016–Present
White III, Luther	President	Randolph College (VA)	1967–1979
White III, Luther	President	Kentucky Wesleyan College (KY)	1979–1988
White, John Brown	President	Wake Forest University (NC)	1848–1853
White, John Brown	President	Almira College (now Greenville University) (IL)	1855–1878
Whitfield, Henry L.	President	Mississippi University for Women (MS)	1907–1920
Wiggins, Norman Adrian	Chancellor/President	Campbell College (previously Campbell University) (NC)	1967–2003
Wilcox, Reed	President	Southern Virginia University (VA)	2014–Present
Wilkinson, Ernest	President	Brigham Young University (UT)	1951–1971
Willets, Edwin	President	Michigan State University (MI)	1885–1889
William, Elisha	President	Yale University (CT)	1726–1739
Williams IV, Alfred	President	River Valley Community College (NH)	2018–Present
Williams, Jr., John	President	Muhlenberg College (PA)	2015–2019
Williams, Gregory H.	President	City University of New York (NY)	2001–2009
Williams, Gregory H.	President	University of Cincinnati (OH)	2009–2012
Williams, H. James	President	Fisk University (TN)	2013–2015
Williams, H. James	President	Mount St. Joseph University (OH)	2016–Present
Williams, John	Interim President	Principia College (IL)	2019–2020
Williams, Joseph R.	President	Michigan State University (MI)	1857–1859
Williams, Phillip	President	University of Montevallo (AL)	2006–2010
Williams, Phillip	President	McNeese State University (LA)	2010–Present
Willits, Edwin	President	Eastern Michigan University (MI)	1883–1885
Willits, Edwin	President	State Agriculture College (Michigan State) (MI)	1885–1889
Wilson, Matthew	President	University of Akron (OH)	2016–2018
Wilson, Matthew	President	Missouri Western State University (MO)	2019–Present
Wilson, Woodrow	President	Princeton University (NJ)	1902–1910
Wippman, David	President	Hamilton College (NY)	2016–Present
Wisenhunt, Denise	Interim President	San Diego City College (CA)	2016–2017
Wiserman, Christine	President	Saint Xavier University (IL)	2010–2016

Name	Position	School	Term of Office
Witherspoon, Gerald	President	Goddard College (VT, WA) (VT)	1970–1975
Woolsey, Theodore Dwight	President	Yale University (CT)	1846–1871
Worthen, Kevin	President	Brigham Young University (UT)	2014–Present
Wyatt, Scott L.	President	Snow College (UT)	2007–2013
Wyatt, Scott L.	President	Southern Utah University (UT)	2013–2021
Wyman, William Stokes	Interim President	University of Alabama (AL)	1879–1880
Wyman, William Stokes	Interim President	University of Alabama (AL)	1885–1886
Wyman, William Stokes	Interim President	University of Alabama (AL)	1889–1890
Wyman, William Stokes	President	University of Alabama (AL)	1901–1902
Wynes, Tim	President	Inver Hills Community College (MN)	2010–2018
Wynes, Tim	President	Dakota County Technical College (MN)	2013–2018
Wynes, Tim	President	Black Hawk College (IL)	2018–Present
Yellen, David	President	Marist College (NY)	2016–2019
Young, Betty	President	Northwest State Community College (OH)	2003–2007
Young, Betty	President	Ashville-Boncombe Tech Community College (NC)	2007–2009
Young, Betty	President	Coleman College for Health Sciences at Houston (TX)	2009–2014
Young, Betty	Interim President	Hocking College (OH)	2014–2014
Young, Betty	President	Hocking College (OH)	2015–Present
Young, Michael	President	University of Utah (UT)	2004–2011
Young, Michael	President	University of Washington (WA)	2011–2015
Young, Michael	President	Texas A&M (TX)	2015–2021
Yudof, Mark	President	University of Minnesota (MN)	1997–2002
Yudof, Mark	Chancellor	University of Texas System (TX)	2002–2008
Yudof, Mark	President	University of California (CA)	2008–2013
Zak, Leocadia	President	Agnes Scott College (GA)	2018–Present
Zeppos, Nicholas	President	Vanderbilt University (TN)	2008–2019

Appendix 2—Lawyer Presidents, 2020 to 2021

Name	Position	School	Term of Office
Allison, Darrell	Chancellor	Fayettville State University (NC)	2021–Present
Archie, Anita	Interim President	Trenholm State Community College (AL)	2020–Present
Ballard-Washington, Kimberly	President	Savannah State University (GA)	2021–Present
Baston, Michael	President	Cuyahoga Community College (OH)	2022–Present
Cage, Ericke S.	Interim President	West Virginia State University (WV)	2021–2022
Cage, Ericke S.	President	West Virginia State University (WV)	2022–Present
Carson, Brad	President	University of Tulsa (OK)	2021–Present
Carter, Laurie	President	Lawrence University (WI)	2021–Present
Caruso, Jr., F. Willis (Bill)	a	DeVry College (National) (IL)	2020–Present
Cawley, Jim	Interim President	Rosemont College (PA)	2022–Present
Cole, Jr., J. Derham	Interim Chancellor	University of South Carolina Upstate (SC)	2020–2021
Collins, Jennifer M.	President	Rhodes College (TN)	2022–Present
Cox, Cathy	President	Georgia College and State University (GA)	2021–Present
Crawford III, James W.	Interim President	Felician University (NJ)	2020–2021
Crawford III, James W.	President	Felician University (NJ)	2021–Present
Delaney, John	Interim President	Flagler College (FL)	2021–2021
Delaney, John	President	Flagler College (FL)	2021–Present
Demleitner, Nora	President	St. John's College (MD)	2022–Present
Doran, Sandra J.	President	Bay Path University (MA)	2020–Present
Easton, Stephen	President	Dickinson State University (ND)	2020–Present
Farmbry, Kyle	President	Guildford College (NC)	2022–Present
Galligan, Jr., Thomas	Interim President	LSU Agricultural and Mechanical College (LA)	2020–Present
Ganther, Felicia, L.	President	Bucks County Community College (PA)	2021–Present
Hamen, Laurie M.	President	Saint Benedict (MN)	2020–Present
Hanycz, Colleen	President	Xavier University (OH)	2021–Present
Harroz, Joseph	President	University of Oklahoma (OK)	2020–Present
Hartzler, Tracy	President	Central New Mexico Community College (NM)	2020–Present

Name	Position	School	Term of Office
Henry, Dennis Mitchell	President	Faulkner University (AL)	2022–Present
Horton, Howard E.	President	Cambridge College (MA)	2020–Present
Hudson, Thomas	Interim President	Jackson State University (MS)	2020–2020
Hudson, Thomas	President	Jackson State University (MS)	2020–Present
Jones, John E.	Interim President	Dickinson College (PA)	2021–2022
Jones, John E.	President	Dickinson College (PA)	2022–Present
Jones, Marcus	President	Northwestern State University (LA)	2021–Present
Kavalhuna, Russell	Chancellor	Virginia Community College System (VA)	2022–Present
Keck, Rachelle (Karstens)	President	Grand View University (IA)	2022–Present
Kelliher, Marsha	President	Simpson College (IA)	2020–Present
Klein, Andy	Interim Chancellor	Indiana University-Purdue University Indianapolis (IN)	2022–Present
Law, Rhea	Interim President	University of South Florida (FL)	2021–2022
Law, Rhea	President	University of South Florida (FL)	2022–Present
Levit, Janet	Interim President	University of Tulsa (OK)	2020–2021
Lewis, Brien	President	Transylvania University (KY)	2020–Present
Litvack, Steven	President	Jersey College (NJ)	Unknown–Present
Magill, Elizabeth	President	University of Pennsylvania (PA)	2022–Present
Mahoney, Joanie	President	SUNY ESF (NY)	2020–Present
McKeegan, John N.	President	Mount Aloysius College (PA)	2020–Present
Mnookin, Jennifer	Chancellor	University of Wisconsin Madison (WI)	2022–Present
Padilla, Jose	President	Valparaiso University (IN)	2021–Present
Parnell, Sean	Chancellor	University of Alaska-Anchorage (AK)	2021–Present
Penalver, Eduardo	President	Seattle University (WA)	2021–Present
Posner, Susan	President	Hofstra University (NY)	2021–Present
Pritchett, Wendell	Interim President	University of Pennsylvania (PA)	2022–2022
Reisberg, Darren	President	Hartwick College (NY)	2022–Present
Richardson, L. Song	President	Colorado College (CO)	2021–Present
Rothman, Jay	President	University of Wisconsin System (WI)	2022–Present
Rougeau, Vincent D.	President	College of the Holy Cross (MA)	2021–Present
Sandoval, Brian	President	University of Nevada (NV)	2020–Present

Name	Position	School	Term of Office
Sawyer, Terrence M.	President	Loyola University Maryland (MD)	2022–Present
Shields, Dennis	President and Chancellor	Southern University System (IA)	2022–Present
Stanley, Deborah F.	Interim Chancellor	SUNY Oswego (NY)	2021–Present
Sulmasy, Glenn M.	President	Nichols College (MA)	2021–Present
Tetlow, Tania	President	Fordham University (NY)	2022–Present
Tuckman, Eric	President	Alhambra Medical University (CA)	Unknown–Present
Vincent, Gregory	President	Talladega College (AL)	2022–Present
Vischer, Rob	Interim President	University of St. Thomas (MN)	2022–Present
Williams, John	President	Principia College (IL)	2020–Present
Wu, Frank	President	Queens College CUNY (NY)	2020–Present
Zdanty, Sophie	Interim Chancellor	Vermont State Colleges System (VT)	2020–Present

Appendix 3—Women Lawyer Presidents by Name, School, School Type, and Location

Name	Position	School	Term of Office
Abdullah, Edythe	Campus President	Florida State College at Jacksonville (FL)	1985–2010
Abdullah, Edythe	President	Essex County College (NJ)	2010–2013
Ambar, Carmen Twillie	President	Douglass College (NJ)	2002–2008
Ambar, Carmen Twillie	President	Cedar Crest College (PA)	2008–2017
Ambar, Carmen Twillie	President	Oberlin College (OH)	2017–Present
Anderson, Michelle	President	Brooklyn College-CUNY (NY)	2016–Present
Arthur, Virginia	President	Metropolitan State University (MN)	2016–Present
Bair, Sheila C.	President	Washington College (MD)	2015–Present
Ballard-Washington, Kimberly	Interim President	Albany State University (GA)	2013–2013
Ballard-Washington, Kimberly	Interim President	Fort Valley State University (GA)	2013–2013
Ballard-Washington, Kimberly	Interim President	Savannah State University (GA)	2019–2021
Baltodano, Josefina Castillo	President	Marian University (WI)	2006–2009
Bekavac, Nancy Y.	President	Scripps College (CA)	1990–2007
Carter, Laurie	President	Shippensburg University of Pennsylvania (PA)	2017–2021
Clark-Artis, Roslyn	President	Florida Memorial University (FL)	2013–2017
Clark-Artis, Roslyn	President	Benedict College (SC)	2017–Present
Cline, Kimberly	President	Mercy College (NY)	2008–2013
Cline, Kimberly	President	Long Island University (NY)	2013–Present
Cordana, Roberta	President	Gallaudet University (DC)	2016–Present
Cordes Larson, Gloria	President	Bentley (MA)	2007–2018
Cox, Cathy	President	Young Harris College (GA)	2007–2017
Cunningham, Paige Comstock	Interim President	Taylor University (IN)	2019–2021
D'Emilio, Deaane Horner	President	Gwynedd Mercy University (PA)	2017–Present
Davis, Joan Y.	Interim President	Shelton State Community College (AL)	2013–2014
Davis, Joan Y.	Chancellor	Delgado Community College (LA)	2014–2018
DeCoudreaux, Alecia A.	President	Mills College (CA)	2011–2016
Doran, Sandra J.	President	American College of Education (IN)	2011–2014

Name	Position	School	Term of Office
Doran, Sandra J.	Interim President	Salem College (NC)	2018–Present
Farenthold, Frances Tarlton "Sissy"	President	Wells College (NY)	1976–1980
Futter, Ellen V.	Acting President/President	Barnard College (NY)	1980–1993
Gabel, Joan T.A.	President	University of Minnesota (MN)	2019–Present
Gann, Pamela B.	President	Claremont McKenna College (CA)	1993–2013
Garrett, Allison	President	Emporia State University (KS)	2016–2021
Garrett, Elizabeth	President	Cornell University (NY)	2015–2016
Glover, Glenda Baskin	President	TN State University (TN)	2013–Present
Godwin, Angeline	President	Ashland Community and Technical College (KY)	1997–2000
Godwin, Angeline	President	Patrick Henry College (VA)	2012–Present
Haddon, Phoebe	Chancellor	Rutgers University-Camden (NJ)	2014–2020
Hamen, Laurie M.	President	Mount Mercy University (IA)	2014–2020
Hanycz, Colleen	President	LaSalle Univeristy (PA)	2015–2021
Hardaway, Patricia	President	Wilberforce University (OH)	2007–2013
Harrison, Valerie	President	Lincoln University (PA)	2014–Present
Herseth Sandlin, Stephanie	President	Augustana University (SD)	2017–Present
Hill, Sister Elizabeth A.	President	St. Joseph's College (NY)	1997–2014
Hillman, Elizabeth	President	Mills College (CA)	2016–Present
Holmes, Barbara A.	President	United Theological Seminary of the Twin Cities (MN)	2012–2016
Holton, Anne	Interim President	George Mason University (VA)	2019–Present
Keck, Rachelle (Karstens)	President	Briar Cliff University (IA)	2018–Present
Kelliher, Marsha	President	Walsh College (MI)	2017–2020
Kneebone, Elaine	Acting President	Henderson State University (AR)	2019–Present
Knight, Bobbie	President	Miles College (AL)	2019–Present
Kyle, Penelope Ward	President	Radford University (VA)	2005–2016
Looney, Susan	President	Reading Area Community College (PA)	2018–Present
Lorimer, Linda	President	Randolph College (VA)	1986–1993
Mason, Karol	President	John Jay (NY)	2017–Present
McClure, Tori Murden	President	Spalding University (KY)	2010–Present
McConnell, Joyce	President	Colorado State (CO)	2019–2022

Name	Position	School	Term of Office
McCormick, Cecilia	President	Elizabethtown College (PA)	2019–Present
McGuire, Patricia	President	Trinity Washington University (DC)	1989–Present
McKenna, Margaret	President	Lesley University (MA)	1985–2007
McKenna, Margaret	President	Suffolk University (MA)	2015–2016
Mooney, Carol Ann	President	Saint Mary's College (IN)	2004–2016
Musterman, Cynthia	President	Stevens-The Institute of Business and Arts (MO)	1999–Present
Napolitano, Janet	President	UC system (CA)	2013–2020
Neimic, Catherine	President and Founder	Phoenix Institute of Herbal Medicine and Accupuncture (AZ)	1996–Present
Newkirk, Krista	President	Converse College (SC)	2016–Present
Nguyen, Thuy Thi	President	Foothills College (CA)	2016–Present
O'Connor, Maureen	President	Palo Alto University (CA)	2016–Present
O'Leary, Hazel	President	Fisk University (TN)	2005–2013
Parker, Ava	President	Palm Beach State College (FL)	2015–Present
Peterson, Shirely	President	Hood College (MD)	1995–2000
Raab, Jennifer	President	Hunter College, CUNY (NY)	2001–Present
Rimai, Monica	Interim President	University of Cincinnati (OH)	2009–2009
Rinehart, Kathleen	President	Cardinal Stritch University (WI)	2018–Present
Rooney, Jo Ann	President	Spalding University (KY)	2002–2010
Rooney, Jo Ann	President	Mount Ida College (MA)	2010–2010
Rooney, Jo Ann	President	Loyola University Chicago (IL)	2016–2022
Scott, Zaldwaynaka 'Z'	President	Chicago State University (IL)	2018–Present
Sea, Brooks	Interim President	Young Harris College (GA)	2017–2017
Smith, Virginia B.	President	Vassar College (NY)	1977–1986
Smith, Virginia B.	Acting President	Mills College (CA)	1990–1990
Snyder, Barbara	President	Case Western Reserve (OH)	2007–Present
Sparks, Laura	President	Cooper Union (NY)	2017–Present
Spencer, Clayton	President	Bates College (ME)	2012–Present
Stanley, Deborah F.	Interim President	SUNY Oswego (NY)	1995–1997
Stanley, Deborah F.	President	SUNY Oswego (NY)	1997–2021
Steinmayer, Janet	President	Mitchell College (CT)	2014–2019
Steinmayer, Janet	President	Lesley University (MA)	2019–Present
Studley, Jamie	President	Skidmore (NY)	1999–2003

Name	Position	School	Term of Office
Sylvester, Esther R.	Interim President	Rosemont College (PA)	1978–1979
Tetlow, Tania	President	Loyola University (LA)	2018–2022
Ulmer, Frances	Chancellor	University of Alaska-Anchorage (AK)	2007–2011
Walsh, Suzannne	President	Bennett College (NC)	2019–Present
Wisenhunt, Denise	Interim President	San Diego City College (CA)	2016–2017
Wiserman, Christine	President	Saint Xavier University (IL)	2010–2016
Young, Betty	President	Northwest State Community College (OH)	2003–2007
Young, Betty	President	Ashville-Boncombe Tech Community College (NC)	2007–2009
Young, Betty	President	Coleman College for Health Sciences at Houston (TX)	2009–2014
Young, Betty	Interim President	Hocking College (OH)	2014–2014
Young, Betty	President	Hocking College (OH)	2015–Present
Zak, Leocadia	President	Agnes Scott College (GA)	2018–Present

Appendix 4—Lawyer Presidents of Community Colleges by Name, School, School Type, and Location

Name	Position	School	Term of Office	School Type
Abdullah, Edythe	President	Essex County College (NJ)	2010–2013	Public
Bailey, Chris	President	Lower Columbia College (WA)	2011–Present	Public
Baker, Bruce	President	Chippewa Valley Technical College (WI)	2007–Present	Public
Baston, Michael	President	Rockland County Community College (NY)	2017–2022	Public
Brainard, Mark	President	Delaware Technical Community College-Terry (DE)	2014–Present	Public
Brown, Keith	President	Jefferson State Community College (AL)	2018–Present	Public
Byas, Renee	Acting Chancellor	Houston Community College (TX)	2013–2014	Public
Caroll, Brian J.	President	Community Christian College (CA)	2017–Present	Private
Cassidy, Joseph	President	Washington County Community College (ME)	2013–2018	Public
Cassidy, Joseph	Interim President	Eastern Maine Community College (ME)	2015–2016	Public
Cassidy, Joseph	President	Southern Maine Community College (ME)	2018–Present	Public
Dalton, Walter	President	Isothermal Community College (NC)	2013–2021	Public
Davis, Bradley	President	West Valley College (CA)	2012–Present	Public
Davis, Joan Y.	Interim President	Shelton State Community College (AL)	2013–2014	Public
Davis, Joan Y.	Chancellor	Delgado Community College (LA)	2014–2018	Public
Denson, Rob	President	Northeast Iowa Community College (IA)	1998–2003	Public
Denson, Rob	President	Des Moines Area Community Colleges (IA)	2003–Present	Private
Donner, Thomas	Interim President	Santa Monica College (CA)	1994–1995	Public
Donner, Thomas	Interim President	Santa Monica College (CA)	2005–2005	Public
Fagg, Jr., Fred D.	President	University of Southern California (CA)	1947–1957	Private
Ferrentino, Robert	President	Montcalm Community College (MI)	2009–Present	Public

Name	Position	School	Term of Office	School Type
Garcia, Joseph A.	President	Pikes Peak Community College (CO)	2001–2006	Public
Godwin, Angeline	President	Ashland Community and Technical College (KY)	1997–2000	Public
Green, O. Jerome	President	Shorter College (AR)	2012–Present	Private
Hespe, David	President	Rowan College at Burlington County (NJ)	2012–2015	Public
Kavalhuna, Russell	President	Henry Ford College (MI)	2018–2022	Public
Klauber, James S.	President	Ownesboro Community and Tech College (KY)	2010–2015	Public
Klauber, James S.	President	John C. Calhoun State Community College (AL)	2015–2018	Public
Klauber, James S.	President	Hagerstown Community College (MD)	2018–Present	Public
Kuttler, Jr., Carl M.	President	St. Petersburg College (FL)	1978–2009	Public
Lambert, Lee D.	President	Shoreline Community College (WA)	2006–2013	Public
Lambert, Lee D.	Chancellor	Pima County Community College (AZ)	2013–Present	Public
Lee, Jay	President	Northeastern Junior College (CO)	2012–Present	Public
Looney, Susan	President	Reading Area Community College (PA)	2018–Present	Public
Mautz, Robert	Chancellor	State University System of Florida (FL)	1968–1975	Public
Meador, Earl W.	Chancellor	South Central Louisiana Technical College (LA)	2012–2017	Public
Meador, Earl W.	Interim Chancellor	Fletcher Technical Community College (LA)	2014–2015	Public
Meador, Earl W.	Chancellor	Northwest Louisiana Technical Community College (LA)	2017–Present	Public
Montgomery, Douglas	President	Blue Ridge Community College (VA)	1966–1968	Public
Montgomery, Douglas	President	Tidewater Community College (VA)	1968–1972	Public
Parish, Michael C.	President	Bay Mills Community College (MI)	2002–Present	Public
Petrizzo, Louis	Interim President	Suffolk County Community College (NY)	2019–2021	Public
Rodriguez, Jorge E. Mojica	President	Humacao Community College (PR)	2003–Present	Private

Name	Position	School	Term of Office	School Type
Sam, David	President	North Harris College (TX)	2000–2007	Private
Sam, David	President	Elgin Community College (IL)	2007–Present	Public
Sanchez, Luis	President	Moorpark College (CA)	2015–2019	Public
Sanchez, Luis	Interim President	Oxnard College (CA)	2019–Present	Public
Shafer, Raymond P.	Interim President	Allegheny Community College (PA)	1985–1986	Public
Siemens, Cornelius Henry	President	Compton College (CA)	1946–1950	Public
Steiner, Stuart	President	Genesee Community College (KY)	1975–2011	Public
Stern, Eliot	President	Saddleback College (CA)	2019–Present	Public
Stith, Jr., Millard "Pete"	President	Saint Paul College (MN)	2013–2016	Public
Thomason, Chris	Chancellor	University of Arkansas Community College at Hope-Texarcana (AR)	2008–Present	Public
Viar, David	President	American River College (CA)	1995–2013	Public
Viar, David	President	Glendale Community College (CA)	2013–Present	Public
Whaley, Chris	President	Roane State Community College (TN)	2012–Present	Public
Williams IV, Alfred	President	River Valley Community College (NH)	2018–Present	Public
Wisenhunt, Denise	Interim President	San Diego City College (CA)	2016–2017	Public
Wynes, Tim	President	Inver Hills Community College (MN)	2010–2018	Public
Wynes, Tim	President	Black Hawk College (IL)	2018–Present	Public
Young, Betty	President	Northwest State Community College (OH)	2003–2007	Public
Young, Betty	President	Ashville-Boncombe Tech Community College (NC)	2007–2009	Public
Young, Betty	President	Coleman College for Health Sciences at Houston (TX)	2009–2014	Public
Young, Betty	Interim President	Hocking College (OH)	2014–2014	Public
Young, Betty	President	Hocking College (OH)	2015–Present	Public

Appendix 5—Lawyer Presidents of Religiously Affiliated Schools by Name, School, and Location

Name	Position	School	Term of Office	School Type
Alanis, Javier	President	Seminary of the Southwest (TX)	2009–Present	Private
Anderson, Hurst Robbins	President	Centenary College (NJ)	1943–1948	Private
Anderson, Hurst Robbins	President	American University (DC)	1952–1968	Private
Armstrong, David	President	Thomas More College (KY)	2013–2018	Private
Armstrong, David	President	St. Thomas University (MN)	2018–Present	Private
Arnold, W. Ellis	President	Lambuth University (TN)	1996–1996	Private
Arnold, W. Ellis	President	Hendrix College (AR)	2019–Present	Private
Baldasare, Paul	President	St. Andrews University (NC)	2006–2020	Private
Baltodano, Josefina Castillo	President	Marian University (WI)	2006–2009	Private
Bartle, Harold Roe	President	Missouri Valley College (MO)	1948–1950	Private
Beauchamp, Rev. E. William	President	University of Portland (OR)	2004–2014	Private
Bennett, James Jefferson	President	Sewanee-The University of the South (TN)	1971–1977	Private
Benton, Andrew K.	President	Pepperdine University (CA)	2000–2019	Private
Black, James D.	President	Union College (KY)	1910–1912	Private
Bowman, Milo Jesse	Interim President	Valparaiso University (IN)	1922–1922	Private
Bradford, James	President	Sattler College (MA)	2018–2019	Private
Brown II., John	President	John Brown University (AR)	1979–1993	Private
Bruntmyer, Eric	President	Hardin-Simmons University (TX)	2016–Present	Private
Burcham, David	Interim President	Loyola Marymount University (CA)	2010–2010	Private
Burcham, David	President	Loyola Marymount University (CA)	2010–2015	Private
Caroll, Brian J.	President	Community Christian College (CA)	2017–Present	Private
Cheek, Jr., King V.	President	Shaw University (NC)	1969–1971	Private
Clark-Artis, Roslyn	President	Florida Memorial University (FL)	2013–2017	Private
Crawford, David	President	McCormack Theological Seminary (IL)	2018–Present	Private

Name	Position	School	Term of Office	School Type
Cunningham, Paige Comstock	Interim President	Taylor University (IN)	2019–2021	Private
Curan, Thomas	President	Rockhurt University (MO)	2006–Present	Private
D'Emilio, Deaane Horner	President	Gwynedd Mercy University (PA)	2017–Present	Private
Darrell, Barton	President	Kentucky Wesleyan College (KY)	2014–2019	Private
Davenport, David	President	Pepperdine University (CA)	1985–2000	Private
Davis, Harwell Goodwin	President	Samford University (also known as Howard College) (AL)	1938–1958	Private
Degnan, Rev Daniel A.	President	Saint Peter's University (NJ)	1990–1995	Private
Desteiguer, John	President	Oklahoma Christian University (OK)	2012–Present	Private
Dodge, Randall	President	Horizon University (IN)	2017–Present	Private
Dunkle, Rev. Kurt H.	President	The General Theological Seminary (NY)	2013–Present	Private
Dunsworth, Richard	Interim President	Millikin University (IL)	2013–2013	Private
Dunsworth, Richard	President	University of the Ozarks (AR)	2014–Present	Private
Dykstra, Kurt	President	Trinity Christian College (IL)	2015–Present	Private
Eck, Daniel	President	Lakeland University (WI)	2013–2017	Private
Eyring, Henry Johnson	President	Brigham Young University-Idaho (ID)	2017–Present	Private
Faison, Jr., Zachary	President	Edward Waters College (FL)	2018–Present	Private
Falwell, Jr., Jerry Lamon	President	Liberty University (VA)	2007–2020	Private
Farris, Michael	President	Patrick Henry College (VA)	2000–2006	Private
Farris, Michael	Chancellor	Patrick Henry College (VA)	2006–2017	Private
Felton, Jr., Herman J.	President	Wilberforce University (OH)	2016–2017	Private
Felton, Jr., Herman J.	President	Wiley College (TX)	2017–Present	Private
Floyd, John Anthony	President	Mars Hill University (NC)	2018–Present	Private
Francis, Norman C.	President	Xavier University of Louisiana (LA)	1968–2015	Private
French, George	President	Miles College (AL)	2006–2019	Private
Funk, Robert N.	Interim President	St. Edwards University (TX)	1998–1998	Private

Name	Position	School	Term of Office	School Type
Fuster, Jamie	President	Pontifical Catholic University of Puerto Rico (PR)	1981–1984	Private
Gallot, Jr., Richard Joseph	President	Grambling State University (LA)	2019–Present	Private
Garvey, John	President	Catholic University of America (DC)	2010–2022	Private
Gash, Jim	President	Pepperdine University (CA)	2019–Present	Private
Godwin, Angeline	President	Patrick Henry College (VA)	2012–Present	Private
Gormley, Ken	President	Duquesne (PA)	2015–Present	Private
Green, O. Jerome	President	Shorter College (AR)	2012–Present	Private
Groves, William P	Chancellor	Antioch University (NH)	2017–Present	Private
Guerry, Alexander	President	Sewanee-The University of the South (TN)	1938–1948	Private
Habecker, Eugene	President	Huntington University (IN)	1981–1991	Private
Habecker, Eugene	President	Taylor University (IN)	2005–2019	Private
Haines, Paul Lowell	President	Taylor University (IN)	2016–2019	Private
Hamen, Laurie M.	President	Mount Mercy University (IA)	2014–2020	Private
Hanley, Dexter L.	President	University of Scranton (PA)	1970–1975	Private
Hanycz, Colleen	President	LaSalle Univeristy (PA)	2015–2021	Private
Hardaway, Patricia	President	Wilberforce University (OH)	2007–2013	Private
Hardin III, Paul	President	Wofford College (SC)	1968–1972	Private
Hardin III, Paul	President	Southern Methodist University (TX)	1972–1974	Private
Hardin III, Paul	President	Drew University (NJ)	1974–1988	Private
Hardy, John Crumpton	President	University of Mary Hardin-Baylor (TX)	1912–1937	Private
Hartzog, Henry	President	Ouachita Baptist University (AR)	1907–1911	Private
Helmer, Robert	President	Lourdes University (OH)	2003–2012	Private
Herseth Sandlin, Stephanie	President	Augustana University (SD)	2017–Present	Private
Hill, Sister Elizabeth A.	President	St. Joseph's College (NY)	1997–2014	Private
Holmes, Barbara A.	President	United Theological Seminary of the Twin Cities (MN)	2012–2016	Private
Hurley, John J.	President	Canisius College (NY)	2010–2022	Private
Jeffcoat, Harold	President	Texas Wesleyan University (TX)	2000–2010	Private
Jeffcoat, Harold	President	Millikin University (IL)	2011–2012	Private
Jewell, Richard G.	President	Grove City College (PA)	2003–2014	Private
Joel, Richard	President	Yeshiva University (NY)	2003–2017	Private

Name	Position	School	Term of Office	School Type
Johnson, Ed	President	Sterling College-Kansas (KS)	1997–2003	Private
Johnson, George R.	President	Lemoyne-Owen College (TN)	1996–2002	Private
Johnston, Bryan M.	President	Saint Martin's University (OR)	2008–2008	Private
Kauffman, Bill	Interim President	St. Louis University (MO)	2013–2014	Private
Keck, Rachelle (Karstens)	President	Briar Cliff University (IA)	2018–Present	Private
Keith, Kent M.	President	Chaminade University of Honolulu (HI)	1989–1995	Private
Keith, Kent M.	President	Pacific Rim Christian University (HI)	2015–Present	Private
Knight, Bobbie	President	Miles College (AL)	2019–Present	Private
La Lumiere, Stanislaus	President	Marquette University (WI)	1887–1889	Private
LaGree, Kevin	President	Simpson College (IA)	1999–2005	Private
Lewis, Brien	President	Catwaba College (NC)	2012–2020	Private
Longstreet, Augustis Baldwin	President	Centenary College (LA)	1849–1849	Private
Lowry III, L. Randolph	President	Lipscomb University (TN)	2005–2021	Private
Ludwick, Richard	President	University of St. Thomas (MN)	2017–Present	Private
Macchiarola, Frank	President	St. Francis College (NY)	1996–2008	Private
Macchiarola, Frank	Chancellor	St. Francis College (NY)	2008–2012	Private
Martin, Daniel	President	Mount Vernon Nazarene University (OH)	2007–2012	Private
Martin, Daniel	President	Seattle Pacific University (WA)	2012–2021	Private
McClure, Tori Murden	President	Spalding University (KY)	2010–Present	Private
McCormick, Samuel	President	Coe College (IA)	1987–1904	Private
McDaniel, Tom J.	President	Oklahoma City University (OK)	2001–2004	Private
McGuire, Patricia	President	Trinity Washigton University (DC)	1989–Present	Private
McNulty, Paul	President	Grove City College (PA)	2014–Present	Private
Mengler, Thomas	President	St. Mary's University (TX) (TX)	2012–Present	Private
Miller, Michael	President	Pfeiffer University (NC)	2010–2014	Private

Name	Position	School	Term of Office	School Type
Mooney, Carol Ann	President	Saint Mary's College (IN)	2004–2016	Private
Mooney, Christopher F.	President	Woodstock College (NY)	1969–1974	Private
Morales, Jose Alberto	President	Pontifical Catholic University of Puerto Rico (PR)	2001–2006	Private
Munsil, Len	President	Arizona Christian University (AZ)	2010–Present	Private
Murrh, William Belton	President	Millsaps College (MS)	1890–1910	Private
O'Brien, Kevin	President	Santa Clara University (CA)	2019–Present	Private
O'Day, Steven	President	Austin College (TX)	2017–Present	Private
O'Hara, William T.	President	Mounty Saint Mary College (NY)	1972–1976	Private
Onders, Bob	President	Alaska Pacific University (AK)	2017–Present	Private
Pearce, Richard	President	Methodist University (NC)	1973–1983	Private
Pearsall, Joel K.	Interim President	Northwest Nazarene University (ID)	2015–2015	Private
Pearsall, Joel K.	President	Northwest Nazarene University (ID)	2016–Present	Private
Peri, Jonathan	President	Manor College (PA)	2015–Present	Private
Perrin, Larry Timothy	President	Lubbock Christian University (TX)	2012–Present	Private
Pistole, John	President	Anderson University (IN)	2015–Present	Private
Pollard, Chip	President	John Brown University (AR)	2004–Present	Private
Price, Alan	President	Ealham College (IN)	2017–2018	Private
Pye, A. Kenneth	President	Southern Methodist University (TX)	1987–1994	Private
Quinn, Kevin	President	University of Scranton (PA)	2011–2017	Private
Rainsford, George Nichols	President	Lynchburg College (VA)	1983–1993	Private
Ray, Alan	President	Elmhurst College (IL)	2008–2015	Private
Rinehart, Kathleen	President	Cardinal Stritch University (WI)	2018–Present	Private
Rooney, Jo Ann	President	Spalding University (KY)	2002–2010	Private
Scanlon, Michael	President	Franciscan University of Steubenville (OH)	1974–2000	Private
Scanlon, Michael	Chancellor	Franciscan University of Steubenville (OH)	2000–2011	Private
Scherrens, Maurice William	President	Newbury College (MA)	2012–Present	Private
Shannon, Jack	President	Christian Brothers University (TN)	2019–Present	Private

Name	Position	School	Term of Office	School Type
Sheridan, Sean	President	Franciscan University of Steubenville (OH)	2013–2019	Private
Sikorsky, Fr. Charles	President	Divine Mercy University (VA)	2007–Present	Private
Slabach, Frederick G.	President	Texas Wesleyan University (TX)	2011–Present	Private
Sloan, Albert J.	Interim President	Miles College (AL)	1989–1989	Private
Sloan, Albert J.	President	Miles College (AL)	1989–2006	Private
Smith, Hildreth	President	Catawba College (NC)	1853–1856	Private
Smith, Rodney	President	Southern Virginia University (VA)	2004–2011	Private
Sorell, Michael	President	Paul Quinn College (TX)	2007–Present	Private
Starcher, Jr., John M.	President	Southside Regional Medical Center-Professional Schools (VA)	2018–Present	Private
Starr, Kenneth	President	Baylor University (TX)	2010–2016	Private
Staton, Robert	President	Presbyterian College (SC)	2015–Present	Private
Sylvester, Esther R.	Interim President	Rosemont College (PA)	1978–1979	Private
Tetlow, Tania	President	Loyola University (LA)	2018–2022	Private
Thierstein, Joel	Interim President	Mount St. Joseph University (OH)	2014–2014	Private
Titus, Steven	President	Midland University (NE)	2002–2007	Private
Titus, Steven	President	Iowa Wesleyan University (IA)	2013–Present	Private
Towey, Jim	President	Saint Vincent College (PA)	2006–2010	Private
Underwood, William	Interim President	Baylor University (TX)	2005–2006	Private
Victor, Michael	President	Mercyhurst University (PA)	2015–2021	Private
Warfield, Ethelbert Dudley	President	Wilson College (PA)	1915–1936	Private
Whitaker, Alexander	President	King University (TN)	2016–Present	Private
White III, Luther	President	Kentucky Wesleyan College (KY)	1979–1988	Private
White, John Brown	President	Almira College (now Greenville University) (IL)	1855–1878	Private
Wiggins, Norman Adrian	Chancellor/President	Campbell College (previously Campbell University) (NC)	1967–2003	Private
Wilcox, Reed	President	Southern Virginia University (VA)	2014–Present	Private
Wilkinson, Ernest	President	Brigham Young University (UT)	1951–1971	Private
Williams, H. James	President	Mount St. Joseph University (OH)	2016–Present	Private

Name	Position	School	Term of Office	School Type
Williams, H. James	President	Mount St. Joseph University (OH)	2016–Present	Private
Williams, John	Interim President	Principia College (IL)	2019–2020	Private
Wiserman, Christine	President	Saint Xavier University (IL)	2010–2016	Private
Worthen, Kevin	President	Brigham Young University (UT)	2014–Present	Private
Zak, Leocadia	President	Agnes Scott College (GA)	2018–Present	Private

Appendix 6—Lawyer Presidents of HBCUs by Name, School, and Location

Name	Position	School	Term of Office	School Type
Alexander, Laurence	President	University of Arkansas at Pine Bluff (AK)	2013–Present	Public
Armbrister, Clarence	President	Johnson C. Smith University (NC)	2018–Present	Private
Ballard-Washington, Kimberly	Interim President	Albany State University (GA)	2013–2013	Public
Ballard-Washington, Kimberly	Interim President	Fort Valley State University (GA)	2013–2013	Public
Ballard-Washington, Kimberly	Interim President	Savannah State University (GA)	2019–2021	Public
Becton, Charles L.	Interim Chancellor	North Carolina Central University (NC)	2012–2013	Public
Becton, Charles L.	Interim Chancellor	Elizabeth City State University (NC)	2013–2014	Public
Capehart, Robin	President	Bluefield State College-Bluefield Campus (WV)	2019–Present	Public
Carter, Lisle C.	President	University of the District of Columbia (DC)	1977–1982	Public
Chambers, Julius L.	Chancellor	North Carolina Central University (NC)	1994–2001	Public
Cheek, Jr., King V.	President	Shaw University (NC)	1969–1971	Private
Cheek, Jr., King V.	President	Morgan State University (MD)	1971–1974	Private
Clark-Artis, Roslyn	President	Florida Memorial University (FL)	2013–2017	Private
Clark-Artis, Roslyn	President	Benedict College (SC)	2017–Present	Private
Davis, Joan Y.	Interim President	Shelton State Community College (AL)	2013–2014	Public
Davis, John W.	President	West Virginia State University (WV)	1919–1953	Public
Faison, Jr., Zachary	President	Edward Waters College (FL)	2018–Present	Private
Felton, Jr., Herman J.	President	Wilberforce University (OH)	2016–2017	Private
Felton, Jr., Herman J.	President	Wiley College (TX)	2017–Present	Private

Name	Position	School	Term of Office	School Type
Francis, Norman C.	President	Xavier University of Louisiana (LA)	1968–2015	Private
French, George	President	Miles College (AL)	2006–2019	Private
French, George	President	Clark Atlanta University (GA)	2019–Present	Private
Gallot, Jr., Richard Joseph	President	Grambling State University (LA)	2019–Present	Private
Green, O. Jerome	President	Shorter College (AR)	2012–Present	Private
Hall, David	President	University Virgin Islands (VI)	2009–Present	Public
Hardaway, Patricia	President	Wilberforce University (OH)	2007–2013	Private
Hardesty, Jr., David S.	President	West Virginia State University (WV)	1995–2007	Public
Harrison, Valerie	President	Lincoln University (PA)	2014–Present	Private
Hill, John H.	President	West Virginia State University (WV)	1894–1898	Public
Knight, Bobbie	President	Miles College (AL)	2019–Present	Private
Langston, John Mercer	Acting President	Howard University (DC)	1872–1872	Private
Langston, John Mercer	President	Virginia State University (VA)	1882–1882	Public
Martin, Jr., Harold	President	Morehouse College (GA)	2017–Present	Private
Mason, Ronald	President	Jackson State University (MS)	2000–2010	Public
Mason, Ronald	President	University of the District of Columbia (DC)	2015–Present	Public
Moron, Alonzo Graseano	Acting President	Hampton University (VA)	1948–1948	Private
Moron, Alonzo Graseano	President	Hampton University (VA)	1949–1959	Private
Nabrit, James	President	Howard University (DC)	1960–1969	Private
O'Leary, Hazel	President	Fisk University (TN)	2005–2013	Private
Sloan, Albert J.	Interim President	Miles College (AL)	1989–1989	Private
Sloan, Albert J.	President	Miles College (AL)	1989–2006	Private
Sorell, Michael	President	Paul Quinn College (TX)	2007–Present	Private
Stith, Jr., Millard "Pete"	President	Saint Paul College (MN)	2013–2016	Public
Swygert, H. Patrick	President	Howard University (DC)	1995–2008	Private
Walsh, Suzannne	President	Bennett College (NC)	2019–Present	Private
Williams, H. James	President	Fisk University (TN)	2013–2015	Private

Appendix 7—Appointments of Lawyer Presidents by Decade

Decade	Name	Position	School	Term of Office
1700s	Leverett, John	President	Harvard University (MA)	1708–1724
1720s	William, Elisha	President	Yale University (CT)	1726–1739
1770s	Madison, Bishop James	President	College of William and Mary (VA)	1777–1812
1780s	Baldwin, Abraham	President	University of Georgia (GA)	1785–1801
1780s	Johnson, William Samuel	President	Columbia University (NY)	1787–1800
1790s	Kerr, David	President	University of North Carolina (NC)	1794–1796
1800s	Meigs, Josiah	President	University of Georgia (GA)	1801–1810
1800s	Messer, Asa	President	Brown University (RI)	1802–1826
1820s	Clark, Peter	President	Washington College (MD)	1829–1832
1820s	Deur, William Alexander	President	Columbia University (NY)	1829–1842
1820s	Quincy III., Josiah	President	Harvard University (MA)	1829–1845
1830s	Barnwell, Robert Woodward	President	South Carolina College (SC)	1833–1841
1830s	Elliott, David	President	Washington College (MD)	1830–1831
1830s	Few, Ignatius Alphonso	President	Emory University (GA)	1836–1839
1830s	Linsley, Joel Harvey	President	Marietta College (OH)	1835–1846
1830s	Longstreet, Augustis Baldwin	President	Emory University (GA)	1839–1839
1830s	Maxwell, William	President	Hampden-Sydney College (VA)	1838–1844
1830s	Pierce, George Foster	President	Georgian Female College (later Wesleyan) (GA)	1838–1840
1830s	Swain, David Lowry	President	University of North Carolina (NC)	1835–1868
1840s	Emory, Robert	Interim President	Dickinson College (PA)	1842–1843
1840s	Emory, Robert	President	Dickinson College (PA)	1845–1847
1840s	Fillmore, Millard	Chancellor	University at Buffalo (NY)	1846–1874
1840s	Hasbrouck, Abraham Bruyn	President	Rutgers University (NJ)	1840–1850
1840s	Longstreet, Augustis Baldwin	President	Centenary College (LA)	1849–1849
1840s	Longstreet, Augustus Baldwin	President	Emory University (GA)	1840–1848
1840s	Moore, Nathaniel Fish	President	Columbia University (NY)	1842–1849
1840s	Pierce, George Foster	President	Emory University (GA)	1848–1854

Decade	Name	Position	School	Term of Office
1840s	Preston, William C.	President	South Carolina College (SC)	1845–1851
1840s	White, John Brown	President	Wake Forest University (NC)	1848–1853
1840s	Woolsey, Theodore Dwight	President	Yale University (CT)	1846–1871
1850s	Frelinghuysen, Theodore	President	Rutgers University (NJ)	1850–1862
1850s	Laws, Samuel	President	Westminster College (MO)	1854–1861
1850s	Longstreet, Augustus Baldwin	President	University of Mississippi (MS)	1850–1850
1850s	Longstreet, Augustus Baldwin	President	South Carolina College (SC)	1856–1856
1850s	Smith, Hildreth	President	Catawba College (NC)	1853–1856
1850s	Welch, Adoniah Strong	President	Eastern Michigan University (MI)	1851–1865
1850s	White, John Brown	President	Almira College (now Greenville University) (IL)	1855–1878
1850s	Williams, Joseph R.	President	Michigan State University (MI)	1857–1859
1860s	Bowman, John Bryan	President	Transylvania University (KY)	1865–1875
1860s	Forsyth, James	President	Rensselaer Polytechnic Institute (NY)	1868–1886
1860s	Magoun, George	President	Grinnell College (IA)	1865–1884
1860s	Smith, Luther M.	President	Emory University (GA)	1867–1871
1860s	Smith, William Russell	President	University of Alabama (AL)	1869–1871
1860s	Sutton, Andrew J.	President	Washington College (MD)	1860–1867
1860s	Welch, Adoniah Strong	President	Iowa State University (IA)	1869–1883
1870s	Battle, Kemp Plummer	President	University of North Carolina (NC)	1876–1891
1870s	Farnsworth, Charles Buchanan	President	Rhode Island School of Design (RI)	1877–1888
1870s	Fowler, Charles Henry	President	Northwestern University (IL)	1873–1876
1870s	Langston, John Mercer	Acting President	Howard University (DC)	1872–1872
1870s	Laws, Samuel	President	University of Missouri (MO)	1876–1889
1870s	Marcy, Oliver	President	Northwestern University (IL)	1876–1881
1870s	Purnell, William Henry	President	University of Delaware (DE)	1870–1875
1870s	Smith, Hildreth	President	Sam Houston State University (TX)	1879–1881
1870s	Wyman, William Stokes	Interim President	University of Alabama (AL)	1879–1880
1880s	Clayton, Henry Delamar	President	University of Alabama (AL)	1886–1889

Decade	Name	Position	School	Term of Office
1880s	Cummings, Joseph	President	Northwestern University (IL)	1881–1890
1880s	Hale, Horace M.	President	University of Colorado-Boulder (CO)	1887–1892
1880s	La Lumiere, Stanislaus	President	Marquette University (WI)	1887–1889
1880s	Lamberton, Robert Alexander	President	Lehigh University (PA)	1880–1893
1880s	Langston, John Mercer	President	Virginia State University (VA)	1882–1882
1880s	Lewis, Burwell Boykin	President	University of Alabama (AL)	1880–1885
1880s	Northrop, Cyrus	President	University of Minnesota (MN)	1884–1911
1880s	Peck, John Hudson	President	Rensselaer Polytechnic Institute (NY)	1888–1901
1880s	Sprague, Carleton	Chancellor	University at Buffalo (NY)	1885–1895
1880s	Sprague, Homer	President	Mills College (CA)	1885–1887
1880s	Sprague, Homer	President	University of North Dakota (ND)	1887–1891
1880s	Tucker, Thomas DeSaille	President	Florida Agricultural and Mechanical University (FL)	1887–1901
1880s	Tyler, Lyon Gardiner	President	College of William and Mary (VA)	1888–1919
1880s	Walker, Francis Amasa	President	Massachusetts Institute of Technology (MA)	1881–1897
1880s	Ward, George Morgan	President	Rollins College (FL)	1886–1902
1880s	Warfield, Ethelbert Dudley	President	Miami University (OH)	1888–1891
1880s	Willets, Edwin	President	Michigan State University (MI)	1885–1889
1880s	Willits, Edwin	President	Eastern Michigan University (MI)	1883–1885
1880s	Willits, Edwin	President	State Agriculture College (Michigan State) (MI)	1885–1889
1880s	Wyman, William Stokes	Interim President	University of Alabama (AL)	1885–1886
1880s	Wyman, William Stokes	Interim President	University of Alabama (AL)	1889–1890
1890s	Dobson, William Davis	President	Truman State University (MO)	1891–1899
1890s	Hartzog, Henry	President	Clemson University (SC)	1897–1902
1890s	Hill, John H.	President	West Virginia State University (WV)	1894–1898
1890s	Hill, Walter Barnard	Chancellor	University of Georgia (GA)	1899–1905
1890s	Kirk, John Robert	President	Truman State University (MO)	1899–1925
1890s	Marcy, Oliver	President	Northwestern University (IL)	1890–1890
1890s	Murrh, William Belton	President	Millsaps College (MS)	1890–1910
1890s	Rogers, Henry Wade	President	Northwestern University (IL)	1890–1900

Appendices | 247

Decade	Name	Position	School	Term of Office
1890s	Taylor, A. N.	President	Northern Arizona University (AZ)	1899–1909
1890s	Warfield, Ethelbert Dudley	President	Lafayette College (PA)	1891–1914
1890s	Weld, Frank	President	Minnesota State University Moorhead (MN)	1899–1920
1900s	Abercrombie, John	President	University of Alabama (AL)	1902–1911
1900s	Bissell, Wilson Shannon	Chancellor	University at Buffalo (NY)	1902–1903
1900s	Drinker, Henry Sturgis	President	Lehigh University (PA)	1905–1920
1900s	Garfield, Henry Augustus	President	Williams College (MA)	1908–1934
1900s	Hardy, John Crumpton	President	Mississippi State University (MS)	1900–1912
1900s	Hartzog, Henry	President	University of Arkansas (AR)	1902–1905
1900s	Hartzog, Henry	President	Ouachita Baptist University (AR)	1907–1911
1900s	Lowell, Lawrence	President	Harvard University (MA)	1909–1933
1900s	McCormick, Samuel	Chancellor	University of Pittsburgh (PA)	1904–1921
1900s	Norton, Charles Phelps	Chancellor	University at Buffalo (NY)	1909–1920
1900s	Tillman, John N.	President	University of Arkansas (AR)	1905–1912
1900s	Whitfield, Henry L.	President	Mississippi University for Women (MS)	1907–1920
1900s	Wilson, Woodrow	President	Princeton University (NJ)	1902–1910
1900s	Wyman, William Stokes	President	University of Alabama (AL)	1901–1902
1910s	Black, James D.	President	Union College (KY)	1910–1912
1910s	Davis, John W.	President	West Virginia State University (WV)	1919–1953
1910s	Goodnow, Frank Johnson	President	Johns Hopkins (MD)	1914–1929
1910s	Hardy, John Crumpton	President	University of Mary Hardin-Baylor (TX)	1912–1937
1910s	Warfield, Ethelbert Dudley	President	Wilson College (PA)	1915–1936
1920s	Baker, Simon Strousse	President	Washington and Jefferson College (PA)	1922–1931
1920s	Beury, Charles Ezra	President	Temple University (PA)	1926–1941
1920s	Bowman, Milo Jesse	Interim President	Valparaiso University (IN)	1922–1922
1920s	Guerry, Alexander	President	University of Chattanooga (TN)	1929–1938
1920s	Hadley, Herbert S.	President	Washington University in St. Louis (MO)	1923–1927
1920s	Hall, Arnold Bennett	President	University of Oregon (OR)	1926–1932

Decade	Name	Position	School	Term of Office
1920s	Hutchins, Robert Maynard	President	University of Chicago (IL)	1929–1945
1920s	Moore, Ernest Carroll	President	University of California, Los Angeles (CA)	1927–1929
1920s	Wells, Rainey T.	President	Murray State University (KY)	1926–1932
1930s	Archer, Sr., Gleason	President	Suffolk University (MA)	1937–1948
1930s	Brett, Sr., Philip Milledoler	Acting President	Rutgers University-Newark (NJ)	1930–1932
1930s	Butts, Alfred Benjamin	Chancellor	University of Mississippi (MS)	1935–1946
1930s	Davis, Harwell Goodwin	President	Samford University (also known as Howard College) (AL)	1938–1958
1930s	Foster, Richard Clark	President	University of Alabama (AL)	1937–1941
1930s	Fulbright, J. William	President	University of Arkansas (AR)	1939–1941
1930s	Gates, Thomas Sovereign	President	University of Pennsylvania (PA)	1930–1944
1930s	Guerry, Alexander	President	Sewanee-The University of the South (TN)	1938–1948
1930s	Harris, Rufus Carrollton	President	Tulane University (LA)	1939–1960
1930s	Knapp, Bradford	President	Texas Tech University (TX)	1932–1938
1930s	Moseley, John Ohleyer	President	University of Central Oklahoma (OK)	1935–1939
1930s	Stearns, Robert	President	University of Colorado-Boulder (CO)	1939–1953
1940s	Anderson, Hurst Robbins	President	Centenary College (NJ)	1943–1948
1940s	Anderson, Hurst Robbins	President	Hamline College (MN)	1948–1952
1940s	Armstrong, Richard H.	President	University of Southern Maine (ME)	1945–1961
1940s	Bartle, Harold Roe	President	Missouri Valley College (MO)	1948–1950
1940s	Burse, Walter	President	Suffolk University (MA)	1948–1954
1940s	Darden, Jr., Colgate Whitehead	President	University of Virginia (VA)	1947–1959
1940s	Fagg, Jr., Fred D.	President	University of Southern California (CA)	1947–1957
1940s	Hutchins, Robert Maynard	Chancellor	University of Chicago (IL)	1945–1951
1940s	Jacobs, Albert C.	Chancellor	University of Denver (CO)	1949–1953
1940s	Lockmiller, David A.	President	University of Chattanooga (TN)	1942–1959

Appendices | 249

Decade	Name	Position	School	Term of Office
1940s	McCormick, James Byron	President	University of Arizona (AZ)	1947–1951
1940s	Moron, Alonzo Graseano	Acting President	Hampton University (VA)	1948–1948
1940s	Moron, Alonzo Graseano	President	Hampton University (VA)	1949–1959
1940s	Moseley, John Ohleyer	President	University of Nevada, Reno (NV)	1944–1949
1940s	Price, James F.	President	Kansas State Teachers College/ Emporia College (KS)	1943–1945
1940s	Price, James F.	Chancellor	University of Denver (CO)	1948–1948
1940s	Siemens, Cornelius Henry	President	Compton College (CA)	1946–1950
1940s	Stassen, Harold	President	University of Pennsylvania (PA)	1948–1953
1950s	Anderson, Hurst Robbins	President	American University (DC)	1952–1968
1950s	Aycock, William Brantley	Chancellor	University of North Carolina (NC)	1957–1964
1950s	Fey, John T.	President	University of Vermont (VT)	1958–1964
1950s	Garside, Charles	Acting President	State University of New York (NY)	1951–1952
1950s	Hawk, Rupert A.	Acting President	Grinnell College (IA)	1954–1955
1950s	Helfferich, Donald L. "Ty"	President	Ursinus College (PA)	1958–1970
1950s	Jacobs, Albert C.	President	Trinity College (CT)	1953–1968
1950s	McFarland, Carl	President	University of Montana (MT)	1951–1958
1950s	Newton, J. Quigg	President	University of Colorado-Boulder (CO)	1956–1963
1950s	Russell, Donald S.	President	University of South Carolina (SC)	1952–1957
1950s	Shepley, Ethan A. H.	Chancellor	Washington University in St. Louis (MO)	1953–1961
1950s	Siemens, Cornelius Henry	President	Humboldt State University (CA)	1950–1973
1950s	Sweavingen, Tilford	President	William Woods College (MI)	1951–1961
1950s	Tweed, Harrison	Acting President	Sarah Lawrence College (NY)	1959–1960
1950s	Wilkinson, Ernest	President	Brigham Young University (UT)	1951–1971
1960s	Adams, Ralph Wyatt	President	Troy University (AL)	1964–1989
1960s	Appel, Anthony R.	President	Franklin and Marshall (PA)	1962–1962
1960s	Bloustein, Edward J.	President	Bennington College (VT)	1965–1971

Decade	Name	Position	School	Term of Office
1960s	Brewster, Jr Kingman	President	Yale University (CT)	1963–1977
1960s	Cheek, Jr., King V.	President	Shaw University (NC)	1969–1971
1960s	Crosby, Harold B.	President	University of Florida (FL)	1964–1974
1960s	Donovan, James	President	Pratt Institute (NY)	1968–1970
1960s	Eliot, Thomas H.	Chancellor	Washington University in St. Louis (MO)	1962–1971
1960s	Ethierington, Edwin	President	Wesleyan University (CT)	1967–1979
1960s	Fenton, John E.	President	Suffolk University (MA)	1965–1970
1960s	Ferguson, Glenn	Chancellor	Long Island University (NY)	1969–1970
1960s	Fey, John T.	President	University of Wyoming (WY)	1964–1966
1960s	Francis, Norman C.	President	Xavier University of Louisiana (LA)	1968–2015
1960s	Godfrey III, Edward S.	President	University of Southern Maine (ME)	1962–1973
1960s	Greenberg, Erwin	President	Worsham College of Mortuary Science (IL)	1961–1979
1960s	Hardin III, Paul	President	Wofford College (SC)	1968–1972
1960s	Harris, Rufus Carrollton	President	Mercer University (GA)	1960–1979
1960s	Huntley, Robert E. R.	President	Washington and Lee University (VA)	1968–1983
1960s	Levi, Edward H.	President	University of Chicago (IL)	1968–1975
1960s	Mautz, Robert	Chancellor	State University System of Florida (FL)	1968–1975
1960s	Montgomery, Douglas	President	Blue Ridge Community College (VA)	1966–1968
1960s	Montgomery, Douglas	President	Tidewater Community College (VA)	1968–1972
1960s	Mooney, Christopher F.	President	Woodstock College (NY)	1969–1974
1960s	Nabrit, James	President	Howard University (DC)	1960–1969
1960s	Olsen, James Karge	President	William Paterson University of New Jersey (NJ)	1968–1972
1960s	Pantzer, Robert T.	President	University of Montana (MT)	1966–1974
1960s	Rendelman, John S.	President	Southern Illinois University-Edwardsville (IL)	1968–1976
1960s	Rexach, Jamie Benitez	President	University of Puerto Rico (PR)	1966–1970
1960s	Rosenblum, Victor	President	Reed College (OR)	1968–1970
1960s	Shaw, Manford A.	President	Westminster College (UT)	1968–1976
1960s	Spangler, James	President	Worsham College of Mortuary Science (IL)	1961–1979

Appendices | 251

Decade	Name	Position	School	Term of Office
1960s	White III, Luther	President	Randolph College (VA)	1967–1979
1960s	Wiggins, Norman Adrian	Chancellor/ President	Campbell College (previously Campbell University) (NC)	1967–2003
1970s	Barry, Jeffrey	President	Walsh College (MI)	1971–1991
1970s	Bennett, James Jefferson	President	Sewanee-The University of the South (TN)	1971–1977
1970s	Bloustein, Edward J.	President	Rutgers University (NJ)	1971–1989
1970s	Bok, Derek	President	Harvard University (MA)	1971–1999
1970s	Bragdon, Paul E.	President	Reed College (OR)	1971–1988
1970s	Brewster, Carroll	President	Hollins University (VA)	1975–1981
1970s	Brickley, James H.	President	Eastern Michigan University (MI)	1975–1978
1970s	Brown II., John	President	John Brown University (AR)	1979–1993
1970s	Campbell, Colin	President	Wesleyan University (CT)	1970–1988
1970s	Carter, Lisle C.	President	University of the District of Columbia (DC)	1977–1982
1970s	Cheek, Jr., King V.	President	Morgan State University (MD)	1971–1974
1970s	Cheek, Jr., King V.	President	Union Insitute and University (OH)	1976–1978
1970s	Crosby, Harold B.	Interim President	Florida International University (FL)	1975–1975
1970s	Crosby, Harold B.	President	Florida International University (FL)	1976–1979
1970s	Drinnon, James E.	Chancellor	University of Tennessee-Chattanooga (TN)	1973–1981
1970s	Emery, Alfred C.	President	University of Utah (UT)	1971–1973
1970s	Farenthold, Frances Tarlton "Sissy"	President	Wells College (NY)	1976–1980
1970s	Ferguson, Glenn	President	Clark University (MA)	1970–1973
1970s	Ferguson, Glenn	President	University of Connecticut (CT)	1973–1978
1970s	Hanley, Dexter L.	President	University of Scranton (PA)	1970–1975
1970s	Hardin III, Paul	President	Southern Methodist University (TX)	1972–1974
1970s	Hardin III, Paul	President	Drew University (NJ)	1974–1988
1970s	Iseman, Joseph S.	Acting President	Bennington College (VT)	1976–1976
1970s	Kinney, RADM, Sheldon H.	President	SUNY Martime College (NY)	1972–1982
1970s	Kuttler, Jr., Carl M.	President	St. Petersburg College (FL)	1978–2009

Decade	Name	Position	School	Term of Office
1970s	Lee, Calvin B.T.	Acting President	Boston University (MA)	1970–1971
1970s	Lee, Calvin B.T.	Chancellor	University of Maryland, Baltimore (MD)	1971–1976
1970s	Lesar, Hiram	Interim President	Southern Illinois University-Carbondale (IL)	1974–1974
1970s	Lesar, Hiram	Interim President	Southern Illinois University-Carbondale (IL)	1979–1980
1970s	Mackey, M. Cecil	President	University of South Florida (FL)	1971–1976
1970s	Mackey, M. Cecil	President	Texas Tech University (TX)	1976–1979
1970s	Mackey, M. Cecil	President	Michigan State University (MI)	1979–1985
1970s	O'Hara, William T.	President	Mounty Saint Mary College (NY)	1972–1976
1970s	O'Hara, William T.	President	Bryant University (RI)	1976–1989
1970s	Pearce, Richard	President	Methodist University (NC)	1973–1983
1970s	Pye, A. Kenneth	Chancellor	Duke University (NC)	1970–1971
1970s	Pye, A. Kenneth	Chancellor	Duke University (NC)	1976–1982
1970s	Rainsford, George Nichols	President	Kalamzoo College (MI)	1972–1983
1970s	Scanlon, Michael	President	Franciscan University of Steubenville (OH)	1974–2000
1970s	Sherman, Max	President	West Texas A&M University (TX)	1977–1982
1970s	Smith, Virginia B.	President	Vassar College (NY)	1977–1986
1970s	Steiner, Stuart	President	Genesee Community College (KY)	1975–2011
1970s	Stevens, Robert	President	Haverford College (PA)	1978–1987
1970s	Stone, Jesse N.	President	Southern University and A&M College (LA)	1974–1985
1970s	Sylvester, Esther R.	Interim President	Rosemont College (PA)	1978–1979
1970s	Trachtenberg, Steven	President	Univeristy of Hartford (CT)	1977–1998
1970s	Vestal, Theodore M. "Ted"	President	California Institute of Integrated Studies (CA)	1979–1983
1970s	Webb, W. Roger	President	Northeastern State University (OK)	1978–1997
1970s	White III, Luther	President	Kentucky Wesleyan College (KY)	1979–1988
1970s	Witherspoon, Gerald	President	Goddard College (VT, WA) (VT)	1970–1975
1980s	Abdullah, Edythe	Campus President	Florida State College at Jacksonville (FL)	1985–2010
1980s	Adamany, David	President	Wayne State University (MI)	1982–1997

Decade	Name	Position	School	Term of Office
1980s	Bepko, Gerald	Chancellor	Indiana University-Purdue University Indianapolis (IN)	1986–2003
1980s	Brewster, Carroll	President	Hobart William Smith Colleges (NY)	1982–1991
1980s	Carothers, Robert L.	President	Southwest Minnesota State University (MN)	1983–1986
1980s	Carothers, Robert L.	Chancellor	Minnesota State University System (MN)	1986–1991
1980s	Criser, Marshall	President	University of Florida (FL)	1984–1989
1980s	Davenport, David	President	Pepperdine University (CA)	1985–2000
1980s	Dybward, Peter	President	The Wright Institute (CA)	1982–Present
1980s	Ehrlich, Thomas	President	Indiana University (IN)	1987–1994
1980s	Ferrero, Ray	CEO	Nova Southeastern University (FL)	1988–2010
1980s	Freedman, James O.	President	University of Iowa (IA)	1982–1987
1980s	Freedman, James O.	President	Dartmouth College (NH)	1987–1998
1980s	Funk, Robert N.	President	Cornish College of the Arts (WA)	1985–1994
1980s	Fuster, Jamie	President	Pontifical Catholic University of Puerto Rico (PR)	1981–1984
1980s	Futter, Ellen V.	Acting President/President	Barnard College (NY)	1980–1993
1980s	Gardner, James A.	President	Lewis and Clark College (OR)	1989–2003
1980s	Gee Gordon, E	President	West Virginia University (WV)	1981–1985
1980s	Gee Gordon, E	President	University of Colorado System (CO)	1985–1990
1980s	Gerety, Tom	President	Trinity College (CT)	1989–1994
1980s	Habecker, Eugene	President	Huntington University (IN)	1981–1991
1980s	Hardin III, Paul	Chancellor	University of North Carolina (NC)	1988–1995
1980s	Haynes, Ulric	Acting President	SUNY College at Old Westbury (NY)	1981–1981
1980s	Heyman, Ira Michael	Chancellor	University of California, Berkeley (CA)	1980–1990
1980s	Horton, Howard E.	President	Massachusetts Communications College/New England Institute of Art (MA)	1988–2000
1980s	Hull, Roger	President	Beloit College (WI)	1981–1990
1980s	Keith, Kent M.	President	Chaminade University of Honolulu (HI)	1989–1995

Decade	Name	Position	School	Term of Office
1980s	Lader, Philip	President	Winthrop University (SC)	1983–1985
1980s	Lapp, Joseph	President	Eastern Memmonite University (PA)	1987–2003
1980s	Liacouras, Peter	President	Temple University (PA)	1981–2000
1980s	Lorimer, Linda	President	Randolph College (VA)	1986–1993
1980s	McCormick, Samuel	President	Coe College (IA)	1987–1904
1980s	McGuire, Patricia	President	Trinity Washigton University (DC)	1989–Present
1980s	McKenna, Margaret	President	Lesley University (MA)	1985–2007
1980s	O'Neil, Robert Marchant	President	University of Wisconsin (WI)	1980–1985
1980s	O'Neil, Robert Marchant	President	University of Virginia (VA)	1985–1990
1980s	Pye, A. Kenneth	President	Southern Methodist University (TX)	1987–1994
1980s	Rainsford, George Nichols	President	Lynchburg College (VA)	1983–1993
1980s	Sargent, David	President	Suffolk University (MA)	1989–2010
1980s	Schmidt, Benno	President	Yale University (CT)	1986–1992
1980s	Shafer, Raymond P.	Interim President	Allegheny Community College (PA)	1985–1986
1980s	Sloan, Albert J.	Interim President	Miles College (AL)	1989–1989
1980s	Sloan, Albert J.	President	Miles College (AL)	1989–2006
1980s	Sovern, Michael	President	Columbia University (NY)	1980–1993
1980s	Stevens, Robert	Chancellor	University of California, Santa Cruz (CA)	1987–1991
1980s	Stoepler, John W.	Interim President	University of Toledo (OH)	1988–1989
1980s	Thornton, Ray	President	Arkansas State University (AR)	1981–1984
1980s	Thornton, Ray	President	University of Arkansas (AR)	1984–1990
1980s	Trachtenberg, Steven	President	George Washington University (DC)	1988–2007
1980s	Verkuil, Paul Robert	President	College of William and Mary (VA)	1985–1992
1990s	Abbott, James	President	University of South Dakota (SD)	1997–2018
1990s	Arnold, W. Ellis	President	Lambuth University (TN)	1996–1996
1990s	Barba, James	President	Albany Medical College (NY)	1995–2020
1990s	Bekavac, Nancy Y.	President	Scripps College (CA)	1990–2007
1990s	Bernstine, Daniel	President	Portland State University (OR)	1997–2007

Appendices | 255

Decade	Name	Position	School	Term of Office
1990s	Bollinger, Lee	President	University of Michigan at Ann Arbor (MI)	1996–2002
1990s	Boren, David	President	University of Oklahoma (OK)	1994–2018
1990s	Brown, Hank	President	University of Northern Colorado (CO)	1998–2002
1990s	Bulger, William	President	University of Massachusetts (MA)	1995–2003
1990s	Carothers, Robert L.	President	University of Rhode Island (RI)	1991–2009
1990s	Casper, Gerhard	President	Stanford University (CA)	1992–2000
1990s	Chambers, Julius L.	Chancellor	North Carolina Central University (NC)	1994–2001
1990s	Cobb, John Whitehouse	President	Naropa University (CO)	1993–2003
1990s	Collens, Lew	President	Illinois Institute of Technology (IL)	1990–2007
1990s	D'Alembert, Talbert "Sandy"	President	Florida State University (FL)	1994–2003
1990s	Davros, Harry	President and CEO	Wade College (TX)	1997–Present
1990s	Degnan, Rev Daniel A.	President	Saint Peter's University (NJ)	1990–1995
1990s	Denson, Rob	President	Northeast Iowa Community College (IA)	1998–2003
1990s	Donner, Thomas	Interim President	Santa Monica College (CA)	1994–1995
1990s	Farish, Donald	President	Rowan University (NJ)	1998–2011
1990s	Frohnmayer, David	President	University of Oregon (OR)	1994–2000
1990s	Funk, Robert N.	Interim President	Sierra Nevada College (NV)	1995–1997
1990s	Funk, Robert N.	Interim President	St. Edwards University (TX)	1998–1998
1990s	Funk, Robert N.	Interim President	Villa Julie College (now Stevenson University) (MD)	1999–2000
1990s	Gann, Pamela B.	President	Claremont McKenna College (CA)	1993–2013
1990s	Gee Gordon, E	President	Ohio State University (OH)	1990–1998
1990s	Gee Gordon, E	President	Brown University (RI)	1998–2000
1990s	Gerety, Tom	President	Amherst College (MA)	1994–2003
1990s	Godwin, Angeline	President	Ashland Community and Technical College (KY)	1997–2000
1990s	Greenwald, Stephen	President	Metropolitan College of New York (NY)	1999–2008

Decade	Name	Position	School	Term of Office
1990s	Greiner, William R.	President	University of Buffalo (NY)	1991–2004
1990s	Hardesty, Jr., David S.	President	West Virginia State University (WV)	1995–2007
1990s	Hill, Sister Elizabeth A.	President	St. Joseph's College (NY)	1997–2014
1990s	Hull, Roger	President	Union College (NY)	1990–2005
1990s	Hunter, James	President	Point Park University (PA)	1995–1997
1990s	Jackson, Thomas H.	President	University of Rochester (NY)	1994–2005
1990s	Johnson, Ed	President	Sterling College-Kansas (KS)	1997–2003
1990s	Johnson, George R.	President	Lemoyne-Owen College (TN)	1996–2002
1990s	Johnson, Jr., Glen D.	President	Southeastern Oklahoma State University (OK)	1997–2006
1990s	Johnston, Bryan M.	Interim President	Willamette University (OR)	1997–1998
1990s	Khaytat, Robert	President	University of Mississippi (MS)	1995–2009
1990s	LaGree, Kevin	President	Simpson College (IA)	1999–2005
1990s	Landsmark, Ted	President	Boston Architectural College (MA)	1997–2004
1990s	Lewis, Ovid C.	President	Nova Southeastern University (FL)	1994–1997
1990s	Macchiarola, Frank	President	St. Francis College (NY)	1996–2008
1990s	Machtley, Ronald	President	Bryant University (RI)	1996–2020
1990s	McPherson, M. Peter	President	Michigan State University (MI)	1993–2004
1990s	Meehan, Martin	Chancellor	University of Massachusetts Lowell (MA)	1995–2003
1990s	Musterman, Cynthia	President	Stevens-The Institute of Business and Arts (MO)	1999–Present
1990s	Neimic, Catherine	President and Founder	Phoenix Institute of Herbal Medicine and Accupuncture (AZ)	1996–Present
1990s	Nelson, Christopher B.	President	St. John's College-Annapolis (MD)	1991–2017
1990s	Nordenberg, Mark	Interim Chancellor	University of Pittsburgh (PA)	1995–1995
1990s	Nordenberg, Mark	Chancellor	University of Pittsburgh (PA)	1996–2014
1990s	Osgood, Russell K.	President	Grinnell College (IA)	1998–2010
1990s	Perry, Audy Michael	Interim President	Marshall University (WV)	1999–2000
1990s	Peterson, Shirely	President	Hood College (MD)	1995–2000
1990s	Pretty, Keith	President	Walsh College (MI)	1999–2006

Appendices | 257

Decade	Name	Position	School	Term of Office
1990s	Quigley, Jr., Kenneth	President	Curry College (MA)	1996–Present
1990s	Rothkopf, Arthur	President	Lafayette College (PA)	1993–2005
1990s	Salmon, Thomas P.	President	University of Vermont (VT)	1991–1997
1990s	Schwarz, Thomas	Acting President	Hamilton College (NY)	1999–1999
1990s	Smith, Virginia B.	Acting President	Mills College (CA)	1990–1990
1990s	Stanley, Deborah F.	Interim President	SUNY Oswego (NY)	1995–1997
1990s	Stanley, Deborah F.	President	SUNY Oswego (NY)	1997–2021
1990s	Stone, Philip	President	Bridgewater College (VA)	1994–2010
1990s	Studley, Jamie	President	Skidmore (NY)	1999–2003
1990s	Sullivan, Timothy J.	President	College of William and Mary (VA)	1992–2005
1990s	Swygert, H. Patrick	President	University at Albany (NY)	1990–1995
1990s	Swygert, H. Patrick	President	Howard University (DC)	1995–2008
1990s	Thompson, Larry	President	Ringling College of Art and Design (FL)	1999–Present
1990s	Traer, James	President	Westminster College (MO)	1993–1999
1990s	Trible, Paul	President	Christopher Newport University (VA)	1996–2022
1990s	Viar, David	President	American River College (CA)	1995–2013
1990s	Vogt, Carl	President	Williams College (MA)	1999–2000
1990s	Webb, W. Roger	President	University of Central Oklahoma (OK)	1997–2011
1990s	Yudof, Mark	President	University of Minnesota (MN)	1997–2002
2000s	Abrams, Norman	President	University of California, Los Angeles (CA)	2006–2007
2000s	Adamany, David	President	Temple University (PA)	2000–2006
2000s	Alanis, Javier	President	Seminary of the Southwest (TX)	2009–Present
2000s	Ambar, Carmen Twillie	President	Douglass College (NJ)	2002–2008
2000s	Ambar, Carmen Twillie	President	Cedar Crest College (PA)	2008–2017
2000s	Bacow, Lawrence	President	Tufts University (MA)	2001–2011
2000s	Bahls, Steven	President	Augustana College (IL)	2003–Present
2000s	Baker, Bruce	President	Chippewa Valley Technical College (WI)	2007–Present
2000s	Baldasare, Paul	President	St. Andrews University (NC)	2006–2020
2000s	Baltodano, Josefina Castillo	President	Marian University (WI)	2006–2009

Decade	Name	Position	School	Term of Office
2000s	Beauchamp, Rev. E. William	President	University of Portland (OR)	2004–2014
2000s	Benton, Andrew K.	President	Pepperdine University (CA)	2000–2019
2000s	Bepko, Gerald	Interim President	Indiana University (IN)	2003–2003
2000s	Black, Robert	Interim President	Rocky Vista University (CO)	2009–2010
2000s	Bogomolny, Robert	President	University of Baltimore (MD)	2002–2014
2000s	Bok, Derek	President	Harvard University (MA)	2006–2007
2000s	Bollinger, Lee	President	Columbia University (NY)	2002–2023
2000s	Bragdon, Paul E.	Interim President	Lewis and Clark College (OR)	2003–2004
2000s	Brand, Jonathan	President	Doane College (NE)	2005–2011
2000s	Braveman, Daan	President	Nazareth College (NY)	2005–2020
2000s	Brown, Hank	President	University of Colorado-Boulder (CO)	2005–2008
2000s	Capehart, Robin	President	West Liberty University (WV)	2007–2015
2000s	Casey, Brian	President	DePauw University (IN)	2008–2016
2000s	Cheek, Jr., King V.	Chancellor	New York College of Health Professionals (NY)	2001–2003
2000s	Chema, Thomas V.	President	Hiram College (OH)	2003–2014
2000s	Cline, Kimberly	President	Mercy College (NY)	2008–2013
2000s	Cordes Larson, Gloria	President	Bentley (MA)	2007–2018
2000s	Cox, Cathy	President	Young Harris College (GA)	2007–2017
2000s	Curan, Thomas	President	Rockhurst University (MO)	2006–Present
2000s	Daniels, Ronald	President	Johns Hopkins (MD)	2009–Present
2000s	Decatur, William	Interim President	University of Toledo (OH)	2000–2001
2000s	Delaney, John	President	University of North Florida (FL)	2003–2018
2000s	Denson, Rob	President	Des Moines Area Community Colleges (IA)	2003–Present
2000s	Diver, Colin	President	Reed College (OR)	2002–2012
2000s	Donner, Thomas	Interim President	Santa Monica College (CA)	2005–2005
2000s	Dunagan, Nick	Chancellor	University of Tennessee-Martin (TN)	2001–2007
2000s	Falwell, Jr., Jerry Lamon	President	Liberty University (VA)	2007–2020
2000s	Farrell, Michael Jospeh	Interim President	Marshall University (WV)	2005–2005

Decade	Name	Position	School	Term of Office
2000s	Farris, Michael	President	Patrick Henry College (VA)	2000–2006
2000s	Farris, Michael	Chancellor	Patrick Henry College (VA)	2006–2017
2000s	Ferrentino, Robert	President	Montcalm Community College (MI)	2009–Present
2000s	Foster, Tim	President	Colorado Mesa Univeristy (CO)	2004–2021
2000s	Freidman, Stephen	President	Pace University (NY)	2007–2017
2000s	French, George	President	Miles College (AL)	2006–2019
2000s	Funk, Robert N.	Interim President	Hood College (MD)	2000–2001
2000s	Galligan, Jr., Thomas	President	Colby-Sawyer College (NH)	2006–2016
2000s	Garcia, Joseph A.	President	Pikes Peak Community College (CO)	2001–2006
2000s	Garcia, Joseph A.	President	Colorado State University-Pueblo (CO)	2006–2010
2000s	Garrison, Michael	President	West Virginia University (WV)	2007–2008
2000s	Gee Gordon, E	President	Vanderbilt University (TN)	2000–2007
2000s	Gee Gordon, E	President	Ohio State University (OH)	2007–2013
2000s	Gregg, John R.	Interim President	Vincennes University (IN)	2003–2004
2000s	Habecker, Eugene	President	Taylor University (IN)	2005–2019
2000s	Hall, David	President	University Virgin Islands (VI)	2009–Present
2000s	Hall, Timothy	President	Austin Peay State University (TN)	2007–2014
2000s	Hardaway, Patricia	President	Wilberforce University (OH)	2007–2013
2000s	Hardin, Lu	President	University of Central Arkansas (AR)	2002–2008
2000s	Helmer, Robert	President	Lourdes University (OH)	2003–2012
2000s	Hill-Kennedy, Scott	Interim President	Ferris State University (MI)	2003–2003
2000s	Hoi, Samuel	President	Otis College of Art and Design (CA)	2000–2014
2000s	Horton, Howard E.	President	Bay State College (MA)	2000–2006
2000s	Horton, Howard E.	President	New England College of Business and Finance (MA)	2006–2020
2000s	Jeffcoat, Harold	President	Texas Wesleyan University (TX)	2000–2010
2000s	Jewell, Richard G.	President	Grove City College (PA)	2003–2014
2000s	Joel, Richard	President	Yeshiva University (NY)	2003–2017
2000s	Johnson, Jr., Glen D.	Chancellor	Oklahoma System of Higher Education (OK)	2007–Present
2000s	Johnston, Bryan M.	President	Saint Martin's University (OR)	2008–2008

Decade	Name	Position	School	Term of Office
2000s	Klein, John E.	President	Randolph College (VA)	2007–2013
2000s	Krislov, Marvin	President	Oberlin College (OH)	2007–2017
2000s	Kyle, Penelope Ward	President	Radford University (VA)	2005–2016
2000s	Lambert, Lee D.	President	Shoreline Community College (WA)	2006–2013
2000s	Leebron, David	President	Rice University (TX)	2004–2022
2000s	Lehman, Jeffrey S.	President	Cornell University (NY)	2003–2005
2000s	Liacouras, Peter	Chancellor	Temple University (PA)	2000–2016
2000s	Lindgren, Robert	President	Randolph College (VA)	2006–Present
2000s	Lowry III, L. Randolph	President	Lipscomb University (TN)	2005–2021
2000s	Macchiarola, Frank	Chancellor	St. Francis College (NY)	2008–2012
2000s	Maniaci, Vincent	President	American International College (MA)	2005–Present
2000s	Martin, Daniel	President	Mount Vernon Nazarene University (OH)	2007–2012
2000s	Mason, Ronald	President	Jackson State University (MS)	2000–2010
2000s	McDaniel, Tom J.	President	Northwestern Oklahoma State University (OK)	2000–2001
2000s	McDaniel, Tom J.	President	Oklahoma City University (OK)	2001–2004
2000s	McDonald, J. Clay	President	Logan University (MO)	2003–Present
2000s	McGlothlin, Michael	Interim President	Appalachian College of Pharmacy (VA)	2005–2006
2000s	McGlothlin, Michael	President	Appalachian College of Pharmacy (VA)	2008–2008
2000s	McGlothlin, Michael	President and CEO	Appalachian College of Pharmacy (VA)	2009–Present
2000s	Mercer, Peter	President	Ramapo College (NJ)	2005–Present
2000s	Milliken, James	President	University of Nebraska (NE)	2004–2014
2000s	Mills, Barry	President	Bowdoin College (ME)	2001–2015
2000s	Mooney, Carol Ann	President	Saint Mary's College (IN)	2004–2016
2000s	Morales, Jose Alberto	President	Pontifical Catholic University of Puerto Rico (PR)	2001–2006
2000s	Nichol, Gene R.	President	College of William and Mary (VA)	2005–2008
2000s	O'Leary, Hazel	President	Fisk University (TN)	2005–2013
2000s	Padilla, Antonio Garcia	President	University of Puerto Rico (PR)	2001–2009
2000s	Parish, Michael C.	President	Bay Mills Community College (MI)	2002–Present
2000s	Perlman, Harvey	Chancellor	University of Nebraska (NE)	2001–2016
2000s	Perry, Audy Michael	President	Marshall University (WV)	2000–2005

Decade	Name	Position	School	Term of Office
2000s	Phillip, George	Interim President	University at Albany (NY)	2007–2009
2000s	Phillip, George	President	University at Albany (NY)	2009–2012
2000s	Pickens, Joe	President	St. John's River State College (FL)	2008–Present
2000s	Pollard, Chip	President	John Brown University (AR)	2004–Present
2000s	Poskanzer, Steven	President	SUNY New Paltz (NY)	2001–2010
2000s	Powers, Jr., William	President	University of Texas at Austin (TX)	2006–2015
2000s	Pretty, Keith	President	Northwood University (MI)	2006–2019
2000s	Raab, Jennifer	President	Hunter College, CUNY (NY)	2001–Present
2000s	Rabinowitz, Stuart	President	Hofstra (NY)	2001–2021
2000s	Rallo, Joseph	President	Angelo State University (TX)	2007–2015
2000s	Ray, Alan	President	Elmhurst College (IL)	2008–2015
2000s	Reveley III, Walter Taylor	President	College of William and Mary (VA)	2008–2018
2000s	Rimai, Monica	Interim President	University of Cincinnati (OH)	2009–2009
2000s	Rodriguez, Jorge E. Mojica	President	Humacao Community College (PR)	2002–Present
2000s	Rooney, Jo Ann	President	Spalding University (KY)	2002–2010
2000s	Rosen, Andrew	President	Kaplan University (IA)	2002–2008
2000s	Rosen, Andrew	CEO and Chairman	Kaplan University (IA)	2003–Present
2000s	Ryan, Barry	President	Agrosy University, Southern CA campuses (CA)	2007–2009
2000s	Ryan, Barry	President and CEO	West Coast University (CA)	2009–2014
2000s	Sam, David	President	North Harris College (TX)	2000–2007
2000s	Sam, David	President	Elgin Community College (IL)	2007–Present
2000s	Scanlon, Michael	Chancellor	Franciscan University of Steubenville (OH)	2000–2011
2000s	Schall, Lawrence M. (Larry)	President	Oglethorpe University (GA)	2005–2020
2000s	Seligman, Joel	President	University of Rochester (NY)	2005–2018
2000s	Sexton, John	President	New York University (NY)	2002–2015
2000s	Shutt, Steven	President	Lake Forest College (IL)	2001–Present
2000s	Sikorsky, Fr. Charles	President	Divine Mercy University (VA)	2007–Present
2000s	Smith, Rodney	President	Southern Virginia University (VA)	2004–2011
2000s	Snyder, Barbara	President	Case Western Reserve (OH)	2007–Present

Decade	Name	Position	School	Term of Office
2000s	Sorell, Michael	President	Paul Quinn College (TX)	2007–Present
2000s	Spaniolo, James	President	University of Texas at Arlington (TX)	2004–2013
2000s	Spectar, Jem	President	University of Pittsburgh-Johnstown (PA)	2007–Present
2000s	Stargardter, Steven	President	John F. Kennedy University (CA)	2004–Present
2000s	Thomason, Chris	Chancellor	University of Arkansas Community College at Hope-Texarcana (AR)	2008–Present
2000s	Titus, Steven	President	Midland University (NE)	2002–2007
2000s	Towey, Jim	President	Saint Vincent College (PA)	2006–2010
2000s	Ulmer, Frances	Chancellor	University of Alaska-Anchorage (AK)	2007–2011
2000s	Underwood, William	Interim President	Baylor University (TX)	2005–2006
2000s	Underwood, William	President	Mercer University (GA)	2006–Present
2000s	Victor, Michael	President	Lake Erie College (OH)	2006–2015
2000s	Williams, Gregory H.	President	City University of New York (NY)	2001–2009
2000s	Williams, Gregory H.	President	University of Cincinnati (OH)	2009–2012
2000s	Williams, Phillip	President	University of Montevallo (AL)	2006–2010
2000s	Wyatt, Scott L.	President	Snow College (UT)	2007–2013
2000s	Young, Betty	President	Northwest State Community College (OH)	2003–2007
2000s	Young, Betty	President	Ashville-Boncombe Tech Community College (NC)	2007–2009
2000s	Young, Betty	President	Coleman College for Health Sciences at Houston (TX)	2009–2014
2000s	Young, Michael	President	University of Utah (UT)	2004–2011
2000s	Yudof, Mark	Chancellor	University of Texas System (TX)	2002–2008
2000s	Yudof, Mark	President	University of California (CA)	2008–2013
2000s	Zeppos, Nicholas	President	Vanderbilt University (TN)	2008–2019
2010s	Abdullah, Edythe	President	Essex County College (NJ)	2010–2013
2010s	Achampong, Francis	Chancellor	Penn State Fayette (PA)	2010–2013
2010s	Achampong, Francis	Chancellor	Penn State Mont Alto (PA)	2013–Present
2010s	Adelman, Michael	President	West Virginia School of Osteopathic Medicine (WV)	2010–2018
2010s	Alexander, Laurence	President	University of Arkansas at Pine Bluff (AK)	2013–Present
2010s	Alger, Jonathan	President	James Madison University (VA)	2012–Present

Appendices | 263

Decade	Name	Position	School	Term of Office
2010s	Ambar, Carmen Twillie	President	Oberlin College (OH)	2017–Present
2010s	Anderson, Michelle	President	Brooklyn College-CUNY (NY)	2016–Present
2010s	Armbrister, Clarence	President	Johnson C. Smith University (NC)	2018–Present
2010s	Armstrong, David	President	Thomas More College (KY)	2013–2018
2010s	Armstrong, David	President	St. Thomas University (MN)	2018–Present
2010s	Arnold, W. Ellis	President	Hendrix College (AR)	2019–Present
2010s	Arthur, Virginia	President	Metropolitan State University (MN)	2016–Present
2010s	Bacow, Lawrence	President	Harvard University (MA)	2018–2023
2010s	Bailey, Chris	President	Lower Columbia College (WA)	2011–Present
2010s	Bair, Sheila C.	President	Washington College (MD)	2015–Present
2010s	Baldwin, James	President	Excelsior College (NY)	2016–2020
2010s	Ballard-Washington, Kimberly	Interim President	Fort Valley State University (GA)	2013–2013
2010s	Ballard-Washington, Kimberly	Interim President	Albany State University (GA)	2013–2013
2010s	Ballard-Washington, Kimberly	Interim President	Savannah State University (GA)	2019–2021
2010s	Baston, Michael	President	Rockland County Community College (NY)	2017–2022
2010s	Becton, Charles L.	Interim Chancellor	North Carolina Central University (NC)	2012–2013
2010s	Becton, Charles L.	Interim Chancellor	Elizabeth City State University (NC)	2013–2014
2010s	Beutler, Randy	President	Southern Oklahoma State University (OK)	2010–Present
2010s	Boehmer, Bob	Interim President	East Georgia State College (GA)	2011–2011
2010s	Boehmer, Bob	President	East Georgia State College (GA)	2012–Present
2010s	Bradford, James	President	Sattler College (MA)	2018–2019
2010s	Brainard, Mark	President	Delaware Technical Community College-Terry (DE)	2014–Present
2010s	Brand, Jonathan	President	Cornell College (IA)	2011–Present
2010s	Brown, Barry	Interim President	Suffolk University (MA)	2010–2012
2010s	Brown, Barry	President	Mount Ida College (MA)	2012–2018
2010s	Brown, Keith	President	Jefferson State Community College (AL)	2018–Present
2010s	Bruntmyer, Eric	President	Hardin-Simmons University (TX)	2016–Present

Decade	Name	Position	School	Term of Office
2010s	Burcham, David	Interim President	Loyola Marymount University (CA)	2010–2010
2010s	Burcham, David	President	Loyola Marymount University (CA)	2010–2015
2010s	Byas, Renee	Acting Chancellor	Houston Community College (TX)	2013–2014
2010s	Capehart, Robin	President	Bluefield State College-Bluefield Campus (WV)	2019–Present
2010s	Caroll, Brian J.	President	Community Christian College (CA)	2017–Present
2010s	Carter, Laurie	President	Shippensburg University of Pennsylvania (PA)	2017–2021
2010s	Casey, Brian	President	Colgate University (NY)	2016–Present
2010s	Cassidy, Joseph	President	Washington County Community College (ME)	2013–2018
2010s	Cassidy, Joseph	Interim President	Eastern Maine Community College (ME)	2015–2016
2010s	Cassidy, Joseph	President	Southern Maine Community College (ME)	2018–Present
2010s	Chodosh, Hiram	President	Claremont McKenna College (CA)	2013–Present
2010s	Clark, Lawrence	President	Louisiana State University in Shreveport (LA)	2014–Present
2010s	Clark-Artis, Roslyn	President	Florida Memorial University (FL)	2013–2017
2010s	Clark-Artis, Roslyn	President	Benedict College (SC)	2017–Present
2010s	Cline, Kimberly	President	Long Island University (NY)	2013–Present
2010s	Cobb, John Whitehouse	Interim President	Naropa University (CO)	2011–2012
2010s	Cohen, David	President	Five Towns College (NY)	2016–Present
2010s	Cordana, Roberta	President	Gallaudet University (DC)	2016–Present
2010s	Courtway, Tom	Interim President	University of Central Arkansas (AR)	2011–2011
2010s	Courtway, Tom	President	University of Central Arkansas (AR)	2011–2016
2010s	Crawford, David	President	McCormack Theological Seminary (IL)	2018–Present
2010s	Cunningham, Paige Comstock	Interim President	Taylor University (IN)	2019–2021
2010s	D' Emilio, Deaane Horner	President	Gwynedd Mercy University (PA)	2017–Present

Decade	Name	Position	School	Term of Office
2010s	Dalton, Walter	President	Isothermal Community College (NC)	2013–2021
2010s	Daniels, Mitchell	President	Purdue (IN)	2013–2022
2010s	Darrell, Barton	President	Kentucky Wesleyan College (KY)	2014–2019
2010s	Davis, Bradley	President	West Valley College (CA)	2012–Present
2010s	Davis, Joan Y.	Interim President	Shelton State Community College (AL)	2013–2014
2010s	Davis, Joan Y.	Chancellor	Delgado Community College (LA)	2014–2018
2010s	DeCoudreaux, Alecia A.	President	Mills College (CA)	2011–2016
2010s	Desteiguer, John	President	Oklahoma Christian University (OK)	2012–Present
2010s	Dimenna, Gary	President	Monmouth University (NJ)	2017–Present
2010s	Dodge, Randall	President	Horizon University (IN)	2017–Present
2010s	Doran, Sandra J.	President	American College of Education (IN)	2011–2014
2010s	Doran, Sandra J.	Interim President	Salem College (NC)	2018–Present
2010s	Dunkle, Rev. Kurt H.	President	The General Theological Seminary (NY)	2013–Present
2010s	Dunsworth, Richard	Interim President	Millikin University (IL)	2013–2013
2010s	Dunsworth, Richard	President	University of the Ozarks (AR)	2014–Present
2010s	Dykstra, Kurt	President	Trinity Christian College (IL)	2015–Present
2010s	Easton, Stephen	Interim President	Dickinson State University (ND)	2019–2020
2010s	Eck, Daniel	President	Lakeland University (WI)	2013–2017
2010s	Eisgruber, Christopher	President	Princeton University (NJ)	2013–Present
2010s	Ellis, David	Interim President	Lewis and Clark College (OR)	2017–2017
2010s	Engler, John	Interim President	Michigan State University (MI)	2018–2019
2010s	Eyring, Henry Johnson	President	Brigham Young University-Idaho (ID)	2017–Present
2010s	Faison, Jr., Zachary	President	Edward Waters College (FL)	2018–Present
2010s	Farish, Donald	President	Roger Williams University (RI)	2011–2018
2010s	Felton, Jr., Herman J.	President	Wilberforce University (OH)	2016–2017
2010s	Felton, Jr., Herman J.	President	Wiley College (TX)	2017–Present
2010s	Ferrero, Ray	Chancellor/CEO	Nova Southeastern University (FL)	2010–2011

Decade	Name	Position	School	Term of Office
2010s	Ferrero, Ray	Chancellor	Nova Southeastern University (FL)	2011–Present
2010s	Finnegan, Patrick	President	Longwood University (VA)	2010–2012
2010s	Fitts, Michael	President	Tulane University (LA)	2014–Present
2010s	Flanagan, David	President	University of Southern Maine (ME)	2014–2015
2010s	Flicker, John	President	Prescott College (AZ)	2014–Present
2010s	Floyd, John Anthony	President	Mars Hill University (NC)	2018–Present
2010s	Follick, Edwin	President	South Baylo University School of Oriental Medicine (CA)	2018–Present
2010s	French, George	President	Clark Atlanta University (GA)	2019–Present
2010s	Frisch, Randy	President	City University of Seattle (WA)	2016–Present
2010s	Gabel, Joan T.A.	President	University of Minnesota (MN)	2019–Present
2010s	Gallot, Jr., Richard Joseph	President	Grambling State University (LA)	2019–Present
2010s	Garrett, Allison	President	Emporia State University (KS)	2016–2021
2010s	Garrett, Elizabeth	President	Cornell University (NY)	2015–2016
2010s	Garvey, John	President	Catholic University of America (DC)	2010–2022
2010s	Gash, Jim	President	Pepperdine University (CA)	2019–Present
2010s	Gee Gordon, E	President	West Virginia University (WV)	2014–Present
2010s	Gerhart, Peter	President	Lake Erie College (OH)	2015–2016
2010s	Glover, Glenda Baskin	President	TN State University (TN)	2013–Present
2010s	Godwin, Angeline	President	Patrick Henry College (VA)	2012–Present
2010s	Gormley, Ken	President	Duquesne (PA)	2015–Present
2010s	Gotanda, John	President	Hawaii Pacific University (HI)	2016–Present
2010s	Green, O. Jerome	President	Shorter College (AR)	2012–Present
2010s	Groves, William P	Chancellor	Antioch University (NH)	2017–Present
2010s	Haddon, Phoebe	Chancellor	Rutgers University-Camden (NJ)	2014–2020
2010s	Haile, Gregory	President	Broward College (FL)	2018–Present
2010s	Haines, Paul Lowell	President	Taylor University (IN)	2016–2019
2010s	Hall, Timothy	President	Mercy College (NY)	2014–Present
2010s	Hamen, Laurie M.	President	Mount Mercy University (IA)	2014–2020
2010s	Hanycz, Colleen	President	LaSalle Univeristy (PA)	2015–2021
2010s	Harpool, David	President	North Central University (Online) (CA)	2015–Present
2010s	Harrison, Valerie	President	Lincoln University (PA)	2014–Present
2010s	Harroz, Joseph	Interim President	University of Oklahoma (OK)	2019–2020

Decade	Name	Position	School	Term of Office
2010s	Haynes, David S.	President	Northern Michigan University (MI)	2012–2014
2010s	Helmer, Robert	President	Baldwin Wallace University (OH)	2012–Present
2010s	Herseth Sandlin, Stephanie	President	Augustana University (SD)	2017–Present
2010s	Hespe, David	President	Rowan College at Burlington County (NJ)	2012–2015
2010s	Hillman, Elizabeth	President	Mills College (CA)	2016–Present
2010s	Hoi, Samuel	President	Maryland Institute College of Art (MD)	2014–Present
2010s	Holmes, Barbara A.	President	United Theological Seminary of the Twin Cities (MN)	2012–2016
2010s	Holton, Anne	Interim President	George Mason University (VA)	2019–Present
2010s	Hurley, John J.	President	Canisius College (NY)	2010–2022
2010s	Hyde, Kevin	Interim President	Florida State College at Jacksonville (FL)	2019–Present
2010s	Iacullo, Steven	President	Health Care Institute (FL)	2014–Present
2010s	Iuliano, Robert	President	Gettysburg College (PA)	2019–Present
2010s	Jeffcoat, Harold	President	Millikin University (IL)	2011–2012
2010s	Jerome, March	President	Monroe College (NY)	2017–Present
2010s	Johnson, Ed	President	Everest College Phoenix and Everest Univeristy Online (AZ)	2011–2015
2010s	Jones, Brian	President	Strayer University (VA)	2015–Present
2010s	Jones, Jr., Glendell	President	Henderson State University (AR)	2012–2019
2010s	Kauffman, Bill	Interim President	St. Louis University (MO)	2013–2014
2010s	Kavalhuna, Russell	President	Henry Ford College (MI)	2018–2022
2010s	Keck, Rachelle (Karstens)	President	Briar Cliff University (IA)	2018–Present
2010s	Keenan, John D.	President	Salem State University (MA)	2017–Present
2010s	Keith, Kent M.	President	Pacific Rim Christian University (HI)	2015–Present
2010s	Kelliher, Marsha	President	Walsh College (MI)	2017–2020
2010s	Klauber, James S.	President	Ownesboro Community and Tech College (KY)	2010–2015
2010s	Klauber, James S.	President	John C. Calhoun State Community College (AL)	2015–2018
2010s	Klauber, James S.	President	Hagerstown Community College (MD)	2018–Present

Decade	Name	Position	School	Term of Office
2010s	Kneebone, Elaine	Acting President	Henderson State University (AR)	2019–Present
2010s	Knight, Bobbie	President	Miles College (AL)	2019–Present
2010s	Krislov, Marvin	President	Pace University (NY)	2017–Present
2010s	Kroger, John	President	Reed College (OR)	2012–2018
2010s	LaForge, William N.	President	Delta State University (MS)	2013–2022
2010s	Lambert, Lee D.	Chancellor	Pima County Community College (AZ)	2013–Present
2010s	Lash, Jonathan	President	Hampshire College (MA)	2011–2018
2010s	Lawrence, Fred	President	Brandeis (MA)	2011–2015
2010s	Lee, Douglas	President	Waynesburg University (PA)	2013–Present
2010s	Lee, Jay	President	Northeastern Junior College (CO)	2012–Present
2010s	Lewis, Brien	President	Catwaba College (NC)	2012–2020
2010s	Lief, Charles	President	Naropa University (CO)	2012–Present
2010s	Loh, Wallace	President	University of Maryland, College Park (MD)	2010–2020
2010s	Looney, Susan	President	Reading Area Community College (PA)	2018–Present
2010s	Ludwick, Richard	President	University of St. Thomas (MN)	2017–Present
2010s	Lugo, Daniel	President	Queens College of Charlotte (NC)	2019–Present
2010s	Malloy, Dannel	Chancellor	University of Maine (ME)	2019–Present
2010s	Martin, Jr., Harold	President	Morehouse College (GA)	2017–Present
2010s	Martin, Daniel	President	Seattle Pacific University (WA)	2012–2021
2010s	Martin, Earl F.	President	Drake University (IA)	2015–Present
2010s	Mason, Karol	President	John Jay (NY)	2017–Present
2010s	Mason, Ronald	President	Southern University System (LA)	2010–2015
2010s	Mason, Ronald	President	University of the District of Columbia (DC)	2015–Present
2010s	McClure, Tori Murden	President	Spalding University (KY)	2010–Present
2010s	McConnell, Glenn F.	President	College of Charleston (SC)	2014–2018
2010s	McConnell, Joyce	President	Colorado State (CO)	2019–2022
2010s	McCormick, Cecilia	President	Elizabethtown College (PA)	2019–Present
2010s	McCormick, Mark	President	Middlesex County College (NJ)	2019–Present
2010s	McDonald, Clay	President	Logan University (MO)	2013–Present
2010s	McKenna, Margaret	President	Suffolk University (MA)	2015–2016
2010s	McNulty, Paul	President	Grove City College (PA)	2014–Present
2010s	Meador, Earl W.	Chancellor	South Central Louisiana Technical College (LA)	2012–2017

Decade	Name	Position	School	Term of Office
2010s	Meador, Earl W.	Interim Chancellor	Fletcher Technical Community College (LA)	2014–2015
2010s	Meador, Earl W.	Chancellor	Northwest Louisiana Technical Community College (LA)	2017–Present
2010s	Mearns, Geoffrey S.	President	Northern Kentucky University (KY)	2012–2017
2010s	Mearns, Geoffrey S.	President	Ball State University (IN)	2017–Present
2010s	Meehan, Martin	President	University of Massachusetts System (MA)	2015–Present
2010s	Mengler, Thomas	President	St. Mary's University (TX) (TX)	2012–Present
2010s	Miller, Michael	President	Pfeiffer University (NC)	2010–2014
2010s	Milliken, James	President	City University of New York (NY)	2014–2018
2010s	Milliken, James	Chancellor	University of Texas System (TX)	2018–Present
2010s	Mills, Barry	Interim Chancellor	University of Massachusetts Boston (MA)	2017–2018
2010s	Morehead, Jere W.	President	University of Georgia (GA)	2013–Present
2010s	Munsil, Len	President	Arizona Christian University (AZ)	2010–Present
2010s	Napolitano, Janet	President	UC system (CA)	2013–2020
2010s	Newkirk, Krista	President	Converse College (SC)	2016–Present
2010s	Nguyen, Thuy Thi	President	Foothills College (CA)	2016–Present
2010s	O'Brien, Kevin	President	Santa Clara University (CA)	2019–Present
2010s	O'Connor, Maureen	President	Palo Alto University (CA)	2016–Present
2010s	O'Day, Steven	President	Austin College (TX)	2017–Present
2010s	Onders, Bob	President	Alaska Pacific University (AK)	2017–Present
2010s	Owens, Steven	Interim President	University of Missouri (MO)	2011–2021
2010s	Oxholm, Carl	President	Arcadia (PA)	2011–2013
2010s	Parker, Ava	President	Palm Beach State College (FL)	2015–Present
2010s	Patterson, Bart	President	Nevada State College (NV)	2011–Present
2010s	Pearsall, Joel K.	Interim President	Northwest Nazarene University (ID)	2015–2015
2010s	Pearsall, Joel K.	President	Northwest Nazarene University (ID)	2016–Present
2010s	Peri, Jonathan	President	Manor College (PA)	2015–Present
2010s	Perrin, Larry Timothy	President	Lubbock Christian University (TX)	2012–Present
2010s	Petrizzo, Louis	Interim President	Suffolk County Community College (NY)	2019–2021

Decade	Name	Position	School	Term of Office
2010s	Pietruszkiewicz, Christopher	President	University of Evansville (IN)	2018–Present
2010s	Pistole, John	President	Anderson University (IN)	2015–Present
2010s	Poskanzer, Steven	President	Carlton College (MN)	2010–Present
2010s	Price, Alan	President	Ealham College (IN)	2017–2018
2010s	Quinn, Kevin	President	University of Scranton (PA)	2011–2017
2010s	Ray, Alan	President	Fisher College (MA)	2017–Present
2010s	Reiss, Mitchell B.	President	Washington College (MD)	2010–2014
2010s	Reveley, IV, W. Taylor	President	Longwood University (VA)	2013–Present
2010s	Richey, James H.	President	Eastern Florida State College (FL)	2012–Present
2010s	Rinehart, Kathleen	President	Cardinal Stritch University (WI)	2018–Present
2010s	Roberts, Gary	President	Bradley University (IL)	2016–Present
2010s	Rooney, Jo Ann	President	Mount Ida College (MA)	2010–2010
2010s	Rooney, Jo Ann	President	Loyola University Chicago (IL)	2016–2022
2010s	Roosevelt, Mark	President	St. John's College (NM)	2016–Present
2010s	Ryan, Barry	Chancellor	Agrosy University (CA)	2014–2015
2010s	Ryan, Barry	President and CEO	United States University (CA)	2015–2016
2010s	Ryan, Barry	President	Sofia University (CA)	2018–2020
2010s	Ryan, James	President	University of Virginia (VA)	2018–Present
2010s	Sanchez, Luis	President	Moorpark College (CA)	2015–2019
2010s	Sanchez, Luis	Interim President	Oxnard College (CA)	2019–Present
2010s	Sands, Harlan	President	Cleveland State University (OH)	2018–Present
2010s	Satterlee, Kevin	President	Idaho State University (ID)	2018–Present
2010s	Scherrens, Maurice William	President	Newbury College (MA)	2012–Present
2010s	Schill, Michael	President	University of Oregon (OR)	2015–Present
2010s	Schmoke, Kurt	President	University of Baltimore (MD)	2014–Present
2010s	Schwarz, Thomas	President	Purchase College-State University of New York (NY)	2013–2019
2010s	Scott, Zaldwaynaka 'Z'	President	Chicago State University (IL)	2018–Present
2010s	Sea, Brooks	Interim President	Young Harris College (GA)	2017–2017
2010s	Shannon, Jack	President	Christian Brothers University (TN)	2019–Present
2010s	Sheilds, Dennis	Chancellor	University of Wisconsin Platteville (WI)	2010–Present

Decade	Name	Position	School	Term of Office
2010s	Sheridan, Sean	President	Franciscan University of Steubenville (OH)	2013–2019
2010s	Shutkin, William	President	Presidio Graduate School (CA)	2011–2016
2010s	Slabach, Frederick G.	President	Texas Wesleyan University (TX)	2011–Present
2010s	Smart, Clifton	Interim President	Missouri State University-Springfield (MO)	2011–2012
2010s	Smart, Clifton	President	Missouri State University-Springfield (MO)	2012–Present
2010s	Smolla, Rodney	President	Furman College (SC)	2010–2013
2010s	Sparks, Laura	President	Cooper Union (NY)	2017–Present
2010s	Spencer, Clayton	President	Bates College (ME)	2012–Present
2010s	St. Amand, Gerry	Interim President	Northern Kentucky University (KY)	2017–Present
2010s	Starcher, Jr., John M.	President	Southside Regional Medical Center-Professional Schools (VA)	2018–Present
2010s	Starr, Kenneth	President	Baylor University (TX)	2010–2016
2010s	Staton, Robert	President	Presbyterian College (SC)	2015–Present
2010s	Steinmayer, Janet	President	Mitchell College (CT)	2014–2019
2010s	Steinmayer, Janet	President	Lesley University (MA)	2019–Present
2010s	Stern, Eliot	President	Saddleback College (CA)	2019–Present
2010s	Stith, Jr., Millard "Pete"	President	Saint Paul College (MN)	2013–2016
2010s	Stone, Philip	President	Sweet Briar College (VA)	2015–2017
2010s	Sullivan, Thomas, E.	President	University of Vermont (VT)	2012–Present
2010s	Syverud, Kent	President	Syracuse University (NY)	2014–Present
2010s	Tetlow, Tania	President	Loyola University (LA)	2018–2022
2010s	Thierstein, Joel	Interim President	Mount St. Joseph University (OH)	2014–2014
2010s	Thierstein, Joel	President	West Virginia Wesleyan College (WV)	2017–Present
2010s	Thompson, Winfred	President	American University of Kuwait (Kuwait)	2013–2013
2010s	Thompson, Winfred	President	American University in Kosovo (Kosovo)	2014–Present
2010s	Thrasher, John E.	President	Florida State University (FL)	2014–2020
2010s	Titus, Steven	President	Iowa Wesleyan University (IA)	2013–Present
2010s	Van Zandt, David	President	The New School (NY)	2011–2020
2010s	Viar, David	President	Glendale Community College (CA)	2013–Present
2010s	Victor, Michael	President	Mercyhurst University (PA)	2015–2021

Decade	Name	Position	School	Term of Office
2010s	Vincent, Gregory	President	Hobart William Smith Colleges (NY)	2017–2018
2010s	Virjee, Framroze	President	California State University Fullerton (CA)	2017–Present
2010s	Walsh, Suzannne	President	Bennett College (NC)	2019–Present
2010s	Weiss, Jeff A.	President	Lesley University (MA)	2016–2018
2010s	Whaley, Chris	President	Roane State Community College (TN)	2012–Present
2010s	Whitaker, Alexander	President	King University (TN)	2016–Present
2010s	Wilcox, Reed	President	Southern Virginia University (VA)	2014–Present
2010s	Williams IV, Alfred	President	River Valley Community College (NH)	2018–Present
2010s	Williams, Jr., John	President	Muhlenberg College (PA)	2015–2019
2010s	Williams, H. James	President	Fisk University (TN)	2013–2015
2010s	Williams, H. James	President	Mount St. Joseph University (OH)	2016–Present
2010s	Williams, H. James	President	Mount St. Joseph University (OH)	2016–Present
2010s	Williams, John	Interim President	Principia College (IL)	2019–2020
2010s	Williams, Phillip	President	McNeese State University (LA)	2010–Present
2010s	Wilson, Matthew	President	University of Akron (OH)	2016–2018
2010s	Wilson, Matthew	President	Missouri Western State University (MO)	2019–Present
2010s	Wippman, David	President	Hamilton College (NY)	2016–Present
2010s	Wisenhunt, Denise	Interim President	San Diego City College (CA)	2016–2017
2010s	Wiserman, Christine	President	Saint Xavier University (IL)	2010–2016
2010s	Worthen, Kevin	President	Brigham Young University (UT)	2014–Present
2010s	Wyatt, Scott L.	President	Southern Utah University (UT)	2013–2021
2010s	Wynes, Tim	President	Inver Hills Community College (MN)	2010–2018
2010s	Wynes, Tim	President	Dakota County Technical College (MN)	2013–2018
2010s	Wynes, Tim	President	Black Hawk College (IL)	2018–Present
2010s	Yellen, David	President	Marist College (NY)	2016–2019
2010s	Young, Betty	Interim President	Hocking College (OH)	2014–2014
2010s	Young, Betty	President	Hocking College (OH)	2015–Present
2010s	Young, Michael	President	University of Washington (WA)	2011–2015
2010s	Young, Michael	President	Texas A&M (TX)	2015–2021
2010s	Zak, Leocadia	President	Agnes Scott College (GA)	2018–Present

Appendix 8—Lawyer Presidents by School Type and Decade, 1700 to 2019

Decade	Name	Public School	Private School	Religiously Affiliated School	Community College	Law School	HBCU School
1700s	Leverett, John		Y			Y	
1720s	William, Elisha		Y			Y	
1770s	Madison, Bishop James	Y				Y	
1780s	Baldwin, Abraham	Y				Y	
1780s	Johnson, William Samuel		Y			Y	
1790s	Kerr, David	Y				Y	
1800s	Meigs, Josiah	Y				Y	
1800s	Messer, Asa		Y				
1820s	Clark, Peter		Y				
1820s	Deur, William Alexander		Y			Y	
1820s	Quincy III., Josiah		Y			Y	
1830s	Barnwell, Robert Woodward	Y				Y	
1830s	Elliott, David		Y				
1830s	Few, Ignatius Alphonso		Y			Y	
1830s	Linsley, Joel Harvey		Y				
1830s	Longstreet, Augustis Baldwin		Y			Y	
1830s	Maxwell, William		Y				
1830s	Pierce, George Foster		Y				
1830s	Swain, David Lowry	Y				Y	
1840s	Emory, Robert		Y			Y	
1840s	Fillmore, Millard	Y					
1840s	Hasbrouck, Abraham Bruyn	Y				Y	
1840s	Longstreet, Augustis Baldwin		Y	Y			
1840s	Longstreet, Augustus Baldwin		Y			Y	
1840s	Moore, Nathaniel Fish		Y			Y	
1840s	Pierce, George Foster		Y			Y	

Decade	Name	Public School	Private School	Religiously Affiliated School	Community College	Law School	HBCU School
1840s	Preston, William C.	Y				Y	
1840s	White, John Brown		Y			Y	
1840s	Woolsey, Theodore Dwight		Y			Y	
1850s	Frelinghuysen, Theodore	Y				Y	
1850s	Laws, Samuel		Y				
1850s	Longstreet, Augustis Baldwin	Y				Y	
1850s	Smith, Hildreth		Y	Y			
1850s	Welch, Adoniah Strong	Y					
1850s	White, John Brown		Y	Y			
1850s	Williams, Joseph R.	Y				Y	
1860s	Bowman, John Bryan		Y				
1860s	Forsyth, James		Y				
1860s	Magoun, George		Y				
1860s	Smith, Luther M.		Y			Y	
1860s	Smith, William Russell	Y				Y	
1860s	Sutton, Andrew J.		Y				
1860s	Welch, Adoniah Strong	Y				Y	
1870s	Battle, Kemp Plummer	Y				Y	
1870s	Farnsworth, Charles Buchanan		Y				
1870s	Fowler, Charles Henry		Y			Y	
1870s	Langston, John Mercer		Y			Y	Y
1870s	Laws, Samuel	Y					
1870s	Marcy, Oliver		Y			Y	
1870s	Purnell, William Henry	Y					
1870s	Smith, Hildreth	Y					
1870s	Wyman, William Stokes	Y				Y	
1880s	Clayton, Henry Delamar	Y				Y	
1880s	Cummings, Joseph		Y			Y	
1880s	Hale, Horace M.	Y				Y	

Decade	Name	Public School	Private School	Religiously Affiliated School	Community College	Law School	HBCU School
1880s	La Lumiere, Stanislaus		Y	Y		Y	
1880s	Lamberton, Robert Alexander		Y				
1880s	Langston, John Mercer	Y					Y
1880s	Lewis, Burwell Boykin	Y				Y	
1880s	Northrop, Cyrus	Y				Y	
1880s	Peck, John Hudson		Y				
1880s	Sprague, Carleton	Y				Y	
1880s	Sprague, Homer	Y	Y			Y	
1880s	Tucker, Thomas DeSaille	Y				Y	
1880s	Tyler, Lyon Gardiner	Y				Y	
1880s	Walker, Francis Amasa		Y				
1880s	Ward, George Morgan		Y				
1880s	Warfield, Ethelbert Dudley	Y					
1880s	Willets, Edwin	Y				Y	
1880s	Willits, Edwin	Y				Y	
1880s	Wyman, William Stokes	Y				Y	
1890s	Dobson, William Davis	Y					
1890s	Hartzog, Henry	Y					
1890s	Hill, John H.	Y					Y
1890s	Hill, Walter Barnard	Y				Y	
1890s	Kirk, John Robert	Y					
1890s	Marcy, Oliver		Y			Y	
1890s	Murrh, William Belton		Y	Y			
1890s	Rogers, Henry Wade		Y			Y	
1890s	Taylor, A. N.	Y					
1890s	Warfield, Ethelbert Dudley		Y				
1890s	Weld, Frank	Y					
1900s	Abercrombie, John	Y				Y	
1900s	Bissell, Wilson Shannon	Y				Y	
1900s	Drinker, Henry Sturgis		Y				

Decade	Name	Public School	Private School	Religiously Affiliated School	Community College	Law School	HBCU School
1900s	Garfield, Henry Augustus		Y				
1900s	Hardy, John Crumpton	Y					
1900s	Hartzog, Henry	Y	Y	Y		Y	
1900s	Lowell, Lawrence		Y			Y	
1900s	McCormick, Samuel	Y				Y	
1900s	Norton, Charles Phelps	Y				Y	
1900s	Tillman, John N.	Y				Y	
1900s	Whitfield, Henry L.	Y					
1900s	Wilson, Woodrow		Y				
1900s	Wyman, William Stokes	Y				Y	
1910s	Black, James D.		Y	Y			
1910s	Davis, John W.	Y					Y
1910s	Goodnow, Frank Johnson		Y				
1910s	Hardy, John Crumpton		Y	Y			
1910s	Warfield, Ethelbert Dudley		Y	Y			
1920s	Baker, Simon Strousse		Y				
1920s	Beury, Charles Ezra	Y				Y	
1920s	Bowman, Milo Jesse		Y	Y		Y	
1920s	Guerry, Alexander	Y					
1920s	Hadley, Herbert S.		Y			Y	
1920s	Hall, Arnold Bennett	Y				Y	
1920s	Hutchins, Robert Maynard		Y			Y	
1920s	Moore, Ernest Carroll	Y				Y	
1920s	Wells, Rainey T.	Y					
1930s	Archer, Sr., Gleason		Y			Y	
1930s	Brett, Sr., Philip Milledoler	Y				Y	
1930s	Butts, Alfred Benjamin	Y				Y	
1930s	Davis, Harwell Goodwin		Y	Y		Y	

Decade	Name	Public School	Private School	Religiously Affiliated School	Community College	Law School	HBCU School
1930s	Foster, Richard Clark	Y				Y	
1930s	Fulbright, J. William	Y				Y	
1930s	Gates, Thomas Sovereign		Y			Y	
1930s	Guerry, Alexander		Y	Y			
1930s	Harris, Rufus Carrollton		Y			Y	
1930s	Knapp, Bradford	Y				Y	
1930s	Moseley, John Ohleyer	Y					
1930s	Stearns, Robert	Y				Y	
1940s	Anderson, Hurst Robbins		Y	Y		Y	
1940s	Armstrong, Richard H.	Y					
1940s	Bartle, Harold Roe		Y	Y			
1940s	Burse, Walter		Y			Y	
1940s	Darden, Jr., Colgate Whitehead	Y				Y	
1940s	Fagg, Jr., Fred D.		Y		Y	Y	
1940s	Hutchins, Robert Maynard		Y			Y	
1940s	Jacobs, Albert C.		Y			Y	
1940s	Lockmiller, David A.	Y					
1940s	McCormick, James Byron	Y				Y	
1940s	Moron, Alonzo Graseano		Y				Y
1940s	Moseley, John Ohleyer	Y				Y	
1940s	Price, James F.	Y	Y			Y	
1940s	Siemens, Cornelius Henry	Y			Y		
1940s	Stassen, Harold		Y			Y	
1950s	Anderson, Hurst Robbins		Y	Y		Y	
1950s	Aycock, William Brantley	Y				Y	
1950s	Fey, John T.	Y					
1950s	Garside, Charles	Y				Y	
1950s	Hawk, Rupert A.		Y				

Decade	Name	Public School	Private School	Religiously Affiliated School	Community College	Law School	HBCU School
1950s	Helfferich, Donald L. "Ty"		Y				
1950s	Jacobs, Albert C.		Y				
1950s	McFarland, Carl	Y				Y	
1950s	Newton, J. Quigg	Y				Y	
1950s	Russell, Donald S.	Y				Y	
1950s	Shepley, Ethan A. H.		Y			Y	
1950s	Siemens, Cornelius Henry	Y					
1950s	Sweavingen, Tilford		Y				
1950s	Tweed, Harrison		Y				
1950s	Wilkinson, Ernest		Y	Y		Y	
1960s	Adams, Ralph Wyatt	Y					
1960s	Appel, Anthony R.		Y			Y	
1960s	Bloustein, Edward J.		Y				
1960s	Brewster, Jr Kingman		Y			Y	
1960s	Cheek, Jr., King V.		Y	Y			Y
1960s	Crosby, Harold B.	Y				Y	
1960s	Donovan, James		Y				
1960s	Eliot, Thomas H.		Y			Y	
1960s	Ethierington, Edwin		Y				
1960s	Fenton, John E.		Y			Y	
1960s	Ferguson, Glenn		Y				
1960s	Fey, John T.	Y				Y	
1960s	Francis, Norman C.		Y	Y			Y
1960s	Godfrey III, Edward S.	Y					
1960s	Greenberg, Erwin		Y				
1960s	Hardin III, Paul		Y	Y			
1960s	Harris, Rufus Carrollton		Y			Y	
1960s	Huntley, Robert E. R.		Y			Y	
1960s	Levi, Edward H.		Y			Y	
1960s	Mautz, Robert	Y			Y	Y	
1960s	Montgomery, Douglas	Y			Y		
1960s	Mooney, Christopher F.		Y	Y			

Decade	Name	Public School	Private School	Religiously Affiliated School	Community College	Law School	HBCU School
1960s	Nabrit, James		Y			Y	Y
1960s	Olsen, James Karge		Y				
1960s	Pantzer, Robert T.	Y				Y	
1960s	Rendelman, John S.	Y					
1960s	Rexach, Jamie Benitez	Y				Y	
1960s	Rosenblum, Victor		Y				
1960s	Shaw, Manford A.		Y				
1960s	Spangler, James		Y				
1960s	White III, Luther		Y				
1960s	Wiggins, Norman Adrian		Y	Y		Y	
1970s	Barry, Jeffrey		Y				
1970s	Bennett, James Jefferson		Y	Y			
1970s	Bloustein, Edward J.	Y				Y	
1970s	Bok, Derek		Y			Y	
1970s	Bragdon, Paul E.		Y				
1970s	Brewster, Carroll		Y				
1970s	Brickley, James H.	Y					
1970s	Brown II., John		Y	Y			
1970s	Campbell, Colin		Y				
1970s	Carter, Lisle C.	Y				Y	Y
1970s	Cheek, Jr., King V.		Y				Y
1970s	Crosby, Harold B.	Y					
1970s	Drinnon, James E.	Y				Y	
1970s	Emery, Alfred C.	Y				Y	
1970s	Farenthold, Frances Tarlton "Sissy"		Y				
1970s	Ferguson, Glenn	Y	Y			Y	
1970s	Hanley, Dexter L.		Y	Y			
1970s	Hardin III, Paul		Y	Y		Y	
1970s	Iseman, Joseph S.		Y				
1970s	Kinney, RADM, Sheldon H.	Y					
1970s	Kuttler, Jr., Carl M.	Y			Y		
1970s	Lee, Calvin B.T.	Y	Y			Y	

Decade	Name	Public School	Private School	Religiously Affiliated School	Community College	Law School	HBCU School
1970s	Lesar, Hiram	Y				Y	
1970s	Mackey, M. Cecil	Y				Y	
1970s	O'Hara, William T.		Y	Y			
1970s	Pearce, Richard		Y	Y			
1970s	Pye, A. Kenneth		Y			Y	
1970s	Rainsford, George Nichols		Y				
1970s	Scanlon, Michael		Y	Y			
1970s	Sherman, Max	Y					
1970s	Smith, Virginia B.		Y				
1970s	Steiner, Stuart	Y			Y		
1970s	Stevens, Robert		Y				
1970s	Stone, Jesse N.	Y				Y	
1970s	Sylvester, Esther R.		Y	Y			
1970s	Trachtenberg, Steven		Y				
1970s	Vestal, Theodore M. "Ted"		Y				
1970s	Webb, W. Roger	Y					
1970s	White III, Luther		Y	Y			
1970s	Witherspoon, Gerald		Y				
1980s	Abdullah, Edythe	Y					
1980s	Adamany, David	Y				Y	
1980s	Bepko, Gerald	Y				Y	
1980s	Brewster, Carroll		Y				
1980s	Carothers, Robert L.	Y				Y	
1980s	Criser, Marshall	Y				Y	
1980s	Davenport, David		Y	Y		Y	
1980s	Dybward, Peter		Y				
1980s	Ehrlich, Thomas	Y				Y	
1980s	Ferrero, Ray		Y			Y	
1980s	Freedman, James O.	Y	Y			Y	
1980s	Funk, Robert N.		Y				
1980s	Fuster, Jamie		Y	Y			
1980s	Futter, Ellen V.		Y				
1980s	Gardner, James A.		Y			Y	
1980s	Gee Gordon, E	Y				Y	

Decade	Name	Public School	Private School	Religiously Affiliated School	Community College	Law School	HBCU School
1980s	Gerety, Tom		Y				
1980s	Habecker, Eugene		Y	Y			
1980s	Hardin III, Paul	Y				Y	
1980s	Haynes, Ulric	Y					
1980s	Heyman, Ira Michael	Y				Y	
1980s	Horton, Howard E.		Y				
1980s	Hull, Roger		Y				
1980s	Keith, Kent M.		Y	Y			
1980s	Lader, Philip	Y					
1980s	Lapp, Joseph		Y				
1980s	Liacouras, Peter	Y				Y	
1980s	Lorimer, Linda		Y				
1980s	McCormick, Samuel		Y	Y			
1980s	McGuire, Patricia		Y	Y			
1980s	McKenna, Margaret		Y				
1980s	O'Neil, Robert Marchant	Y				Y	
1980s	Pye, A. Kenneth		Y	Y		Y	
1980s	Rainsford, George Nichols		Y	Y			
1980s	Sargent, David		Y			Y	
1980s	Schmidt, Benno		Y			Y	
1980s	Shafer, Raymond P.	Y			Y		
1980s	Sloan, Albert J.		Y	Y			Y
1980s	Sovern, Michael		Y			Y	
1980s	Stevens, Robert	Y					
1980s	Stoepler, John W.	Y				Y	
1980s	Thornton, Ray	Y				Y	
1980s	Trachtenberg, Steven		Y			Y	
1980s	Verkuil, Paul Robert	Y				Y	
1990s	Abbott, James	Y				Y	
1990s	Arnold, W. Ellis		Y	Y			
1990s	Barba, James		Y				
1990s	Bekavac, Nancy Y.		Y				
1990s	Bernstine, Daniel	Y					
1990s	Bollinger, Lee	Y				Y	

Decade	Name	Public School	Private School	Religiously Affiliated School	Community College	Law School	HBCU School
1990s	Boren, David	Y				Y	
1990s	Brown, Hank	Y					
1990s	Bulger, William	Y				Y	
1990s	Carothers, Robert L.	Y					
1990s	Casper, Gerhard		Y			Y	
1990s	Chambers, Julius L.	Y				Y	Y
1990s	Cobb, John Whitehouse		Y				
1990s	Collens, Lew		Y			Y	
1990s	D'Alembert, Talbert "Sandy"	Y				Y	
1990s	Davros, Harry		Y				
1990s	Degnan, Rev Daniel A.		Y	Y			
1990s	Denson, Rob	Y			Y		
1990s	Donner, Thomas	Y			Y		
1990s	Farish, Donald	Y					
1990s	Frohnmayer, David	Y				Y	
1990s	Funk, Robert N.		Y	Y			
1990s	Gann, Pamela B.		Y				
1990s	Gee Gordon, E	Y	Y			Y	
1990s	Gerety, Tom		Y				
1990s	Godwin, Angeline	Y			Y		
1990s	Greenwald, Stephen		Y				
1990s	Greiner, William R.	Y				Y	
1990s	Hardesty, Jr., David S.	Y					Y
1990s	Hill, Sister Elizabeth A.		Y	Y			
1990s	Hull, Roger		Y				
1990s	Hunter, James		Y				
1990s	Jackson, Thomas H.		Y				
1990s	Johnson, Ed		Y	Y			
1990s	Johnson, George R.		Y	Y			
1990s	Johnson, Jr., Glen D.	Y					
1990s	Johnston, Bryan M.		Y			Y	
1990s	Khaytat, Robert	Y				Y	
1990s	LaGree, Kevin		Y	Y			
1990s	Landsmark, Ted		Y				

Decade	Name	Public School	Private School	Religiously Affiliated School	Community College	Law School	HBCU School
1990s	Lewis, Ovid C.		Y			Y	
1990s	Macchiarola, Frank		Y	Y			
1990s	Machtley, Ronald		Y				
1990s	McPherson, M. Peter	Y				Y	
1990s	Meehan, Martin	Y					
1990s	Musterman, Cynthia		Y				
1990s	Neimic, Catherine		Y				
1990s	Nelson, Christopher B.		Y				
1990s	Nordenberg, Mark	Y				Y	
1990s	Osgood, Russell K.		Y				
1990s	Perry, Audy Michael	Y					
1990s	Peterson, Shirely		Y				
1990s	Pretty, Keith		Y				
1990s	Quigley, Jr., Kenneth		Y				
1990s	Rothkopf, Arthur		Y				
1990s	Salmon, Thomas P.	Y					
1990s	Schwarz, Thomas		Y				
1990s	Smith, Virginia B.		Y				
1990s	Stanley, Deborah F.	Y					
1990s	Stone, Philip		Y				
1990s	Studley, Jamie		Y				
1990s	Sullivan, Timothy J.	Y				Y	
1990s	Swygert, H. Patrick	Y	Y			Y	Y
1990s	Thompson, Larry		Y				
1990s	Traer, James		Y				
1990s	Trible, Paul	Y					
1990s	Viar, David	Y			Y		
1990s	Vogt, Carl		Y				
1990s	Webb, W. Roger	Y					
1990s	Yudof, Mark	Y				Y	
2000s	Abrams, Norman	Y				Y	
2000s	Adamany, David	Y				Y	
2000s	Alanis, Javier		Y	Y			
2000s	Ambar, Carmen Twillie		Y				
2000s	Bacow, Lawrence		Y			Y	

Decade	Name	Public School	Private School	Religiously Affiliated School	Community College	Law School	HBCU School
2000s	Bahls, Steven		Y				
2000s	Baker, Bruce	Y			Y		
2000s	Baldasare, Paul		Y	Y			
2000s	Baltodano, Josefina Castillo		Y	Y			
2000s	Beauchamp, Rev. E. William		Y	Y			
2000s	Benton, Andrew K.		Y	Y		Y	
2000s	Bepko, Gerald	Y				Y	
2000s	Black, Robert		Y				
2000s	Bogomolny, Robert	Y				Y	
2000s	Bok, Derek		Y			Y	
2000s	Bollinger, Lee		Y			Y	
2000s	Bragdon, Paul E.		Y			Y	
2000s	Brand, Jonathan		Y				
2000s	Braveman, Daan		Y				
2000s	Brown, Hank	Y				Y	
2000s	Capehart, Robin	Y					
2000s	Casey, Brian		Y				
2000s	Cheek, Jr., King V.		Y				
2000s	Chema, Thomas V.		Y				
2000s	Cline, Kimberly		Y				
2000s	Cordes Larson, Gloria		Y				
2000s	Cox, Cathy		Y				
2000s	Curan, Thomas		Y	Y			
2000s	Daniels, Ronald		Y				
2000s	Decatur, William	Y				Y	
2000s	Delaney, John	Y					
2000s	Denson, Rob		Y		Y		
2000s	Diver, Colin		Y				
2000s	Donner, Thomas	Y			Y		
2000s	Dunagan, Nick	Y					
2000s	Falwell, Jr., Jerry Lamon		Y	Y		Y	
2000s	Farrell, Michael Jospeh	Y					
2000s	Farris, Michael		Y	Y			
2000s	Ferrentino, Robert	Y			Y		

Decade	Name	Public School	Private School	Religiously Affiliated School	Community College	Law School	HBCU School
2000s	Foster, Tim	Y					
2000s	Freidman, Stephen		Y			Y	
2000s	French, George		Y	Y			Y
2000s	Funk, Robert N.		Y				
2000s	Galligan, Jr., Thomas		Y				
2000s	Garcia, Joseph A.	Y			Y		
2000s	Garrison, Michael	Y				Y	
2000s	Gee Gordon, E	Y	Y			Y	
2000s	Gregg, John R.	Y					
2000s	Habecker, Eugene		Y	Y			
2000s	Hall, David	Y					Y
2000s	Hall, Timothy	Y					
2000s	Hardaway, Patricia		Y	Y			Y
2000s	Hardin, Lu	Y					
2000s	Helmer, Robert		Y	Y			
2000s	Hill-Kennedy, Scott	Y					
2000s	Hoi, Samuel		Y				
2000s	Horton, Howard E.		Y				
2000s	Jeffcoat, Harold		Y	Y		Y	
2000s	Jewell, Richard G.		Y	Y			
2000s	Joel, Richard		Y	Y		Y	
2000s	Johnson, Jr., Glen D.	Y					
2000s	Johnston, Bryan M.		Y	Y			
2000s	Klein, John E.		Y				
2000s	Krislov, Marvin		Y				
2000s	Kyle, Penelope Ward	Y					
2000s	Lambert, Lee D.	Y			Y		
2000s	Leebron, David		Y				
2000s	Lehman, Jeffrey S.		Y			Y	
2000s	Liacouras, Peter	Y				Y	
2000s	Lindgren, Robert		Y				
2000s	Lowry III, L. Randolph		Y	Y			
2000s	Macchiarola, Frank		Y	Y			
2000s	Maniaci, Vincent		Y				
2000s	Martin, Daniel		Y	Y			

Decade	Name	Public School	Private School	Religiously Affiliated School	Community College	Law School	HBCU School
2000s	Mason, Ronald	Y					Y
2000s	McDaniel, Tom J.	Y	Y	Y			
2000s	McDonald, J. Clay		Y				
2000s	McGlothlin, Michael		Y				
2000s	Mercer, Peter		Y				
2000s	Milliken, James	Y				Y	
2000s	Mills, Barry		Y				
2000s	Mooney, Carol Ann		Y	Y			
2000s	Morales, Jose Alberto		Y	Y			
2000s	Nichol, Gene R.	Y				Y	
2000s	O'Leary, Hazel		Y				Y
2000s	Padilla, Antonio Garcia	Y				Y	
2000s	Parish, Michael C.	Y			Y		
2000s	Perlman, Harvey	Y				Y	
2000s	Perry, Audy Michael	Y					
2000s	Phillip, George	Y					
2000s	Pickens, Joe	Y					
2000s	Pollard, Chip		Y	Y			
2000s	Poskanzer, Steven	Y					
2000s	Powers, Jr., William	Y				Y	
2000s	Pretty, Keith		Y				
2000s	Raab, Jennifer	Y				Y	
2000s	Rabinowitz, Stuart		Y			Y	
2000s	Rallo, Joseph	Y					
2000s	Ray, Alan		Y	Y			
2000s	Reveley III, Walter Taylor	Y				Y	
2000s	Rimai, Monica	Y				Y	
2000s	Rodriguez, Jorge E. Mojica		Y		Y		
2000s	Rooney, Jo Ann		Y	Y			
2000s	Rosen, Andrew		Y				
2000s	Ryan, Barry		Y				
2000s	Sam, David	Y	Y		Y		
2000s	Scanlon, Michael		Y	Y			

Decade	Name	Public School	Private School	Religiously Affiliated School	Community College	Law School	HBCU School
2000s	Schall, Lawrence M. (Larry)		Y				
2000s	Seligman, Joel		Y				
2000s	Sexton, John		Y			Y	
2000s	Shutt, Steven		Y				
2000s	Sikorsky, Fr. Charles		Y	Y			
2000s	Smith, Rodney		Y	Y			
2000s	Snyder, Barbara		Y			Y	
2000s	Sorell, Michael		Y	Y			Y
2000s	Spaniolo, James	Y					
2000s	Spectar, Jem	Y					
2000s	Stargardter, Steven		Y				
2000s	Thomason, Chris	Y			Y		
2000s	Titus, Steven		Y	Y			
2000s	Towey, Jim		Y	Y			
2000s	Ulmer, Frances	Y					
2000s	Underwood, William		Y	Y		Y	
2000s	Victor, Michael		Y				
2000s	Williams, Gregory H.	Y				Y	
2000s	Williams, Phillip	Y					
2000s	Wyatt, Scott L.	Y					
2000s	Young, Betty	Y			Y		
2000s	Young, Michael	Y				Y	
2000s	Yudof, Mark	Y				Y	
2000s	Zeppos, Nicholas		Y			Y	
2010s	Abdullah, Edythe	Y			Y		
2010s	Achampong, Francis	Y					
2010s	Adelman, Michael		Y				
2010s	Alexander, Laurence	Y					Y
2010s	Alger, Jonathan	Y					
2010s	Ambar, Carmen Twillie		Y				
2010s	Anderson, Michelle	Y				Y	
2010s	Armbrister, Clarence		Y				Y
2010s	Armstrong, David		Y	Y		Y	
2010s	Arnold, W. Ellis		Y	Y			
2010s	Arthur, Virginia	Y					

Decade	Name	Public School	Private School	Religiously Affiliated School	Community College	Law School	HBCU School
2010s	Bacow, Lawrence		Y			Y	
2010s	Bailey, Chris	Y			Y		
2010s	Bair, Sheila C.		Y				
2010s	Baldwin, James		Y				
2010s	Ballard-Washington, Kimberly	Y					Y
2010s	Baston, Michael	Y			Y		
2010s	Becton, Charles L.	Y				Y	Y
2010s	Beutler, Randy	Y					
2010s	Boehmer, Bob	Y					
2010s	Bradford, James		Y	Y			
2010s	Brainard, Mark	Y			Y		
2010s	Brand, Jonathan		Y				
2010s	Brown, Barry		Y			Y	
2010s	Brown, Keith	Y			Y		
2010s	Bruntmyer, Eric		Y	Y			
2010s	Burcham, David		Y	Y		Y	
2010s	Byas, Renee	Y			Y		
2010s	Capehart, Robin	Y					Y
2010s	Caroll, Brian J.		Y	Y	Y		
2010s	Carter, Laurie	Y					
2010s	Casey, Brian		Y				
2010s	Cassidy, Joseph	Y			Y		
2010s	Chodosh, Hiriam		Y				
2010s	Clark, Lawrence	Y					
2010s	Clark-Artis, Roslyn		Y	Y			Y
2010s	Cline, Kimberly		Y				
2010s	Cobb, John Whitehouse		Y				
2010s	Cohen, David		Y				
2010s	Cordana, Roberta		Y				
2010s	Courtway, Tom	Y					
2010s	Crawford, David		Y	Y			
2010s	Cunningham, Paige Comstock		Y	Y			
2010s	D'Emilio, Deaane Horner		Y	Y			

Appendices

Decade	Name	Public School	Private School	Religiously Affiliated School	Community College	Law School	HBCU School
2010s	Dalton, Walter	Y			Y		
2010s	Daniels, Mitchell		Y				
2010s	Darrell, Barton		Y	Y			
2010s	Davis, Bradley	Y			Y		
2010s	Davis, Joan Y.	Y			Y		Y
2010s	DeCoudreaux, Alecia A.		Y				
2010s	Desteiguer, John		Y	Y			
2010s	Dimenna, Gary		Y				
2010s	Dodge, Randall		Y	Y			
2010s	Doran, Sandra J.		Y				
2010s	Dunkle, Rev. Kurt H.		Y	Y			
2010s	Dunsworth, Richard		Y	Y			
2010s	Dykstra, Kurt		Y	Y			
2010s	Easton, Stephen	Y					
2010s	Eck, Daniel		Y	Y			
2010s	Eisgruber, Christopher		Y				
2010s	Ellis, David		Y			Y	
2010s	Engler, John	Y				Y	
2010s	Eyring, Henry Johnson		Y	Y		Y	
2010s	Faison, Jr., Zachary		Y	Y			Y
2010s	Farish, Donald		Y			Y	
2010s	Felton, Jr., Herman J.		Y	Y			Y
2010s	Ferrero, Ray		Y			Y	
2010s	Finnegan, Patrick	Y					
2010s	Fitts, Michael		Y			Y	
2010s	Flanagan, David	Y					
2010s	Flicker, John		Y				
2010s	Floyd, John Anthony		Y	Y			
2010s	Follick, Edwin		Y				
2010s	French, George		Y				Y
2010s	Frisch, Randy		Y				
2010s	Gabel, Joan T.A.	Y				Y	
2010s	Gallot, Jr., Richard Joseph		Y	Y			Y
2010s	Garrett, Allison	Y					

Decade	Name	Public School	Private School	Religiously Affiliated School	Community College	Law School	HBCU School
2010s	Garrett, Elizabeth		Y			Y	
2010s	Garvey, John		Y	Y		Y	
2010s	Gash, Jim		Y	Y		Y	
2010s	Gee Gordon, E	Y				Y	
2010s	Gerhart, Peter		Y				
2010s	Glover, Glenda Baskin	Y					
2010s	Godwin, Angeline		Y	Y			
2010s	Gormley, Ken		Y	Y		Y	
2010s	Gotanda, John		Y				
2010s	Green, O. Jerome		Y	Y	Y		Y
2010s	Groves, William P		Y	Y			
2010s	Haddon, Phoebe	Y				Y	
2010s	Haile, Gregory	Y					
2010s	Haines, Paul Lowell		Y	Y			
2010s	Hall, Timothy		Y				
2010s	Hamen, Laurie M.		Y	Y			
2010s	Hanycz, Colleen		Y	Y			
2010s	Harpool, David		Y				
2010s	Harrison, Valerie		Y				Y
2010s	Harroz, Joseph	Y				Y	
2010s	Haynes, David S.	Y					
2010s	Helmer, Robert		Y				
2010s	Herseth Sandlin, Stephanie		Y	Y			
2010s	Hespe, David	Y			Y		
2010s	Hillman, Elizabeth		Y				
2010s	Hoi, Samuel		Y				
2010s	Holmes, Barbara A.		Y	Y			
2010s	Holton, Anne	Y				Y	
2010s	Hurley, John J.		Y	Y			
2010s	Hyde, Kevin	Y					
2010s	Iacullo, Steven		Y				
2010s	Iuliano, Robert		Y				
2010s	Jeffcoat, Harold		Y	Y			
2010s	Jerome, March		Y				
2010s	Johnson, Ed		Y				

Decade	Name	Public School	Private School	Religiously Affiliated School	Community College	Law School	HBCU School
2010s	Jones, Brian		Y				
2010s	Jones, Jr., Glendell	Y					
2010s	Kauffman, Bill		Y	Y		Y	
2010s	Kavalhuna, Russell	Y			Y		
2010s	Keck, Rachelle (Karstens)		Y	Y			
2010s	Keenan, John D.	Y					
2010s	Keith, Kent M.		Y	Y			
2010s	Kelliher, Marsha		Y				
2010s	Klauber, James S.	Y			Y		
2010s	Kneebone, Elaine	Y					
2010s	Knight, Bobbie		Y	Y			Y
2010s	Krislov, Marvin		Y			Y	
2010s	Kroger, John		Y				
2010s	LaForge, William N.	Y					
2010s	Lambert, Lee D.	Y			Y		
2010s	Lash, Jonathan		Y				
2010s	Lawrence, Fred		Y				
2010s	Lee, Douglas		Y				
2010s	Lee, Jay	Y			Y		
2010s	Lewis, Brien		Y	Y			
2010s	Lief, Charles		Y				
2010s	Loh, Wallace	Y				Y	
2010s	Looney, Susan	Y			Y		
2010s	Ludwick, Richard		Y	Y		Y	
2010s	Lugo, Daniel		Y				
2010s	Malloy, Dannel	Y				Y	
2010s	Martin, Jr., Harold		Y				Y
2010s	Martin, Daniel		Y	Y			
2010s	Martin, Earl F.		Y			Y	
2010s	Mason, Karol	Y				Y	
2010s	Mason, Ronald	Y				Y	Y
2010s	McClure, Tori Murden		Y	Y			
2010s	McConnell, Glenn F.		Y				
2010s	McConnell, Joyce	Y				Y	
2010s	McCormick, Cecilia		Y				

Decade	Name	Public School	Private School	Religiously Affiliated School	Community College	Law School	HBCU School
2010s	McCormick, Mark	Y					
2010s	McDonald, Clay		Y				
2010s	McKenna, Margaret		Y			Y	
2010s	McNulty, Paul		Y	Y			
2010s	Meador, Earl W.	Y			Y		
2010s	Mearns, Geoffrey S.	Y				Y	
2010s	Meehan, Martin	Y				Y	
2010s	Mengler, Thomas		Y	Y		Y	
2010s	Miller, Michael		Y	Y			
2010s	Milliken, James	Y				Y	
2010s	Mills, Barry	Y				Y	
2010s	Morehead, Jere W.	Y				Y	
2010s	Munsil, Len		Y	Y			
2010s	Napolitano, Janet	Y				Y	
2010s	Newkirk, Krista		Y				
2010s	Nguyen, Thuy Thi	Y					
2010s	O'Brien, Kevin		Y	Y		Y	
2010s	O'Connor, Maureen		Y				
2010s	O'Day, Steven		Y	Y			
2010s	Onders, Bob		Y	Y			
2010s	Owens, Steven	Y				Y	
2010s	Oxholm, Carl		Y				
2010s	Parker, Ava	Y					
2010s	Patterson, Bart	Y					
2010s	Pearsall, Joel K.		Y	Y			
2010s	Peri, Jonathan		Y	Y			
2010s	Perrin, Larry Timothy		Y	Y			
2010s	Petrizzo, Louis	Y			Y		
2010s	Pietruszkiewicz, Christopher		Y				
2010s	Pistole, John		Y	Y			
2010s	Poskanzer, Steven		Y				
2010s	Price, Alan		Y	Y			
2010s	Quinn, Kevin		Y	Y			
2010s	Ray, Alan		Y				
2010s	Reiss, Mitchell B.		Y				

Appendices | 293

Decade	Name	Public School	Private School	Religiously Affiliated School	Community College	Law School	HBCU School
2010s	Reveley, IV, W. Taylor	Y					
2010s	Richey, James H.	Y					
2010s	Rinehart, Kathleen		Y	Y			
2010s	Roberts, Gary		Y				
2010s	Rooney, Jo Ann		Y			Y	
2010s	Roosevelt, Mark		Y				
2010s	Ryan, Barry		Y				
2010s	Ryan, James	Y				Y	
2010s	Sanchez, Luis	Y			Y		
2010s	Sands, Harlan	Y				Y	
2010s	Satterlee, Kevin	Y				Y	
2010s	Scherrens, Maurice William		Y	Y			
2010s	Schill, Michael	Y				Y	
2010s	Schmoke, Kurt	Y				Y	
2010s	Schwarz, Thomas	Y					
2010s	Scott, Zaldwaynaka 'Z'	Y					
2010s	Sea, Brooks		Y				
2010s	Shannon, Jack		Y	Y			
2010s	Sheilds, Dennis	Y					
2010s	Sheridan, Sean		Y	Y			
2010s	Shutkin, William		Y				
2010s	Slabach, Frederick G.		Y	Y		Y	
2010s	Smart, Clifton	Y					
2010s	Smolla, Rodney		Y				
2010s	Sparks, Laura		Y				
2010s	Spencer, Clayton		Y				
2010s	St. Amand, Gerry	Y				Y	
2010s	Starcher, Jr., John M.		Y	Y			
2010s	Starr, Kenneth		Y	Y		Y	
2010s	Staton, Robert		Y	Y			
2010s	Steinmayer, Janet		Y				
2010s	Stern, Eliot	Y			Y		
2010s	Stith, Jr., Millard "Pete"	Y			Y		Y
2010s	Stone, Philip		Y				
2010s	Sullivan, Thomas, E.	Y					

Decade	Name	Public School	Private School	Religiously Affiliated School	Community College	Law School	HBCU School
2010s	Syverud, Kent		Y			Y	
2010s	Tetlow, Tania		Y	Y		Y	
2010s	Thierstein, Joel		Y	Y			
2010s	Thompson, Winfred		Y				
2010s	Thrasher, John E.	Y				Y	
2010s	Titus, Steven		Y	Y			
2010s	Van Zandt, David		Y				
2010s	Viar, David	Y			Y		
2010s	Victor, Michael		Y	Y			
2010s	Vincent, Gregory		Y				
2010s	Virjee, Framroze	Y					
2010s	Walsh, Suzannne		Y				Y
2010s	Weiss, Jeff A.		Y				
2010s	Whaley, Chris	Y			Y		
2010s	Whitaker, Alexander		Y	Y			
2010s	Wilcox, Reed		Y	Y			
2010s	Williams IV, Alfred	Y			Y		
2010s	Williams, Jr., John		Y				
2010s	Williams, H. James		Y	Y			Y
2010s	Williams, John		Y	Y			
2010s	Williams, Phillip	Y					
2010s	Wilson, Matthew	Y				Y	
2010s	Wippman, David		Y				
2010s	Wisenhunt, Denise	Y			Y		
2010s	Wiserman, Christine		Y	Y			
2010s	Worthen, Kevin		Y	Y		Y	
2010s	Wyatt, Scott L.	Y					
2010s	Wynes, Tim	Y			Y		
2010s	Yellen, David		Y				
2010s	Young, Betty	Y			Y		
2010s	Young, Michael	Y				Y	
2010s	Zak, Leocadia		Y	Y			

Appendix 9—Lawyer Presidents and Where They Attended Law School, 1900–2019

Name	School Attended	Degree Earned
Abbott, James	University of South Dakota School of Law	JD
Abdullah, Edythe	University of Florida College of Law	JD
Abercrombie, John	University of Alabama School of Law	JD
Abrams, Norman	University of Chicago Law School	JD
Achampong, Francis	University of London	JD
Adamany, David	Harvard Law School	JD
Adams, Ralph Wyatt	University of Alabama School of Law	LLB
Adams, Ralph Wyatt	University of Alabama School of Law	LLD
Adelman, Michael	University of Toledo College of Law	JD
Alanis, Javier	University of Texas School of Law	JD
Alexander, Laurence	Tulane University	JD
Alger, Jonathan	Harvard Law School	JD
Ambar, Carmen Twillie	Columbia Law School	JD
Anderson, Hurst Robbins	University of Michigan Law School	JD
Anderson, Michelle	Yale Law School	JD
Appel, Anthony R.	Unknown	JD
Archer, Sr., Gleason	Boston University School of Law	LLB
Armbrister, Clarence	University of Michigan Law School	JD
Armstrong, David	Cleveland-Marshall College of Law	JD
Armstrong, Richard H.	Unknown	
Arnold, W. Ellis	University of Arkansas at Little Rock-School of Law	JD
Arthur, Virginia	Washington College of Law at American University	JD
Aycock, William Brantley	University of North Carolina School of Law	JD
Bacow, Lawrence	Harvard Law School	JD
Bahls, Steven	Northwestern University School of Law	JD
Bailey, Chris	University of Washington School of Law	JD
Bair, Sheila C.	University of Kansas School of Law	JD
Baker, Bruce	Marquette University Law School	JD
Baker, Simon Strousse	University of Pittsburgh School of Law	LLB
Baldasare, Paul	University of North Carolina School of Law	JD
Baldwin, James	Albany Law School	JD
Ballard-Washington, Kimberly	Texas Southern University	JD
Baltodano, Josefina Castillo	Unknown	JD

Name	School Attended	Degree Earned
Barba, James	Notre Dame Law School	JD
Barry, Jeffrey	University of Michigan Law School	JD
Bartle, Harold Roe	Hamilton College of Law	JD
Baston, Michael	Brooklyn Law School	JD
Beauchamp, Rev. E. William	Notre Dame Law School	JD
Becton, Charles L.	Duke University School of Law	JD
Bekavac, Nancy Y.	Yale Law School	JD
Bennett, James Jefferson	University of Alabama School of Law	JD
Benton, Andrew K.	Oklahoma City University School of Law	JD
Bepko, Gerald	ITT Chicago Kent School of Law	JD
Bernstine, Daniel	Northwestern University School of Law	JD
Beury, Charles Ezra	Harvard Law School	JD
Beutler, Randy	Taft Law School	JD
Bissell, Wilson Shannon	Unknown	
Black, James D.	Unknown	
Black, Robert	University of Baltimore School of Law	JD
Bloustein, Edward J.	Cornell Law School	LLB
Boehmer, Bob	University of Oregon School of Law	JD
Bogomolny, Robert	Harvard Law School	LLB
Bok, Derek	Harvard Law School	JD
Bollinger, Lee	Columbia Law School	JD
Boren, David	University of Oklahoma College of Law	JD
Bowman, Milo Jesse	Indiana School of Law	JD
Bradford, James	Vanderbilt Law School	JD
Bragdon, Paul E.	Yale Law School	JD
Brainard, Mark	Widener University Law School	JD
Brand, Jonathan	Cornell Law School	JD
Braveman, Daan	University of Pennsylvania Law School	JD
Brett, Sr., Philip Milledoler	New York Law School	LLB
Brewster, Carroll	Yale Law School	LLB
Brewster, Jr Kingman	Harvard Law School	JD
Brickley, James H.	University of Detroit	JD
Brown II., John	University of Arkansas School of Law	JD
Brown, Barry	Harvard Law School	JD
Brown, Hank	University of Colorado Law School	JD
Brown, Keith	University of Alabama School of Law	JD

Name	School Attended	Degree Earned
Bruntmyer, Eric	Baylor Law School	JD
Bulger, William	Boston College Law School	JD
Burcham, David	Loyola Law School	JD
Burse, Walter	Harvard Law School	JD
Butts, Alfred Benjamin	Yale Law School	JD
Byas, Renee	Texas Southern University	JD
Campbell, Colin	Columbia Law School	JD
Capehart, Robin	Unknown	JD
Caroll, Brian J.	University of San Francisco	JD
Carothers, Robert L.	University of Akron School of Law	JD
Carter, Laurie	Rutgers School of Law	JD
Carter, Lisle C.	St. John's University School of Law	JD
Casey, Brian	Stanford Law School	JD
Casper, Gerhard	University of Hamburg	JD
Cassidy, Joseph	University of Maine School of Law	JD
Chambers, Julius L.	University of North Carolina School of Law	JD
Cheek, Jr., King V.	University of Chicago Law School	JD
Chema, Thomas V.	Harvard Law School	JD
Chodosh, Hiriam	Yale Law School	JD
Clark, Lawrence	John Marshall Law School	JD
Clark-Artis, Roslyn	West Virginia University College of Law	JD
Cline, Kimberly	Hofstra Law School	JD
Cobb, John Whitehouse	Columbia Law School	JD
Cohen, David	New York Law School	JD
Collens, Lew	University of Chicago Law School	JD
Cordana, Roberta	University of Wisconsin Law School	JD
Cordes Larson, Gloria	University of Virginia School of Law	JD
Courtway, Tom	University of Arkansas School of Law	JD
Cox, Cathy	Mercer University School of Law	JD
Crawford, David	Georgetown University Law Center	JD
Criser, Marshall	Florida State University: College of Law	JD
Crosby, Harold B.	University of Florida College of Law	JD
Cunningham, Paige Comstock	Northwestern University School of Law	JD
Curan, Thomas	Columbus School of Law at Catholic University of America	JD
D' Emilio, Deaane Horner	University of Pittsburgh School of Law	JD

Name	School Attended	Degree Earned
D'Alembert, Talbert "Sandy"	University of Flordia	JD
Dalton, Walter	University of North Carolina School of Law	JD
Daniels, Ronald	University of Toronto	JD
Daniels, Mitchell	Georgetown University Law Center	JD
Darden, Jr., Colgate Whitehead	Columbia Law School	LLB
Darrell, Barton	University of Louisville School of Law	JD
Davenport, David	University of Kansas School of Law	JD
Davis, Bradley	Syracuse University College of Law	JD
Davis, Harwell Goodwin	University of Alabama School of Law	LLB
Davis, Joan Y.	University of Alabama School of Law	JD
Davis, John W.	Washington and Lee University School of Law	JD
Davros, Harry	Baylor Law School	JD
DeCoudreaux, Alecia A.	Indiana School of Law	JD
Decatur, William	Ohio State University Moritz College of Law	JD
Degnan, Rev Daniel A.	Seton Hall University School of Law	JD
Delaney, John	Unknown	JD
Denson, Rob	Florida State University: College of Law	JD
Desteiguer, John	Pepperdine Law	JD
Dimenna, Gary	Syracuse University College of Law	JD
Diver, Colin	Harvard Law School	LLB
Dodge, Randall	Indiana University Maurer School of Law	JD
Donner, Thomas	Southwestern University School of Law	JD
Donovan, James	Harvard Law School	LLB
Doran, Sandra J.	Syracuse University College of Law	JD
Drinker, Henry Sturgis	University of Pennsylvania Law School	JD
Drinnon, James E.	University of Tennessee College of Law	JD
Dunagan, Nick	University of Missouri School of Law	JD
Dunkle, Rev. Kurt H.	University of Florida College of Law	JD
Dunsworth, Richard	University of Illinois at Urbana-Champaign	JD
Dybward, Peter	Yale Law School	JD
Dykstra, Kurt	Marquette University Law School	JD
Easton, Stephen	Stanford Law School	JD
Eck, Daniel	Indiana University Maurer School of Law	JD
Ehrlich, Thomas	Harvard Law School	JD
Eisgruber, Christopher	University of Chicago Law School	JD
Eliot, Thomas H.	Harvard Law School	JD

Name	School Attended	Degree Earned
Ellis, David	University of Oregon School of Law	JD
Emery, Alfred C.	University of Utah	JD
Engler, John	Thomas M. Cooley Law School	JD
Ethierington, Edwin	Yale Law School	JD
Eyring, Henry Johnson	Brigham Young University	JD
Fagg, Jr., Fred D.	Northwestern University School of Law	JD
Faison, Jr., Zachary	University of Georgia School of Law	JD
Falwell, Jr., Jerry Lamon	University of Virginia School of Law	JD
Farenthold, Frances Tarlton "Sissy"	University of Texas School of Law	JD
Farish, Donald	University of Missouri School of Law	JD
Farrell, Michael Jospeh	University of West Virginia College of Law	JD
Farris, Michael	Gonzaga University	JD
Felton, Jr., Herman J.	Levin College of Law, Univ, of FL	JD
Fenton, John E.	Suffolk University Law School	JD
Ferguson, Glenn	University of Pittsburgh School of Law	JD
Ferrentino, Robert	Thomas M. Cooley Law School	JD
Ferrero, Ray	Florida State University: College of Law	JD
Fey, John T.	University of Maryland School of Law	LLB
Finnegan, Patrick	University of Virginia School of Law	JD
Fitts, Michael	Yale Law School	JD
Flanagan, David	Boston College Law School	JD
Flicker, John	William Mitchell College of Law	JD
Floyd, John Anthony	Campbell University School of Law	JD
Follick, Edwin	California College of Law & Blackstone Law	LLB/JD
Foster, Richard Clark	Harvard Law School	LLB
Foster, Tim	University of Denver College of Law	JD
Francis, Norman C.	Loyola University	JD
Freedman, James O.	Yale Law School	JD
Freidman, Stephen	Harvard Law School	JD
French, George	Miles Law School	JD
Frisch, Randy	Thomas Jefferson School of Law	JD
Frohnmayer, David	University of California Berkeley Law	JD
Fulbright, J. William	George Washington University	JD
Funk, Robert N.	University of Oregon School of Law	JD
Fuster, Jamie	University of Puerto Rico School of Law	JD

Name	School Attended	Degree Earned
Futter, Ellen V.	Columbia Law School	JD
Gabel, Joan T.A.	University of Georgia School of Law	JD
Galligan, Jr., Thomas	Seattle University School of Law	JD
Gallot, Jr., Richard Joseph	Southern University Law Center	JD
Gann, Pamela B.	Duke University School of Law	JD
Garcia, Joseph A.	Harvard Law School	JD
Gardner, James A.	Yale Law School	JD
Garfield, Henry Augustus	Columbia Law School	Attended for one year
Garrett, Allison	Tulsa Law School	JD
Garrett, Elizabeth	University of Virginia School of Law	JD
Garrison, Michael	West Virginia University College of Law	JD
Garside, Charles	Cornell Law School	JD
Garvey, John	Harvard Law School	JD
Gash, Jim	Pepperdine Law	JD
Gates, Thomas Sovereign	University of Pennsylvania Law School	LLB
Gee Gordon, E	Columbia Law School	JD
Gerety, Tom	Yale Law School	JD
Gerhart, Peter	Columbia Law School	JD
Glover, Glenda Baskin	Georgetown University Law Center	JD
Godfrey III, Edward S.	Columbia Law School	JD
Godwin, Angeline	Thomas M. Cooley Law School	JD
Goodnow, Frank Johnson	Columbia Law School	LLB
Gormley, Ken	Harvard Law School	JD
Gotanda, John	University of Hawaii Richardson School of Law	JD
Green, O. Jerome	University of Arkansas at Little Rock-School of Law	JD
Greenberg, Erwin	Unknown	
Greenwald, Stephen	New York University School of Law	JD
Gregg, John R.	Indiana University Robert H. McKinney School of Law	JD
Greiner, William R.	Yale Law School	JD
Groves, William P	Ohio State University Moritz College of Law	JD
Guerry, Alexander	Chattanooga Law School	LLB
Habecker, Eugene	Temple University Beasley School of Law	JD
Haddon, Phoebe	Duquesne University School of Law	JD
Hadley, Herbert S.	Northwestern University School of Law	JD

Name	School Attended	Degree Earned
Haile, Gregory	Columbia Law School	JD
Haines, Paul Lowell	Indiana University Maurer School of Law	JD
Hall, Arnold Bennett	University of Chicago Law School	JD
Hall, David	University of Oklahoma College of Law	JD
Hall, Timothy	University of Texas School of Law	JD
Hamen, Laurie M.	DePaul University College of Law	JD
Hanley, Dexter L.	Harvard Law School	LLB
Hanycz, Colleen	Dalhousie University (Nova Scotia)	JD
Hardaway, Patricia	Cardozo School of Law	JD
Hardesty, Jr., David S.	Harvard Law School	JD
Hardin III, Paul	Duke University School of Law	JD
Hardin, Lu	University of Arkansas School of Law	JD
Hardy, John Crumpton	Millsaps College	JD
Harpool, David	University of Missouri-Columbia	JD
Harris, Rufus Carrollton	Yale Law School	JD
Harrison, Valerie	Villanova University School of Law	JD
Harroz, Joseph	Georgetown University Law Center	JD
Hartzog, Henry	Mercer University School of Law	LLD
Hawk, Rupert A.	John Marshall Law School	JD
Haynes, David S.	Thomas M. Cooley Law School	JD
Haynes, Ulric	Yale Law School	JD
Helfferich, Donald L. "Ty"	Yale Law School	JD
Helmer, Robert	University of Toledo College of Law	JD
Herseth Sandlin, Stephanie	Georgetown University Law Center	JD
Hespe, David	Rutgers Law School-Newark	JD
Heyman, Ira Michael	Yale Law School	JD
Hill, Sister Elizabeth A.	St. John's University School of Law	JD
Hill-Kennedy, Scott	University of Arizona	JD
Hillman, Elizabeth	Yale Law School	JD
Hoi, Samuel	Columbia Law School	JD
Holmes, Barbara A.	Mercer University School of Law	JD
Holton, Anne	Harvard Law School	JD
Horton, Howard E.	Suffolk University Law School	JD
Hull, Roger	University of Virginia School of Law	JD
Hull, Roger	Yale Law School	LLB
Hunter, James	University of Pittsburgh School of Law	JD

Name	School Attended	Degree Earned
Huntley, Robert E. R.	Washington and Lee University School of Law	JD
Hurley, John J.	Notre Dame Law School	JD
Hutchins, Robert Maynard	Yale Law School	LLB
Hyde, Kevin	Florida State University: College of Law	JD
Iacullo, Steven	Thomas Jefferson School of Law	JD
Iseman, Joseph S.	Yale Law School	JD
Iuliano, Robert	University of Virginia School of Law	JD
Jackson, Thomas H.	Yale Law School	JD
Jacobs, Albert C.	Oxford University	BCL
Jeffcoat, Harold	University of Leicester College of Law (UK)	JD
Jerome, March	University of Pennsylvania Law School	JD
Jewell, Richard G.	University of Michigan Law School	JD
Joel, Richard	New York University School of Law	JD
Johnson, Ed	Columbia Law School	JD
Johnson, George R.	Columbia Law School	JD
Johnson, Jr., Glen D.	Oklahoma City University School of Law	JD
Johnston, Bryan M.	Loyola University-Chicago	JD
Jones, Brian	UCLA	JD
Jones, Jr., Glendell	University of Arkansas School of Law	JD
Kauffman, Bill	University of Pittsburgh School of Law	JD
Kavalhuna, Russell	Thomas M. Cooley Law School	JD
Keck, Rachelle (Karstens)	University of Iowa College of Law	JD
Keenan, John D.	Suffolk University Law School	JD
Keith, Kent M.	University of Hawaii Richardson School of Law	JD
Kelliher, Marsha	South Texas College of Law	JD
Khaytat, Robert	University of Mississippi School of Law	JD
Kinney, RADM, Sheldon H.	George Washington University	JD
Klauber, James S.	University of South Carolina School of Law	JD
Klein, John E.	University of Michigan Law School	JD
Knapp, Bradford	University of Michigan Law School	JD
Kneebone, Elaine	University of Arkansas-Fayetteville	JD
Knight, Bobbie	Birmingham School of Law	JD
Krislov, Marvin	Yale Law School	JD
Kroger, John	Harvard Law School	JD
Kuttler, Jr., Carl M.	Stetson University College of Law	JD
Kyle, Penelope Ward	University of Virginia School of Law	JD

Name	School Attended	Degree Earned
LaForge, William N.	Mississippi Law School	JD
LaGree, Kevin	Harvard Law School	JD
Lader, Philip	Harvard Law School	JD
Lambert, Lee D.	Seattle University School of Law	JD
Landsmark, Ted	Yale Law School	JD
Lapp, Joseph	Chicago-Kent	JD
Lash, Jonathan	Columbus School of Law at Catholic University of America	JD
Lawrence, Fred	Yale Law School	JD
Lee, Calvin B.T.	NYU School of Law	JD
Lee, Douglas	University of West Virginia College of Law	JD
Lee, Jay	University of North Dakota School of Law	JD
Leebron, David	Harvard Law School	JD
Lehman, Jeffrey S.	University of Michigan Law School	JD
Lesar, Hiram	University of Illinois College of Law	JD
Levi, Edward H.	University of Chicago Law School	JD
Lewis, Brien	University of Toronto	JD
Lewis, Ovid C.	Rutgers School of Law	JD
Liacouras, Peter	University of Pennsylvania Law School	JD
Lief, Charles	University of Colorado Law School	JD
Lindgren, Robert	Florida State University: College of Law	JD
Lockmiller, David A.	Cumberland University School of Law	JD
Loh, Wallace	Yale Law School	JD
Looney, Susan	Widener University Law School	JD
Lorimer, Linda	Yale Law School	JD
Lowell, Lawrence	Harvard Law School	JD
Lowry III, L. Randolph	Hamline University School of Law	JD
Ludwick, Richard	Indiana University Law School	JD
Lugo, Daniel	University of Minnesota Law School	JD
Macchiarola, Frank	Columbia Law School	LLB
Machtley, Ronald	Suffolk University Law School	JD
Mackey, M. Cecil	University of Alabama School of Law	JD
Malloy, Dannel	Boston College Law School	JD
Maniaci, Vincent	University of San Francisco	JD
Martin, Jr., Harold	Yale Law School	JD
Martin, Daniel	University of Kansas School of Law	JD

Name	School Attended	Degree Earned
Martin, Earl F.	University of Kentucky School of Law	JD
Mason, Karol	University of Michigan Law School	JD
Mason, Ronald	Columbia Law School	JD
Mautz, Robert	Yale Law School	BA
McClure, Tori Murden	University of Louisville School of Law	JD
McConnell, Glenn F.	University of South Carolina School of Law	JD
McConnell, Joyce	Antioch Law School	JD
McCormick, Cecilia	Delaware Law School	JD
McCormick, James Byron	Illinois Wesleyan University	LLB
McCormick, Mark	New York University School of Law	JD
McCormick, Samuel	Unknown	
McDaniel, Tom J.	University of Oklahoma College of Law	JD
McDonald, Clay	Valpraiso Law School	JD
McDonald, J. Clay	Valpraiso Law School	JD
McFarland, Carl	University of Montana School of Law	LLB
McGlothlin, Michael	College of William and Mary	JD
McGuire, Patricia	Georgetown University Law Center	JD
McKenna, Margaret	Southern Methodist University	JD
McNulty, Paul	Capital University Law School	JD
McPherson, M. Peter	Washington College of Law at American University	JD
Meador, Earl W.	Loyola University New Orleans College of Law	JD
Mearns, Geoffrey S.	University of Virginia School of Law	JD
Meehan, Martin	Suffolk University Law School	JD
Mengler, Thomas	University of Texas School of Law	JD
Mercer, Peter	University of Western Ontario Law School	JD
Miller, Michael	Wake Forest University School of Law	JD
Milliken, James	New York University School of Law	JD
Mills, Barry	Columbia Law School	JD
Montgomery, Douglas	Harvard Law School	JD
Mooney, Carol Ann	Notre Dame Law School	JD
Mooney, Christopher F.	University of Pennsylvania Law School	JD
Moore, Ernest Carroll	Ohio Normal University	LLB
Morales, Jose Alberto	Unknown	
Morehead, Jere W.	University of Georgia School of Law	JD
Moron, Alonzo Graseano	Harvard Law School	LLB
Moseley, John Ohleyer	Austin College	LLD

Name	School Attended	Degree Earned
Moseley, John Ohleyer	University of Oklahoma College of Law	JD
Munsil, Len	Arizona State University	JD
Musterman, Cynthia	Washington University School of Law	JD
Nabrit, James	Northwestern University School of Law	JD
Napolitano, Janet	University of Virginia School of Law	JD
Neimic, Catherine	University of California Hastings College of Law	JD
Nelson, Christopher B.	Utah College of Law	JD
Newkirk, Krista	William and Mary College of Law	JD
Newton, J. Quigg	Yale Law School	JD
Nguyen, Thuy Thi	UCLA	JD
Nichol, Gene R.	University of Texas School of Law	JD
Nordenberg, Mark	University of Wisconsin Law School	JD
Norton, Charles Phelps	Unknown	
O'Brien, Kevin	University of Florida College of Law	JD
O'Connor, Maureen	University of Arizona	JD
O'Day, Steven	Temple University Beasley School of Law	JD
O'Hara, William T.	Georgetown University Law Center	JD
O'Leary, Hazel	Rutgers Law School-Newark	JD
O'Neil, Robert Marchant	Harvard Law School	LLB
Olsen, James Karge	University of Chicago Law School	JD
Onders, Bob	University Wyoming Law	JD
Osgood, Russell K.	Yale Law School	JD
Owens, Steven	Wake Forest University School of Law	JD
Oxholm, Carl	Harvard Law School	JD
Padilla, Antonio Garcia	University of Puerto Rico School of Law	JD
Pantzer, Robert T.	University of Montana School of Law	LLB
Parish, Michael C.	Thomas M. Cooley Law School	JD
Parker, Ava	Florida State University: College of Law	JD
Patterson, Bart	Duke University School of Law	JD
Pearce, Richard	Stetson University College of Law	JD
Pearsall, Joel K.	Willamette University College of Law	JD
Peri, Jonathan	Widener University Law School	JD
Perlman, Harvey	University of Nebraska	JD
Perrin, Larry Timothy	Texas Tech University	JD
Perry, Audy Michael	University of West Virginia College of Law	LLB
Peterson, Shirely	NYU School of Law	JD

Name	School Attended	Degree Earned
Petrizzo, Louis	University of Toledo College of Law	JD
Phillip, George	Western New England School of Law	JD
Pickens, Joe	Florida State University: College of Law	JD
Pietruszkiewicz, Christopher	Loyola University New Orleans College of Law	JD
Pistole, John	Indiana University Robert H. McKinney School of Law	JD
Pollard, Chip	Harvard Law School	JD
Poskanzer, Steven	Harvard Law School	JD
Powers, Jr., William	Harvard Law School	JD
Pretty, Keith	Thomas M. Cooley Law School	JD
Price, Alan	Harvard Law School	JD
Price, James F.	Stanford Law School	JD
Pye, A. Kenneth	Georgetown University Law Center	JD
Quigley, Jr., Kenneth	Villanova University School of Law	JD
Quinn, Kevin	University of California Berkeley Law	JD
Raab, Jennifer	Harvard Law School	JD
Rabinowitz, Stuart	Columbia Law School	JD
Rainsford, George Nichols	Yale Law School	JD
Rallo, Joseph	Western New England School of Law	JD
Ray, Alan	University of California Hastings College of Law	JD
Reiss, Mitchell B.	Columbia Law School	JD
Rendelman, John S.	University of Illinois College of Law	JD
Reveley III, Walter Taylor	University of Virginia School of Law	JD
Reveley, IV, W. Taylor	University of Virginia School of Law	JD
Rexach, Jamie Benitez	Georgetown University Law Center	LLB
Richey, James H.	Ohio State University Moritz College of Law	JD
Rimai, Monica	University of Michigan Law School	JD
Rinehart, Kathleen	Marquette University Law School	JD
Roberts, Gary	Stanford Law School	JD
Rodriguez, Jorge E. Mojica	Unknown	JD
Rooney, Jo Ann	Boston University School of Law	JD
Roosevelt, Mark	Harvard Law School	JD
Rosen, Andrew	Yale Law School	JD
Rosenblum, Victor	Columbia Law School	LLB
Rothkopf, Arthur	Harvard Law School	JD
Russell, Donald S.	University of South Carolina School of Law	LLB

Name	School Attended	Degree Earned
Ryan, Barry	University of California Berkeley Law	JD
Ryan, James	University of Virginia School of Law	JD
Salmon, Thomas P.	Boston College Law School	JD
Sam, David	University of Akron School of Law	JD
Sanchez, Luis	McGeorge Law School	JD
Sands, Harlan	George Mason University	JD
Sargent, David	Suffolk University Law School	JD
Satterlee, Kevin	University of Idaho	JD
Scanlon, Michael	Harvard Law School	JD
Schall, Lawrence M. (Larry)	University of Pennsylvania Law School	JD
Scherrens, Maurice William	George Washington University	JD
Schill, Michael	Yale Law School	JD
Schmidt, Benno	Columbia Law School	JD
Schmoke, Kurt	Harvard Law School	JD
Schwarz, Thomas	Fordham Law School	JD
Scott, Zaldwaynaka 'Z'	Indiana University Law School	JD
Sea, Brooks	Georgia State	JD
Seligman, Joel	Harvard Law School	JD
Sexton, John	Harvard Law School	JD
Shafer, Raymond P.	Yale Law School	JD
Shannon, Jack	University of Pennsylvania Law School	JD
Shaw, Manford A.	University of Utah	JD
Sheilds, Dennis	University of Iowa College of Law	JD
Shepley, Ethan A. H.	Washington University	JD
Sheridan, Sean	University of Pittsburgh School of Law	JD
Sherman, Max	University of Texas School of Law	JD
Shutkin, William	University of Virginia School of Law	JD
Shutt, Steven	University of Pennsylvania Law School	JD
Siemens, Cornelius Henry	University of California	LLD
Sikorsky, Fr. Charles	University of Maryland School of Law	JD
Slabach, Frederick G.	University of Mississippi School of Law	JD
Sloan, Albert J.	Miles Law School	JD
Smart, Clifton	University of Arkansas School of Law	JD
Smith, Rodney	Brigham Young University	JD
Smith, Virginia B.	University of Washington School of Law	JD
Smolla, Rodney	Duke University School of Law	JD

Name	School Attended	Degree Earned
Snyder, Barbara	University of Chicago Law School	JD
Sorell, Michael	Duke University School of Law	JD
Sovern, Michael	Columbia Law School	JD
Spangler, James	Unknown	
Spaniolo, James	University of Michigan Law School	JD
Sparks, Laura	University of Pennsylvania Law School	JD
Spectar, Jem	University of Maryland School of Law	JD
Spencer, Clayton	Yale Law School	JD
St. Amand, Gerry	Unknown	JD
Stanley, Deborah F.	Syracuse University College of Law	JD
Starcher, Jr., John M.	University of Toledo College of Law	JD
Stargardter, Steven	University of Washington School of Law	JD
Starr, Kenneth	Duke University School of Law	JD
Stassen, Harold	University of Minnesota Law School	LLB
Staton, Robert	University of South Carolina School of Law	JD
Stearns, Robert	Columbia Law School	JD
Steiner, Stuart	University of Baltimore School of Law	JD
Steinmayer, Janet	University of Chicago Law School	JD
Stern, Eliot	University of Michigan Law School	JD
Stevens, Robert	University of Oxford	BCL
Stith, Jr., Millard "Pete"	College of William and Mary	JD
Stoepler, John W.	University of Toledo College of Law	JD
Stone, Jesse N.	Southern University Law Center	JD
Stone, Philip	University of Virginia School of Law	JD
Studley, Jamie	Harvard Law School	JD
Sullivan, Thomas, E.	Indiana University Law School	JD
Sullivan, Timothy J.	Harvard Law School	JD
Sweavingen, Tilford	Texas Christian University	JD
Swygert, H. Patrick	Howard University	JD
Sylvester, Esther R.	Villanova University School of Law	JD
Syverud, Kent	University of Michigan Law School	JD
Tetlow, Tania	Unknown	JD
Thierstein, Joel	Syracuse University College of Law	JD
Thomason, Chris	University of Arkansas at Little Rock-School of Law	JD
Thompson, Larry	Ohio State University Moritz College of Law	JD
Thompson, Winfred	George Washington University	JD

Name	School Attended	Degree Earned
Thornton, Ray	University of Arkansas-Fayetteville	JD
Thrasher, John E.	Florida State University: College of Law	JD
Tillman, John N.	Unknown	
Titus, Steven	Marquette University Law School	JD
Towey, Jim	Florida State University: College of Law	JD
Trachtenberg, Steven	Yale Law School	JD
Traer, James	University of Michigan Law School	JD
Trible, Paul	Washington and Lee University School of Law	JD
Tweed, Harrison	Harvard Law School	JD
Ulmer, Frances	University of Wisconsin Law School	JD
Underwood, William	University of Illinois College of Law	JD
Van Zandt, David	Yale Law School	JD
Verkuil, Paul Robert	University of Virginia School of Law	JD
Vestal, Theodore M. "Ted"	Yale Law School	JD
Viar, David	Drake University School of Law	JD
Victor, Michael	Duquesne University School of Law	JD
Vincent, Gregory	Ohio State University Moritz College of Law	JD
Virjee, Framroze	University of California Hastings College of Law	JD
Vogt, Carl	University of Texas School of Law	JD
Walsh, Suzannne	Case Western Reserve	JD
Warfield, Ethelbert Dudley	Columbia Law School	LLB
Webb, W. Roger	University of Oklahoma College of Law	JD
Weiss, Jeff A.	Harvard Law School	JD
Wells, Rainey T.	Unknown	Studied law
Whaley, Chris	University of Tennessee College of Law	JD
Whitaker, Alexander	University of Virginia School of Law	JD
White III, Luther	Washington and Lee University School of Law	JD
Whitfield, Henry L.	Millsaps College	JD
Wiggins, Norman Adrian	Wake Forest University School of Law	LLB
Wilcox, Reed	Harvard Law School	JD
Wilkinson, Ernest	George Washington University	JD
Williams IV, Alfred	University of Illinois at Urbana-Champaign	JD
Williams, Jr., John	Harvard Law School	JD
Williams, Gregory H.	George Washington University	JD
Williams, H. James	Georgetown University Law Center	JD

Name	School Attended	Degree Earned
Williams, H. James	Georgetown university Law Center	JD
Williams, John	George Washington University	JD
Williams, Phillip	Columbia Law School	JD
Wilson, Matthew	Temple University Beasley School of Law	JD
Wilson, Woodrow	University of Virginia School of Law	JD
Wippman, David	Yale Law School	JD
Wisenhunt, Denise	Columbus School of Law at Catholic University of America	JD
Wiserman, Christine	Marquette University Law School	JD
Witherspoon, Gerald	University of Chicago Law School	JD
Worthen, Kevin	Brigham Young University	JD
Wyatt, Scott L.	University of Utah	JD
Wyman, William Stokes	University of Alabama School of Law	JD
Wynes, Tim	St. Louis University School of Law	JD
Yellen, David	Cornell Law School	JD
Young, Betty	Capital University Law School	JD
Young, Michael	Harvard Law School	JD
Yudof, Mark	University of Pennsylvania Law School	JD
Yudof, Mark	University of Pennsylvania Law School	LLB
Zak, Leocadia	Northeastern University School of Law	JD
Zeppos, Nicholas	University of Wisconsin Law School	JD

Bibliography

"125 Years of History." *Johnson University*. Accessed September 9, 2021. https://history.johnsonu.edu/timeline.html.

"2017 Overview, Minority Presidents, Demographics." *American Council on Education*. Accessed August 29, 2021. https://www.aceacps.org/minority-presidents/#demographics.

"2017 Overview, Women Presidents." *American Council on Education*. Accessed August 29, 2021. https://www.aceacps.org/women-presidents/.

"2022 Best Law Schools (Ranked in 2021)." *U.S. News and World Report*. Accessed September 13, 2021. https://www.usnews.com/best-graduate-schools/top-law-schools/law-rankings.

"2020 Vision for Leadership Conference at Baylor Law, Day 1—Session 1, Reflections on the Challenges Facing Legal Education and Leadership Lessons from the Challenges of 2020." Transcript. *Baylor Law*. Last modified September 22, 2020. Accessed September 30, 2021. https://www.baylor.edu/law/doc.php/364677.pdf.

"2020 Vision for Leadership Conference at Baylor Law, Law School Deans Panel: Leadership Programing in Law Schools, Monday, September 14, 2020." Transcript. *Baylor Law*. Last modified September 22, 2020. Accessed September 30, 2021. https://www.baylor.edu/law/doc.php/364678.pdf.

"7 College Presidents Share Their Biggest Challenges for 2020." *Higher Ed Dive*. Last modified February 6, 2020. Accessed August 31, 2021. https://www.highereddive.com/news/7-college-presidents-share-their-biggest-challenges-for-2020/571856/.

"75th Anniversary of the GI Bill." *U.S. Department of Veterans Affairs*. Accessed August 30, 2021. https://benefits.va.gov/gibill/75th-anniversary.asp.

"ABA Model Rules of Professional Conduct, Rule 1.1, Competence Comment." *American Bar Association*. Accessed August 31, 2021. https://www.americanbar.org/groups/professional_responsibility/publications/model_rules_of_professional_conduct/rule_1_1_competence/comment_on_rule_1_1/.

"ABA National Lawyer Population Survey: Lawyer Population by State." *American Bar Association*. Last modified 2021. Accessed September 22, 2021. https://www.americanbar.org/content/dam/aba/administrative/market_research/2021-national-lawyer-population-survey.pdf.

ABA Standards Committee. Memorandum to the Council (Council on Legal Education), "Proposed Changes to Standards 205, 206, 303, 507 and 508," May 7, 2021. Accessed August 31, 2021. https://www.americanbar.org/content/dam/aba/administrative/legal_education_and_admissions_to_the_bar/council_reports_and_resolutions/may21/21-may-standards-committee-memo-proposed-changes-with-appendix.pdf.

"About the American Bar Association, ABA Timeline." *American Bar Association*. Accessed September 1, 2021. https://www.americanbar.org/about_the_aba/timeline/.

Age Discrimination in Employment Act, 29 U.S.C. §621.

Allied News (Grove City, PA). "McNulty Chosen as GCC President." May 28, 2014. Accessed September 22, 2021. https://www.alliednews.com/news/local_news/mcnulty-chosen-as-gcc-president/article_afada688-78c3-5f36-8551-43229559448f.html.

Altbach, Philip G. "From Revolution to Apathy: American Student Activism in the 1970s." *Higher Education* 8, no. 6 (November 1979): 609–626. https://www.jstor.org/stable/3446222.

"American Bar Association, Resolution (Adopting the Model Rule for Minimum Legal Education and Accompanying Report)." *American Bar Association*. Last modified February 6, 2017. Accessed August 31, 2021. https://www.americanbar.org/content/dam/aba/directories/policy/2017_hod_midyear_106.pdf.

Americans with Disabilities Act of 1990, 42 U.S.C. §12101 et seq. (2008).

Areen, Judith, and Peter F. Lake. *Higher Education and the Law*. 2nd ed. University Casebook Series. N.p.: Foundation Press, 2014.

Association of Governing Boards of Universities and Colleges. *Policies, Practices, and Composition of Governing and Foundation Boards 2016*. N.p.: AGB Press, 2016. Accessed January 2019. https://agb.org/product/policies-practices-and-composition-of-governing-and-foundation-boards-2016/.

Baldwin, Simeone E. "The Founding of the American Bar Association." *American Bar Association Journal* 3 (1917): 658–695. Accessed September 1, 2021. https://digitalcommons.law.yale.edu/cgi/viewcontent.cgi?referer=https://www.google.com/&httpsredir=1&article=5323&context=fss_papers.

Barkan, Steven M. "The First Conference of Religiously Affiliated Law Schools: An Overview." *Marquette Law Review* 78, no. 2 (Winter 1995): 247–254. https://scholarship.law.marquette.edu/cgi/viewcontent.cgi?article=1568&context=mulr.

Beardsley, Scott Cochran. "The Rise of the Nontraditional Liberal Arts College President: Context, Pathways, Institutional Characteristics, Views of Search Firm Executives, and Lessons Learned by Presidents Making the Transitions." PhD diss., University of Pennsylvania, Philadelphia, PA, 2015. https://www.proquest.com/dissertations-theses/rise-nontraditional-liberal-arts-college/docview/1727125953/se-2?accountid=30558.

Bentley, Melinda J. "Ethics: The Ethical Implications of Technology in Your Law Practice: Understanding the Rules of Professional Conduct Can Prevent Potential Problems." *The MissouriBar*, February 17, 2020. Accessed August 31, 2021. https://news.mobar.org/ethics-the-ethical-implications-of-technology-in-your-law-practice-understanding-the-rules-of-professional-conduct-can-prevent-potential-problems/.

Berman, Jillian. "Why States Are Cutting Back on Higher Education Funding." *MarketWatch*. Last modified January 7, 2017. Accessed September 22, 2021. https://www.marketwatch.com/story/why-states-are-cutting-back-on-higher-education-funding-2016-01-07.

Bickel, Robet D., and Peter H. Ruger. "The Ubiquitous College Lawyer." *Chronicle of Higher Education*. Last modified June 25, 2004. Accessed August 31, 2021. https://www.chronicle.com/article/the-ubiquitous-college-lawyer/.

Bok, Derek. "The American System of Higher Education." In his *Higher Education in America*, 9–27. Revised ed. The William G. Bowen Memorial Series in Higher Education. N.p.: Princeton University Press, 2013. https://doi.org/10.2307/j.ctv7h0rts.34.

Bound, John, and Sarah Turner. "Going to War and Going to College: Did World War II and the G.I. Bill Increase Educational Attainment for Returning Veterans?" *Journal of Labor Economics* 20, no. 4 (October 2002): 784–815. https://www.jstor.org/stable/pdf/10.1086/342012.pdf.

"Browse Law Schools by State." *Law School Numbers*. Accessed September 2, 2021. http://schools.lawschoolnumbers.com/states.

Burt, Chris. "Becker College Will Permanently Close after 237 Years, but Esports Will Survive." *University Business*, March 29, 2021. Accessed August 29, 2021. https://universitybusiness.com/becker-college-will-permanently-close-after-237-years/?eml=20210330&oly_enc_id=9918E4543589E5D.

Bump, Bethany, "UAlbany Pays Over $200k for Presidential Search Consultant," *Times Union*, February 22, 2017. Accessed October 22, 2022. https://www.timesunion.com/local/article/UAlbany-pays-over-200K-for-presidential-search-10951363.php.

"Cambridge College Launches Cambridge College Global, New Online Division for New Markets with a Global Reach." *Cambridge College*. Last modified May 13, 2021. Accessed September 22, 2021. https://www.cambridgecollege.edu/news/cambridge-college-launches-cambridge-college-global.

Camera, Lauren. "The Higher Education Apocalypse: A Steady Drip of Crises in Massachusetts and across New England May Just Signal Its Arrival." *U.S. News & World Report*. Last modified March 22, 2019. Accessed August 29, 2021. https://www.usnews.com/news/education-news/articles/2019-03-22/college-closings-signal-start-of-a-crisis-in-higher-education.

Campanile, Carl, and Bernadette Hogan. "SUNY Campuses Prepare for 25 Percent Cut in State Aid amid Pandemic." *New York Post*, September 27, 2020. Accessed October 14, 2020. https://nypost.com/2020/09/27/suny-campuses-face-25-percent-cut-in-state-aid-amid-pandemic/.

Carlton, Genevieve. "Student Activism in College A History of Campus Protests." *Best Colleges* (blog). Entry posted May 18, 2020. Accessed September 1, 2021. https://www.bestcolleges.com/blog/history-student-activism-in-college/.

Caron, Paul. "There Are Now 27 Black Women Law School Deans." *TaxProf Blog*. Entry posted May 5, 2021. Accessed September 2, 2021. https://taxprof.typepad.com/taxprof_blog/2021/05/there-are-now-27-black-women-law-school-deans.html.

Cengage. "1878–1899: Education: Overview." *Encyclopedia.com*. Accessed September 1, 2021. https://www.encyclopedia.com/history/news-wires-white-papers-and-books/1878-1899-education-overview.

Center for Women's History and Leadership. "Biography." *Frances Willard, House Museum and Archives*. Accessed September 9, 2021. https://franceswillardhouse.org/frances-willard/biography/.

Chou, Paul Hsun-Ling. "The Dark Spots on the Ivory Tower: Leaders in Higher Education Are Facing More Scrutiny, Higher Stress and Lower Job Security." *Korn Ferry*. Accessed August 31, 2021. https://www.kornferry.com/insights/this-week-in-leadership/the-dark-spots-on-the-ivory-tower.

Clark, Kristin Hodge, and Brandon D. Daniels. *Top Strategic Issues Facing HBCUs, Now and into the Future*. Washington, DC: Association of Governing Boards of Universities and Colleges, 2014. https://eric.ed.gov/?id=ED549731.

"C|M|Law P. Kelly Tompkins Leadership and the Law Program." *Cleveland-Marshall College of Law*. Accessed September 29, 2021. https://www.law.csuohio.edu/academics/leadership.

"College Administrator Data/Turnover Rates 2018–Present." *HigherEd Direct*. Last modified March 31, 2021. Accessed August 30, 2021. https://hepinc.com/newsroom/college-administrator-data-turnover-rates-2018-present/?utm_source=Iterable&utm_medium=email&utm_campaign=campaign_2175853_nl_Daily-Briefing_date_20210402&cid=db&source=ams&sourceId=4587547.

College of Charleston. "President Elect Glenn McConnell: Lt. Gov. Glenn McConnell Is 22nd President of College of Charleston." News release. Accessed September 22, 2021. https://cofc.edu/president-elect/.

"Commission on Women in the Profession." *American Bar Association.* Accessed September 9, 2021. https://www.americanbar.org/groups/diversity/women/about_us/.

Connecticut General Assembly Office of Legislative Research. *Exemptions from the Higher Education Licensing Process for Religious Colleges.* By Rute A. Pinhel. Report no. 2007-R-0023. January 9, 2007. Accessed September 2, 2021. https://www.cga.ct.gov/2007/rpt/2007-R-0023.htm.

Court of Appeals, State of New York. "Rule 520.16, Pro Bono Requirement for Bar Admission" (22 N.Y. Comp. Codes R. & Regs. §520.16 [last amended 2012, current through October 15, 2020]). *Westlaw, New York Codes, Rules and Regulations.* Accessed September 1, 2021. https://govt.westlaw.com/nycrr/Document/I14be86f14dbb11e2b9e30000845b8d3e?viewType=FullText&originationContext=documenttoc&transitionType=CategoryPageItem&contextData=(sc.Default).

"COVID-19, Stay Informed with the Latest Enrollment Information: Spring 2021 Enrollment (As of March 25)." National Student Clearinghouse Research Center. Last modified April 29, 2021. Accessed August 29, 2021. https://nscresearchcenter.org/stay-informed/.

Crittenden, Jack. "Law School Faculties 40% Larger than 10 Years Ago." *The National Jurist.* Last modified March 9, 2010. Accessed September 2, 2021. http://www.nationaljurist.com/content/law-school-faculties-40-larger-10-years-ago.

Curriden, Mark. "CEO, Esq." *ABA Journal,* May 1, 2010. Accessed August 30, 2021. https://www.abajournal.com/magazine/article/ceo_esq/.

"Dalton Selected as Isothermal's Next President." *Tryon Daily Bulletin,* March 15, 2013. Accessed October 10, 2022. https://www.tryondailybulletin.com/2013/03/15/dalton-selected-as-isothermals-next-president/.

Daniels, Nick, and Zoe Lescaze. "The Evolution of a Leader: Barry Mills as President." *The Bowdoin Orient,* December 10, 2010. Accessed October 22, 2022, https://bowdoinorient.com/bonus/article/5878.

Dean, James. "Peñalver, Law School Dean, Named Seattle University President." *Cornell Law School.* Last modified October 22, 2020. Accessed September 2, 2021. https://www.lawschool.cornell.edu/news/penalver-law-school-dean-named-seattle-university-president/.

Delabbio, Daryl, and Louann Palmer. "A 360° View of Non-Traditional University Presidents." *Academic Leadership: The Online Journal* 7, no. 1 (Winter 2009). Accessed August 30, 2021. https://scholars.fhsu.edu/cgi/viewcontent.cgi?article=1245&context=alj.

Deloitte's Center for Higher Education Excellence, and Georgia Tech's Center for 21st Century Universities. *Pathways to the University Presidency: The Future of Higher Education Leadership.* N.p.: Deloitte Universisty Press, 2017. Accessed August 31, 2021. https://www2.deloitte.com/us/en/insights/industry/public-sector/college-presidency-higher-education-leadership.html.

Doyle, Jeff. "Should We Believe Scott Galoway's Predictions of Soon-To-Perish Colleges." *University Business.* Last modified July 27, 2020. Accessed August 29, 2021. https://universitybusiness.com/should-we-believe-scott-galloways-predictions-of-soon-to-perish-colleges/.

Dunham, Stephen S. "Government Regulation of Higher Education: The Elephant in the Middle of the Room." *Journal of College and University Law* 36, no. 1 (2009): 749–790. https://heinonline.org/HOL/Print?collection=journals&handle=hein.journals/jcolunly36&id=799.

Dykstra, Jason G. "Teasing the Arc of Electric Spark: Fostering and Teaching Creativity in the Law School Curriculum." *Wyoming Law Review* 20, no. 1 (2020): 1–42. Accessed September 30, 2021. https://scholarship.law.uwyo.edu/cgi/viewcontent.cgi?article=1427&context=wlr.

Easterbrook, Gregg. "Who Needs Harvard?" *Brookings*. Last modified October 1, 2004. Accessed September 9, 2021. https://www.brookings.edu/articles/who-needs-harvard/.

Ellsworth, Frank L., and Martha A. Burns. *Student Activism in American Higher Education*. Student Personnel Series 10. Washington, D.C: American College Personnel Association, 1970. Accessed September 1, 2021. http://story.myacpa.org/img/carousel/STUDENT%20ACTIVISM%20IN%20AMERICAN%20HIGHER%20EDUCATION.pdf.

Equal Employment Opportunity Act of 1972, Pub. L. No. 92–261, 86 Stat. 103 (March 24, 1972). (Amending the Civil Rights Act of 1964.)

"Faculty and Staff: Harry Davros." *Wade College*. Accessed September 22, 2021. https://www.wadecollege.edu/about/faculty_and_staff.

FaegreDrinker. "Partner Lowell Haines to Become President of Taylor University." January 21, 2016. Accessed October 20, 2022. https://www.faegredrinker.com/en/about/news/2016/1/partner-lowell-haines-to-become-president-of-taylor-university.

Field, Kelly. "The Successful President of Tomorrow: The Five Skills Future Leaders Will Need." *Chronicle of Higher Education*, 2019.

Flowers, Deidre B. "The Launching of the Student Sit-in Movement: The Role of Black Women at Bennett College." *The Journal of African American History* 90, no. 1/2 (Winter 2005): 52–63. https://www.jstor.org/stable/20063975.

Gagliardi, Jonathan S., Lorelle L. Espinosa, Jonathan M. Turk, and Morgan Taylor. *American College President Study 2017*. American College President Study Series 8. Washington, DC: American Council on Education, TIAA Institute, 2017. Accessed November 14, 2021. https://www.aceacps.org/.

Galloway, Scott. "U.SS University." *No Mercy/No Malice*. Last modified July 17, 2020. Accessed August 29, 2021. https://www.profgalloway.com/uss-university/.

Gardella, Adriana. "The Secret of Lawyers-Turned-Entrepreneurs?" *Forbes*. Last modified April 10, 2015. Accessed September 1, 2021. https://www.forbes.com/sites/adrianagardella/2015/04/10/the-secret-of-lawyers-turned-entrepreneurs/?sh=24e83d067cec.

Geiger, Roger L. "The First Century of the American College, 1636–1740." In his *The History of American Higher Education: Learning and Culture from the Founding to World War II*, 1–32. Princeton: Princeton University Press, 2014. Accessed September 1, 2021. http://assets.press.princeton.edu/chapters/s10320.pdf.

Greenberg, Susan. "3 Campuses Unite to Become Vermont State University." *Inside Higher Ed*. Last modified October 1, 2021. Accessed November 8, 2021. https://www.insidehighered.com/quicktakes/2021/10/01/3-campuses-unite-become-vermont-state-university?utm_source=Inside+Higher+Ed&utm_campaign=903c7d9065-DNU_2021_COPY_02&utm_medium=email&utm_term=0_1fcbc04421-903c7d9065-199790317&mc_cid=903c7d9065&mc_eid=ef35c4ecbc.

"The Greensboro Sit-Ins: Nearly Four Decades Ago, Well-Mannered, Well-Dressed, and Courteous Black College Kids Launched a Lunch Counter Revolution in the United States." *The Journal of Blacks in Higher Education* 15 (Spring 1997): 135. https://www.jstor.org/stable/i348963.

Hardesty, Nancy A. "Willard, Frances Elizabeth (1839–98)." In *Handbook of Women Biblical Interpreters*, edited by Marion Ann Taylor and Agnes Choi. Ada, MI: Baker

Publishing Group, 2012. https://search.credoreference.com/content/entry/bpgwomen/willard_frances_elizabeth_1839_98/0.

Harno, Albert J. *Legal Education in the United States.* San Francisco: Bancroft-Whitney Company, 1953.

Harris, Adam. "Who Wants to Be a College President? Probably Not Many Qualified Candidates." *The Atlantic*, January 24, 2019. Accessed November 12, 2021. https://www.theatlantic.com/education/archive/2019/01/how-politics-are-reshaping-college-presidency/581077/.

The Harvard Crimson (Boston, MA). "Colleges in the Colonial Times. A Lecture by Prof. Tyler—Harvard's Tariff for College Sins." April 20, 1883. Accessed September 30, 2021. https://www.thecrimson.com/article/1883/4/20/colleges-in-the-colonial-times-prof/.

Harvard Square. "Janet L. Steinmayer Named Lesley University's Seventh President." July 10, 2019. Accessed October 20, 2022. https://www.harvardsquare.com/janet-l-steinmayer-named-lesley-universitys-seventh-president/.

Harvard University, Columbia University, John Hopkins University, The University of Chicago, and University of California. Letter, "The Letter of Invitation to the Founding Conference of AAU," January 1900. Accessed September 1, 2021. https://www.aau.edu/sites/default/files/AAU%20Files/Key%20Issues/Budget%20%26%20Appropriations/FY17/Invit.pdf. The original document is in the AAU archive in the Special Collections of the Milton S. Eisenhower Library at The Johns Hopkins University.

Hatch, Orrin. "Protecting Freedom of Speech Where It Matters Most, on the College Campus." *National Review*, February 7, 2018. Accessed September 1, 2021. https://www.nationalreview.com/2018/02/free-speech-college-campuses-legislation-ensure-it/.

Hechinger, Grace. "Clark Kerr, Leading Public Educator and Former Head of California's Universities, Dies at 92." *New York Times*, December 23, 2003. https://www.nytimes.com/2003/12/02/us/clark-kerr-leading-public-educator-former-head-california-s-universities-dies-92.html.

Heineman, Ben W., Jr. "Lawyers as Leaders." *Yale Law Journal Forum* 116, no. 30 (February 16, 2007). Accessed September 30, 2021. https://www.yalelawjournal.org/forum/lawyers-as-leaders.

Henahan, David, "SUNY Interim Chancellor Clark Appoints George M. Philip as University at Albany Officer in Charge: Clark to Recommend Philip as Interim President to SUNY Board," *University at Albany*, October 3, 2007. Accessed October 22, 2022. https://www.albany.edu/campusnews/releases_414.htm.

Hernández, Christine, and Annie Martínez. "Leading the Way to a Diversity-Focused CLE Requirement." *Colorado Lawyer*. Last modified December 2020. Accessed August 31, 2021. https://k794ovkhls2hdtl419uu4dcd-wpengine.netdna-ssl.com/wp-content/uploads/2020/11/Dec2020_Welcome-PM.pdf.

Hersch, Joni, and W. Kip Viscusi. "Law and Economics as a Pillar of Legal Education." *Review of Law and Economics* 8, no. 2 (October 2012): 487–510. Accessed September 9, 2021. https://law.vanderbilt.edu/files/archive/2012_Hersch&Viscusi_Law-and-Economics-as-a-Pillar-of-Legal-Education_RLE-Oct-2012.pdf.

Hess, Abigail Johnson. "Harvard Business School Professor: Half of American Colleges Will Be Bankrupt in 10–15 Years." *CNBC Make It: Careers*. Last modified August 30, 2018. Accessed August 29, 2021. https://www.cnbc.com/2018/08/30/hbs-prof-says-half-of-us-colleges-will-be-bankrupt-in-10-to-15-years.html.

Higher Education Act of 1965, Pub. L. No. 89–329, 86 Stat. 1219 (November 8, 1965). (Codified as amended 20 U.S.C. §1001 et seq.)

Hodge-Clark, Kristin, and Brandon D. Daniels. "Top Strategic Issues Facing HBCUs, Now and into the Future." *American Association of Governing Boards of Universities and Colleges*, 2014, 1–16. https://eric.ed.gov/?id=ED549731.

Honan, William H. "An Icon of State Politics is Picked to Lead U. Mass." *New York Times*, November 29, 1995. https://timesmachine.nytimes.com/timesmachine/1995/11/29/issue.html.

Hong, Nicole, William K. Rosenblaum, and Ben Protess. "Court Suspends Giuliani's Law License, Citing Trump Election Lies." *New York Times*, June 24, 2021. Accessed September 30, 2021. https://www.nytimes.com/2021/06/24/nyregion/giuliani-law-license-suspended-trump.html.

Horowitz, Helen Lefkowitz. "The 1960s and the Transformation of Campus Cultures." *History of Education Quarterly* 26, no. 1 (Spring 1986): 1–38. https://www.jstor.org/stable/368875.

Horvath, Ginny Schaefer, and Maya Ranchod. "Sharpening the Lens for Hiring Leaders." *2020 Vision Academic Search*. Last modified 2020. Accessed August 31, 2021. https://academicsearch.org/wp-content/uploads/formidable/8/ASI-2020-Vision-Article.pdf.

Hunt, Thomas C. "National Defense Education Act, United States [1958]." *Britannica*. Last modified August 26, 2021. Accessed September 30, 2021. https://www.britannica.com/topic/National-Defense-Education-Act.

Hunter, Glen. "Lunch with D CEO: Michael J. Sorrell, the President of Paul Quinn College Talks Innovation in Education." Business. *D Magazine*, November 2016. Accessed November 14, 2021. https://www.dmagazine.com/publications/d-ceo/2016/november/lunch-with-d-ceo-michael-j-sorrell/.

Hunter College. "Office of the President, Biography: About President Raab, the 13th President of Hunter College." *Hunter*. https://hunter.cuny.edu/about/leadership/president/bio/.

Hutcheson, Philo A. *A People's History of American Higher Education*. New York: Routledge, 2020.

Hylton, J. Gordon. "What Should Be the Prerequisites for Becoming a Law Professor." *Marquette University Law School Faculty Blog*. Entry posted September 8, 2011. Accessed September 9, 2021. https://law.marquette.edu/facultyblog/2011/09/what-should-be-the-prerequisites-for-becoming-a-law-professor/.

Indiana University Center for Post Secondary Research. "CCIHE 2018 Public Data File." *Carnegie Classifications of Institutions of Higher Education*. Last modified 2018. http://carnegieclassifications.iu.edu/downloads/CCIHE2018-PublicDataFile.xlsx.

Indiana University Center for Postsecondary Research. "Distribution of Institutions and Enrollments by Classification Category." *CCIHE2018 Summary Tables*. Last modified 2018. Accessed September 22, 2021. https://view.officeapps.live.com/op/view.aspx?src=https%3A%2F%2Fcarnegieclassifications.iu.edu%2Fdownloads%2FCCIHE2018-SummaryTables.xlsx&wdOrigin=BROWSELINK.

———. "2018 Update Facts & Figures." *Carnegie Classification of Institutions of Higher Education*. Last modified March 19, 2021. Accessed August 31, 2021. https://carnegieclassifications.iu.edu/downloads/CCIHE2018-FactsFigures.pdf.

"Institute for Lawyer Leadership Education." *Santa Clara University School of Law*. Accessed September 29, 2021. https://law.scu.edu/leadership/leadership-institute-info/.

"Institute for Professional Leadership Preparting." *University of Tennessee Knoxville College of Law*. Accessed September 29, 2021. https://law.utk.edu/programs/leadership/.

Ivory, Joanne L. "A Review of Nontraditional Presidents in Higher Education: Benefits and Challenges of Change Agents in Colleges and Universities." PhD diss., Benedictine University, Lisle, IL, 2017. https://www.proquest.com/dissertations-theses/review-nontraditional-presidents-higher-education/docview/1914898658/se-2?accountid=30558.

"John Leverett, Educator, Lawyer, Politician." *Prabook*. Accessed September 1, 2021. https://prabook.com/web/john.leverett/2231353.

Johnson, Jermaine. "Led by Lawyers: Perceptions of Legal Training and Experience and Their Effect upon Leadership." PhD diss., Iowa State University, Ames, IA, 2017. https://lib.dr.iastate.edu/etd/16725/.

Johnson, Julie. "The Law; Universities Looking to Lawyers for Leadership." *New York Times*, December 25, 1987, sec. B, 12. https://www.nytimes.com/1987/12/25/us/the-law-universities-looking-to-lawyers-for-leadership.html.

Kaplin, William A., and Barbara A. Lee. *The Law of Higher Education*. 5th ed. N.p.: Jossey-Bass, 2013.

Kerr, Clark, and Marian L. Gade. *The Many Lives of Academic Presidents*. Washington, DC: Association of Governing Boards of Universities and Colleges, 1986. Accessed August 30, 2021. https://files.eric.ed.gov/fulltext/ED267704.pdf.

Klein, Laura B. "Understanding the Experiences of Non-Traditional University Leadership in Higher Education: A Qualitative Study Using a Triangular Theoretical Approach." PhD diss., Oakland University, Rochester, MI, 2016. Accessed October 30, 2019. https://www.proquest.com/dissertations-theses/understanding-experiences-non-traditional/docview/1826914039/se-2?accountid=30558.

LaBaree, David F. "Learning to Love the Bomb: The Cold War Brings the Best of Times to American Higher Education." In *Discourses of Change and Changes to Discourse*, edited by Paul Smeyers and Marc Depaepe, 101–117. Vol. 9 of *Educational Research*. N.p.: Springer International Publishing, 2016.

Larson, Gloria. "From 'Recovering Lawyer' to University President: Q and A with Gloria Larson." *HuffPost*, August 16, 2017. Accessed August 30, 2021. https://www.huffpost.com/entry/from-recovering-lawyer-to-university-president-q_b_599451d4e4b0a88ac1bc38a4?guccounter=1.

Law.com. "If It's a New Law Dean, It's Likely and Woman." March 30, 2017. Accessed September 22, 2021. https://www.law.com/sites/almstaff/2017/03/30/if-its-a-new-law-dean-its-likely-a-woman/.

"Leadership Competency Matrix." Table. *Columbia University*. Accessed September 28, 2021. https://leadership-initiative.law.columbia.edu/sites/default/files/content/FINAL_Leadership%20Competency%20Matrix.pdf.

"Leadership Development." *Baylor Law*. Accessed September 29, 2021. https://www.baylor.edu/law/currentstudents/index.php?id=935914.

Leading as Lawyers (blog). Accessed September 30, 2021. https://leadingaslawyers.blog/posts/.

"Leading Differently across Difference: National Conference on Training Lawyers as Leaders." *Hofstra University Maurice A. Deane School of Law, Freedman Institute*. Accessed September 29, 2021. https://freedmaninstitute.hofstra.edu/events/leading-differently-across-difference-a-national-conference-on-training-lawyers-as-leaders/#cle-materials.

Lee, Barbara A. "Fifty Years of Higher Education Law: Turning the Kaleidoscope." *Journal of College and University Law* 36, no. 3 (2010): 649–690. https://heinonline.org/HOL/Print?collection=journals&handle=hein.journals/jcolunly36&id=699.

Lennon, Tiffani. *Benchmarking Women's Leadership in the United States.* Denver, CO: Colorado Women's College, University of Denver, 2013. https://www.issuelab.org/resources/26706/26706.pdf.

Lesley University, "Janet L. Steinmayer, Lesley University's Seventh President," April 23, 2019. Accessed October 20, 2022. https://lesley.edu/news/janet-l-steinmayer.

Lipton, Jacqueline. "Non-Traditional Law Deans and Tenure." *The Faculty Lounge* (blog). Entry posted October 3, 2009. Accessed September 2, 2021. https://www.thefacultylounge.org/2009/10/nontraditional-law-deans-and-tenure.html.

Lombardo, Lynn M. "A Comprehensive Examination of Student Unrest at Buffalo State College, 1966–1970." Master's thesis, Buffalo State College, Buffalo, NY, 2011. https://digitalcommons.buffalostate.edu/cgi/viewcontent.cgi?article=1005&context=buffstate-history.

Louie, David M. "Leadership in Public Service." In *Leadership for Lawyers*, edited by Francisco Ramos, Jr, 63–69. Elmhurst, IL: Federation of Defense & Corporate Counsel, 2017. Accessed September 9, 2021. https://cdn.ymaws.com/thefederation.site-ym.com/resource/resmgr/docs/Leadeship_for_Lawyers_Dec2017/V1.02_Leadership_for_Lawyers.pdf.

Macauley, Don. "What Is A Lawyer's Duty Of Technology Competence?" *National Jurist*, February 2, 2019. Accessed August 31, 2021. http://www.nationaljurist.com/smartlawyer/what-lawyers-duty-technology-competence.

Martin, Rodger. "So You Want to Become a College President." *Inside Higher Ed.* Last modified March 19, 2018. Accessed September 13, 2021. https://www.insidehighered.com/advice/2018/03/19/myths-and-misconceptions-about-presidential-searches-opinion.

McBain, Lesley, Harold V. Hartley, III, Kerry E. Pannell, and Katherine M. Whatley. *A Study of Chief Academic Officers at Independent Colleges and Universities, 2009–2019.* N.p.: Council of Independent Colleges, 2019. Accessed September 13, 2021. https://www.cic.edu/r/cd/Pages/cao-report-2019.aspx.

McKenna, Laura. "Why Are Fewer College Presidents Academics?" *The Atlantic*, December 3, 2015. Accessed August 30, 2021. https://www.theatlantic.com/education/archive/2015/12/college-president-mizzou-tim-wolfe/418599/.

Mertz, Elizabeth, Katherine Barnes, and Wamucii Njogu. *After Tenure: Post-Tenure Law Professors in the United States.* American Bar Foundation, 2011. Accessed October 30, 2019. http://www.americanbarfoundation.org/uploads/cms/documents/after_tenure_report-_final-_abf_4.1.pdf.

Mitchell, Michael, Michael Leachman, and Kathleen Masterson. "A Lost Decade in Higher Education Funding: State Cuts Have Driven Up Tuition and Reduced Quality." *Center on Budget and Policy Priorities.* Last modified August 23, 2017. Accessed September 22, 2021. https://www.cbpp.org/research/state-budget-and-tax/a-lost-decade-in-higher-education-funding.

"Mitchell E. Daniels, Jr.: Biography." *Purdue University: Office of the President.* Accessed September 22, 2021. https://www.purdue.edu/president/about/biography.php.

"Model Rule for Minimum Continuing Legal Education." *American Bar Association.* Last modified February 6, 2017. Accessed August 31, 2021. https://www.americanbar.org/content/dam/aba/directories/policy/2017_hod_midyear_106.pdf.

Moody, Josh. "A Guide to the Changing Number of U.S. Universities: The U.S. Department of Education Lists Nearly 4000 Degree-Granting Academic Institutions." *U.S. News and World Report, Best Colleges.* Last modified April 27, 2021. Accessed August 29, 2021. https://www.usnews.com/education/best-colleges/articles/how-many-universities-are-in-the-us-and-why-that-number-is-changing.

Moran, Lyle. "Lawyers Find Their Skill Sets Make Them Ideal Candidates for College Presidencies." *ABA Journal*, April/May 2021, 55–61.

Morgan, Thomas D. "The Changing Face of Legal Education: Its Impact on What It Means to Be a Lawyer." *Akron Law Review* 45, no. 4 (2011–2012): 811–842.

Muir, Ronda. "Emotional Intelligence for Lawyers." *ABA Career Center* (blog). Accessed September 1, 2021. https://www.americanbar.org/careercenter/blog/emotional-intelligence-for-lawyers/.

National Association of College and University Attorneys. Accessed August 31, 2021. https://www.nacua.org/about-nacua.

Nguyen, Thomas T. "Perceptions of Lawyers on Career Transition, Transferable Skills, and Prepartion for Community College Leadership." PhD diss., Florida Atlantic University, Boca Raton, FL, 2014. https://www.proquest.com/dissertations-theses/perceptions-lawyers-on-career-transition/docview/1547946174/se-2?accountid=30558.

"Non-ABA-Approved Law Schools." *Law School Admission Council*. Accessed September 30, 2021. https://www.lsac.org/choosing-law-school/find-law-school/non-aba-approved-law-schools.

"Nora Demleitner Appointed President of St. John's College, Annapolis." *St. John's College*. Last modified September 24, 2021. Accessed November 8, 2021. https://www.sjc.edu/news/nora-demleitner-appointed-president-st-johns-college-annapolis.

"Office of the President, Barry Mills (2001–2015)." *Bowdoin*. Accessed October 22, 2022. https://www.bowdoin.edu/president/past-presidents/mills.html.

"Office of the President, Meet President Krisolv." *Pace University*. Accessed September 9, 2021. https://www.pace.edu/president/meet-president-krislov.

Olsen, Keith W. "The G.I. Bill and Higher Education: Success and Surprise." *American Quarterly* 25, no. 5 (1973): 596–610. https://www.jstor.org/stable/2711698.

Padilla, Laura M. "A Gendered Update on Women Law Deans: Who, Where, Why, and Why Not?" *Journal of Gender, Social Policy & the Law* 15, no. 3 (2007): 443–546. Accessed September 22, 2021. https://digitalcommons.wcl.american.edu/cgi/viewcontent.cgi?referer=https://www.google.com/&httpsredir=1&article=1253&context=jgspl.

Parker, Reed. "Taylor University Appoints Interim President." August 2, 2019. Accessed October 2022. https://www.insideindianabusiness.com/articles/taylor-university-appoints-interim-president.

Peri, Jonathan. "The Wisdom of Employed General Counsel in Higher Education." *Widener Law Journal* 18, no. 1 (2008): 191–203. https://heinonline.org/HOL/Page?handle=hein.journals/wjpl18&id=193&collection=journals.

"President Emeritus James J. Barba." *Albany Medical College*. Accessed September 22, 2021. https://www.amc.edu/leadership/jamesjbarba/index.cfm.

"Program on Law and Leadership." *The Ohio State University Moritz College of Law*. Accessed September 29, 2021. https://moritzlaw.osu.edu/faculty-and-research/program-law-and-leadership.

Queenan, Rosemary, and Mary Walsh. "Leadership Courses: Paving the Path for Future Attorneys." *Best Practices for Legal Education* (blog). Entry posted January 30, 2019. Accessed September 30, 2021. https://bestpracticeslegaled.com/2019/01/30/leadership-courses-paving-the-way-for-future-attorneys/.

Quinlan, Casey. "Universities Run Into Problems When They Hire Presidents from the Business World." *Think Progress*. Last modified March 7, 2016. Accessed September 29, 2021. https://archive.thinkprogress.org/universities-run-into-problems-when-they-hire-presidents-from-the-business-world-a66b2739c1a/.

Rabner, Stuart, Chief Justice, and Glen A. Grant, J.A.D. "Notice to the BAR and Order" (Continuing Legal Education Requirement of Two Hours [per Two-year Reporting Cycle] of Courses in Diversity, Inclusion, and Elimination of Bias; Judiciary to Offer Real-time Virtual Courses on Implicit Bias and Elimination of Bias). *Supreme Court of New Jersey.* Last modified October 20, 2020. Accessed August 31, 2021. https://www.njcourts.gov/notices/2020/n201021e.pdf?c=c2f.

Rash, Jennifer David. "Judson College Board of Trustees Votes to Close School." *The Alabama Baptist,* May 6, 2021. Accessed August 29, 2021. https://thealabamabaptist.org/judson-college-board-votes-to-close-school/.

Redden, Elizabeth. "A Cross-Town Acquisition." *Inside Higher Ed.* Last modified July 2, 2021. Accessed August 29, 2021. https://www.insidehighered.com/news/2021/07/02/delaware-state-university-finalizes-acquisition-neighboring-wesley-college?utm_source=Inside+Higher+Ed&utm_campaign=01799623bd-DNU_2021_COPY_02&utm_medium=email&utm_term=0_1fcbc04421-01799623bd-197546157&mc_cid=01799623bd&mc_eid=8696d9ba4f.

Reed, Alfred Z. *Review of Legal Education in the United States and Canada for the Years 1926 and 1927.* New York City: The Carnegie Foundation for the Advancement of Teaching, 1928. Accessed September 1, 2021. https://www.americanbar.org/content/dam/aba/publications/misc/legal_education/Standards/standardsarchive/1926_1927_review.pdf.

Rehabilitation Act of 1973, Pub. L. No. 93–112, 87 Stat. 355 (September 26, 1973). (Codified as amended 29 U.S. C. §701 et seq.)

Rhode, Deborah. "Section on Leadership: Message from the Chair, 2018." *The Association of American Law Schools.* Last modified November 1, 2018. Accessed September 2, 2021. https://sectiononleadership.org/2018/11/.

———. *Lawyers as Leaders.* New York: Oxford University Press, 2013.

Rhodes, Dawn. "Chicago State Picks Zaldwaynaka 'Z' Scott as New President." *Chicago Tribune,* May 9, 2018. Accessed October 10, 2022, https://www.chicagotribune.com/news/ct-met-chicago-state-university-z-scott-president 20180509-story.html.

Robinson, Gray. "Family Lawyers and Emotional Intelligence." *Family Lawyer Magazine.com,* August 26, 2021. Accessed September 1, 2021. https://familylawyermagazine.com/family-lawyers-and-emotional-intelligence/.

Ryssdal, Kai. "COVID-19: Some Small Colleges Are Closing their Doors for Good amid Pandemic." August 20, 2020. In *Marketplace,* narrated by Sasha Asianian. Podcast, audio. Accessed August 29, 2021. https://www.marketplace.org/2020/08/20/some-small-colleges-closing-for-good-covid19/.

Salkin, Patricia E. "In Tough Times, Schools Look to Lawyers to Lead." *Trusteeship,* May/June 2021, 28–32.

———. "Lawyers Are Leading Higher Education as Advocates Call for More Formal Leadership Training in Legal Education." *Best Practices for Legal Education* (blog). Entry posted February 18, 2021. Accessed September 29, 2021. https://bestpracticeslegaled.com/2021/02/18/lawyers-are-leading-higher-education-as-advocates-call-for-more-formal-leadership-training-in-legal-education/.

Salkin, Patricia E., and Pamela Ko. "Should I Stay or Should I Go? Student Housing, Remote Instruction, Campus Policies." *The Urban Lawyer* 50, no. 3 (February 2021): 371–399. https://papers.ssrn.com/sol3/papers.cfm?abstract_id=3748864.

Santistevan, Ryan. "Concordia College to Close: Iona College to Acquire Bronxville Campus." *Iohud*, January 28, 2021. Accessed August 29, 2021. https://www.lohud.com/story/news/education/2021/01/28/concordia-college-closes-iona-college-acquires-bronxville-campus/4292059001/.

Schaefer, Paul. "Leadership Education in Law School: You're Already Providing It." *Best Practices for Legal Education* (blog). Entry posted January 16, 2019. Accessed September 30, 2021. https://bestpracticeslegaled.com/2019/01/16/leadership-education-in-law-school-youre-already-providing-it/.

Schmidt, Peter. "A Lawyer Takes an Uncommon Path to a University Presidency." *Chronicle of Higher Education*, January 1, 2012. Accessed August 31, 2021. https://www.chronicle.com/article/a-lawyer-takes-an-uncommon-path-to-a-university-presidency/.

Schmotter, James W. "Ministerial Careers in Eighteenth-Century New England: The Social Context, 1700–1760." *Journal of Social History* 9, no. 2 (Winter 1975): 249–267. http://www.jstor.org/stable/3786254.

Schnackner, Bill. "In Historic Vote, State System of Higher Education Sets Plan in Motion to Combine 6 Schools into 2." *Pittsburg Post-Gazette*, April 28, 2021. Accessed August 30, 2021. https://www.post-gazette.com/news/education/2021/04/28/California-Clarion-Edinboro-university-colleges-merger-Pennsylvania-State-System-of-Higher-Education-Bloomsburg-Lock-Haven-Mansfield/stories/202104280084?utm_source=Iterable&utm_medium=email&utm_campaign=campaign_2277141_nl_Daily-Briefing_date_20210429&cid=db&source=ams&sourceId=4587547.

"Section on Leadership." *Association of American Law Schools*. Accessed September 2, 2021. https://www.aals.org/sections/list/leadership/.

Section on Legal Education and Admission to the Bar. "List of ABA Approved Law Schools." *American Bar Association*. Accessed September 2, 2021. https://www.americanbar.org/groups/legal_education/resources/aba_approved_law_schools/.

———. "Various Statistics on ABA Approved Law Schools." *American Bar Association*. Accessed September 2, 2021. https://www.americanbar.org/groups/legal_education/resources/aba_approved_law_schools/.

Seltzer, Rick. "Defending Nontraditional Presidents." *Inside Higher Ed*. Last modified August 30, 2017. Accessed September 29, 2021. https://www.insidehighered.com/news/2017/08/30/new-book-examines-developments-hiring-nontraditional-college-presidents.

———. "Dickinson Plans Unique Presidential Transition." *Inside Higher Ed*. Last modified May 17, 2021. Accessed September 9, 2021. https://www.insidehighered.com/news/2021/05/17/board-chair-plans-two-year-interim-presidency-dickinson-college?utm_source=Inside+Higher+Ed&utm_campaign=00369dca8f-DNU_2021_COPY_02&utm_medium=email&utm_term=0_1fcbc04421-00369dca8f-198501589&mc_cid=00369dca8f&mc_eid=3e858f3f7a.

Siegel, Andrew. "'To Learn and Make Respectable Hereafter:' The Litchfield Law School in Cultural Context." *New York University Law Review* 73 (December 1998): 1978–2028. Accessed September 1, 2021. https://digitalcommons.law.seattleu.edu/faculty/644/.

Sloan, Karen. "ABA Pushes Forward With Racism Training Requirement for Law Schools." *Law.com*, May 17, 2021. Accessed August 31, 2021. https://www.law.com/2021/05/17/aba-pushes-forward-with-racism-training-requirement-for-law-schools/.

———. "Meet the Record-Setting Number of Incoming Women Law Deans." *Law.com*, April 3, 2019. Accessed September 2, 2021. https://www.law.com/2019/04/03/meet-the-record-setting-number-of-incoming-women-law-deans/.

Smith, J. Clay, Jr. *Emancipation: The Making of the Black Lawyer, 1844–1944*. Philadelphia: University of Pennsylvania Press, 1993.

Smola, Jennifer. "Urbana University in Ohio Closing due to Coronavirus Challenges, Low Enrollment." *Cincinnati.com: The Enquirer*, April 22, 2020. Accessed September 1, 2021. https://www.cincinnati.com/story/news/2020/04/22/urbana-university-ohio-closing-permanently-coronavirus/3002171001/.

"Status and Trends in the Education of Racial and Ethnic Minorities" (Snapshot: Enrollment in Historically Black Colleges and Universities, Hispanic Serving Institutions, and Tribal Colleges). *National Center for Education Statistics*. Last modified 2017. Accessed September 9, 2021. https://nces.ed.gov/pubs2010/2010015/indicator6_24.asp#snapshot.

Stern, Hal S. "Law Dean L. Song Richardson Named President of Colorado College." UCI Office of the Provost and Executive Vice Chancellor. Accessed September 2, 2021. https://provost.uci.edu/2020/12/09/law-dean-l-song-richardson-named-president-of-colorado-college/.

Stevens, Robert Bocking. *Law School: Legal Education in America from the 1850s to the 1980s*. Chapel Hill, NC: University of North Carolina Press, 1983.

Strauss, Valerie. "Lawyers Are Leading U.S. Colleges and Universities More than Ever Before. Is That Good or Bad for Higher Education?" *Washington Post*, January 15, 2020. Accessed August 30, 2021. https://www.washingtonpost.com/education/2020/01/15/lawyers-are-leading-us-colleges-universities-more-than-ever-before-is-that-good-or-bad-higher-education/.

Strikwerda, Carl J. "Do Deans Make Better Presidents?" *Inside Higher Ed*. Last modified February 17, 2017. Accessed September 13, 2021. https://www.insidehighered.com/advice/2017/02/02/encouraging-both-deans-and-provosts-become-college-presidents-essay#:~:text=Working%20or%20consulting%20with%20provosts,Provosts%20handle%20internal%20matters.&text=Deans%2C%20by%20contrast%2C%20especially%20at,like%20presidents%20of%20small%20colleges.

"Table 6. Employed Persons by Detailed Occupation, Race, and Hispanic or Latino Ethnicity, 2008 Annual Averages." Table. U.S. Department of Labor, Labor Force Characteristics by Race and Ethnicity, 2008, Report 1020, 16. *U.S. Bureau of Labor Statistics*, November 2009. Accessed September 9, 2021. https://www.americanbar.org/content/dam/aba/administrative/market_research/cpsaat11.pdf.

"Table 317.50. Degree-Granting Postsecondary Institutions That Have Closed Their Doors, by Control and Level of Institution: 1969–1970 through 2018–2019." Table. *National Center for Education Statistics: Digest of Education Statistics*. Accessed August 29, 2021. https://nces.ed.gov/programs/digest/d19/tables/dt19_317.50.asp?current=yes.

"Table 317.40. Degree-Granting Postsecondary Institutions and Enrollment in These Institutions, by Enrollment Size, Control, and Classification of Institution: Fall 2017." Table. *National Center for Education Statistics: Digest of Education Statistics*. Accessed September 2, 2021. https://nces.ed.gov/programs/digest/d18/tables/dt18_317.40.asp.

"Table 3. Number and Percentage Distribution of Title IV Institutions, by Control of Institution, Degree-Granting Status, and Levels of Offering: United States, Academic Year 2014–15." Table. Fall 2014 Web Tables, *National Center for Education Statistics*, 2017. Accessed September 2, 2021. https://nces.ed.gov/Datalab/TablesLibrary/TableDetails/12132?rst=true.

"Talking Points: State Authorization of Religious Colleges." *WCET*. Last modified January 2016. Accessed September 2, 2021. https://wcet.wiche.edu/documents/talking-points/state-auth-religious-colleges.

Thelin, John R. *A History of American Higher Education*. 3rd ed. Baltimore, MD: John Hopkins University Press, 2019.

Thelin, John R., Jason R. Edwards, Eric Moyen, Joseph B. Berger, and Maria Vita Calkins. "Higher Education in the United States: Historical Development, System." *Education Encyclopedia—StateUniversity.com*. https://education.stateuniversity.com/pages/2044/Higher-Education-in-United-States.html.

Title IX of Educational Amendments of 1972, Pub. L. No. 92–318, 86 Stat. 235 (June 22, 1972). (Codified as amended 20 U.S.C. §§1681–1688.)

Title VII, Civil Rights Act of 1964, Pub. L. No. 88–352, 78 Stat. 253 (July 2, 1964). (Codified as amended 42 U.S.C. §2000e et seq.)

Tobin, Jonathan. "Q&A: Lawyer as Entrepreneur." *Law Technology Today*. Last modified April 17, 2015. Accessed September 1, 2021. https://www.lawtechnologytoday.org/2015/04/qa-lawyer-as-entrepreneur/.

Trachtenberg, Stephen Joel, Gerald B. Kauvar, and E. Grady Bougue. *Presidencies Derailed: Why University Leaders Fail and How to Prevent It*. N.p.: John Hopkins University Press, 2013.

Turk, Jonathan. "ACPS Data Request." Email message to author. February 21, 2020.

———. "ACPS Data Request." Email message to author. February 28, 2020.

UC Berkeley, Public Affairs. "Janet Napolitano Selected as New UC president." News release. July 12, 2013. Accessed September 24, 2021. https://news.berkeley.edu/2013/07/12/janet-napolitano-selected-as-new-uc-president/.

University of Georgia, Communications. "Cathy Cox Named President of Georgia College & State University." News release. August 19, 2021. Accessed September 22, 2021. https://www.usg.edu/news/release/cathy_cox_named_president_of_georgia_college_state_university.

University of Southern Maine, Office of Public Affairs. "Former Connecticut Governor Dannel Malloy to Lead University of Maine System." News release. May 30, 2019. Accessed September 22, 2021. https://usm.maine.edu/publicaffairs/former-connecticut-governor-dannel-malloy-lead-university-maine-system.

U.S. Department of Education. "DataLab." *IES-NCES National Center for Education Statistics*. Accessed November 14, 2021. https://nces.ed.gov/Datalab/TablesLibrary/TableDetails/12129?releaseYear=0&dataSource=IPEDS&subjectId=2&topicId=3&rst=true.

———. *Reform in American Public Higher Education*. By Harriett J. Robles. Research report no. ED 426746. 1998. Accessed November 8, 2021. https://files.eric.ed.gov/fulltext/ED426746.pdf.

U.S. Department of Health Education and Welfare. *The Report of the President's Commission on Campus Unrest*. Report no. ED083899. Washington, DC: U.S. Government Printing Office, 1970. Accessed November 8, 2021. https://files.eric.ed.gov/fulltext/ED083899.pdf.

Valparaiso University. "Valparaiso University Names New President." December 2, 2020. Accessed October 10, 2022, https://www.valpo.edu/news/2020/12/02/valparaiso-university-names-new-president/.

Vedder, Richard. "Training To Be a College President." *Forbes*. Last modified August 30, 2016. Accessed September 1, 2021. https://www.forbes.com/sites/ccap/2016/08/30/training-to-be-a-college-president/?sh=cd7c7a171a1f.

Wall, Seth P. "Characteristics of Nontraditional College and University Presidents in New England." PhD diss., New England College, Henniker, NH, 2015. https://www.proquest.com/dissertations-theses/characteristics-nontraditional-college-university/docview/1682466631/se-2?accountid=30558.

Weiss, Jack M. "A Causerie on Selecting Law Deans in an Age of Entrepreneurial Deaning." *Louisiana Law Review* 70, no. 3 (Spring 2010): 923–944. Accessed September 2, 2021. https://digitalcommons.law.lsu.edu/cgi/viewcontent.cgi?article=6345&context=lalrev.

"What Are the Characteristics of a Good Leader?" *Center for Creative Leadership*. Accessed November 15, 2021. https://www.ccl.org/articles/leading-effectively-articles/characteristics-good-leader/.

The White House Project Report: Benchmarking Women's Leadership. New York: White House Project, 2009. Accessed September 9, 2021. https://www.in.gov/icw/files/benchmark_wom_leadership.pdf.

Whitford, Emma. "Frank Assessment from a Private College." *Inside Higher Ed*. Last modified May 15, 2020. Accessed August 29, 2021. https://www.insidehighered.com/news/2020/05/15/wells-college-exemplifies-which-institutions-stand-lose-most-pandemic.

———. "Saint Leo University to Merge with Marymount California." *Inside Higher Ed*. Last modified July 30, 2021. Accessed August 30, 2021. https://www.insidehighered.com/news/2021/07/30/saint-leo-university-will-acquire-marymount-california?utm_source=Inside+Higher+Ed&utm_campaign=46c2c0cfa1-DNU_2021_COPY_02&utm_medium=email&utm_term=0_1fcbc04421-46c2c0cfa1-199790317&mc_cid=46c2c0cfa1&mc_eid=ef35c4ecbc.

Wilson, Le Von E. "The Value of Law-Related Education for Faculty and Academic Administrators in Higher Education: The Challenge of Educating Educators." *Academy of Educational Leadership Journal* 11, no. 1 (2007): 25–41. https://www.proquest.com/docview/214227083/fulltextPDF/58F2C2FFC6AC453DPQ/1?accountid=30558.

WVTM 13 Digital. "Dr. Bobbie Knight Names Permanent President of Miles College." Updated March 8, 2020. Accessed October 21, 2022. https://www.wvtm13.com/article/interim-president-selected-for-miles-college/28441645#.

Zarling, Patti. "'Sad Situation': Manitowoc Mayor, College Leaders React to Holy Family College Closing." *Herald Times Reporter*. Last modified May 6, 2020. Accessed August 29, 2021. https://www.htrnews.com/story/news/2020/05/06/manitowoc-holy-family-college-closing-mayor-justin-nickels-leaders-react/5171455002/.

Index

Academic Search, 1, 26, 56, 190
Albany Medical College, 126
Alger, Jonathan, 136–137
Allen, Macon Bolling, 85
American Association of Law Schools (AALS), 44, 46, 57, 193
American Association of University Professors, 17
American Bar Association, 27–28, 30, 44–45, 86, 151–152, 189, 192
American College President Study, 1, 10, 95, 98, 154, 188
American Council on Education, 1, 10, 77, 98, 150, 154, 188
Americans with Disabilities Act (ADA), 20
Areen, Judith, 57
Association of Governing Boards, 23–24, 85, 143
Artis, Roslyn Carter, 9

Barba, James, 126
Barden, Dennis, 136
Barnard College, 189
Bay State College, 127
Baylor Law School, 193, 195
Beardsley, Scott, 2, 92
Becker College, 4
Bekavac, Nancy, 189
Benedict College, 9, 20
Bentley University, 9
Boel, Werner, 56–57
Bollinger, Lee, 58
Bowdoin College, 144
Brown University, 34
Bulger, William, 116, 120

Cambridge College, 127
CARES Act, 6
Carnegie Classification, 60, 65, 75, 77–78
Carter, Laurie, 134
Christensen, Clayton, 3
Chou, Paul Hsun-Ling, 25–26
Center for College Affordability and Productivity, 31
Chicago State University, 144
Civil Rights, 19–20, 27, 32, 39–43, 136
Civil Rights Act, 18
Claremont McKenna College, 189
Clinton, Hillary Rodham, 189
College of Charleston, 117
College of Philadelphia, 43
College of William and Mary, 32–34, 43
Colorado College, 58
Columbia University, 33–35, 58, 94
Columbia University School of Law, 94
Community Colleges, 48–49, 51, 54, 56, 60, 72–73, 77, 80–82, 100–101, 103, 106–108, 113–114, 122–124, 128, 132, 140, 149, 232
Concordia College, 5
Cornell Law School, 58, 94
Council of Independent Colleges (CIC), 110, 143
COVID-19, 1, 3, 4, 6, 20–21, 59, 134, 136
Cox, Cathy, 116
Cunningham, Paige Comstock, 145

Dalton, Walter, 144
Daniels, Mitch, 116
Dartmouth College, 23, 33
Davros, Harry, 126

Delaware State University, 5
Demleitner, Nora, 9
Dickerson, Darby, 193
Dickinson College, 33, 35, 142
Dykstra, John, 194

Eaton, Nathaniel, 39
Ehrlich, Thomas, 22
Eisgruber, Christopher, 15
Ekman, Richard, 143
Equal Employment Opportunity Act, 18

Field, Kelly, 14–15
Folt, Carol, 25
Free Speech, 18–20, 41–42, 51, 90, 117, 136
Futter, Ellen V., 189

Galloway, Scott, 3
Gann, Pamela, 189
Gee, E. Gordon, 24
General Counsel, 16, 21–22, 92, 99, 134–141, 148, 175, 177–180, 183
Georgia College and State University, 117
GI Bill, 39
Government Lawyer, 16, 115, 117–119, 144
Grove City College, 117

Haines, Paul Lowell, 145
Harvard Law School, 43, 94
Harvard University, 23, 33–34, 85
HBCUs, 84–85, 242
HEERF Act, 6
Heineman, Ben, Jr., 194
Hersch, Joni, 97
Higher Education Act, 6, 18, 21
Holy Family College, 5
Horton, Howard, 126
Horvath, Ginny Schaefer, 26, 29
Howard, William (Bill), 56
Hunter College, 126, 189

Isothermal College, 144

Jackson State, 41
James Madison University, 136
Johns Hopkins, 17, 23
Jones, John E. III, 142–143
Julliard School, 134
Judson College, 5

Kent State, 41
Kerr, Clark, 18, 22
Kishore, Maya Ranchod, 26
Knight, Bobbie, 145
Krislov, Marvin, 138

Langston, John Mercer, 86
Larson, Gloria Cordes, 9
Law Dean, 9, 46, 51–58, 60, 102–106, 108, 169–171, 183, 190
Legal Education, 26–28, 43–46, 58, 190, 192–193
Lesley Univeristy, 145
Leverett, John, 33
Lewis, William Henry, 86
Litchfield Law School, 43
Lorimer, Linda, 189
Louie, David M., 118–119

MacMurray College, 5
Malloy, Dannel P., 116, 119
Mamlet, Robin, 191
Martin, Roger, 91
Marymount California University, 5
Massachusetts Communication College, 127
McConnell, Glenn, 117
McGuire, Patricia, 189
Miles College, 145
Mills Barry, 144
Mitchell College, 145
Moravian college, 91
Morrill Land Grant Act, 35–36

Napolitano, Janet, 117
National Association of College and University Attorneys, 21–22, 134
National Defense Education Act, 17
New England College of Business and Finance, 127
New England Institute of Art, 127
New York University, 15, 23, 94, 195

Oberlin College, 138
Oglethorpe College, 9

Pace University, 138
Paul Quinn College, 126
Pell Grant, 17–18
Penalver, Eduardo, 58
Pennsylvania State University, 5
Philip, George, 145
President's Commission on Campus Unrest, 41 Princeton University, 15, 23
Provost, 9, 15, 23, 45–46, 60, 98, 110–115, 172–174, 183, 188

Raab, Jennifer, 126, 189
Randolph College, 189
Randolph, Edwin Archer, 86
Randolph-Macon College, 91, 189
Rehabilitation Act, 18
Reeve, Judge Tapping, 43
Religiously Affiliated Institutions, 50, 52, 54, 57, 74–75, 84, 104, 108–109, 114–115, 124–125, 128, 133, 140–141, 150
R.H. Perry & Associates, 91
Rhode, Deborah, 192, 194
Richardson, L. Song, 58
Ruffin, George Lewis, 85
Rutgers University, 35, 136

St. John's College (Annapolis), 9
Saint Leo University, 5

Schall, Lawrence, 9, 97
Scott, Zaldwaynaka, 144
Seattle University, 58
Scripps College, 189
Shippensburg University, 134
Skidmore College, 189
Smith, J. Clayton, 85
Sorrell, Michael, 126
State University of New York, 4, 26, 145
Stead, Ronald, 24
Steiner, David, 135
Steinmayer, Janet, 145
Stover, Henry, 143
Studley, Jamie, 189

Taylor University, 145
Teague, Leah, 193
Title IX, 18–20, 51, 134
Trinity College, 189
Tobin, Bradley, 193
Trustee, 20, 25, 91–92, 119–120, 127, 136, 142–150, 175–186
Tucker, St. George, 43
Turk, Jonathan, 98, 150

UIC John Marshall, 193
Urbana University, 5
University of Athens, 33
University of California, 18, 22, 25, 41, 58, 94, 117
University of Indiana, 22–23
University of Maine, 116, 119
University of Maryland, 43
University of Massachusetts, 116, 120
University of Michigan School of Law, 58
University of Missouri, 15
University of North Carolina, Chapel Hill, 25
University of Pennsylvania, 3, 33–34, 94, 187–188
University of Pennsylvania School of Law, 94

University of Virginia, 40, 94
University of Wisconsin-Madison, 41
U.S. News & World Report, 94

Vedder, Ricahrd, 31
Vermont State College System, 6
Vietnam, 39–43
Viscusi, kip, 97

Wade College, 126
Weintraub, Ruth, 22
Wells College, 5
Wesley College , 5

White House Project, 186–187
Wickersham, George, 86
Williams, Elisha, 33
Wilson, Woodrow, 15
WittKieffer, 56, 136
Wolfe, Timothy, 15
Wythe, George, 43

Yale Law School, 85, 94
Yale University, 33, 35
Young Harris College, 117

Zemsky, Robert, 3

www.ingramcontent.com/pod-product-compliance
Lightning Source LLC
Chambersburg PA
CBHW070749230426
43665CB00017B/2309